THE CONSTITUTIONAL DIMENSION OF EUROPEAN CRIMINAL LAW

Criminal law is one of the most rapidly changing areas of contemporary EU law and integration. The Treaty of Lisbon has elevated it to a central place in the constitution of the EU, within the dynamic area of freedom, security and justice. The phenomenon of EU criminal law as such is, however, far from new but has developed on an ad hoc basis, not least as a result of the case law of the European Court of Justice. Central to the Court's reasoning in this area has been the principle of effectiveness. A main theme running through the book is, therefore, the role of the axiom of effectiveness, which is critically examined, with particular attention to its use by the European Court of Justice in recent leading cases. This book explores the constitutional principles underlying it, both those determining the substantive values it embodies, and those determining its scope and extent. Other chapters consider the phenomenon of preventative criminalisation at EU level and the protection of subsidiarity and proportionality in EU criminal law. The balance between effective EU action, proper control of competence and adequate protection of individual rights is of growing importance as EU criminal law expands, but, as this book suggests, has not yet been fully articulated or entrenched by the institutions of the EU.

Volume 30 in the series Modern Studies in European Law

Modern Studies in European Law
Recent titles in this series:

Unfair Contract Terms in European Law: A Study in Comparative and EC Law *Paolisa Nebbia*

Energy Security: The External Legal Relations of the European Union with Major Oil and Gas Supplying Countries *Sanam S Haghighi*

EU Criminal Law *Valsamis Mitsilegas*

Effective Judicial Protection and the Environmental Impact Assessment Directive in Ireland *Áine Ryall*

Network-Based Governance in EC Law: The Example of EC Competition and EC Communications Law *Maartje de Visser*

Legitimacy in EU Cartel Control *Ingeborg Simonsson*

Mixed Agreements Revisited: The EU and its Member States in the World *Edited by Christophe Hillion and Panos Koutrakos*

Reflexive Governance: Redefining the Public Interest in a Pluralistic World *Edited by Olivier De Schutter and Jacques Lenoble*

The Impact of EU Law on Minority Rights *Tawhida Ahmed*

Direct Investment, National Champions and EU Treaty Freedoms: From Maastricht to Lisbon *Frank S Benyon*

The Cyprus Issue: The Four Freedoms in a Member State under Siege *Nikos Skoutaris*

The European Union and Global Emergencies: A Law and Policy Analysis *Edited by Antonis Antoniadis, Robert Schütze and Eleanor Spaventa*

Public Liability in EU Law: *Brasserie, Bergaderm* and Beyond *Pekka Aalto*

Professional Services in the EU Internal Market: Quality Regulation and Self-Regulation *Tinne Heremans*

Environmental Integration in the EU's External Relations: Beyond Multilateral Dimensions *Gracia Marín Durán and Elisa Morgera*

For the complete list of titles in this series, see 'Modern Studies in European Law' link at www.hartpub.co.uk/books/series.asp

The Constitutional Dimension of European Criminal Law

Ester Herlin-Karnell

• HART •
PUBLISHING
OXFORD AND PORTLAND, OREGON
2012

Published in the United Kingdom by Hart Publishing Ltd
16C Worcester Place, Oxford, OX1 2JW
Telephone: +44 (0)1865 517530
Fax: +44 (0)1865 510710
E-mail: mail@hartpub.co.uk
Website: http://www.hartpub.co.uk

Published in North America (US and Canada) by
Hart Publishing
c/o International Specialized Book Services
920 NE 58th Avenue, Suite 300
Portland, OR 97213-3786
USA
Tel: +1 503 287 3093 or toll-free: (1) 800 944 6190
Fax: +1 503 280 8832
E-mail: orders@isbs.com
Website: http://www.isbs.com

British Library Cataloguing in Publication Data
Data Available

ISBN: 978-1-84946-176-4

Typeset by Hope Services, Abingdon
Printed and bound in Great Britain by
TJ International Ltd, Padstow, Cornwall

Preface and Acknowledgements

In this book, I examine the progression to supranational criminal law and how effectiveness has driven this trend. In this EU constitutional tale, I investigate the phenomenon of a European criminal law based on 'effectiveness' by first tracing the notion of effective enforcement and thereafter exploring the constitutional question of effectiveness in a transnational setting. In particular, I endeavour to show the dynamics of effectiveness as a competence question by telling the *Commission v Council* (environmental crimes) story. In addition, I ask to what extent the Lisbon Treaty has provided for the proper groundwork in this area.

This book is initially based on my doctorial thesis recommended for the DPhil at Oxford University on 3 December 2009. I am extremely grateful to Steve Weatherill for all his guidance and help. I am indebted to him for having accepted me as a DPhil student in 2005 and for having offered an intellectually challenging but very friendly environment at Somerville College. Without him this book would not have come into existence. I am also very grateful to my DPhil examiners Paul Craig and Valsamis Mitsilegas not only for inspiring my way of thinking about law, but also for their very useful comments in the viva that greatly improved this manuscript and gave me the confidence to write this book.

I would also like to thank Andrea Biondi for encouraging me at various stages in my academic life and for reading parts of the book and being the person who originally inspired me to embark on the DPhil journey. Moreover, I would like to thank Gareth Davies for his thought-provoking discussions, insightful comments and his mentorship at the VU University of Amsterdam. I am particularly grateful to Theodore Konstadinides for his invaluable comments and encouragement while drafting this book. Thanks also to Gerard Conway, Christina Eckes and Tarcisio Gazzini for helpful suggestions on various aspects of this book. I also thank Harry Panagopulos for help with proof reading of the initial DPhil thesis on which this book is based. Last but not least, I thank Richard Hart and the staff at Hart Publishing, for believing in this project and for their patience with the submission of the manuscript.

In Oxford thanks are due to many. I would especially like to thank Nina Bausek, Sanja Bogojevic, Alica Hinarejos, Jan Komarek, Dorota Leczykiewicz, Vanessa Mak and Katja Ziegler for having been part of a stimulating and unique study setting in Oxford. I am also grateful to Jenny Dix and Katja Ziegler (again) at the Institute of European and Comparative Law for having given me the opportunity to continue to visit the Bodleian Law Library as an academic visitor, with the kind support from the Royal Swedish Academy grant.

But most of all I thank my parents for their love and support and for keeping me up-to-date on horses. Special thanks are also due to my brother for supplying me with the best equestrian hoof care.

Amsterdam, July 2011
Ester Herlin-Karnell

Table of Contents

Table of Cases

CASES BEFORE THE COURT OF JUSTICE OF THE EUROPEAN UNION AND THE GENERAL COURT

CASES BEFORE THE EUROPEAN COURT OF HUMAN RIGHTS

NATIONAL CASES

English courts

German Constitutional Court

Table of Treaties, Conventions and other Legislative Instruments

TREATIES AND CONVENTIONS

PROTOCOLS

EU SECONDARY LEGISLATION

Directives

Regulation

Framework decisions

EU decisions

EU documents

Miscellaneous documents

NATIONAL LEGISLATION AND LEGISLATIVE INSTRUMENTS

UK legislation

Swedish legislation

Danish and Finnish legislation

1

Introduction

I. INTRODUCTION

THIS BOOK EXAMINES the constitutional dimension of European criminal law. The specific focus of the book is the competence question in EU criminal law and how effectiveness has driven its constitutional adaptation and development. The book considers the vertical delimitation of powers between the EU and its Member States. The concept of European criminal law has always been very patchy and has only gained impetus in recent years. Prior to the entry into force of the Lisbon Treaty, criminal law was primarily a third pillar intergovernmental matter within the framework of the Treaty of Amsterdam. The major issue, therefore, was the horizontal delimitation of powers between the former first and third pillars in the EU. This book investigates the development of criminal law in the EU from the failure of the Constitutional Treaty in 2005, to the entry into force of the Lisbon Treaty in 2009, which elevated criminal law to a central constitutional position. However, in spite of the non-ratification and ill-fated destiny of the Constitutional Treaty in 2005 and the uncertain wait for the Lisbon Treaty, the European Court of Justice concluded that there could be an EU supranational competence if this was needed to safeguard the environment effectively. Without doubt, few cases concerning criminal law in a European context have received as much attention as Case C-176/03, *Commission v Council*[1] (hereafter Case C-176/03), which highlighted the general problem of the delimitation of competences between the former first and third pillars and stated that criminal law could be a matter for the EU legislator if the principle of full effectiveness so required. So, until recently, criminal law in the EU context straddled in the border between the first and the third pillars but could be considered to fall within the scope of the first pillar if this was required for the EU law to be fully effective. This case opened up a vague and ill-defined competence in this judicial area which fuelled a debate concerning the exact limits of competence.[2] The aim of this book is, therefore, to explore the meaning of 'effectiveness' and examine how it has been used as an authority of EU law to open up areas thought to lie – in part or in

[1] Case C-176/03 *Commission v Council* [2005] ECR I-7879.

[2] eg V Mitsilegas, 'The Transformation of Criminal Law in the Area of Freedom, Security and Justice' (2007) 26 *Yearbook of European Law* 1 and S Peers, 'EU Criminal Law and the Treaty of Lisbon' (2008) 33 *European Law Review* 507.

whole – within the autonomy of Member States. This raises several issues. For example, is the concept of 'effectiveness' in EU law different from 'effectiveness' in criminal law? Is it possible to simply translate the harmonisation of trade standards into the harmonisation of criminal provisions? Clearly, these issues also illuminate the difficult question of how to reconcile effective EU action with respect for human rights in criminal law matters at the EU level.

Moreover, as will be explained, the principle of effectiveness has primarily and traditionally been seen as a question of the enforcement of EU legal rights in national courts. However, the judgment in Case C-176/03 could also be interpreted to mean that showing the 'effectiveness' of an EU rule is a precondition to establishing the EU's competence to act in the first place. These questions are important to analyse. The reason for this is twofold – first criminal law is very different, for example, from private law in its power to impose 'legitimate violence' on individuals and therefore a cautious approach should be taken to avoid the inflationary use or abuse of the criminal law. Secondly, it is dangerous to view the principle of effectiveness as a carte blanche for harmonisation, as this would run counter to the concept of conferred powers as stipulated in Article 5(1–2) Treaty on European Union (TEU) and Article 7 Treaty on the Functioning of the European Union (TFEU).

This book seeks to examine the principle of effectiveness, which has become the key drive in the pursuit of the constitutional evolution of European criminal law. More specifically, the book investigates the constitutional implications of reasoning based on 'effectiveness' and how it has developed from an enforcement issue in European law to a more independent principle at the constitutional level when justifying EU powers. The main theme running through this book is the tension between effectiveness concerns and the legitimacy question of EU criminal law. It is argued that criminal law at the EU level has developed rapidly without taking the time to reflect on the premises on which it is based. The contention is that the EU has pushed forward with criminal law initiatives leading to the development of a preventive regime, while the protection of the individual has been largely left behind. Thus, in order to understand the changes for the criminal law as brought by the Lisbon Treaty it is necessary to put it into context. This book serves that purpose. It will embark on a constitutional tour of EU criminal law and explain how the principle of effectiveness has driven this whole area forward. The Lisbon Treaty solves, to some extent, the big question of whether a competence to harmonise criminal law at the supranational level exists by simply asserting that it does. In other words, the Lisbon Treaty provides for a specific basis for such a crime-fighting mission by listing a whole range of crime-fighting activities as set out in Articles 82 and 83 TFEU. The main question is how to decide and monitor the contours of these provisions and how to ensure that procedural rights in criminal law are protected.

This short introduction intends to offer some preliminary background information as to why such a study is important.

II. BRIEF COMMENT ON THE HISTORY OF EU CRIMINAL LAW

When discussing the concept of European criminal law it is easy to get the impression that it is the result of the general success of the EU. However, viewed from a historical perspective it is actually quite difficult to find a sensible meaning for the 'Europeanisation' of a criminal law which is already 'European', having been inspired by ideas developed during the Enlightenment.[3] Nevertheless, there are considerable differences between the different Member States. It is, moreover, precisely the combination of these 'cultural similarities' and 'cultural disparities' that makes the concept of European criminal law so complex. For example, it is often pointed out that there is currently insufficient mutual trust between the Member States that have divergent criminal laws, to justify the application of the internal market principle of mutual recognition to the field of EU criminal law.[4]

In any case, until recently, the assumption was that criminal law fell outside the legislative competence of the EU. Indeed, criminal law was initially of little interest to the EU legislator who was more concerned with the notion of free movement and the functioning and establishment of the internal market. There was, in short, no need to interfere in the sensitive field of criminal law. As stated though above, the current 'Europeanisation' of criminal law is not a new phenomenon, as the general lines of the future orientation of a 'European criminal law' were already the basis for Kant's *Perpetual Peace* in 1795.[5] Therefore, although criminal law is a fairly recent actor on the Union stage in terms of 'EU criminal law', the notion of 'European' criminal law as such is far from new. After all, it should be recalled that there was a time when 'Europe' represented a more enlightened and proportionate penal system than the national systems.[6] For example, the Enlightenment brought with it a criminal law system more inspired by humanism and the introduction of the principles of proportionality and legality.[7] Today, in slightly exaggerated terms, the opposite appears to be the case, with EU law running the risk of relying on the appealing concept of enforcement at the possible expense of sufficient legal safeguards.[8] This is especially true, as will be discussed below, in the areas of combating terrorism, money laundering, and in crime

[3] See eg, C Harding, 'The Identity of European Law: Mapping out the European Legal Space' (2000) 5 *European Law Journal* 128; K Nuotio, 'The Emerging Concept of European Criminal Law' in P Asp (ed) *Festskrift till Nils Jareborg* (Uppsala, Iustus, 2002) 531 and V Mitsilegas, *EU Criminal Law* (Oxford, Hart Publishing, 2009).

[4] eg For the concept of mutual recognition see, of course, Case 120/78 Cassis de Dijon [1979] ECR 649. For on overview of mutual recognition and EU criminal law see S Peers *EU Justice and Home Affairs* (Oxford, Oxford University Press, 2011) ch 9 and Mitsilegas (n 3 above) 115.

[5] I Kant, *Perpetual Peace and Other International Essays* (Indianapolis, Hackett Publishing, 1983) also cited in U Sieber, 'Memorandum avseende en europeisk modellstrafflag' (1997) 84 *Nordisk Tidskrift for Kriminalvidenskab* 237.

[6] See eg, H Jung, 'Criminal Justice – A European Perspective' (1993) *Criminal Law Review* 237.

[7] Generally, A Norrie, *Crime, Reason and History* (London, Butterworths, 2001) ch 1.

[8] eg in the context of EU counter-terrorism legislation, Statewatch report 'The exceptional and draconian become the norm' available at www.statewatch.org/analyses/exceptional-and-draconian.pdf (last accessed January 2012).

prevention at the EU level, where the notion of effectiveness seems to play an increasingly dominant role in the legislative debate.

III. STRUCTURE OF THE BOOK

In examining these issues, this book starts by looking at the famous patchwork pattern of criminal law in the EU and how it was formed. The development of EU criminal law will be explored against the general background of the impact of effectiveness as both an enforcement mechanism and a competence parameter. It also highlight the fact that there is no clear-cut division between enforcement and competence issues and that effectiveness is a chameleonic concept. Yet, the problem is that it is far from clear that effectiveness in criminal law mirrors 'effectiveness' as interpreted by the Court or the European Commission. We will begin this exercise by tracing the EU colonisation of criminal law in chapter two, outlining the journey of criminal law in the EU to show how it has emerged from a third pillar issue to a supranational question. In addition, chapter two considers the implications of the Lisbon Treaty by introducing the main changes in criminal law as well as the extended jurisdiction of the Court in this area.

A. Effectiveness as Enforcement

In chapter three, the principle of effectiveness is examined in further detail. In doing so this chapter considers the meaning of effectiveness in EU law generally by tracing its origin in the classic EU context before applying it to the former third pillar, and subsequently to the area of freedom, security and justice (AFSJ) following the Lisbon Treaty. It is argued that there has been an implementation imbalance within the former EU third pillar between the attractiveness of effective enforcement of EU law, and the dangers of one-sided integration where legal protection of the individual is neglected, despite this being an area where such safeguards are most needed. In addition, this chapter discusses the extent to which the Lisbon Treaty has changed the framework of criminal law. It then investigates 'effectiveness' as a general principle of criminal law and cautiously argues that this principle is a tricky parameter when deciding on criminalisation.

B. Constitutional Effectiveness

This book then scrutinises effectiveness as a constitutional axiom. Chapter four maps the development of the principle of effectiveness in EU law as a constitutional principle for confirming competences. This is in many ways the chapter on which the book is based, as it attempts to construct a theoretical framework for the analysis of effectiveness in EU criminal law. In particular, the chapter examines Case C-176/03 more closely and considers how the Court established a new meaning of 'effectiveness' in their reading of the case and its wider implications. Part I introduces the topic of this chapter and explains the conundrums of effectiveness by analysing it in the light of the conferral of powers in the EU. Although the focus is on criminal law, the aim is to construct a broader setting in order to show the underlying concerns permeating this area. In so doing, the chapter seeks to illuminate the wider question of European powers. Arguably, it is necessary to look at the background picture before looking more specifically at the details of European criminal law and the question of competences. In other words, the aim is to place the notion of a supranational criminal law competence in context. Hence, the chapter covers the general constitutional questions in the EU, such as the objectives of the EU and the conferral of competences.

An important aim of this chapter is to track the objectives of the EU in the light of the effectiveness principle. Part II of the chapter serves this purpose. In particular, this part of the chapter sets out to explore the dynamics and the history of the wide-ranging former portal provision of the *acquis communautaire*, ex Article 47 TEU and to consider what we can learn from it with respect to the Lisbon Treaty. The purpose of doing so is to investigate how criminal law was already being transferred prior to the Lisbon Treaty as part of the Court of Justice's heavy reliance on the effectiveness principle coupled with the wide contours of the *acquis communautaire*. Thus, part II seeks to tie this question to the constitutional question of effectiveness in the EU and show how the competence threshold was being manipulated to extend into new areas. The section considers how much has really changed in this area since the entry into force of the Lisbon Treaty. The intention is to show that even though it is true that Opinion 2/94[9] was clear that the objectives of the Treaty cannot be expanded by themselves, the meaning of this assertion remained unclear, as in practice the scope of this provision remained unstable, as was demonstrated by the *Kadi* case.[10] In particular, this part of the chapter tries to explain that the issue of what is to be counted as an EU objective revealed a similar vagueness to that of the effectiveness principle, where the effectiveness imperative has become part of the EU objectives. The chapter also analyses the new Article 13 TEU and the question of institutional balance and the continuing aspirations for effectiveness.

Part III of chapter four then investigates the constitutional scope of Article 114 TFEU, and thereby briefly dissects the myriad of legal scholarship here. More specifically, this part intends to explore how much weight Case C-176/03 could bear before collapsing under Article 114 TFEU. In doing so, this study focuses on the snowball effect of this ruling and the eagerness to legislate that followed in its wake. Moreover, the part examines the Article 114 TFEU conundrums by looking specifically at the market concept in the context of the possibilities of harmonising criminal law by scrutinising the notions of obstacles to trade and the

[9] Opinion 2/94 *Accession to the ECHR* [1996] ECR I-1759.

[10] Case C-415/05P *Kadi and Al Barakaat International Foundation v Council and Commission* [2008] ECR I-6351.

distortion of competition. The starting point for this discussion is naturally the new *lex specialis* function of Article 83 TFEU and the boundaries of the notion of EU criminal law particularly with regard to how far it will be possible to rely on Article 114 TFEU in the future. Yet although Lisbon provides for quite strictly drafted provisions on criminal law competence, it has also resulted in slippery provisions that would allow legislation 'when necessary' for the effective implementation of an EU policy which has been the subject of harmonisation measures as stipulated in Article 83 TFEU.

In part IV the issues of subsidiarity and proportionality are explored in the context of European criminal law in order to show that these principles appear to play a less significant role in EU criminal law as well as in the mainstream EU framework. This is particularly alarming as the very notions of subsidiarity and proportionality should be reflected in the *ultima ratio* of criminal law. This chapter also discusses the new function of the national parliaments in this area as well as problems with penal populism and the wider issues of balancing in the AFSJ and the extent to which criminal law is different from other areas.

Part V of this chapter links such reasoning to the flexibility provision of enhanced cooperation. The purpose is to show the dangers in 'moving forward' blindly at the expense of adequate attention being paid to what such cooperation means from the perspective of coherence. This part of the chapter examines the mechanisms of enhanced cooperation with regard to criminal law and the emergency brake in particular and argues that the emergency brake provided by the Lisbon Treaty might not be significant in practice as nine Member States can always move forward by establishing automatic enhanced cooperation. This part also discusses the meaning of the imperative of loyalty in this area and to what extent the proportionality principle could play a role here in future as better recognising the sensitive nature of criminal law cooperation.

Finally, part VI of the chapter provides some thoughts on the wider constitutional debate which underpins this area as initiated by the Laeken Declaration and taken further in the discussion on the Lisbon Treaty, by highlighting the bigger question of the need for broad flexible competence provisions. Specifically this part of the chapter seeks to bring us back to the discussion on the objectives of the EU and the issue of the future of the EU project more broadly. The chapter concludes by drawing together the findings of the chapter.

C. The Development of EU Precautionary Criminalisation and the Fight against Money Laundering

Chapter five sets out to analyse the EU's security agenda, which plays an increasingly significant role in the EU's policy within the AFSJ. More particularly, the chapter aims to discuss it in the light of risk regulation and the effectiveness principle. The intention is to investigate what happens in practice in the intersection between national criminal law and EU measures and two case studies are discussed. Chapter five deals specifically with EU financial crimes and the EU suppression of money laundering. The Third Money Laundering Directive[11] introduces a risk-based approach as well as the inclusion of the financing of terrorism within its scope. This poses numerous challenges not least because money laundering and the financing of terrorism, although sometimes related, do not necessarily show the same (criminological) pattern. It will be shown that 'risk' in EU law is not necessarily the same as 'risk' in criminal law despite the EU's heavy reliance on the concept. The Third Money Laundering Directive introduces a risk-based approach to suspicious transactions but this book examines 'risk' as a much wider concept connected to the question of paternalism and whether the EU should be involved in these issues at all. In particular, this part of the chapter tries to demonstrate that the driving notions behind the EU's agenda in this area are risk and security coupled with effectiveness concerns. It is argued that the EU's approach here has led – and could lead – to precautionary criminalisation at the EU level. Such a development is a dangerous trend as it seems to push criminal law in the direction of harsher law. Thereafter, this chapter sets out to briefly look at the (repealed) Counterfeiting and Piracy Directive[12] as an example of an early aspiration of creating a EU supranational criminal law. In doing so the purpose is to illuminate any difficulties from the perspective of national criminal law and the question of criminal law liability for legal persons. This chapter also discusses the notion of a protective regime at the EU level by not only linking the chapter back to the debate on Article 114 TFEU and the justification for harmonisation on the basis of 'confidence in the market' but also confronting it with the notion of paternalistic legislation in criminal law.

Finally, chapter six looks more closely at the implementation of the Third Money Laundering Directive in the UK and Sweden and what challenges it poses in practice.

D. The Lisbon Treaty and Criminal Law: Old Problems and New Challenges

In chapter seven the book explores to what extent the Lisbon Treaty currently provides for a sufficient structure for EU criminal law. Although the Lisbon Treaty has greatly improved the situation by granting competences and providing for the adoption of legal safeguards for the individual, it does not mean that the framework drawn up by the Lisbon Treaty constitutes the ideal solution to EU criminal law. Therefore, this chapter discusses the Lisbon Treaty from the perspective of EU criminal law and asks if it offers anything new. The answer is both yes and no. The Lisbon Treaty draws attention to the EU's legal values and

[11] Directive (EC) 2005/60 on the prevention of the use of the financial system for the purpose of money laundering and terrorist financing [2005] OJ L60/309.

[12] Proposal for a Directive (COM (2006) 168 final, on criminal measures aimed at ensuring the enforcement of intellectual property rights. Later withdrawn by the Commission, see OJ C252, 18 September 2010.

officially promotes the Charter of Fundamental Rights as a legal source of interpretation as well as ensuring the EU's future accession to the European Convention on Human Rights (ECHR). Moreover, the Lisbon Treaty provides for the possibility of approximation of legal safeguards as well as bringing the 'emergency brake' (initially invented by the Constitutional Treaty) back in. The emergency brake is important as it provides for the possibility of a constraint to be implemented if a criminal law legislative measure is considered to affect fundamental aspects of a Member State national criminal law system. This chapter also looks at the new role of the Court of Justice, as well as the new expedited procedure, and tentatively asks if the Court of Justice could (and should) become a criminal law court and the difficulties it faces in this judicial domain.

IV. FINAL REMARKS

This book tries to clarify the puzzling issue of the distribution of competences in the EU by focusing on criminal law and the notion of effectiveness as the key principle in this area. Whilst it is true that the Lisbon Treaty has largely solved the question of whether there is any competence in criminal law at the supranational level, by listing it as one of the EU's objectives in the TFEU, such a Treaty reformation has not solved the larger issue of EU criminal law. For example, it remains unclear to what extent the EU could legislate in criminal law or to what degree such harmonisation could take place outside the *lex specialis* provisions in Title V of the TFEU. In addition, and as already noted above, a study of the impact of the effectiveness principle and how it has transferred criminal law at the EU level is of utmost importance. It illustrates the ambiguity of the Treaty framework for the competence monitoring much more broadly. Thus, it tells us about the future scope of the new Treaty articles on criminal law where 'effectiveness' still plays a key role.

However, the underlying constitutional debate permeating this whole field is the fact that although there is no need to finalise the European project, which is a process under constant dynamic flux, this is not the whole story. [13] The point is rather that the criminal law is fundamentally ill-suited for clear-cut analogies with the internal market. The reason for this is that the criminal law handles a different kind of 'freedom' from that at the heart of the EU project, in that it can cause harm by depriving people of their liberty through sanctioned punishment. Another very important component, and as will be explored more fully below, is the function of the principle of legality in criminal law, which requires certainty and specific underlying qualities in the law in question. From the perspective of EU law, this touches on the rather provocative issue of the extent to which the EU should have any legislative competence in criminal law which creates the need for

[13] S Weatherill, 'Is constitutional finality feasible or desirable? On the case for European Constitutionalism and the European Constitution' (2002) available at www.wiso.uni-hamburg.de/fileadmin/sowi/politik/governance/ConWeb_Papers/conweb7-2002.pdf (accessed January 2012).

a strictly laid down competence in the name of legitimacy without bringing the EU to a halt. In other words, there appears to be a clash between the principle of legality in criminal law and the need to maintain the dynamic nature of EU law. This theme was considered at the general level in the Laeken Declaration[14] and remains highly topical as regards the future interpretation of the new competence provisions as created by the Lisbon Treaty in this area.

It will become clear that the phenomenon of EU criminal law is highly complex. The very idea of it reveals the vulnerability of the credentials of EU action based on the principle of effectiveness and the respect for the attribution of powers, while at the same time it concerns a matter which is very different from, say, the labelling of tobacco products.[15] As explained, the Lisbon Treaty has provided a whole new framework for the development of criminal law at the EU level in Title V of the TFEU. In spite of this, it merely draws up a skeleton for the development of criminal law at the EU level, leaving it largely unexplored. Clearly, the protection of the individual should constitute the main theme in the emergence of EU criminal law. As will be argued below, an accompanying rule of thumb should equally be the EU principles of subsidiarity and proportionality, long reflected in the *ultima ratio* of criminal law. Nevertheless, EU legislative practice paints a different picture. Here the most appealing notion of forward thinking appears to assume that better EU regulation means more criminal law. Indeed, the field of EU criminal law has been the textbook example of creeping competence in action and offers a good constitutional test case. Accordingly, this book explores and guides the reader through different notions of 'effectiveness' in EU law, and the issues of EU legislative competence and 'over-criminalisation' by scrutinising an area which has become one of the most important issues in contemporary European integration discourse.

[14] European Council at Laeken 2001.

[15] Case C-376/98 *Germany v Parliament and Council* [2000] ECR I-8419.

2

The Journey of Criminal Law in the EU

I. INTRODUCTION

THIS CHAPTER PROVIDES an overview of the relationship between European law and criminal law and aims to guide the reader through the journey of criminal law in the EU's institutions from the Maastricht Treaty to the Lisbon Treaty via the case law of the European Court of Justice. The specific focus of the chapter is the transformation of criminal law in the EU and the impact of the Lisbon Treaty.

The first part of this chapter focuses on the question of the general influence of EU law on national criminal law. Thereafter, it deals with EU criminal law cooperation based on the concept of mutual recognition and how it emerged within the sphere of the former third pillar, while the third part introduces the topic of the emerging phenomenon of EU supranational criminal law. More specifically, the structure of the first part of the chapter is as follows. First, the chapter provides a brief overview of the concept of European criminal law. Secondly, it examines EU law influence on national criminal law. Thereafter, the chapter will try to explore critically the principle of legality as a general principle and its significance to both EU law and criminal law. The second part briefly considers the former third pillar. This part covers the third pillar judgments in *Pupino*, *Advocaten voor de Wereld* and *Dell'Orto*.[1] In doing so, the chapter supplies some preliminary thoughts on the history of *communautaire* reasoning in the former third pillar and introduces the question of how much Community law could legitimately be transferred to the third pillar arena prior to the Lisbon Treaty. Subsequently, the third part introduces the high profile rulings of Case C-176/03 and the *Ship source pollution* case,[2] which constitute the main source of guidance when navigating the Court's use of effectiveness as a constitutional principle. Thereafter, the chapter charts the main changes introduced by the Lisbon Treaty and concludes by discussing the Stockholm programme[3] as well as recent case law in this area.

[1] Case C-105/03 *Pupino* [2005] ECR I-5285; Case C-303/05 *Advocaten voor de Wereld* [2007] ECR I-3633; Case C-467/05 *Giovanni Dell'Orto* [2007] ECR I-5557.

[2] Case C-176/03 *Commission v Council* [2005] ECR I-7879; Case C-440/05 *Commission v Council* [2007] ECR I-9097.

[3] The Stockholm programme – An open and secure Europe serving and protecting the citizen (Council of the European Union Brussels, 2 December 2009), available at http://register.consilium.europa.eu/pdf/en/09/st17/st17024.en09.pdf? (last accessed January 2012).

Thus the chapter seeks to introduce the relevant developments in EU criminal law in a largely chronological way.

A caveat should perhaps be expressed before starting. As this is an introductory chapter it has to be brutally selective. I have, therefore, chosen to focus on aspects which provide the best illustrations of the characteristic and challenging patch-work relationship between European law and criminal law. This means that the chapter will not, for example, analyse the merits of a European Public Prosecutor although the possibility of such a prosecutor will be touched upon briefly in chapter seven. Neither will this chapter penetrate the tangled system of the so-called administrative sanctions (in the area of competition or agriculture law, for example) as any such interpretation would be far beyond the scope of this chapter. The reason that they have been mentioned briefly is to try to show from an academic perspective that when discussing sanctions, discourse has traditionally concerned two different levels of sanctions and provisions. On the one hand, the so-called administrative sanctions at the supranational level, which are regarded as non-criminal law by EU institutions but which are extremely hard to distinguish from 'criminal law' *stricto sensu*, and on the other hand the Community law influence of Article 4(3) TEU and the principle of loyalty more generally. The Lisbon Treaty has modified this distinction by creating a new legal framework making it possible for the EU legislator to rely on criminal sanctions directly.

II. WHAT IS AT STAKE?

The entry into force of the Lisbon Treaty has changed the framework and possibilities of the development of EU criminal law. Gone is the long-lived and awkward cross-pillar character of EU criminal law, where it was seen mainly as a third pillar intergovernmental issue but also partly as a first pillar question.[4] In understanding the constitutional dynamics which have shaped the development of EU criminal law, it is necessary to take a short historical detour to explain how criminal law reached the EU stage in the first place.

Generally speaking, criminal law as a European issue entered the EU scene in connection with the entry into force of the Maastricht Treaty in 1993. Subsequently, the Amsterdam Treaty of 1999 clarified the EU's objectives in the justice and home affairs (JHA) sphere and created the concept of an area of freedom, security and justice (AFSJ).[5] However, the third pillar allowed for a limited involvement by the European Parliament in the legislative process and could easily be criticised for creating a democratic deficit and for a lack of transparency in the lawmaking. Moreover, the Court's jurisdiction within this pillar has been very restricted and based on a voluntary declaration by the Member

[4] N Neagu, 'Entrapment between Two Pillars: The European Court of Justice Rulings in Criminal Law' (2009) 15 *European Law Journal* 536.

[5] However, it also further 'intergovernmentalised' the criminal law when it moved the former third pillar area of immigration and asylum and civil law to the first pillar sphere.

States to confer such jurisdiction (ex Article 35 TEU).[6] Therefore, from an EU law perspective, the former third pillar framework was never considered to be an ideal counterpart to the first pillar (EC) sphere.[7] However, the Member States were concerned about retaining their competences in the extremely sensitive area of justice and home affairs, which is the reason why this field – or its EU subculture – has persisted. In any case, shortly after the entry into force of the Treaty of Amsterdam, the consequential Tampere Council of 1999 and the subsequent Hague programme[8] took the notion of European criminal law one step further by introducing the adoption of the internal market formula of 'mutual recognition' into the third pillar.[9] This concept has remained the main engine of development although there has also been extensive legislation in the area, particularly in the fields of terrorism, organised crime and illicit drug trafficking, in accordance with the relevant provisions. Moreover, a new JHA programme was recently crafted – the Stockholm programme – to replace the previous Hague agenda.[10] The Stockholm programme sets out a very ambitious AFSJ schema. It is the latest development in the creation of an AFSJ and stipulates a number of goals to be achieved in the AFSJ field, and these will be discussed in further detail in section G below.[11]

Although it is true that since its early days the EU has lacked a legislative competence in criminal law, the question of to what extent such a conclusion was universally correct was still left quite open even after the entry into force of the Maastricht Treaty and the creation of the third pillar. Consequently, when the Treaty of Amsterdam came into force it became clear that there was no explicit EC legislative power in criminal law, as ex Articles 280(4) EC (now Article 325 TFEU) and ex Article 135 EC (now Article 33 TFEU) indicated a fairly strict division of powers, namely that administrative sanctions were part of EC law and that criminal measures were left to the Member States or could – in the EU context – only be taken within the framework of the third pillar (Articles 29 to 31(e) EU). In addition, criminal law was not on the – admittedly rather undefined – competence list as provided by ex Articles 2 and 3 EC of the former EC Treaty. Therefore, this remained the main opinion until the landmark Case C-176/03 judgment changed this paradigm by stating that criminal law could be a matter for the EU

[6] For a comment, eg S Peers, *EU Justice and Home Affairs* (Oxford, Oxford University Press, 2011) ch 2.

[7] S Lavenex, 'Justice and Home Affairs' in H Wallace et al (eds) *Policy-Making in the European Union* (Oxford, Oxford University Press, 2010) ch 19.

[8] European Council Tampere 1999 and 'The Hague Programme: Strengthening Freedom, Security and Justice in the EU' [2005] OJ C53/1.

[9] Peers (above n 6) ch 8.

[10] S Peers, 'The EU's JHA Agenda for 2009' available at www.statewatch.org/analyses/eu-sw-analysis-2009-jha-agenda.pdf (last accessed January 2012). The Stockholm programme – An open and secure Europe serving and protecting the citizen (Council of the European Union Brussels, 2 December 2009).

[11] For EU criminal law developments in the run up to the Lisbon Treaty and after its enter into force, see eg, P Beauvais, 'Droit penal de l'Union européen' (2010) 46 *Revue trimestrielle de droit européen* 722, V Mitsilegas, 'European Criminal Law and Resistance to Communautarisation after Lisbon' (2010) 1 *New Journal of European Criminal Law* 456 and C Rijken, 'Re-balancing Security and Justice: Protection of Fundamental Rights in Police and Judicial Cooperation in Criminal Matters' (2010) 47 *CML Rev* 1455.

legislator if the principle of effectiveness so required. As will be demonstrated, this has not only been a question of whether criminal law belonged in the first or the third pillar, that is it is not simply a 'battle of the pillars' question. After all, the third pillar granted a very limited competence (such as rules to combat illicit drug trafficking, terrorism, organised crime and crime prevention) although notions as vague as 'organised crime' have been interpreted rather widely. Instead, the real question was whether an EC/EU competence existed at all. As noted, the Lisbon Treaty altered the situation dramatically by explicitly listing a set of EU crimes and thereby including it in the core of the Treaties, the TFEU and giving it the full jurisdiction of the Court of Justice.

Nevertheless, one of the major problems in dealing with criminal law in the European arena has been – and still is – that the EU is not a state and accordingly classical ways of legitimising the use of criminal law are not sufficient.[12] Some alternative models have to be constructed as the issues at stake go to the very heart of human rights protection and concern the core of state sovereignty.[13] In this respect, it has been suggested that what is needed is an approach more similar to international criminal law, where the division between internal and external is fluid.[14] After all, the very concept of mutual recognition as discussed below, could perhaps be said to lie along the same lines in blurring the national and European legal boundaries. However, the notion of European criminal law is much more multifaceted and raises familiar questions, not only about where national sovereignty ends and Union law begins[15] but also about EU legitimacy and accountability more broadly. These issues will be addressed throughout this chapter.

A. The Framework of EU Criminal Law prior to the Lisbon Treaty

As implied, the phenomenon of EU criminal law has been a hot topic for a long time. Traditionally, the debate has tended to focus on two separate questions. First, the controversial EU administrative sanctions system, as mentioned above,[16] and the question of whether these sanctions, contrary to their 'administrative'

[12] The classic definition is provided by M Weber: 'a territory, a people and a political class exercising monopoly over the legitimate use of violence', M Weber, *Economy and Society* (Berkeley, CA,, California University Press, 1978). For a recent account of criminal law as transnational law see, J Safferling 'Europe as Transnational Law – A Criminal Law for Europe: Between National Heritage and Transnational Necessities' (2009) 10 *German Law Journal* 1383.

[13] eg H Jung, 'L'Etat et moi: Some Reflections on the Relationship between the Criminal Law and the State' (1998) 6 *European Journal of Crime, Criminal Law and Criminal Justice* 208.

[14] E Guild, 'Crime and the EU's Constitutional Future in an Area of Freedom, Security and Justice' (2004) 10 *ELJ* 224.

[15] An expression used by Peers in his 2000 and 2006 editions of *EU Justice and Home Affairs* (2006 edn above n 6) ch 8.

[16] Administrative sanctions is not a term used in the UK, where they are referred to as non-criminal penalties with strict liability, see eg, C Harding, 'Exploring the Intersection of European Law and National Criminal Law' (2000) 25 *EL Rev* 374.

label, should properly be viewed as falling under the criminal law in accordance with the criteria laid down by the European Court of Human Rights (ECtHR) in the case law on Article 6 European Convention on Human Rights (ECHR) (which would ensure the right to a fair trial and a subjective fault element).[17] In this regard, it is worth mentioning that in the early 1990s it was still unclear whether the EU had the competence to prescribe 'non-criminal' sanctions at all.[18] The issue of whether the EU was entitled to create its own 'quasi penal system' was raised in Case C-240/90, *Germany v Commission*,[19] where the Court came to the teleological, or perhaps convenient, conclusion that the measures were needed to secure the internal market and were therefore within its competence.[20] A useful example of the Court's reliance on administrative sanctions is the *Maizena* case.[21] Here the Court simply concluded that the penalty in issue was not of a criminal law nature. The Court did not explain its distinction any further but agreed that in some cases, where a 'penalty' has some characteristics of criminal law, it would be possible to make an analogy to the ECHR and defence rights as traditionally provided in criminal law proceedings. Obviously, the advantage of administrative sanctions is that by not treating them as criminal sanctions, measures could be taken relatively smoothly within the first pillar and the notion of strict liability applies. Nevertheless, administrative sanctions have been severely criticised for constituting a kind of 'competence creep' into the sphere of penal law and in this way creating a supranational system of sanctions through the EU legal back door.[22]

A second and ideological question persisted of where to place the criminal law within the European machinery more generally. As noted, the previous third pillar had been criticised for its lack of transparency and minimal judicial control. Moreover, the hazy concept of trust is often considered as too vague to act as the basis for mutual recognition.[23] For example, it is frequently argued that, contrary to its proclamation in the EU Treaty, the EU does not constitute an AFSJ, as the safeguards for the individual are not adequately protected and the focus on security seems to dominate over the concept justice and freedom.[24] Nevertheless, according to some criminal law scholars, the lack of legitimacy would render the

[17] eg *Engel and others v Netherlands* Series A, No 22; [1979–1980], more generally G Corstens and J Pradel, *European Criminal Law* (The Hague, Kluwer Law Publishing, 2002).

[18] N Haekkerup, *Controls and Sanctions in the EU Law* (Copenhagen, Djoef Publishing, 2001) 161.

[19] Case C-240/90 *Germany v Commission* [1992] ECR I-05383.

[20] AG Jacobs stated in his Opinion of 3 June 1992, 'certainly EC law in its present state does not confer on the Commission, the CFI or the ECJ the function of a criminal tribunal. It should however be noted that that would in itself not preclude the EC from harmonizing the criminal laws of the Member States if that were necessary to attain one of the objectives of the Community'.

[21] Case C-137/85 *Maizena* [1987] ECR I-4587. See also Case C-210/00 *KCH* [2002] ECR I-06453.

[22] P Albrecht and S Braum, 'Deficiencies in the Development of European Criminal Law' (1999) 5 *European Law Journal* 293.

[23] See eg, S Douglas-Scott, 'The Rule of Law in the EU – Putting the Security into the 'Area of Freedom, Security and Justice' (2004) 29 *EL Rev* 219.

[24] S Aleagere and M Leaf, 'Mutual Recognition in European Judicial Cooperation: A step too far too soon?' (2004) 11 *European Law Journal* 200.

transfer of the criminal law to the supranational level impossible.[25] Furthermore, such scholars argue that criminalisation based on political opportunism and populism in order to secure EU goals is simply not a sound enough justification for the relocation of the criminal law to the supranational level. European law experts have, on the contrary, contested the democratic deficit in general terms and celebrated the notion of 'democracy beyond the nation state': that is, as the EU is not a state (with no demos), traditional explanations of democracy were to be adapted accordingly (as the whole purpose of the EU is multilevel governance).[26] In particular, the Commission appears to have viewed the criminal law as the answer to problems with European integration – the missing link for the 'final completion' of the single market.[27] Consequently, the 'race to the bottom' argument has frequently been put forward in this area as the justification for extending EU competence into the field of criminal law to address the possible risk of 'jurisdiction shopping'.

As shown above, the issue of a European criminal law is a heated topic which is far from decided and far from easy and which will continue to fuel a highly complex debate in the near future. The notion of criminal law in the EU and how such a competence could or should be construed, is part of the greater issue about the function of the EU itself – how to generate trust and confidence in the EU and the familiar question of the legitimacy of EU action. Moreover, it is about how to link the principles of criminalisation to the European project. These questions are explored, taken up and integrated in the following chapters.

The next section aims to look more closely at the traditional EU influence over the criminal law and in particular the impact of Article 4(3) TEU. It highlights the potential range of matters which may be judged to fall within the ambit of the Community and for which the Member States had never originally contemplated ceding national control such as the sensitive area of criminal law. It also illuminates the depth of the challenge that EU law presents for criminal law and vice versa.

B. The Search for Effective Sanctions

The Court of Justice has never hesitated to play an intrusive role when stating that the effectiveness of EU law cannot vary according to the various jurisdictions of national law.[28] This has led to a considerable process of harmonisation of national

[25] M Kaiafa Gbandi, 'The Development towards Harmonization within Criminal Law in the European Union – A Citizen's Perspective' (2001) 7 *European Journal of Crime, Criminal Law and Criminal Justice* 239.

[26] On multilevel governance see eg, I Pernice 'Multilevel Constitutionalism in the European Union' (2002) 27 *EL Rev* 511.

[27] Commission to the European Parliament and the Council on the implications of the Court's judgment of 13 September 2005, (Communication) COM (2005) 583 final 2, 24 November 2005, discussed below.

[28] eg, Case C-82/71 *Sail* [1972] ECR I-00119.

criminal laws, with norms either being set aside by EU law (the so-called negative effect) or given extended scope (the so-called positive effect) in the pursuit of European goals. Accordingly, while there has been a presumption that criminal law was a matter for the Member States, this presumption could – as in all other areas of EU law – be rebutted where its operation affected the pursuit of Community policies such as the smooth operation of the market. Clearly, competence boundaries have been easily blurred in this area.

i. Positive Effect

The principle of loyalty (ex Article 10 EC now Article 4(3) TEU) in interaction with the general principles of EU law, has constituted the corollary of the classic relationship between national criminal law and the EU. After all, the principle of loyalty obliged Member States to ensure compliance with EU law. Thus it could be said that the principle of loyalty identified a constitutional dynamic which indirectly provided what the EC Treaty lacked.[29]

The most celebrated example of 'positive effect'[30] in the form of a tangible 'Community law/criminal law principle' authored by the Court is the so-called *Greek Maize* judgment.[31] Briefly, this case concerned fraud against the European Community where the Court held that even though the choice of penalties remained within the discretion of the Member States, the Member States must ensure that infringements of Community law are penalised under conditions, both procedural and substantive, which are analogous to those applicable to infringements of national law of a similar nature and importance and which, in any event, make the penalty effective, proportionate and dissuasive. These requirements have since been confirmed in numerous cases (for example, *Nunes and de Matos*,[32] *Commission v France*[33] and the *Nisselli* case)[34] where the demands for effective, proportionate and dissuasive sanctions and the principle of assimilation have been frequently repeated as a kind of Community mantra. It could be argued that 'dissuasive and proportionate' are oxymoronic concepts. After all, it is far from clear what the Court means when it refers to these requirements. Nonetheless, according to one commentator the notion of an EU sanction should be understood as:

[29] JT Lang, 'The Duties of Cooperation of National Authorities and Courts under Article 10 EC' (2001) 26 *EL Rev* 84.

[30] I have chosen the word 'effect' here since this is the common term used in legal doctrine when discussing EC law in relation to criminal law but it could equally be referred to as 'integration' or 'influence'. See eg, Corstens and Pradel (above n 17).

[31] Case C-68/88 *Commission v Greece* [1989] ECR 1-2965, §24.

[32] Case C-186/98 *Nunes and de Matos* [1999] ECR I-4883.

[33] Case C-333/99 *Commission v France* [2001] ECR I-1025.

[34] Case C-457/02 *Antonio Nisselli* [2004] ECR I-10853.

> In penal practice (as distinct from theorizing), proportionality and dissuasion may be importantly linked: a measure may not be dissuasive unless it is proportionate, since excessive severity or leniency may both undermine future compliance . . . it may be argued that proportionality and dissuasion merely enlarge upon what is inherent in the concept of an effective sanction.[35]

And yet the exact contours of an EU law sanction are arguably still not very clear. Although it is true that this may be regarded as one of the characteristics, or the result of the principle of loyalty, that is, that it is flexible but imprecise,[36] it presupposes that we have an accepted definition of 'dissuasiveness' and 'effectiveness' in the first place. Thus the crucial question may be whether, in practice, Member States have a real choice in refraining from harmonising their criminal laws while still providing for 'dissuasive and effective' sanctions.[37] It should also be noted that the Court has explicitly stated that there is no obstacle to strict liability in EU law as long as there are genuine and sufficient safeguards for the individual in accordance with the principle of proportionality.[38] Nevertheless, arguably the crux of the issue is that the EU principle of proportionality is slightly different from proportionality as a criminal law principle in a strict sense. More specifically, the EU legal principle requires proportionality between 'means and ends', meaning that measures must be 'necessary and appropriate'. In this way, this principle is prospective and therefore different from the criminal law principle of proportionality which is retrospective, that is, it requires that the penalty is proportionate to the severity of the infringement in question.[39] The EU principle can take into account additional factors such as aggravated harm, which means that this principle is often more severe than the criminal law principle of proportionality. In this connection, it has been observed that the Court sometimes mixes these principles and that such confusion could lead to uncertainty and create discrimination where none was intended.[40] Indeed, the very interaction of EU law and national criminal law has been chaotic.

However, the main significance of Article 4(3) TEU is its underlying message of loyalty a Member State cannot choose to do nothing about a certain situation just because the national law is toothless. After all, the classic loyalty principle requires Member States to amend any conflicting legislation in accordance with the *Greek Maize*[41] formula outlined above, taking measures 'which in any event make the penalty dissuasive, effective and proportionate'. The most common and plausible

[35] C Harding, 'European Regimes of Crime Control: Objectives, Legal Bases and Accountability' (2000) 7 *Maastrict Journal of European and Comparative Law* 224.

[36] AG Kokott appears more certain, Case C-403/02 *Berlusconi and others* [2005] ECR I-3565, opinion delivered on 14 October 2004, § 88–90.

[37] T Elhom, *EU Svieg* (Copenhagen, Jurist, 2002) ch 9.

[38] Case C-326/88 *Hansen & Son* [1990] ECR I-2911.

[39] P Asp, *EG: S Sanktionsrätt* (Uppsala, Iustus,1998) ch 4, who gives the following cases as examples: for an application of criminal law principle of proportionality, Case C-326/88 *Hansen & Son* [1990] ECR I-2911, and for an example of administrative proportionality, Case C-137/85 *Maizena* [1987] ECR I-4587.

[40] ibid.

[41] Case C-68/88 *Commission v Greece* [1989] ECR I-2965.

view of an effective sanction is thus that in practice these principles need to be considered in conjunction with the non-discrimination principle – but in any event they must be 'effective' (which, as will be shown in chapter three, is a relative matter).[42] Therefore, there may be a risk of this coexistence of effective sanctions and harmonisation that it has the tendency to push criminal law in the direction of more severe sanctions.[43] In addition, it could create the risk of double procedures, as the notion of *ne bis in idem* only applies to criminal law (as stipulated in Article 50 of the EU Charter of Fundamental Rights ('the Charter'). Even though it is true that the EU law principle of proportionality could come to the rescue here by requiring that the measure in question be proportionate, in practice, it still leaves much uncertainty.[44] Thus, it should be noted that with the entry into force of the Lisbon Treaty and thereby the legally binding status of the Charter, Article 49 (3) makes it clear that the severity of penalties must not be disproportionate to the criminal offence.

ii. Negative Effect

As seen above, the principle of loyalty can have the effect of requiring Member States to provide sanctions 'positively' although it can also prevent them from imposing sanctions if such sanctions would hinder the smooth running of the internal market. More specifically, the negative effect or influence refers to the obligation on Member States to set aside provisions incompatible with EU law and, moreover, to repeal any such provision in order to preserve legal certainty. The case law of the Court in this area is well known and fairly consistent.[45] For example, in the *Cowan* case the Court concluded that

> although in principle criminal legislation and the rules of criminal procedure are matters for which the Member States are responsible, Community law sets certain limits to their power and such legislation may not restrict the fundamental freedoms guaranteed by the Community.[46]

This is basic and not particularly controversial although – since from a European perspective it delivers a clear message – national regimes should not render the freedoms recognised by the Treaty illusory, and no discrimination on the ground of nationality may apply. This is the EU law requirement of non-discrimination. In any case, it is perhaps of more importance that the negative effect is also of interest to the individual, while the above outlined positive effect is generally

[42] C Harding, 'Member State Enforcement of European Community Measures: The Chimera of Effective Enforcement' (1997) 4 *Maastricht Journal of European and Comparative Law* 5.

[43] Asp (above n 39).

[44] See also COM (2005) 696, 23 December 2005. This major topic in EU criminal law, the *ne bis in idem* rule, will not be dealt with here, owning to considerations of space, but they will be touched upon in various sections below, Joint Cases C-187/01 and C-385/01 *Gözütok and Brugge* [2003] ECR I-1354.

[45] eg Case 203/80 *Casati* [1981] ECR 2595; Case C-163/94 *Sanz de Lera* [1995] ECR I-04821; Case C-348/96 *Donatella Calfa* [1999] ECR I-11.

[46] Case C-186/87 *Cowan v Le Trésor Public* [1986] ECR 195.

directed to the national legislator (since only the legislator is entitled to decide what should be criminalised).[47] Interestingly, the concept of a crime is examined similarly to a breach of EU law, which means that a violation has first to be established and then the possible justifications are examined.[48] This is especially relevant in the context of criminal law defences (for example, in the expulsion cases). Therefore, the possibility of 'euro-defence' is a reality and the principle of loyalty required the Member States to consider it. This is the negative – albeit very positive for the defendant – influence of the loyalty obligation. Nonetheless, EU law in national criminal law proceedings appears to resemble the well-known 'Jack-in-the-Box Theory' of Community law, in that it can pop up unexpectedly and cause alarm.[49] The next subsection will look more closely at the principle of legality as it forms an integral part of the 'negative' influence of EU law and constitutes a fundamental principle of importance in both EU law and criminal law.

iii. *The Principle of Legality*

The principle of legality is a *sine qua non* for any discussion of criminal law, procedural or substantive – including at the European level.[50] Indeed, it has become increasingly difficult, as is the case with fundamental rights (and human rights) in general,[51] to know what counts as a general principle of EU law and what counts as a fundamental principle of criminal law. This subsection will briefly compare the notion of legality as a principle of criminal law with legality as a European law concept. One of the first significant cases at the EU level was *Kent Kirk*[52] which concerned the retroactive application of a regulation. The Court's message in this case was clear:

> The principle that penal provisions may not have retroactive effect is one which is common to all the legal orders of the member states and is enshrined in article 7 of the European Convention for the protection of human rights and fundamental freedoms as a fundamental right; it takes its place among the general principles of law whose observance is ensured by the Court of Justice (paragraph 22).

Accordingly, an important issue here is in what way the principle of legality in criminal law differs from the principle of legality in European law, if at all. This is doubtless a huge question which far exceeds the ambit of this limited analysis. Nevertheless, it is useful to dip into it. For example, regarding legality as an abstract principle, in EU law doctrine it is often argued that legal certainty (as

[47] M Delmas-Marty, 'The European Union and Penal Law' (1998) 4 *European Law Journal* 87.

[48] I borrow this example from P Asp *EU & Straffrätten* (Uppsala, Iustus, 2002) ch 1.

[49] T Wilhelmsson, 'Jack-in-the-Box Theory of European Community Law' in Krämer et al (eds), *Law and Diffuse Interests in the European Legal Order* (Baden-Baden, Nomos, 1997).

[50] This section is drawing on E Herlin-Karnell, 'Recent Developments in the Area of European Criminal Law' (2007) 14 *Maastricht Journal of European and Comparative Law* 15. On legality see eg, A Ashworth, *Principles of Criminal Law* (Oxford, Oxford University Press, 2006) ch 2.

[51] eg Case 60/00 *Mary Carpenter* [2002] ECR 1-6279 and *Bosphorus v Ireland* (45036/98) (2006) 42 EHRR 1.

[52] Case C-63/83 *Kent Kirk* [1984] ECR 2689.

forming part of legality) is not so meaningful as an abstract principle and that it should rather be attributed in every concrete case (on a case-by-case basis).[53] The situation is, however, crucially different in the context of criminal law where legal certainty is presupposed as far as possible, also at a more abstract level where the system in question needs to be compliant with legality in its own right. Hence a case-by-case approach is not sufficient in this area. Before looking more closely at the possible clash of norms between EU law and national criminal law, the basics of the legality principle will be explained.

iv. Legality: The Fundamentals

The principle of legality is enshrined in Article 7 ECHR and Article 49 of the Charter which stipulate the ban on retroactive criminal law. Indeed, this is the cornerstone of modern criminal law. However, the principle of legality is more complex than a simple prohibition of retroactive criminal law; the notion of legality is a conjunction of intertwined principles. Briefly, the principles are as follows: there can be no crime without written law; there can be no retroactive criminal law; there should be maximum certainty[54] and there can be no crime by analogy.[55] In this way the principle of legality as a general principle of EU and criminal law helps to control EU institutions and the legislator. There is no doubt that the principle of legality is of great relevance for the individual at the European level, as in a situation of unclear regulations or unimplemented directives it could operate as a basis for avoiding criminal liability. Furthermore, criminal law has, due to the ban on retroactivity, avoided the debate on the doctrine of consistent interpretation since, in contrast to the concept of direct effect, the rule of interpretation in conformity with directives is generally not restricted to cases where the rights of citizens are advanced.[56] In any case, a fifth principle is often added to the four axioms of legality stated above. This is the possibility of relying on a more lenient provision at the time of sentencing and is common in many European legal traditions and furthermore, as noted, is affirmed in Article 49 of the Charter.[57] Nevertheless, such use of retroactive lenient legislation goes further than Article 7 ECHR, which 'only' stipulates the ban on retroactive criminal law. Consequently, it could be argued that the more lenient provision principle does not constitute a component of the 'core legality rule' and is therefore not an absolute right but an extended version of it. The reason for using it stems from the purpose and function of criminal law, that is once a legislator changes his or her opinion of what

[53] S Prechal, *Directives in EC Law* (OUP Oxford 2005) 203.

[54] eg *Kokkinakis v Greece*, ECHR, Series A, No 260-A, 1993, *Cantoni v France*, ECHR, Reports 1996-V and cf eg Joined Cases C-74/95 and 129/95, *Criminal Proceedings against X* [1996] ECR I-6609 and Case C-354/95 *National Farmers' Union* [997] ECR I-4559.

[55] D Frände, *Den straffrättsliga legalitetsprincipen* (Ekenäs, Juridiska Föreningens i Finland, Publikationsserie No 52, 1989).

[56] See eg, Prechal (above n 53).

[57] See also International Covenant of Civil and Political Rights, GA Res 2200A (XXI) of 16 December 1966, Art 15.

action should be made criminal, there is no point in punishing 'old' wrongdoing.[58] Therefore, Article 49(1) of the Charter expressly mentions the possible use of favourable retroactive law.[59]

The question of the application of the more lenient provision was highlighted in the *Berlusconi* judgment. The *Berlusconi*[60] case is interesting because it illuminated a clash between the positive and negative influence of Article 4(3) TEU. This time 'new' national law represented the more lenient provision but such an application would have been in breach of EU law. In brief, Berlusconi was charged with having published false company documents. The offences at issue were defined within the framework of Directive 68/151/EEC, but newly introduced Italian legislation significantly relaxed the previous implementing provisions. For example, the new law introduced a much shorter limitation period and sanctions which could be automatically considered as suspended sentences meaning, in practice, that no punishment was given. The Italian criminal code contains a so-called mitigation statute (allowing the application of a new lenient criminal law at the time of sentencing) but the new provisions clearly run counter to the directive at issue so the question arose as to whether it would amount to a breach of EU law to rely on the new mitigated legislation.

What happened next in this confrontation of effective sanctions versus the use of a more lenient national criminal law provision at the time of sentencing? The answer is that nothing happened. The Court completely avoided this burning issue. Even though it is true that it would have been impossible to use an individual as a 'test case', some clarification regarding Article 4(3) TEU and the two sides of the same coin – positive and negative effect – would have been very useful. In this regard, it has been suggested that the Court (because of this peculiar situation with EU law set aside at the national level) should have focused on the loyalty obligation and its requirement for an effective sanction as trumping an incompatible newer national law.[61] Moreover, a further issue arises, namely why is the 'positive effect' considered stronger than the 'negative effect' when they both act to enforce Community law? Indeed, this is the almost schizophrenic function of the blurred concept of loyalty as a legal tool. For example, what would have been the result if the setting had been different? If the Italian law had not referred to the possible use of a more lenient criminal law, would such a possibility still have constituted a general principle of EU law? Article 49 of the Charter now tells us that it would.[62] It is, however, worth mentioning the fact that there is no authority to support the position that the use of a more lenient provision would form part of, for example, English law and that accordingly there may be a risk that English defendants are disadvantaged compared to those accused on the Continent.[63] It

[58] Ashworth (above n 50).

[59] See also Art 15(1) Covenant of Civil and Political Rights and Art 24 of the Rome (ICC) Statute.

[60] Joined Cases C-387/02, C-391/02 and C-403/02 *Silvio Berlusconi & others* [2005] ECR I-3565.

[61] A Biondi and R Mastroianni, Case Comment (2006) 43 *CML Rev* 550.

[62] Interestingly, this exception refers to national law and international law but not to EU law as such.

[63] E Baker, 'Taking European Criminal Law Seriously' (1998) *Crim LR* 361.

will be interesting to see the impact of the Charter in this respect. It is anticipated that this kind of clash will once again come under the European spotlight, as this breed of Europeanised criminal law appears set for dynamic evolution. Arguably, the *Berlusconi* case illuminates not only the dual function of Article 4(3) TEU but also the political sensitivity of the question.

In any case, the Court had previously stated that there is no restriction on using a more favourable EU law measure at the time of sentencing if that is possible under national law. This has not been explicitly considered as a general principle of EU law, but rather as being in line with Article 4 (3) and the notion of loyalty.[64] After all, cases such as *Bordessa*[65] and *Awoyemi*[66] made clear that an individual could rely on the direct effect of a directive before the deadline for transposition has passed, if that is possible according to a Member State's national legislation concerning the retroactive effect of a more favourable provision. However, the Court did not explicitly refer to the Charter, which, as already explained, referred to the possible use of the more lenient provision, which invites speculation as to whether this decision represented an implied interpretation of it.[67] In a recent case relating to the possibility of relying on the more lenient provision, the Court left it to the national court to ensure that such a possibility was a reality (in the context of the Returns Directive[68]) by stressing that the more lenient provision forms part of the constitutional traditions of the Member States.[69] The Court held that a severe penalty would be liable to delay an enforcement of a return decision and would therefore be in contradiction to EU law. Interestingly, however, there was no mention of the Charter or of the requirement of a proportionate penalty by any source of (explicit) analogy in this case.[70]

III. THE HISTORIC THIRD PILLAR WEB AND THE CONCEPT OF MUTUAL RECOGNITION

It could appear slightly strange to discuss the former third pillar only now when this is the legal sphere which previously formed the core of the notion of European criminal law. The reason for this is twofold: first and obviously, the first and the third pillars have always been very closely interlinked and constantly interacted in EU criminal matters. Secondly, the purpose of this chapter has been to provide a background to the Case C-176/03 judgment and it therefore seemed logical to allow the third pillar and the 'failure' of the Constitutional Treaty in 2005 to set

[64] Peers (above n 6) ch 8.

[65] Case C-416/93 *Bordessa* [1995] ECR I-361.

[66] Case C-230/97 *Awoyemi* [1998] ECR I-06781.

[67] As it would have become binding if the Constitutional Treaty had entered into force. As noted above, with the entry into force of the Lisbon Treaty the Charter is now legally binding.

[68] Directive 2008/115/EC on common standards and procedures in Member States for returning illegally staying third-country nationals [2008] OJ L348/98.

[69] See also Case C-61/11 PPU, *El Dridi*, judgment delivered on 28 April 2011, see also Case C-420/06 *Jager* [2008] ECR I-1315.

[70] See the discussion in ch 4 Part IV.

the final scene – while bearing in mind all the points outlined above on the influence of EU law on national criminal law – before entering the dynamics of supranational criminal law.

Thus, as already noted, criminal law cooperation within the third pillar increased significantly in the effort to combat terrorism, particularly in the aftermath of the terrorist attacks of 9/11. As implied above, cooperation so far has mainly focused on the 'combat' aspect, largely leaving the rights of the defendant behind.[71] One of the first instruments to be agreed upon in this new wave of further criminal law cooperation was the European Arrest Warrant (EAW) Framework Decision.[72] This measure replaced the traditional extradition procedures with ones securing 'surrender' in accordance with the theme of mutual recognition, which, in practice, meant that the legal power in these matters shifted from politicians to judges.[73] The EAW abolished the requirement for dual criminality for certain crimes by introducing the concept of mutual recognition in the area of prosecutions based on the notion of hypothetical trust between Member States. Nevertheless, mutual recognition of judicial decisions across the Member States presupposes a climate of trust between the domestic legal orders which appears particularly difficult to achieve in an area as sensitive as criminal law. Therefore, it can readily be argued, as so many commentators have already done, that criminal law – unlike the creation of an integrated market – demands a common set of generally applicable standards and meta-standards.[74] After all, generally speaking, criminal law deals with the deprivation of liberty, in contrast to the imperative of EU free movement.

Furthermore, one problem which arises when discussing the notion of EU criminal law cooperation is that there is no definition of 'mutual recognition' in the field of criminal law. This lack of conceptualisation has previously been considered as constituting a significant lacuna in EU criminal law cooperation.[75] Even so, this alleged gap in certainty has not been remedied in the Lisbon Treaty. Furthermore, there has always been a clear willingness among Member States to use mutual recognition as a way of avoiding legislation in this area. Nevertheless,

[71] eg Peers (above n 6); V Mitsilegas, 'The Constitutional Implications of Mutual Recognition' (2006) 43 *CML Rev* 1277; V Mitsilegas, 'The third wave of third pillar law. Which direction for EU criminal justice?' (2009) 34 *EL Rev* 523.

[72] 2002/584/JHA [2002] OJ L190/1, on the EAW.

[73] eg Peers (above n 6) ch 9, V Mitsilegas, 'The Transformation of Criminal Law in the Area of Freedom, Security and Justice' (2007) 26 *Yearbook of European Law* 1 as well as V Mitsilegas, *EU Criminal Law* (Oxford, Hart Publishing, 2009) and S Lavenex, 'Mutual Recognition and the Monopoly of Force: Limits of the Single Market Analogy' (2007) 14 *Journal for European Environmental and Planning Law* 762. For recent works on mutual recognition in EU criminal law see in particular, A Suominen, *The European Arrest Warrant and its Implementation in the Nordic Countries* (PhD thesis, Bergen University, 2011) and M Fichera, 'The Implementation of the European Arrest Warrant in the European Union: Law, Policy and Practice' (Antwerp, Intersentia, 2011).

[74] eg Guild (above n 14).

[75] It has furthermore been suggested that a way of remedying the ambiguity that characterised the CT in this respect would be to settle on only one language when issuing documents such as warrants. A Klip, 'The Constitution for Europe and Criminal Law: A Step not Far Enough?' Editorial (2005) 12 *Maastricht Journal of European and Comparative Law* 115.

in the wake of the *Pupino* case,[76] what was at stake is specifically the obligation to adopt Community-based reasoning in the former third pillar and the issue of the extent to which one could simply adopt 'trade-based' principles in the area of criminal law and hence change the notion of extradition to that of surrender. In this regard it is often pointed out that there is currently insufficient mutual trust between the Member States and no adequate European regime for the protection of human rights within the former third pillar to justify such an analogy with the internal market and mutual recognition.[77]

The next section examines a case which demonstrates that the failure of the Constitutional Treaty (CT) was not significant as the course of navigation had already been set. It also highlights the complex function of legality as involving more than a question of substantive criminal law.

A. *Pupino* and the Quest for 'Depillarisation'/Effectiveness[78]

The *Pupino* case has become one of the most debated cases in EU constitutional law and EU criminal law in particular.[79] For this reason, a short summary of the facts should suffice. Briefly, Pupino was charged with using physical violence against pupils under five years old. Under the Italian law in question, evidence does not have to be subject to cross-examination at oral hearings if the case concerned violence or sexual offences involving minors. The prosecution stated that this should apply as the case involved minors. Pupino, in defence, argued that the disputed provision did not apply as the case did not concern sexual violence. A Framework Decision (2001/220/JHA)[80] on the standing of victims required Member States to provide protection for those giving evidence in court by enabling witnesses to testify but not appearing in person in court. Hence, the national court asked the CJEU whether they were required to interpret the Italian law in the light of the Framework Decision. AG Kokott again answered in the affirmative. More concretely, she stated that the principle of loyalty in ex Article 10 EC (now Article 4(3) TEU) from some axiomatic principles, namely that 'obligations must be fulfilled and damaging measures refrained from without needing to be expressly mentioned'.[81] The Court agreed and ruled that it would be very difficult for the EU to carry out its tasks effectively if the principle of loyal cooperation requiring in particular that Member States take all appropriate measures, general

[76] Case C-105/03 *Pupino* [2005] ECR I-5285.

[77] Peers (above n 6).

[78] This section draws largely on Herlin-Karnell (above n 50) and 'In the Wake of Pupino: Advocaten voor de Wereld and Dell'Orto' (2007) 8 *German Law Journal* 1147.

[79] For a survey of different interpretations of the *Pupino* case, see G Martinico, 'From the Constitution for Europe to the Reform Treaty: A Literature Survey on European Constitutional Law' in (2009) *Perspectives on Federalism* available at www.on-federalism.eu/attachments/024_download.pdf (last accessed January 2012).

[80] Framework Decision 2001/220/JHA on the standing of victims in criminal proceedings [2001] OJ L82.

[81] Opinion of AG Kokott delivered on 11 November 2004.

or particular, to ensure the fulfilment of their obligations under EU law were not also binding in the third pillar. Consequently, the measure at issue was accorded, not direct effect – which had been explicitly excluded by ex Article 34 EU – but 'indirect effect' for the sake of the effectiveness of EU law.

What then of legal certainty here? The Framework Decision in question introduced rules which offered protection to the witness or plaintiff by laying down certain and objective rules for giving evidence by means other than appearing in court. Arguably, such rules should be interpreted in the light of the general requirement for a fair trial as promoting objectivity in the manner in which hearings take place. In short, Article 6(2)–(3) ECHR states that everyone charged with a criminal offence shall be presumed innocent until proved guilty according to law and shall have the right to examine, or have examined, any witnesses against him or her. In this connection, suffice it to say that the rules regarding evidence are to be construed in such a way that the defendant is treated fairly by the authorities and the courts, that the notion of presumption of innocence is closely linked to the Article 6(1) ECHR imperative of objectivity. The procedural notion of legality comes into play here. There is no explicit general right to 'expect' a strictly laid down evidence procedure what matters is that the evidence at issue is collected and considered on an objective basis.[82] Expressed differently, the crucial matter is that the defendant be treated fairly and have the right to a defence and that the burden of proof is placed – with limited exceptions – on the prosecutor. This is the function of legality as both a procedural and a substantive principle.[83] Accordingly, the possible confusion or danger as regards the application of legality arises, it is submitted, when it is less clear whether the notion of a fair trial is fulfilled in the context of, for example, an arrest warrant prompting compliance with the *Pupino* rule. It is important to keep in mind that the use of the Framework Decision in question concerned ways of taking evidence involving young children. In other words, the notion of 'mutual trust' between Member States was not really put to the test. The significance of *Pupino* will depend to a large extent upon the specific circumstances of the case at issue. Needless to say, this is not an easy task for the Court and such an exercise casts a harsh light on criminal law policy questions which should not be underestimated. In any event, the underlying rationale should offer rather more 'in favour of the individual' and rather less 'in favour of the EU'.

This brings us to the next step of the present analysis. It is arguably necessary to investigate recent developments in the wake of *Pupino*.

[82] It is also important that any uncertainties are interpreted in favour of the defendant. See eg, Ashworth (above n 50).

[83] For a slightly different view see V Mitselegas, 'Constitutional Principles of the European Community and European Criminal Law' (2007) 9 *European Journal of Law Reform* 303, who does not seem to draw any distinction between procedural and substantive legality from the perspective of legal certainty.

B. *Advocaten voor de Wereld* and the EAW

As indicated above, the adoption of the EAW and the concept of mutual recognition constituted a revolution in EU criminal law procedure. Several Constitutional courts in Europe have either declared the national law implementing the EAW unconstitutional (for example in Germany and Cyprus),[84] or upheld it as part of the process of criminal law cooperation in Europe (for example in the Czech Republic).[85] The challenges to the constitutionality of the EAW have concerned the EU measure itself or the national measure implementing it, or its application to a particular case. In *Advocaten voor de Wereld*, the Court had to tackle probably the most difficult issue of them all – the constitutionality of the EU instrument itself. There is, for example, no general human rights exception in the EAW, even though the preamble uses the language of human rights by highlighting the importance of fundamental rights. In other words, the recital appears to envisage a refusal to surrender in a number of situations not reflected in the substantive provisions of the Framework Decision. At issue here is the extent to which the preamble permits a judge to refuse to surrender a person on account of the risk that the conditions in the issuing state with regard to any or every feature of the impending trial do not measure up to the judge's view of the requirements of fairness.[86] It can, therefore, be argued that, despite the lack of a general human rights exception, an insistence on explicit compliance with the Charter and the ECHR is possible under the preamble of the EAW. Such an interpretation would not, to borrow an expression from the House of Lords in the *Dabas* case concerning the national court's interpretation methods and the EAW, 'cross the Rubicon'; that is, it would not be incompatible with the spirit of EU law.[87]

In any case, the judgment in *Advocaten voor de Wereld* constitutes the first test case of the validity of the EAW Framework Decision at the EU level.[88]

Briefly, Advocaten voor de Wereld was a non-profit making association that brought an action in Belgium for annulment of the EAW Framework Decision. One of the questions asked by the national court[89] – and arguably the most interesting and important one – was whether the EAW breaches the principle of

[84] Mitsilegas (above n 71).

[85] eg E Guild (ed) *Constitutional Challenges to the EAW* (The Hague, TMC Asser, 2006) and Evan Sliedreigt and N Keijzer (eds) *The EAW in Practice* (The Hague, Asser press 2009).

[86] N Fennelly, 'The European Arrest Warrant: Recent Developments' (2007) 8 *ERA Forum* 519.

[87] *Dabas (Appellant) v High Court of Justice, Madrid (Respondent)* (Criminal Appeal from Her Majesty's High Court of Justice) [2007] UKHL 6, 28 February 2007. E Herlin-Karnell, 'The Swedish Supreme Court and the European Arrest Warrant' (2007) 8 *Europarattslig tidskrift* 883.

[88] *Advocaten voor de Wereld*, [2007] ECR I-3633, Opinion of AG Colomer delivered on 12 September 2006. S Peers, 'Salvation outside the Church: Judicial Protection in the Third Pillar after the *Pupino* and *Segi* Judgments' (2007) 44 *CML Rev* 883. E Spaventa 'Remembrance of Principles Lost: on Fundamental Rights, the Third Pillar and the Scope of Union Law' (2006) 25 *YEL* 153.

[89] The other questions asked was whether the EAW should have been adopted as a Convention rather than as a Framework Decision and whether the EWA breached the principles of equality and non-discrimination.

legality in criminal law.[90] The Court concluded that the EAW did not breach the principle of legality. In reaching that conclusion,[91] the Court broke its silence on the Charter[92] and stated that, 'by virtue of [ex Article 6 EU], the Union is founded on the principle of the rule of law and it respects fundamental rights'. Furthermore, the Court stipulated that even if the Member States were to reproduce the list of categories of offences set out in the Framework Decision word-for-word for the purposes of its implementation, the actual definition of those offences and the penalties applicable are those which follow from the law of 'the issuing Member State'. Such reasoning, as already noted, could be said to be in line with the traditional definition of 'mutual recognition', previously developed in the context of internal market law. Nonetheless, the crux has been that the notion of 'trust' was abandoned; that is it does not remedy the lack of maximum certainty in criminal law. It is true that the Court did not express an explicit view as to whether the list of EAW crimes (with no dual criminality) met the requirement of legality in criminal law in general. The only matter of concern is, according to the Court, the law of the issuing state which is safeguarded or supervised by the general protection of human rights in the EU and, more specifically, by the Charter. It is disappointing that the Court did not provide more enlightening legal reasoning as to why the EAW – as it currently stands – is reconcilable with legality and fundamental rights more broadly. In this way the Court has adopted a very narrow definition of legality. At issue here is the risk that an excessive focus on enforcement could easily create a harmful relationship between national law and EU law. More specifically, such an imbalanced enforcement could undermine national procedural safeguards in criminal law, resulting in some Member States in less clear cases (concerning the 'pliable' notion of a fair trial) choosing to comply with fidelity at the possible expense of the individual – and procedural – legality.[93]

C. *Dell'Orto* and the Wider Constitutional Question

In *Dell'Orto*[94] the Court was again confronted by the Framework Decision on the protection of victims (as in *Pupino*) and the setting was again Italy. However, *Dell'Orto* had a further component: the Framework Decision in question was supplemented by a Directive on state compensation for victims.[95] This Directive required Member States to establish a compensation scheme but left the method for doing so to the national systems. Although there already is a degree of approximation in this field due to a Council of Europe Convention, the EU measures in issue have been criticised as being too vague, leaving room for questions of

[90] Herlin-Karnell (above n 78).
[91] Or to initially establish its jurisdiction.
[92] Also eg C-540/03 *Parliament v Council* [2006] ECR I-5769.
[93] See also Mitsilegas (above n 71).
[94] Case C-467/05 *Giovanni Dell'Orto* [2007] ECR I-5557.
[95] Directive 2004/80/EC [2004] OJ L261/15.

interpretation.[96] More specifically, the question asked by the national court was whether the right to compensation from the offender applied to any party affected by the crime in question, and whether the Italian court could interpret 'victim of crime' in light of this Directive, even though these measures were adopted after the crime at issue had been committed. However, *Dell'Orto* did not constitute a battering ram of first pillar reasoning applied to the former third pillar. Instead, the Court in this case took a step back. According to the Court, the issue was obvious – the Directive and the Framework Decision were so different that 'not even supposing that the Directive was capable of having any effect on the interpretation of the provision of a framework decision . . . [they] are not on any analysis linked in a manner which could call for a uniform interpretation in question'.[97] The Italian courts appear here to be in sympathy with the EU Court – engaging in a harmonious interpretation of EU law – but also also appears to be an area characterised by ad hoc solutions. More recently, however, in *Katz*,[98] – again concerning the Framework Decision on the standing of victims, this time on the possibility of interpreting a substitute private prosecutor as a 'private prosecutor' in order to grant testimony rights in accordance with Hungarian law – the Court did not stretch the wording of the instrument in question to insist on such an interpretation. Nevertheless, the Court applied the same standards as those provided by the ECHR in insisting on the right to give testimony by some means. In addition, while the Court in *Advocaten voor de Wereld* appears to have been wearing 'blinkers' as regards the current problems with mutual recognition in criminal law, the judgments in *Dell'Orto* and *Katz* are much more cautious, though it is true that this does not rule out more extensive application of the reasoning in *Pupino* should the facts differ. This issue will be addressed in further detail in chapter three, the purpose here being simply to give an outline of EU criminal law in its very patchy glory.

As seen above, the development of EU criminal law has been 'two-dimensional'. On the one hand, it showed the impact of the criminal law procedural law regime and third pillar cooperation. On the other hand, it showed the influence on national law stemming from the Article 4(3) TEU obligation and effective enforcement more generally. As implied above, the notion of European criminal law has lately, and perhaps more dramatically, also become a question of legislative competence at the supranational level. Hence the next Part addresses the supranational arena. Indeed, remarkable rulings within the area of environmental crime confirm that the Court is on a 'mission': it insists on a communitarisation of the third pillar and when possible an allocation of competences in favour of the supranational sphere in the spirit of ex Article 47 EU.

This introductory chapter now turns to the milestone decision of Case C-176/03 – the starting point of this book – and the developments that followed in its immediate wake.

[96] Peers (above n 6).

[97] Case C-467/05 *Giovanni Dell'Orto* [2007] ECR I-5557.

[98] Case C-404/07 *Katz* [2008] I-7607.

IV. SUPRANATIONAL CRIMINAL LAW

This part introduces the notion of supranational criminal law as developed in the environmental criminal law sphere. As already stated, few cases have received as much attention as Case C-176/03,[99] as the case illuminated the general problem of the delimitation of competences between the former first and the third pillars. As this judgment is so crucial to the development of EU criminal law at the supranational level, it deserves a short reiteration despite being currently one of the best known cases in contemporary EU law.[100]

A. Effectiveness Revised: *Commission v Council*

The story of Case C-176/03 started with an initiative by Denmark for a proposal for a Framework Decision on the protection of the environment through criminal law.[101] Subsequently, the Commission made two proposals for a Directive that would oblige Member States to take criminal law action for the protection of the environment.[102] This Directive was noteworthy because it challenged the previous assumption that the EC has no legislative competence in the field of criminal law. As a response to the actions taken by the Commission, the Council decided to adopt a Framework Decision (based on the above mentioned, but now amended, initiative by Denmark)[103] with the same purpose as the Directive, that is to safeguard the environment through the use of criminal law, but leaving the choice of criminal and/or non-criminal penalties to Member States. This spurred the Commission not only to amend its proposals, which – as expected – had been rejected by the Council, to 'defeat' the Framework Decision but also to bring an action for annulment against the Council for having intruded on its domain.

In his Opinion AG Colomer summarised a very interesting, although sometimes neglected, dimension of this judgment. He stipulated: 'The present dispute brings into play another issue, which affects not so much the Member States as their citizens: their right that it be democratically elected representatives who determine criminal offences, which translates in legal terms as the principle of the

[99] Case C-176/03 *Commission v Council* [2005] ECR I-7879.

[100] E Herlin-Karnell, '*Commission v Council*: Some Reflections on Criminal Law in the First Pillar' (2007) 15 *European Public Law* 69; C Tobler, Annotation 'Case 176/03' (2006) 43 *CML Rev* 835; K Apps, 'Case C-176/03, *Commission v Council*: Pillars Askew: Criminal Law EC-Style', (2006) *Columbia Journal of European Law* 625; Mitsilegas *EU Criminal Law* (above n 73); and H Labayale, 'L'ouverture de la jarred de Pandore: reflexions sur la competene de la Communaute en materiere penale' (2006) *Cashiers de droit Europeen* 382.

[101] Framework Decision on combating environmental crime, [2000] 383/JHA, OJ L39/4. Drawing on Herlin-Karnell (ibid) and above n 50.

[102] Proposal for a Directive on the Protection of the Environment through Criminal Law [2001] OJ C180E/238 and amended Proposal [2003] OJ C020E/284.

[103] Council Framework Decision 2003/80/JHA [2003] OJ L29/55.

legality of criminal law. . ..'[104] On the one hand, he argued that it might be a step too far and too soon to rule that the criminal law 'belongs' in the first pillar. On the other hand, he suggested that this would guarantee respect for the principle of legality.

The Court took the same route but went even further in stating (paragraphs 47–48):

> As a general rule, neither criminal law nor the rules of criminal procedure fall within the Community's competence . . . however the last mentioned findings do not prevent the Community legislator, when the application of effective, proportionate and dissuasive criminal penalties by the competent national authorities is an essential measure for combating serious environmental offences, from taking measures which relate to the criminal law of the Member States which it consider necessary in order to ensure that rules which it lays down on environmental protection are fully effective.

The Court concluded that the aim of the Framework Decision in question was the protection of the environment through criminal law sanctions, which was something for the Community, as the protection of the environment is one of the Community's objectives (ex Article 175 EC now Article 192 TFEU). Consequently, the Court clarified that, in accordance with ex Article 47 EU which safeguarded the former first pillar from intruding on second and third pillar measures, this was the end of the discussion: criminal law was a question for the supranational legislator.

What then makes this case so interesting? After all, the ruling was not a very big step from Article 4(3) TFEU (ex Article 10 EC) and the long-standing mantra of effective, proportionate and dissuasive sanctions. Nevertheless, and as will be discussed below, every discussion regarding EU law competence has to start with Article 5(1) TEU and the principle of attributed competences. However, in the present case the Court appears to use 'effectiveness' as the key threshold to be crossed before an EU competence to take measures relating to criminal law is established. As will be explored in subsequent chapters, this presents difficulties as effectiveness is a very slippery notion. Moreover, it is far from clear that criminal law is 'effective' as a means of social control. It is submitted that the Court's reasoning is actually rather murky, delving into extremely muddy waters. Although it is true that the case concerned the environmental sphere, it is by now obvious that this judgment greatly exceeded the limited terrain of the environment, with a much wider constitutional dimension. Thus, it should be recalled that in the immediate 'celebratory waves' of this judgment, the Commission presented a communication that paved the way for the general harmonisation of criminal law at the EU level. For this reason, the next section briefly introduces this proposal as it highlights the eagerness for EU institutionalisation of criminal law even in the absence of a constitutional document.

[104] Opinion of AG Colomer delivered on 26 May 2005, para 77.

B. The Commission's Communication

As noted, in the wake of the outcome of Case C-176/03, the Commission presented a communication[105] which suggested that the delimitation of power between the first and the third pillars had been resolved once and for all by the judgment in Case C-176/03. According to the Commission, the same reasoning could therefore automatically be extended to, for example, the Article 114 TFEU (ex Article 95 EC) doctrine on the establishment and functioning of the internal market. The impact of Article 114 TFEU will be discussed extensively in chapter four and the purpose here is simply to very briefly outline this communication in order to see the background picture. In this communication the Commission argued that 'in the light of the judgment, when criminal law measures are needed to ensure the effectiveness of Community law, it is for the Community legislator, and for it alone, to adopt such measures'. Nevertheless, this communication ensures that the EU should only act if two conditions – necessity and consistency – are met. Moreover, the Commission stipulated that any use of criminal law must be justified by the need to make the Community policy in question effective on a case-by-case basis. The problem was, however, that it did not evaluate the issue of what counts as 'effectiveness' to make it duly justified. The Commission's communication, however, essentially followed the same pattern as a string of cases including *Pupino* and Case C-176/03 discussed above, which were delivered as seemingly symbolic decisions which insisted on constitutional changes even in the absence of the Constitutional Treaty. Even though the eventual ratification of the subsequent Lisbon Treaty remained uncertain for some time, what was certain was the Court's unambiguous willingness to favour the supranational level, with the reason for such development appearing to rest on an exercise in effectiveness. Clearly, the evolution of EU criminal law has been turbulent.

C. The *Ship Source Pollution* Ruling

Although this case – the first follow-up to Case C-176/03 – will be scrutinised more fully below in connection with the discussion of the constitutional use of 'effectiveness', it is worth briefly setting out here the characteristics of this ruling. It should perhaps be pointed out that the background to the *Ship source pollution* judgment was much less dramatic than that provided by Case C-176/03. Instead, in the *Ship source pollution* case[106] the Framework Decision in question was intended to supplement the Directive on ship source pollution and on the introduction of penalties for infringements with a view to strengthening maritime safety, by approximating the legislation of the Member States, and was consequently not, in contrast

[105] Above n 27.

[106] *Ship source pollution* (above n 2) concerning Directive (EC) 35 [2005] OJ L255 based on Article 80(2) EC, and amended by Directive 2009/123/EC [2009] OJ L280/52.

to Case C-176/03, aimed at competing as a legal instrument with respect to competence.[107] This Framework Decision was based on ex Articles 31(1)(e) EU and 34(2)(b) EU. Briefly, it laid down rules which obliged the Member States to provide for criminal penalties and to take all measures necessary to ensure that offences in breach of the Directive, including aiding and abetting such activity, were punished by effective, proportionate and dissuasive criminal penalties. The Framework Decision also prescribed minimum sentences of imprisonment for intentionally committed crimes and stipulated that Member States were to lay down the measures necessary to ensure that persons could be held legally liable and punished by adequate penalties or measures. However, as noted, the Directive in question was also a significant actor in the game and stressed the importance of safeguards for the environment through the use of criminal law as a part of the EU's maritime safety policy. More specifically, the Directive stipulated that Member States should ensure that ship source discharges of polluting substances were regarded as infringements if committed with intent, recklessly or by serious negligence. Given that there was an obvious overlap between the measures at issue, the Commission argued that the first pillar and the Directive were the correct legal platform from which to approach environmental criminal law.

AG Mazak provided a thoughtful opinion on this case in which he recognised the complexities of the principle of effectiveness. In paragraph 114 of the Opinion he stated that:

> It ought not be concealed, however, that the competence of the Community in relation to criminal law as established by the Court in Case C-176/03 reveals on closer inspection certain conceptual flaws, which make it difficult, as the present case shows, to ascertain whether in a concrete case the conditions for the exercise of that competence are fulfilled.

The essence of such reasoning will be explored below. Despite this reasoning, the Court in this case simply followed the Case C-176/03 route and reiterated the requirement for full effectiveness of EU law. Still, the Court made it clear that the power to decide on the type and level of the criminal law penalties did not fall within the EU's competence, which meant that contrary to the spirit of ex Article 47 EU those provisions in the Framework Decision were not adopted.[108] Nevertheless, it is interesting to note that in both of these cases the newly-evaluated loyalty principle – in the context of the third pillar as regards the possible effectiveness of a Framework Decision as innovated in *Pupino* – was not mentioned at all. Again, this suggests that the Court was taking the effectiveness of supranational sanctions for granted, as automatically trumping any third pillar instruments.

[107] For comments, S Peers, 'The European Community's Criminal Law Competence: The Plot Thickens' (2008) 33 *EL Rev* 399; and the author's case note in (2008) 14 *European Public Law* 533.

[108] Paragraph 70 of the judgment.

D. The Failed Attempt to Transfer the Third Pillar via a Bridging Clause

As an interesting historical development it is worth noting that the Commission, apart from having introduced the above mentioned communication in the direct aftermath of Case C-176/03, also took the opportunity to state that this landmark ruling had done surprisingly little.[109] Therefore, in 2006 the Commission introduced a proposal for transferring the third pillar into the first pillar. This communication 'Implementing the Hague Programme: the way forward'[110] was especially interesting – despite it having been put on ice to give the CT a little bit more 'reflection' time[111] – for criminal law and was in many ways an extended version of the earlier 'A citizens agenda – delivering results for Europe'.[112] Consequently, it appears likely that if the Lisbon Treaty had remained in cold storage, the possibility of transfer via a bridging clause would have been a legal reality. According to the Commission, use of ex Article 42 EU would ensure the ambitious goal of better decision-making and increased efficiency and transparency, and would breed trust and accountability. More precisely, it would guarantee a 'European dimension of the legislative proposals[113] through the right of initiative of the Commission and the use of effective impact assessment tools and favouring high standard achievements through the QMV[114] system'. In any event, it should be observed that there were considerable differences between this communication and the Lisbon Treaty. For example, an Article 42 EU decision would not have given the EU any powers other than those that ex Articles 29 to 31 EU already granted, and it would not have given the EU any explicit mandate to create a European Public Prosecutor. Another difference from the failed CT was the possibility of so-called 'opt-outs' (and opt-ins) for some Member States as well as the opportunity to establish enhanced cooperation for a 'multi-speed' Europe in criminal law. Furthermore, it is not certain how far the Court's jurisdiction would reach into criminal matters (as noted, the Court's jurisdiction is currently limited under Article 35 EU) on the basis of ex Article 67(2) EC.[115] Another significant difference between the bridging clause, ex Article 42 TEU, and the CT was the

[109] See the preamble to Commission, 'Implementing The Hague Programme: the way forward' (Communication), COM (2006) 331 final.

[110] Commission, 'Implementing The Hague Programme: the way forward' (Communication), COM (2006) 331 final.

[111] Outvoted during informal discussions in the European Council Tampere, 27 September 2006 available at www.eu2006/fi/news (last accessed 1 September 2008).

[112] Commission, 'A Citizens Agenda, Delivering Results for Europe' (Communication), COM (2006) 211 final.

[113] COM (2006) 331 final (n 111 above); and for a good overview, House of Lords, European Union Committee, 42 report of session 2005–06, *The Criminal Law Competence of the European Community.*

[114] Qualified Majority Voting in the Council and Co-decision with the European Parliament, which was not possible in the third pillar, where decision making requires unanimity in the Council and only consultation of the EP.

[115] Article 67(2) EC explicitly required the Council to 'adapt' the provisions relating to the Court's jurisdiction after an initial transition period of five years, which ended on 1 May 2004. The Council did not take such a decision. COM (2006) 346 final.

availability of emergency brakes, where a Member State could apply the brakes if proposed legislation were considered too sensitive from the perspective of the fundamental principles of criminal law.

E. The Changes brought by the Lisbon Treaty: Introduction

As outlined above, the general assumption before the entry into force of the Lisbon Treaty was that the EU – first pillar – lacked a competence in criminal law and accordingly that the criminal law was the subject for third pillar cooperation under the Amsterdam Treaty.[116] However, as explained, the Court had already transferred parts of the criminal law in case C-176/03 by an extensive interpretation of 'effectiveness' as the main constitutional criterion for subjecting criminal law to the supranational level.

Clearly, the Lisbon Treaty changes this whole framework by explicitly transferring criminal law to the supranational level. It is fitting to begin by setting out the basic legal framework of criminal law after Lisbon, even though these questions will be discussed in greater detail in chapter seven. The crucial provisions for criminal law are Articles 82 (procedural criminal law) and 83 TFEU (substantive criminal law). These provisions, however, must be read in the light of chapter 1 of Title V of the TFEU, which sets out the general goals to be achieved in this area as stipulated in Article 67 TFEU. More specifically, Article 67 TFEU states that the EU shall constitute an AFSJ with respect for fundamental rights and the different legal systems and traditions of the Member States. Moreover, it holds that the Union shall endeavour to ensure a high level of security through measures to prevent and combat crime, racism and xenophobia, and through measures to encourage coordination and cooperation between police and judicial authorities and other competent authorities, as well as through the mutual recognition of judgments in criminal matters and, if necessary, through the harmonisation of criminal laws.

In any case, the changes brought by Articles 82 and 83 TFEU are so important that they need to be set out in detail.

i. Article 82 TFEU: Procedural Criminal Law

Article 82(1) TFEU stipulates that judicial cooperation in criminal matters shall be based on the principle of mutual recognition and should include the harmonisation of the laws and regulations of Member States in the areas referred to in paragraph 2 of the same article. Paragraph 2, in turn, states that the EP and the Council may establish minimum rules to the extent necessary to facilitate mutual recognition of judgments and judicial decisions, and police and judicial cooperation in criminal matters having a cross-border dimension. Such rules shall take

[116] Arts 29–31 EU.

into account the differences between the legal traditions and systems of Member States. The provision of Article 82 TFEU then sets out a list of areas within the EU's competence for legislation, such as the mutual admissibility of evidence between Member States, the rights of individuals in criminal procedure, and provisions regarding the rights of victims. Furthermore, the article contains a so-called 'general clause' in Article 82(2)(d) which states that any other specific aspect of criminal procedure which the Council has identified in advance by decision (unanimity would apply here) would qualify for future approximation. Finally, this general clause states that the adoption of the minimum rules referred to in this paragraph should not prevent Member States from maintaining or introducing a higher level of protection for individuals.

The substantive competence provision of Article 83 TFEU concerns the interaction between EU legislation and criminalisation, to which we now turn.

ii. Article 83 TFEU: Substantive Criminal Law

Article 83(1) TFEU deals with the regulation of substantive criminal law and stipulates that the European Parliament and the Council may establish minimum rules concerning the definition of criminal law offences and sanctions in the area of particularly serious crime with a cross-border dimension resulting from the nature or impact of such offences or from a special need to combat them on a common basis. Thereafter, this provision sets out a list of crimes in which the EU shall have legislative competence, such as terrorism, organised crime and money laundering. It also states that the Council may identify other possible areas of crime which meet the cross-border and seriousness criteria. Also, and interestingly, paragraph 2 of this article states that the possibility exists for harmonisation if that proves essential to ensure the effective implementation of an EU policy in an area which has already been subject to harmonisation measures. This represents to a large extent a codification of Case C-176/03 with its wide interpretation of the principle of effectiveness. It is therefore discussed in detail below.

iii. Enhanced Cooperation and Emergency Brakes

A significant change introduced by the Lisbon Treaty (and invented by the CT) is the 'one-step backwards, two steps forwards' mechanisms. This is the emergency brake and accelerator procedure. More specifically, both Articles 82(2) and 83(1) and (2) provide in their respective paragraph 3 for the possibility of applying an emergency brake if the law in question would affect fundamental aspects of a Member State's criminal justice system. More specifically, if such an emergency brake scenario arises, a Member State may request that the measure be referred to the European Council. In that case, the ordinary legislative procedure is suspended, and after discussion and 'in case of a consensus, the European Council shall, within four months of this suspension, refer the draft back to the Council, which shall terminate the suspension of the ordinary legislative procedure'. There is, however, no such opportunity with respect to the notion of mutual recognition, which will remain the main theme in EU criminal law cooperation. Obviously, the notion of an emergency brake looks attractive to Member States with a strong relationship between the criminal law and the nation state and hence allays Member State anxiety about the loss of their national sovereignty in criminal law matters.

Nevertheless, whether or not a single Member State pulls the emergency brake, the Lisbon Treaty provides for the opportunity of enhanced cooperation for the remaining Member States (nine or more) under Article 20 TEU and Article 329 TFEU. Although it is true that an emergency brake scenario will generate fragmentation, it is submitted that the problem is more fundamental than that. The crux is that the mere inclusion of an emergency brake does not automatically constitute a guarantee of successful European criminal law. These issues are investigated in detail in chapters four and seven.

F. Extended Jurisdiction

Perhaps one of the most significant improvements as introduced by the Lisbon Treaty, in general, is the extension of the Court's jurisdiction to also cover the former third pillar area.[117] It is one of the most important constitutional restructurings under the Lisbon Treaty. It should perhaps be recalled, and as noted above, that prior to the entry into force of the Lisbon Treaty, such jurisdiction was based on a voluntary declaration by Member States as to whether to accept such jurisdiction in accordance with Article 35 TEU.[118] The Lisbon Treaty changes this, as it significantly extends the Court's jurisdiction within the AFSJ field.[119] Nevertheless, as stated, the Lisbon Treaty Protocol No 36 on Transitional Provisions provides a five-year transition – or alteration – period before the existing third pillar instruments are treated in the same way as TFEU instruments.

Therefore, despite the entry into force of the Lisbon Treaty and, thereby, the merging of the pillars, there will remain 'echoes' of the third pillar in terms of the transitional protocol and its five-year transition period. Obviously, this means that the Commission will not have the power to bring infringement procedures against Member States as regards alleged breaches of pre-existing measures during this period.[120] It also means that the complex inter-pillar structure that has

[117] eg A Hinarejos, *Judicial Control in the European Union* (Oxford, Oxford University Press, 2009); S Peers *EU Justice and Home Affairs* (Oxford, Oxford University Press, 2011); P Craig, *The Lisbon Treaty* (Oxford, Oxford University Press, 2010).

[118] eg E Denza, *The Intergovernmental Pillars of the European Union* (Oxford, Oxford University Press, 2002) ch 9.

[119] See, however, Art 10 of the Protocol on transitional provisions attached to the Lisbon Treaty.

[120] S Peers, 'EU Criminal Law and the Treaty of Lisbon' (2008) 33 *EL Rev* 507.

characterised European criminal law will remain until the end of 2014. Accordingly, as a result of the transitional rules, there will be mixed jurisdiction over different measures concerning the same subject matter, and the most feasible regime (and most favourable from the perspective of the individual) should then be preferred. The crucial question seems to concern the definition of when an act is 'amended'. It has been suggested that, in the absence of any *de minimis* rule or any indication that acts are in any way severable as regards the Court's jurisdiction, any amendment – no matter how minor – would suffice.

But most importantly, the Lisbon Treaty introduces the possibility of expedited procedures for persons in custody. More specifically, the Lisbon Treaty stipulates in Article 267 TFEU that, if a question is raised in a case pending before a court or tribunal of a Member State in relation to a person in custody, the Court shall act with a minimum of delay. This is obviously an extremely important change and reflects the debate on speedier justice in Europe. Briefly, it should be noted that according to Article 275 TFEU the Court will still not have the power to review the validity or proportionality of operations carried out by the police or other law enforcement agencies of a Member State or the exercise of responsibilities incumbent upon Member States with regard to the maintenance of law and order and the safeguarding of internal security. It has been suggested, however, that this seems redundant as the Court cannot review internal situations even under the traditional first pillar.[121] Arguably, the new concept of 'national security' and the legal rules attached to it in these provisions will provoke great difficulty of interpretation.[122] This issue is discussed in detail in chapter seven.

G. The Stockholm Programme

As noted at the outset of this chapter, the recent Stockholm programme[123] is the latest Justice and Home Affairs agenda and the follow-up to the previous Hague programme. It represents an important step in the direction of more criminal law at the EU level and should be viewed in the context of the entry into force of the Lisbon Treaty. The Commission's communication title 'An area of freedom, security and justice serving the citizen' COM (2009) 262/4 and 'Delivering an area of freedom, security and justice for Europe's citizens Action Plan Implementing the Stockholm Programme' COM (2010) 171 on the implementation of the Stockholm programme are instructive here. These documents point to the current success of EU involvement in the present area. Nonetheless, they also indicate that the desired progress has been comparatively slow in the criminal law area because of the limited jurisdiction of the Court prior to the Lisbon Treaty (and since Commission has been unable to bring infringement proceedings), which

[121] N Grief, 'EU Law and Security' (2007) 33 *EL Rev* 752.

[122] C Ladenburger, 'Police and Criminal Law in the Treaty of Lisbon' (2008) 4 *European Constitutional Law Review* 20.

[123] The Stockholm programme (above n 3).

has led to considerable delay in the transposition of EU legislation at national level. However, the Stockholm programme states that the main focus for the future is building a citizen's Europe. As is explained in later chapters, this may seem somewhat contradictory in the context of the increased focus on security and effectiveness in this area and in the Stockholm programme in particular.

The remaining part of this chapter sets out some of the major developments in the area of EU criminal law after the entry into force of, and in the run up to, the Lisbon Treaty.

H. The ECHR and the Legally Binding Status of the Charter of Fundamental Rights: Comment

As a result of the entry into force of the Lisbon Treaty, the EU will now be legally capable of acceding to the ECHR and shall accede to it. Thus, the new Article 6(2) TEU adds that such accession shall not affect the EU's competences as defined in the Treaties. Such an accession would also require unanimity in the Council and ratification by Member States. It is clear that this accession has great symbolic value, particularly in the area of criminal law. Similarly, as mentioned, the Charter of Fundamental Rights has finally become legally binding, even if it is 'dismissed' to one of the numerous protocols annexed to the Treaty. It should perhaps be mentioned that the Court has long shown a stubborn unwillingness to refer to the Charter as a valid source of interpretation, but, as mentioned above, has more recently changed its view.[124] Although the Charter has now become legally binding, it is stated in Article 6 TEU that the provisions of the Charter shall not extend the EU's competences. Also, Article 51 of the Charter makes it clear that the Charter is directed at the Union's institutions and to Member States when they are implementing EU law.[125]

However, even if the Charter is applied when it is implementing EU law, it still has an important function as a source of interpretation. As for criminal law, Articles 47 to 49 of the Charter have a huge influence as they set the framework for the EU's action in this area. It is, therefore, likely that the binding status of the Charter will thus have a real impact on criminal law. It could, therefore, be argued that the Charter not only underlines and clarifies the legal status and freedoms of the EU's citizens facing the institutions of the Union,[126] but also gives the Union and, in particular, the policies regarding the AFSJ, a new normative foundation.

[124] eg Case C-303/05 *Advocaten voor de Wereld* judgment of 3 May 2007 not yet reported. See also, Case C-275/06 *Productores de Música de España (Promusicae)* judgment of 29 January 2008 not yet reported; Case C-450/06 *Varec SA* [2008] ECR I-581.

[125] For a more detailed account on the Charter, see eg M Dougan, 'The Treaty of Lisbon 2007: Winning Minds, Not Hearts,' (2008) 45 *CML Rev* 613 and P Craig, *The Lisbon Treaty, Law, Politics and Treaty Reform* (Oxford, Oxford University Press, 2010) ch 6.

[126] I Pernice, 'The Treaty of Lisbon and Fundamental Rights' in S Griller and Z Ziller (eds) *The Lisbon Treaty EU Constitutionalism without a Constitutional Treaty?* (New York, Springer, 2008) 235.

I. Criminal Law and the Autonomous European Legal Order

Apart from the legal developments in this area referred to above, there have been a few high-profile cases delivered in respect of the EAW, in particular. One of the most interesting recent cases in the run-up to the Lisbon Treaty is the *Wolzenburg*[127] ruling delivered in October 2009. This case concerned the EAW[128] and the opportunity for Member States to refuse to surrender a person under Article 4(6) EAW, under which the Netherlands had chosen such an opt-out. As explained above, what makes the EAW instrument particularly controversial is that it abolished the requirement of dual criminality for a list of 32 crimes as part of the adoption of the mutual recognition template in this area. This dual criminality rule has previously been intrinsic to the law on extradition as touching upon the core of nation state sovereignty. Therefore, the basic idea of the EAW is mutual recognition based on the notion of 'trust' of arrest warrants between Member States, in order to eliminate the previous extremely long and complicated extradition procedures. There is, however, the opportunity under the EAW to refuse to surrender a person, but only under very limited circumstances. For example, there are possibilities to refuse to surrender a person where the crime in question is statute barred, or does not constitute a crime in the executing state, or if the EAW has been issued for the purposes of execution of a custodial sentence or a detention order and the person in question is resident in the executing state and that state undertakes to execute the sentence or detention order in accordance with its domestic law. The *Wolzenburg* case concerned the possibility of serving a custodial suspended sentence in the executing host state.

In short, the question arose as to whether it constituted discrimination to distinguish between a state's own nationals and non-nationals in this regard. In other words, the core question was whether the required period of residence of the person requested for surrendering in the executing state counted as 'staying' or 'residing' so as to be treated in the same way as nationals. Secondly, the question arose of whether an additional administrative burden – such as a residence permit – was in line with the axiom of non-discrimination in EU law. The Court made it clear that the non-discrimination axiom was applicable in the (now former) third pillar area as there is a clear free movement dimension to the EAW. Nevertheless, in the *Wolzenburg* case this did not help the appellant since the Court concluded that a five-year residency requirement was not disproportionate in the context of the possibility of serving a custodial sentence in the host state. This was clear-cut Directive 2004/38/EC[129] reasoning on citizenship rights and free movement. Nonetheless, the establishment of the non-discrimination axiom

[127] Case C-123/08 *Wolzenburg* delivered on 6 October 2009 not yet reported, commented by the author 'European Arrest Warrant Cases and the Principles of Non-discrimination and EU Citizenship' (2010) 73 *Modern Law Review* 824.

[128] Council Framework Decision on the European arrest warrant and the surrender procedures between Member States [2002] OJ L190/1 of 13 June 2002.

[129] OJ L229/35.

and the very implications of the possibility of relying on citizenship rights in the third pillar have arguably a significantly symbolic message. In the context of the EAW, this has important implications from the perspective of rehabilitation issues and the possibility of integrating into society.[130] Moreover, it is quite obvious that the notion of non-discrimination is also of the utmost importance in criminal law cooperation as forming part of the concept of a fair trial in a broad sense. Yet what remains controversial is the application of the mutual recognition principle, developed within the framework of the internal market, to criminal law. The 'trust building'[131] mission of establishing the legitimacy of EU criminal law cooperation by assuming trust has taken place at the expense of adequate human rights protection in this area.[132] This has posed the question the extent to which the EAW was based on 'blind recognition'.

Nevertheless, in the recent *IB* judgment[133] concerning the operation of the EAW and trial in absentia, the Court confirmed that mutual recognition is not absolute. In paragraph 50 of this judgment the Court pointed out that while it is true that the EAW is based on the principle of mutual recognition, as is clear from Article 3 to 5 of the framework decision, that recognition does not mean that there is an absolute obligation to execute an arrest warrant that has been issued. The Court pointed to the importance of allowing some national discretion in this area and particularly the importance of enabling particular weight to be given to the possibility of increasing the chances of the persons sought for an arrest warrant to reintegrate into society. The Court held that against this background it should also include a sentence imposed in absentia as there was nothing to indicate that the EU legislator wished to exclude trials in absentia from the scope of the possibilities of including extra procedural safeguards in this area.

Moreover, in the *Mantello*[134] case concerning the scope of the mandatory options for non-executions of arrest warrants under Article 3(2) of the EAW Framework Decision the Court stated that the interpretation of *ne bis in idem* in Europe should be given an autonomous interpretation. Furthermore, the Court held that the question of whether a person has been 'finally' judged should be determined by the law of the Member State in which the judgment in issue was delivered. In the light of the fact that Article 50 of the Charter sets out the right not to be punished twice, such a reaffirmation of *ne bis in idem* appears to be uncontroversial. Instead, as explained, what remains controversial is the very operation of the mutual recognition principle in this area.

[130] Case C-123/08 *Wolzenburg* Opinion of AG Bot delivered on 24 March 2009.

[131] Joined Cases C-187/01 and C-385/01 *Criminal Proceedings against Hüseyin Gözütok and Klaus Brügge* [2003] ECR I-1354.

[132] See eg, V Mitsilegas, *EU Criminal Law* (Oxford, Hart Publishing, 2009) ch 3 and L Marin, 'The European Arrest Warrant and Domestic Legal Orders. Tensions between Mutual Recognition and Fundamental Rights: the Italian Case' (2008) 15 *Maastrict Journal of European and Comparative Law* 473.

[133] Case C-306/09 *IB* delivered on 21 October 2010 not yet reported. For a case comment, see A Suominen (2011) *Juridiska Foreningen Tidskrift* 122.

[134] Case C-261/09 *Mantello* 7 September 2010 not yet reported.

Therefore, although criminal law has been relocated in terms of Treaty changes, it is perhaps still too early to talk about an autonomous interpretation of it that fully respects defence rights and the adequate protection of the individual. This will remain work in progress for the EU for a considerable time.

V. CONCLUSION

This chapter has tried to explain and thereby highlight, former, recent and current developments in EU criminal law as well introducing the Lisbon Treaty. It has served as an introduction to the events that transformed the criminal law in the EU. The chapter has also highlighted the patchwork development of EU criminal law as it has straddled the border between the first and the third pillars. What has been clear until recently is that the method for enforcing Community law was through the national criminal law systems – though claused by the principle of loyalty and moreover the imperative of non-discrimination and effective sanctions. Things have since changed dramatically since. Even before the entry into force of the Lisbon Treaty, the pioneering Case C-176/03 judgment had significantly revised this assumption. More explicitly, it moved the boundary of creeping competence between Member States and the former EC by relying on ex Article 47 EU as the master provision of the Treaties and by also finding an extensive reach to legislative competences attributed to the first pillar. In doing so, the Court has granted the EU legislator a more independent power in the pursuit of the 'effectiveness' of EU law. This poses difficulties, as the notion of effectiveness is a very imprecise measure for competence monitoring. Subsequent chapters will now turn to the notion of 'effectiveness' and examine it in the light of EU constitutional law while keeping criminal law as the main theme.

Thus, subsequent chapters will look more closely at the competence question in EU criminal law. The underlying question is as follows: to what extent has the Lisbon Treaty changed the competence web? Expressed differently, the question arises to what degree the previous competence debate has been finally settled and in particular, the impact of the principle of effectiveness in this regard. In investigating this issue this exercise starts by looking at the effectiveness principle as an enforcement mechanism. Consequently, this book embarks on a constitutional journey by telling the narrative of European criminal law and how effectiveness has driven this constitutional streamlining.

3

Chasing (Traditional) Effectiveness

I. INTRODUCTION

THIS CHAPTER PROVIDES a clarifying account of the notion of effectiveness as an enforcement mechanism and aims to supply an overview of the principle of effectiveness when viewed from the traditional 'effective enforcement' perspective. As was shown in chapter two, the principle of effectiveness has recently enjoyed a renaissance within the sphere of the former third pillar as initiated by the *Pupino* case.[1] Therefore, the purpose of this section is to provide a sketch of enforcement in contemporary EU law. This legal depiction has come to increasingly overlap with the question of *communautaire* competence creep and the blurred dividing line between the notion of enforcement and competence reasoning, *stricto sensu.*

Accordingly, this chapter looks at EU enforcement law in general and is not confined to the still embryonic area of EU criminal law. It maps out a theoretical framework before moving on to the constitutional dynamics of EU legislative competences, as developed in Case C-176/03.

The first part of this chapter charts the traditional effective enforcement doctrine by tracing the classical definitions of effectiveness as a question of enforcement of Community rights. Hence this chapter aims to scan the main scholarship on effective enforcement in EU law in order to paint the background to the Court's reference to 'effectiveness'. The second part examines the meaning of enforcement in the area of freedom, security and justice (AFSJ). In doing so it also touches upon the former third pillar area and the impact of the *Pupino* ruling. Finally, this chapter offers some tentative thoughts on 'effectiveness' as a criminalisation principle. The issue of 'symbolic criminal law' in particular, as a justification for EU legislation, is questionable, as it seems to run counter to the assumption in EU law that the principle of effectiveness should be based on objective criteria. Put another way, this chapter sets the scene by considering the concept of EU effectiveness as an enforcement mechanism, before embarking on an exploration of the constitutional dimension of the effectiveness axiom. The reason for this approach is that the criminal law is a 'new' actor at the EU level and, moreover, there seems to be a tendency to treat criminal law as analogous to the areas already within the full scope of EU legal power. As explained in the pre-

[1] Case C-105/03 *Pupino* [2005] ECR I-5285.

vious chapters, this is an unwise stance to adopt as criminal law is different from anything the EU legislator has previously experienced: it concerns the deprivation of freedom, the governing of 'morals' and dangerous behaviour.

The Lisbon Treaty introduced a new concept in Article 13 TEU. This provision stipulates that the EU shall ensure the consistency, effectiveness and continuity of its policies and actions. Nevertheless, the argument presented here is that the main concern and driving force in this area has always been the effectiveness criteria. In verifying this argument it is, however, necessary to take a short detour into the history of effectiveness and how it has developed as an enforcement mechanism for EU integration.

II. THE PRINCIPLE OF EFFECTIVENESS

The notion of effectiveness as a legal principle is far from new and can also be found prominently in international law. In this judicial sphere 'effectiveness' constitutes a fairly straightforward concept often used as an argument for justifying the effective control of a certain territory.[2] In the context of EU law the principle of effectiveness seems considerably more complex. Yet, when interacting with the overarching message of supremacy, it is generally considered one of the EU's imperatives. Indeed, there is no doubt that 'effectiveness' is of crucial importance to the survival of the EU legal system through its role as an extended EU law control instrument policing the national legal spheres.[3] As such it forms the basis of the concept of effective judicial protection in EU law.

A common starting point when trying to understand the meaning of any word is obviously a dictionary. There one encounters notions such as 'powerful, successful, able and competent' as synonyms for effectiveness. In other words, 'effectiveness' symbolises something highly desirable.[4] In any case, in the EU setting it is sometimes argued that the fact that the aspiration for 'effectiveness' of EU law relies on the principle of effectiveness, is its main weakness.[5] Moreover, there is a surprising vagueness about the meaning of effective enforcement. As noted, this chapter examines the notion of effectiveness first tracing the classic EU law definitions of it. The aim of this chapter is, furthermore, to highlight the importance of distinguishing between different EU law concepts of effectiveness, starting with the orthodox definition of effectiveness as an integral part of Article 4(3) TEU and the obligation of loyalty towards the EU.

[2] eg M Shaw, *International Law* (Oxford, Oxford University Press, 2003) 842–43.

[3] S Weatherill, *Law and Integration in the European Union* (Oxford, Clarendon Press, 1995) 116–21.

[4] Oxford Dictionary and Thesaurus (Oxford, Oxford University Press, 2009).

[5] F Snyder, 'The Effectiveness of European Community Law: Institutions, Process, Tools and Techniques' (1993) 56 *MLR* 19.

A. The Concept of Effective Enforcement

The principle of loyalty, codified in Article 4(3) TEU, has always played a crucial role in shaping the contours of the effectiveness of EU law.[6] For example, it has given birth to the doctrine of indirect effect.[7] Nonetheless, there is more to the notion of enforcement than Article 4(3) TEU and its message of fidelity reveals.

It is often said that the Court of Justice considers effectiveness as its main criterion in the interpretation of EU law.[8] Perhaps one could even speak of 'hermeneutic effectiveness'. However, it is equally often argued that the Court should choose a consistent philosophy to underpin this concept. For example, it has been observed that legitimate doubt can be entertained as to whom the effectiveness requirement is addressed: does it mean 'effective' from the perspective of the person concerned or 'effective' from the point of view of protecting the maximum enforcement of Community law?[9] In any event, and more pertinently to the present discussion, it is often suggested that the Court's use of Article 4(3) TEU violates the principle of separation of powers.[10] Indeed, Article 4(3) TEU has always been considered as a rather narrow basis from which to justify such activity,[11] with a constitutional ambiguity of the same quality as the competence provisions of Articles 114 and 352 TFEU (discussed below). Moreover, it is frequently argued that the increasingly broad interpretation of Article 4(3) TEU may have reached its limits, as any further extension could undermine the legitimacy of the Court without necessarily achieving additional general social and political results.[12] Yet the reach of Article 4(3) TEU is constantly being expanded, despite the consensus that the Court is only effective if national courts and authorities are willing to abide by and enforce its decisions.[13] One could perhaps ask why the Court has not heeded such criticism and exercised greater self-restraint in discovering loyalty-related obligations.[14] As Weatherill once said, 'the great genius of the European Court has been to lure national courts into doing its bidding'.[15] After all, the attractiveness of Article 4(3) TEU is precisely its constitutional, manipulative

[6] J Temple Lang, 'The Developments of the Court of Justice on the Duties of Cooperation of National Authorities and Community Institutions under Article 10 EC' (2008) 31 *Fordham International Law Journal* 1483. For a recent analysis on loyalty see also, E Neframi, 'The Duty of Loyalty: Rethinking its Scope through its Application in the Field of EU External Relations' (2010) 47 *CML Rev* 323.

[7] eg Case C-106/89 *Marleasing* [1990] ECR I-4135.

[8] A Biondi, Annotation, *Mûnoz* (2003) 40 *CML Rev* 1241.

[9] S Prechal, 'EC Requirement for an Effective Remedy' in J Lonbay and A Biondi (eds), *Remedies for Breach of EC Law* (Chichester, Wiley, 1997) ch 1.

[10] See eg, P Eeckhout, 'The European Court of Justice and the Legislator' (1998) 17 *Yearbook of European Law* 1.

[11] Snyder (above n 5).

[12] A Ward, 'Effective Sanctions in EC Law: A Moving Boundary in the Division of Competences' (1995) 1 *European Law Journal* 205.

[13] ibid.

[14] E Hinton, 'Strengthening the Effectiveness of Community Law: Direct Effect, Article 5 EC and the European Court of Justice' (1998–99) 31 *NYU Journal of International Law and Politics* 307.

[15] S Weatherill, 'Addressing Problems of Imbalanced Implementation in EC Law' in C Kilpatrick et al (eds), *The Future of Remedies in Europe* (Oxford, Hart Publishing, 2000) 87.

vagueness. So the Court has on the one hand derived a specific obligation from the principle of effectiveness, and on the other hand used the effectiveness principle to constrain the autonomy of Member States in the name of effectiveness.[16]

Nevertheless, in the *Pfeiffer* judgment[17] the Court attempted to put an end to the absence of any explicit legal basis for indirect effect besides the general obligation of loyalty by stating that the requirement that national law be interpreted in conformity with Community law was 'inherent in the Treaty'. Admittedly, *Francovich*[18] already claimed that state liability was inherent in the Treaty. Although the enforcement of Community law has since the early days constituted an imperative for the EU project, it seems that the Court is still testing the possible boundaries of 'effectiveness'. One difficulty with the search for effectiveness is, however, that the EU and national perspectives on effectiveness may differ, since the former needs to take into account the requirement of a consistent system of enforcement throughout the community territory.[19] This means – somewhat paradoxically – that effectiveness is not a 'uniform' concept. On the contrary, effectiveness may have very different 'qualities' depending on what the EU is trying to achieve. As highlighted in the introduction to this book, the question arises of whether the concept of 'effectiveness' in European law is different from 'effectiveness' in criminal law.

B. What is EU Effectiveness?

It has been observed that the effectiveness of EU law is primarily an issue of public policy and secondly a question of how to theorise it.[20] The 'effective' use of effectiveness as a means for public policy may sound self-evident, taking into consideration its great success in the European project; however, it is not, in fact, a simple task. Nevertheless, effectiveness is clearly relative – it is not so much a question of 'effective or not' as of 'how effective'.[21] Consequently, the notion of ad hoc and sectoral approaches is often put forward as an explanation for the Court's somewhat patchy case law.[22] Others have described 'effectiveness' as simply requiring the proper application of Community law.[23] Obviously, it is easy to become caught in circular reasoning here.

[16] Neframi (above n 6).

[17] Case C-397/01 *Pfeiffer* [2004] ECR I-8835.

[18] Cases C-6 and C-9/90 *Francovich* [1991] ECR I-5357.

[19] eg M Dougan, *National Remedies before the Court of Justice* (Oxford, Hart Publishing, 2004) ch 2.

[20] Snyder (above n 5).

[21] C Harding, 'Member State Enforcement of European Community Measures: The Chimera of Effective Enforcement' (1997) 4 *Maastrict Journal of European and Comparative Law* 5.

[22] eg Dougan (above n 19), see also Armin von Bogdandy, 'Founding Principles' in von Bogdandy and J Bast, *European Constitutional Law* (Munich/Oxford, Hart Publishing / Ch Beck/ Nomos, 2011) 29.

[23] Hinton (above n 14).

In any case, 'effectiveness' as referred to by the Court is an umbrella label which, generally speaking, requires that national remedies and procedural rules must not, in practice, render their beneficiaries' enjoyment of Community rights excessively difficult. However, effectiveness can also constitute a governing principle for deciding whether Community action in a given area is justified at all.[24] Moreover, it has been argued that the principle of effectiveness and 'effective judicial protection' are not entirely the same.[25] Indeed, it is difficult to draw a clear distinction between effective enforcement and the principle of effectiveness concerning EU rights: they are clearly not exactly the same, yet they are difficult to separate. After all, it would be rather odd to refer to sanctions as 'rights' from the perspective of the individual. What is perhaps of more significance for our purposes is that the Court has had recourse to the concept of individual rights under the weight of two imperatives in particular. The first imperative was the need to provide a justification for legal activity.[26] The second imperative was to persuade national judges to adopt and develop their roles as Community judges and hence to make clear that human rights in particular were adequately protected at the EU level.[27] Many commentators have nevertheless suggested that legal certainty would be improved if the Court were to formulate a specific provision to rely on Community law as such instead of the rather murky concept of 'rights'.[28] Others have argued that a balanced approach rather than the effectiveness test would be more sophisticated as, among other things, it would offer more familiar guidelines by operating like a 'normal' proportionality test and would thus provide a proper test for assessing the consistency of domestic rules within Community law.[29] The Lisbon Treaty has now introduced an explicit legal basis for effective judicial protection. This is the new provision of Article 19 TEU which states that Member States shall provide sufficient remedies to ensure effective legal protection in the fields covered by EU law. In addition, Article 47 of the EU Charter of Fundamental Rights ('the Charter') states that everyone has the right to an effective remedy. The key issue then becomes how vigorously the Court should scrutinise the national standards in question.[30]

Thus, the next section provides a brief overview of the shifting contours of the landscape of the Court's remedies. The intention of this chapter is to demonstrate not only the multifaceted notion of effectiveness as an enforcement question but also the Court's somewhat unsteady approach in this area. This is necessary in

[24] Similarly, see M Accetto and S Zleptnig, 'The Principle of Effectiveness: Rethinking Its Role in Community Law' (2005) 11 *European Public Law* 375 and M Ross, 'Effectiveness in the European Legal Order(s): Beyond Supremacy to Constitutional Proportionality' (2006) 31 *EL Rev* 476.

[25] S Prechal, *Directives in EC law* (Oxford, Oxford University Press, 2005) ch 6–7.

[26] eg Dougan (above n 19).

[27] A Ward, 'The Case for Uniform Remedies' in J Prinssen and A Schrauwen (eds), *Direct Effect, Rethinking a Classic of EC Legal Doctrine* (Groningen, Europa Law Publishing, 2002) ch 11.

[28] eg Prechal (above n 9).

[29] W van Gerven, 'Of Rights, Remedies and Procedures' (2000) 37 *CML Rev* 501 and W Van Gerven, 'Harmonization of Private Law: Do we really need it?' (2004) 41 *CML Rev* 505.

[30] P Craig, *EU Administrative Law* (Oxford, Oxford University Press, 2006) 814.

order to set the scene for the constitutional discussion of the evolution of EU criminal law. The aim is simply to provide a general overview of effectiveness as an enforcement matter. In particular, the intention is to highlight the different phases in the Court's approach to the degree of intervention in the context of the effectiveness principle.

C. The Fundamentals of Enforcement

It may appear superfluous to set out a short history of the basic EU law on remedies. The reason for doing so here is to provide sufficient background information for a more detailed examination of the meaning and scope of the principle of effectiveness as something more than a question of enforcement. In other words, we need to outline the general picture to understand 'effectiveness' in its traditional enforcement sense. Clearly, the Court has been highly innovative in developing the legal basis for its system of judicial protection. Consequently, there is a vast amount of scholarship on the subject, with academics passionately dissecting the Court's somewhat rollercoaster approach to this field.[31]

Although the Court had declared – before Article 19 TEU and the Lisbon Treaty allowed for such protection – that the right to judicial protection is one of the general principles of law stemming from the constitutional traditions of Member States, the law on remedies is far from clear. In this area, the Court has, as usual, relied on its old allies, the rule of law, non-discrimination and effectiveness.[32] In this context the principle of effectiveness is often described as an axiom which bypasses national standards and makes constitutional ideas into living truths.[33] The purpose here is certainly not to reiterate the debate on how directives affect individuals. Suffice it to say that case law on directives has received wide criticism for its uncertainty and for having denied horizontal direct effect, as well as for sometimes distinguishing between apparently similar cases.[34] For instance, it is often held that it would have been more logical to recognise horizontal direct effect instead of developing new doctrines such as incidental direct effect.[35]

Accordingly, in the early days of the Community the principle of effectiveness justified only limited patterns of Community intervention, where the key theme was the question of reasonableness when judging the non-discrimination rule.[36] It is generally considered that this phase did not require the Member States to create any new sanctions so long as EU law was not treated less favourably than national

[31] eg Dougan (above n 19).

[32] Hinton (above n 14).

[33] T Tridimas, *General Principles of EU Law* (Oxford, Oxford University Press, 2006) ch 9.

[34] eg Case C-91/92 *Faccini Dori* [1994] ECR I-3325; and on incidental direct effect eg, Case C-194/94, *CIA Security* [1996] ECR I-2201. For commentary, eg P Craig, 'The Legal Effects of Directives: Policy, Rules and Exceptions' (2009) 34 *EL Rev* 349; S Drake, 'Twenty years after *von Colson*: The Impact of Indirect Effect on the Protection of the Individual's Community Rights' (2005) 30 *EL Rev* 329.

[35] Craig (ibid) 803.

[36] Dougan (above n 19).

law (the principle of equivalence).[37] However, subsequent case law changed course. More specifically, it shifted from pursuing the notions of non-discrimination and minimum protection to the more independent imperative of effectiveness.[38] This so-called middle period of jurisprudence dating from the mid 1980s to the early 1990s is often described as a fairly wild period where the Court set out to establish the doctrine of effective enforcement. In a number of important cases such as *von Colson*,[39] the Court stepped in and made clear that directives were aimed at conferring 'real and effective judicial protection'. In these cases, the Court elaborated the principle of effectiveness further and held, inter alia, that the duty to refrain from taking national action liable to compromise the result sought by a directive applied also in cases where the implementation time of the EU legislation at issue was still running. Clearly, as indicated, Article 4(3) TEU and the ideas of effectiveness have been one of the most useful instruments in the EU legal tool kit. Moreover, most of the subject areas at issue concerned social policy, which made it politically possible to play a more dominant role.[40] In addition, the above-mentioned landmark ruling of *Francovich*[41] was delivered in this new wave of 'intervention fever'. Suffice it to say that this ruling dramatically – and perhaps elegantly[42] – created the possibility of state liability for Member State failure to comply with EU law and the consequent deprivation of the rights of individuals under EU law.

Nevertheless, the law on effective enforcement did not stagnate. From early 1993 the Court explored new paths. This frequently celebrated period from the early 1990s until more recently is characterised by the Court's attempt to strike a more nuanced balance between national autonomy/sovereignty and EU law intervention using an orthodox pattern of negative law. According to Tridimas, the underlying rational for this more relaxed attitude was that matters now appeared to be legally settled.[43] Yet, it could easily be concluded that the Court only partially retreated. For example, gender discrimination and state aid[44] were appropriate for continued intervention but, for instance, employment law[45] was not.[46] This approach is often termed 'selective deference' as the Court seems to have left more discretion to the national courts and was thereby being more cautious about when

[37] Case C-39/73, *Rewe* [1973] ECR 1039.

[38] ibid.

[39] Case C-14/83 *von Colson* [1984] ECR 1891. See eg P Craig and G De Burca *EU Law, Text Cases and Materials* (Oxford, Oxford University Press 2011) 201.

[40] Dougan (above n 19). See already, J Weiler, 'The Transformation of Europe' (1990–91) 100 *Yale Law Journal* 2400.

[41] Joined Cases C-6 and C-9/90 *Francovich* [1991] ECR I-5357.

[42] A Biondi, '*Francovich* Fifteen Years Later' in M Maduro (ed) *The Past and Future of EU Law, The Classics of EU Law revisited on the 50th Anniversary of the Rome Treaty* (Oxford, Hart Publishing, 2010) 413.

[43] T Tridimas, 'Liability for Breach of Community Law: Growing up or Mellowing Down?' (2001) 38 *CML Rev* 301.

[44] Dougan (above n 19) 211. Also, Case C-119/05 *Lucchini* [2007] ECR I-000.

[45] See, however, in a different context Case C-438/05 *Viking Line* [2007] ECR I-000; and Case C-341/05 *Laval* [2007] ECR I-000.

[46] Dougan (above n 19).

to intrude.[47] It has been claimed that this period should not be taken as evidence of retreat and illustrates rather the directed use of judicial power as a legal system matures.[48] According to some commentators, the general approach now followed by the Court when applying the principle of effectiveness could be compared to the 'objective justification' test in internal market free movement law which consists of a presumption of national autonomy coupled with the principle of equivalence and a more or less ad hoc requirement of 'effectiveness'. Thus, an important – yet difficult – task is to identify the exact scope of national autonomy.[49] This is obviously a tricky exercise.

Nonetheless, in the context of indirect effect in several more recent rulings, such as *Pfeiffer*[50] – and also in the context of general principles of EU law and possible horizontality in the *Mangold*[51] ruling – the Court has given surprisingly strong guidance to national courts as to how national law should be interpreted when giving effect to Community law.[52] The case of *Mangold* in particular has cast doubts on exactly how far reasoning based on effectiveness can go.[53] Here, the Court explored a new route by looking at the general aim of a directive as reflected in the general principles of EU law.[54] According to one commentator, it has done so in order to avoid the strong criticism of case law with respect to the effects of unimplemented directives by enforcing general principles of EU law which the measure at stake already embodied.[55] It has even been argued that the case law of remedies has come of age and that we are consequently entering a fourth phase.[56] Such a fourth phase appears dominated by ad hoc and effectiveness approaches. *Kükükdeveci*[57] represents perhaps the latest attempt by the Court to stabilise the scope of the general principle (against age discrimination) which it introduced in *Mangold*.[58] In *Kükükdeveci* the Court stated that

> The need to ensure the full effectiveness of the principle of non-discrimination on grounds of age, as given expression in Directive 2000/78, means that the national court, faced with a national provision falling within the scope of European Union law which it considers to be incompatible with that principle, and which cannot be interpreted in conformity with that principle, must decline to apply that provision.[59]

[47] Tridimas (above n 42).

[48] ibid.

[49] Dougan (above n 19).

[50] Case C-397/01, *Pfeiffer* [2004] ECR I-8835.

[51] Case C-144/04, *Mangold v Helm* [2005] ECR I-9981.

[52] M Dougan, 'When Worlds Collide! Competing Visions of the Relationship between Direct Effect and Supremacy' (2007) 44 *CML Rev* 931.

[53] Ross (above n 24).

[54] Among the many commentators, see eg M Dougan, 'Legal Developments' (2006) 44 *Journal of Common Market Studies* 119 and several contributions in U Bernitz et al (eds) *The General Principles of EC Law in the Process of Development* (The Hague, Kluwer Law International 2008).

[55] ibid.

[56] Drake (above n 33).

[57] Case C-555/07 *Kükükdeveci* judgment of 19 January 2010 not yet reported.

[58] S Peers, Case note (2010) 35 *EL Rev* 849.

[59] Paragraph 53 of the judgment.

So in this case not only was the Charter given a free-standing value as source of interpretation (that is beyond the limits set by Article 51 and the requirement of an implementing measure in the Member State in order to trigger Charter rights) but 'effectiveness' concerns also appear to have played a key role.[60]

Moreover, in *Unibet* the Court made it clear that EU law requires that national rules do not undermine the right to effective judicial protection, by stipulating that ordinary national rules on interim relief will apply to claims based on Community law.[61] In this ruling, the Court emphasised the constitutional status of effective judicial protection as an overriding consideration by expressly linking such an obligation to Article 47 of the Charter, which provides the right to an effective remedy. Another interesting example here is *Coleman*,[62] where 'effectiveness' was used to insist that a broad interpretation of a directive cover an employee who was not herself disabled, but was the victim of undesired conduct amounting to harassment related to the disability of her child. In reaching this conclusion the Court revised the burden of proof: 'the effective application of the principle of equal treatment then requires that the burden of proof should fall on the respondents'. Arguably, this case is a good example of how 'effectiveness' is used by the Court as a driving principle to progress matters, if there is nothing else at issue.[63] Nevertheless, it should be noted that in the *Van der Weerd* case,[64] the Court specified that effectiveness does not always extend so far as to require a national court, in the context of civil litigation, to raise a plea of its own motion based on Community law, irrespective of the importance of the provision in question.

Accordingly, the Court's case law on remedies illustrates that we are dealing with a multifaceted concept of 'effectiveness'. From the traditional effective enforcement angle, it was recently re-emphasised that it is doubtful whether 'effectiveness' constitutes the right label, as effectiveness in the context of state liability means judicial protection of rights while effectiveness as a compliance question constitutes an enforcement issue.[65] Conversely, effectiveness could simply be accepted as a changeable concept and as such capable of use in a multitude of ways by the Court – this latter approach appears to be more accurate and is therefore the one advocated here.

[60] See Editorial 'The Scope of Application of the General Principles of Union Law' (2010) 47 *CML Rev* 1589.

[61] Case C-432/05 *Unibet v Justitiekanslern* [2007] ECR I-2271. For example, A Ward, 'National and EC Remedies under the EC Treaty' in C Barnard and O Odudu, *The Outer Limits of EU Law* (Oxford, Hart Publishing, 2009) 329.

[62] Case C-303/06 *Coleman* judgment of 17 July 2008 not yet reported, concerning Directive 2000/78 establishing a general framework for equal treatment in employment and occupation OJ L 303/16.

[63] Paras 57–63 of the judgment.

[64] Case C-222/05 *Van der Weerd* [2007] ECR 4233.

[65] eg P Nebbia, 'Do the Rules on State Aid have a Life on their Own? National Procedural Autonomy and Effectiveness in the Lucchini Case' (2008) 33 *EL Rev* 427; M Accetto and S Zleptnig, 'The Principle of Effectiveness: Rethinking Its Role in Community Law' (2005) 11 *European Public Law* 375.

i. Short Comment on Non-discrimination and Uniformity

A question that has occupied legal scholars for quite some time is how to view the tangled relationship between effectiveness, uniformity and non-discrimination (also discussed in chapter two in the context of sanctions). For example, Ward has emphasised that the principle of non-discrimination poses the biggest potential threat to national autonomy in the area of EU remedies, as this principle is extremely far reaching in the national sphere by virtue of its spill-over effect.[66] A contrary argument is that it is the principle of effectiveness itself that poses the greatest danger to national sovereignty rather than the more 'neutral' non-discrimination rule. Indeed, this is also a view Ward appears to have endorsed more recently.[67] In any event, others[68] have argued that the relationship between non-discrimination and effectiveness could be fairly easily resolved by means of a balancing test between the two, which is a joint task of the Court and the national courts as Community law remains dependent on the national legal environment. Moreover, the Court seems to find it important that the principles at issue are part of the legal heritage common to Member States.[69] As pointed out by one commentator, in the *Paquay*[70] judgment the Court seems to have opened up a further dimension to the principle of non-discrimination by insisting that remedies and procedural rules were applicable not only to comparable EU and national actions but also to EU rights where the latter are of similar importance. Notwithstanding this, it could be argued that the uniformity and consistency of EU law are largely a symbolic concept closely connected to the notion of citizenship and as such simply part of a wider integrationist project to 'make Europe more relevant to its citizens'.[71] But does it necessarily have to be different from effectiveness? And why is this important to the present work on EU criminal law? Again, the purpose here is to highlight the complex function of effectiveness and more specifically how such an 'effectiveness' principle has emerged within the EU legal order.

Finally, it is commonly held that effectiveness, consistency and uniformity are interlinked and yet are not the same concept in this traditional EU sense. In other words, their relationship is far from clear-cut. A common view seems to be, however, that uniformity and effectiveness are ultimately and fundamentally about ensuring the integrity of the Community legal order as a whole so that although not uniformly applied, it nevertheless retains the greatest possible 'consistency' or

[66] A Ward, *Judicial Review and the Rights of Private Parties in EC Law* (Oxford, Oxford University Press, 2000) 328.

[67] A Ward, Case note *Willy Kempter* (2008) 33 *EL Rev* 739.

[68] See eg, M Claes, *The National Court's Mandate in the European Constitution* (Oxford, Hart Publishing, 2006).

[69] Prechal (above n 24).

[70] Case C-460/06 *Paquay* [2007] ECR I-8511, see M Dougan 'The Vicissitudes of Life at the Coalface: Remedies and Procedures for enforcing Union Law before the National Courts' in G De Burca and P Craig, *The Evolution of EU Law* (Oxford, Oxford University Press, 2011) 407.

[71] C Harlow, 'A Common European Law of Remedies?' in Kilpatrick et al (above n 15).

'coherence'.[72] Therefore, it appears as if what matters depends not so much on the principle of uniformity as on the imperative of effectiveness, which determines the quality of EU supervision over national judicial systems rather than its uniformity as such. Nevertheless, uniformity as a legal concept is always in the background. One problem when trying to pin down the requirement of uniformity is that the Court itself rarely articulates it.[73] Indeed, it seems as though 'effectiveness', involving consistency and uniformity, has become one big legal cluster, with this group of 'effectiveness' concepts having important repercussions on the debate about enforcement.

ii. The Enforcement Debate

As should be obvious by now, the Court's approach in the area of enforcement of Community law has not been entirely consistent. According to Dougan, this has created an 'enforcement deficit' through undesirable inequalities in the standards of judicial protection, which is especially significant as the Community has evolved into a more complex entity than integration through law permits, characterised by varying degrees of integration and differentiation across different policy fields. For this reason, Dougan has suggested that uniformity should be interpreted selectively.[74] More specifically, the point of the sectoral approach is that it can be used as an analytical tool. What seems clear then is that the debate about improving the enforcement of EU law is intensely political.[75] In particular, as noted, it appears much easier to enforce negative law via the judiciary than to enact positive law through the legislator. This really is the core of what could be referred to as the 'implementation imbalance'.[76] The problem is that imbalanced implementation pushed forward through negative law runs the risk of requiring overly harsh intervention, as it demands that the EU decides on the content of a harmonised regime. Such imbalanced implementation is particularly problematic when applied in the sensitive area of criminal law.

This brings us to the former third pillar sphere and the new enforcement battlefield within the EU. The next part introduces the complexities of this area. It also illustrates the difficulty of drawing a line between the issue of enforcement as discussed above and legislative competence matters in the context of effectiveness. In doing so, the section critically examines the principle of fidelity and the role it has played as the mechanism of the EU's cross-pillar integration by focusing on the *Segi* judgment as the starting point.[77] More specifically, this section tentatively asks whether it was wise to extend such a loyalty principle into to the murky landscape of the former third pillar. It is interesting to take a historic approach in

[72] Accetto and Zleptnig (above n 63) and S Besson, 'From European Integration to European Integrity: Should European Law Speak with Just One Voice?' (2004) 10 *ELJ* 257.

[73] Dougan (above n 19) ch 5.

[74] ibid.

[75] Weatherill (above n 15).

[76] ibid.

[77] Case C-354/04, C-355/04P *Segi and others* ECR [2007] I-6157.

considering the five-year Transitional Protocol No 36 as attached to the Lisbon Treaty, as some of the cross-pillar characteristics will remain during this transition period. Moreover, it is necessary to understand the history of the *communautairisation* of the former third pillar as such an understanding can help to pin down the possible boundaries of effectiveness in this field for the future AFSJ.

III. EFFECTIVE ENFORCEMENT OUTSIDE THE EU'S TRADITIONAL BORDERS

The section aims to clarify how the effective enforcement discourse could fit into the EU tapestry created by *Pupino* and help us to understand the rapid developments in this area.[78] As stated, Article 19 TEU and the right to effective judicial protection now also applies to the former third pillar. In addition, as noted, Article 47 of the Charter makes it clear that everyone has the right to an effective remedy. Although it is true that ex Article 3 EU already allowed for the notion of consistency within the wider ambit of EU law, there was no explicit support for the application of the EC doctrine of effective enforcement within the third pillar before the Lisbon Treaty entered into force. The principle of loyalty is now expressly applicable to the AFSJ as guided by Article 4(3) TEU. Furthermore, as indicated, Article 13 TEU ensures that the EU shall have an institutional framework which shall aim not only to promote its values and advance its objectives but also to ensure the consistency, effectiveness and continuity of its policies and actions. However, the question of *communautaire* reasoning in the AFSJ is a far more complicated process than the mere adoption of a supranational model. Expressed differently, there are difficulties that could arise when one adopts traditional Community reasoning developed within the former first pillar to the AFSJ and criminal law in particular, without a fully formed regime of defence rights in this field. Hence, this is an area which has focused to a large extent on enforcement, but at the EU level has largely left behind accompanying safeguards of the individual. The next section will examine this argument in greater detail.

A. The Renaissance of the 'Implementation Imbalance' in EU Law[79]

When trying to identify the contours of effectiveness and the role it has played in the development of the enforcement doctrine within the previous third pillar and EU criminal law cooperation, it is necessary to consider the application of the notion of loyalty and Article 4(3) TEU. As explained in chapter two, the *Pupino* case extended reasoning based on loyalty and effectiveness to the former third

[78] Case C-105/03 *Criminal Proceedings against Maria Pupino* [2005] ECR I-5285.

[79] Draws on E Herlin-Karnell, 'The Question of Communautaire Reasoning in the Third Pillar – The Judgment in *Segi* and Beyond', (2008) 19 *Kings Law Journal* 624. I have borrowed this implementation imbalance term from S Weatherill, 'Addressing Problems of Imbalanced Implementation in EC Law' in C Kilpatrick et al (eds) *The Future of Remedies in Europe* (Oxford, Hart Publishing, 2000) 87.

pillar. Therefore, it is useful to take a short historical detour and examine EU terrorist cases. For example, in the *Segi*[80] ruling the Court referred to *Pupino* and the imperative of loyalty but to some extent left its meaning unexplained. More explicitly, the Court stated that it would be inappropriate, from the perspective of loyalty and the reciprocal duty between the Community and the Member States that Article 4(3) TEU constitutes, to insist on a general right to a fair trial at the EU level, if such a right would be contrary to the mutual interest of the Member States and the Union (that is in the EU's efforts to combat terrorism). However, the Court pointed out that this rule did not apply if a competent national authority had not assessed the alleged terrorist involvement in question. The Court subsequently opened the (now former) third pillar door – which as noted in chapter two had been largely closed as it granted a very limited jurisdiction to the Court – by concluding that jurisdiction was possible despite the fact that the interpretation of a 'common position', as in the case at issue, did not fall under the limited list set out in ex Article 35 EU. Nevertheless, the case of *Segi* has arguably had a more extensive impact on the notion of EU criminal law in general – and had constitutional implications, which far exceed the limited terrain of the terrorist cases. Consequently, this ruling posed important questions with respect to the right to challenge a measure before a court and also put the credentials of reasoning drawn from Article 4(3) TEU into the third pillar spotlight. In order to understand the notion of loyalty in the present setting it seems appropriate to also look briefly at the *OMPI* judgments.[81] Here the General Court (then the Court of First Instance), with surprising confidence, ruled that the principle of loyalty was especially binding in the third pillar area.[82] The meaning of the phrase 'especially binding in the third pillar' has been of crucial concern. Despite the fact that this question was never fully answered by the Court, it is easy to argue that absent a more ambitious approach to the safeguards for the individual – also in the post Lisbon era – the imbalance in EU criminal law cooperation, with the increased focus on loyalty and effectiveness, risks rendering the EU project far from an area of freedom and justice.

As explained in the previous chapter, when dealing with criminal law – procedural and substantive – the principle of legality is axiomatic. It is true that the Court has recognised the principle of legality as an EU law principle (also codified in Article 49 of the Charter), and in several judgments – such as *Pupino* itself – has also stated that there was no obligation to interpret national law *contra legem*.[83] However, as already implied, the issue is far more complicated when dealing with procedural legality in the context of criminal law cooperation. Still at the European

[80] Case C-354/04, C-355/04P *Segi v Council* ECR [2007] I-6157; eg S Peers, 'Salvation outside the Church: Judicial Protection in the Third Pillar after the *Pupino* and *Segi* Judgments' (2007) 44 *CML Rev* 883.

[81] Case T-228/02, *OMPI* [2006] ECR II-4665 and subsequently Case T-256/07 *OMPI II*, judgment of 23 October 2008, not yet reported. See also T-284/08 *OMPI III* judgment of 4 December 2008, not yet reported.

[82] Case T-228/02, *OMPI* [2006] ECR II-4665 § 123.

[83] eg Case C-80/86 *Kolpinghuis Nijmegen* [1987] ECR 3969.

level, this crucial principle seems to have been increasingly often dismissed as a merely substantive matter lacking importance in the area of EU criminal law proceedings.[84] At stake here is what has been referred to as the shield and sword function of criminal law, that is that any enforcement mechanism in criminal law procedure must be accompanied by adequate protection.[85] At the EU level, it appears as though the shield has been lost in the effective enforcement fight across the EU's borders.

Furthermore, the question of *communautaire* reasoning in the former third pillar highlighted an academic community divided into two camps – either in support of full supremacy in the name of EU protection of rights,[86] or taking a more cautious line of reasoning in support of the still intergovernmental structure of the third pillar.[87] In any case, all the arguments seemed united in the call for the constitutional adaptation of the pillars. However, even from a purely EU law perspective, the Court's reasoning in *Pupino* was thin when compared with a landmark ruling such as *Costa v ENEL*.[88] Nonetheless, all things considered, and regardless of how EU law developed traditionally (that is through a highly imaginative or active Court), it should be re-emphasised that EU criminal law should not simply be treated as though it were a normal policy among others, because there are clear limits to the single market analogy in this area.[89]

Again, this demonstrates the very complicated function of Article 4(3) TEU, which is not simply an enforcement mechanism, but is also a many-headed beast with far from unambiguous consequences when applied outside its traditional supranational domain. It also illuminates, as will be discussed in chapter four, and as recognised by AG Mengozzi in his opinion in *Segi*,[90] the somewhat blurred division between enforcement questions and issues of competence. This poses difficulties, as effectiveness is a very slippery concept in itself.

In any event, the Lisbon Treaty improves this situation of effective legal protection within the AFSJ, as explained in chapter two, by extending the jurisdiction of

[84] K Lenearts and T Corthaut, 'Of Birds and Hedges: The Role of Primacy in invoking Norms of EU Laws', (2006) 31 *EL Rev* 287; S Prechal, 'Direct Effect, Indirect Effect, Supremacy and the Evolving Constitution of the European Union' in C Barnard (ed) *The Fundamentals of EU Law Revisited* (Oxford, Oxford University Press, 2007) ch 3.

[85] More generally, A Weyembergh, *L'harmonisation des legislation pénals: Condition de l'espace penal Européen et révélateur de ses tensions* (Brussels, University of Brussels, 2004).

[86] eg Lenearts and Corthaut (above n 82).

[87] Peers (above n 78).

[88] Case C-6/64 *Costa v ENEL* [1964] ECR 585.

[89] Briefly, it should also be noted that AG Mengozzi in *Segi* argued that the *Foto-Frost* rule [Case 314/85 *Foto-Frost* [1987] ECR 4199], that the national courts have no jurisdiction themselves to declare that acts of Community institutions are invalid, did not apply in the third pillar because the two main assumptions on which this rule was based were not transferable. First, while the Community system offers a complete system of remedies, judicial protection in the third pillar is strictly limited. Secondly, the main purpose of the preliminary ruling procedure under Art 234 EC is to ensure that Community law is applied uniformly by national courts, and Art 35 TEU cannot accomplish this task to the same extent. On this see eg C Eckes, *EU Counter-Terrorist Policies and Fundamental Rights* (Oxford, Oxford University Press, 2009) ch 2.

[90] Case C-354/04, C-355/04P *Segi v Council* ECR [2007] I-6157, Opinion of AG Mengozzi delivered on 26 October 2006.

the Court of Justice to cover the former third pillar arena. Further, Article 75 TFEU makes it clear that restrictive measures against individuals must entail necessary legal safeguards and be subject to judicial review. Nonetheless, the question of what 'necessary' legal safeguards really means remains. In the light of the fact that Articles 2 and 6 of the TEU state that the EU is founded on respect for human rights, the standard in question should be sufficiently high. It should also be recalled that the EU's values are set out at length in the preamble of the Lisbon Treaty and that these values include respect for human rights and the rule of law. In other words, although it is true that these values are very broadly defined and that it is, therefore, difficult to pin down their exact meaning, there is no doubt that at its core these values ensure respect for human rights at the EU level.[91]

The following and final section provides some general reflections on the issue of effectiveness as a guiding principle for criminalisation. The reason for this is, as noted, that effectiveness within the theory of criminal law is as complex as it is within EU law discourse itself. In particular, the following section will try to confront effectiveness in criminal law with effectiveness as interpreted by the Court in Case C-176/03. The aim is to demonstrate the absence of robustness in the Court's reasoning when taking the effectiveness of EU law as a given.

IV. EFFECTIVENESS AS A GENERAL PRINCIPLE OF CRIMINAL LAW

While previous sections have focused on the effectiveness in EU law as traditionally interpreted, that is, as a question of enforcement albeit with tentacles extending into the former third pillar sphere, this section turns to criminal law and very briefly looks at the meaning of effectiveness there. The purpose is to provide a background to the constitutional discussion in the following chapters. Indeed, when thinking about the eager adoption of effectiveness in the context of the Court's case law, it might appear somewhat surprising that by contrast most criminal lawyers and criminologists agree on the assumption that criminal law is not always effective as a means of social control.[92] Nevertheless, as noted in chapter two, the judgment in Case C-176/03 seems to be based on the presumption that criminal law is effective per se, and this is where EU law and criminal law create not only friction but also misunderstandings when they are brought together.

[91] Moreover, some further guidance as regards the proper meaning of these safeguards in this area is given in declaration 25 on Arts 75 and 215 TFEU. This declaration emphasises that importance of the protection of the due process rights of the individuals or entities concerned, a thorough judicial review of decisions imposing restrictive measures, and the need to base these decisions on clear and distinct criteria.

[92] See eg, the discussion in the introductory chapter to RA Duff et al (eds), *The Boundaries of the Criminal Law* (Oxford, Oxford University Press, 2011) with further references and an excellent introduction to different theories of criminalisation. See also D Husak, *Overcriminalization* (Oxford, Oxford University Press, 2008).

A. The Ultimate Legal Threat – Is it Effective?

> Perhaps the nearest thing to a genuinely [ineffective and] unforeseeable prohibition in the history of English law was the form of treason which consisted of 'imagining' the death of the King.[93]

The principle of effectiveness in criminal law is a very broad subject with deep philosophical underpinnings. In short, it encompasses a restrictive policy that states that the criminal law should not be used if it cannot be effective in controlling conduct, and an expansive policy that states that criminal law should be used if it is the most efficient and cost-effective means of controlling conduct.[94] Generally, effectiveness as a principle for criminalisation is discussed in terms of positive or negative legitimacy where effectiveness is viewed as a limiting factor with claims that no criminalisation can be justified unless it can be expected to be effective.[95] Nevertheless, the idea of effectiveness being a template for criminalisation is not generally considered to be a justification for legislation.[96] Indeed, most criminal law scholars would argue that a normative theory of criminal law requires that criminalisation should be based on the 'wrongfulness' of the offence in issue rather than the effectiveness criteria as such.[97] Accordingly, 'effectiveness' would enter the arena in the decision as to whether to exercise any legislative power. As will be explained in chapter four, this is how EU law used to be, that is the principle of effectiveness has been part of the subsidiarity and proportionality test in whether to exercise any competences. In the EU context, the problem is that the effectiveness principle has found its way prematurely onto the agenda by asking: 'Can we do this?' instead of later asking 'Should we do this?' It goes without saying that this is problematic in criminal law policy matters.

B. Effectiveness in the Context of Case C-176/03[98]

In connection with the pre-judgment debate on the possible outcomes of Case C-176/03, one commentator stated that the idea that criminal law is always the most effective weapon with which to protect the environment is naïve, since administrative sanctions are often more efficient.[99] The key argument was that the Commission and the Court assume that the simple imposition of criminal penalties in legislation will also render it effective. The point is that an administrative

[93] N Walker, *Punishment, Danger and Stigma: The Morality of Criminal Justice* (Oxford, Blackwell, 1980) cited in C Lernestedt, *Kriminalisering: problem och principer* (Uppsala, Iustus, 2003) ch 1.

[94] Lernestedt, ibid.

[95] J Schonsheck, *On Criminalisation* (The Hague, Kluwer, 1994) ch 3.

[96] ibid

[97] Duff (above n 92).

[98] Draws upon E Herlin-Karnell, '*Commission v Council*: Some Reflections on Criminal Law in the First Pillar' (2007) 13 *European Public Law* 69.

[99] M Faure, 'European Environmental Criminal Law: Do we really Need it?'(2004) 13 *European Environmental Law Review* 18.

sanction with strict liability would be much more effective than criminal law with the associated 'awkward' requirement of a subjective fault element in terms of intent which would have to be 'beyond reasonable doubt'.

When discussing criminalisation, it is, however, commonly held that the burden of proof of the effectiveness and necessity of a suggested measure should be on those who wish to criminalise the action in question and not on those who wish to leave it free of such restrictions.[100] This is an expression of the *ultima ratio* principle (that the criminal law should be the last resort) and this principle reflects a minimalist, subsidiarity-like approach to criminal law. A further issue, closely related to effectiveness, is the question of symbolism. It should perhaps be recalled that AG Colomer in his Opinion in Case C-176/03 stipulated that when an act is prohibited in criminal terms, it is held to merit the most severe punishment because it transgresses the fundamental tenets of the legal system and includes an ethical dimension to the issues at stake.[101] This is clearly an important matter because if it is 'enough' to see European criminal law as a 'symbol' in order to fulfil the requirement of effectiveness, it contradicts the EU law assumption that the principle of effectiveness should be based upon objective criteria. Consequently, it seems vital to understand what we mean by the notion of 'symbolic criminal law' at the European level. More specifically, one could ask whether symbolic criminal legislation really does ensure the effective protection of the environment, as in Case C-176/03, or if it is rather the symbolic labelling of perpetrators which is the aim. Naturally, this opens up the bigger question of the kind of criminal law theory that the above statements are based upon with respect to the nature of a crime.[102] Because criminal law inevitably generates a kind of a 'stigma' and therefore becomes a 'symbol', it should not be the main or only criterion for criminalisation in general, as this can easily lead to 'over criminalisation' which may become counterproductive.[103] And indeed, criminal law sanctions should be the law's ultimate threat. Nevertheless, an important dimension is perhaps neglected. That is that one cannot simply decide to call something an administrative sanction if, in reality, it is a criminal law sanction. The reason for this is, as mentioned in chapter two, that the case law of the European Court of Human Rights concerning the proper scope of Article 6 European Convention on Human Rights[104] stipulates an autonomous interpretation of what is to be regarded as criminal law. This is something that the EU has been severely criticised for, that is,

[100] See eg, Schonsheck (above n 93) and J Feinberg, *Offense to Others* (Oxford, Oxford University Press, 1986).

[101] N Jareborg, 'What kind of Criminal Law Do We Want?' in A Snare (ed) *Beware of Punishment: On the Utility and Futility of Criminal Law, Scandinavian Studies in Criminology* (Oslo, Scandinavian Studies in Criminology, 1995) 17.

[102] For a more sophisticated discussion of criminal law theories see eg Duff et al (n 90), discussing the rise of legal moralism in criminal law and possible problems with such an approach.

[103] This discussion concerns victimless crimes. However, the importance of symbolic criminal law is eg discussed by A Ashworth, *Principles of Criminal Law* (Oxford, Oxford University Press) ch 2.

[104] Starting with *Engel and others v Netherlands* Series A, No 22; [1979–80]1 ECHR 647, 20/04/1977 and *Orzuk v Germany*, Series A, No 73; [1984] 6 EHRR 365, 21/02/1984.

using administrative sanctions as a competence creep into the criminal law field.[105] As will be shown in chapter four, there will always be a delicate balance to be struck between ensuring that the EU complies with the *ultima ratio* and at the same time not over-relying on regulatory sanctions or other coercive non-criminal measures (such as preventive orders with no guarantee of fair trial).[106]

In any case, it would be natural to expect that some kind of empirical data in support of the Court's conclusions on the 'fully effective dogma' as stipulated in Case C-176/03 would have been required here. However, no such data appears to form a part of the Court's reasoning. Even if there were empirical data to hand, the evaluation of such data would obviously vary according to what theory is adopted for the purposes of such an evaluation. For example, if the idea of the provision at issue is dissuasiveness, then data could be collected at a fairly early stage after the criminalisation in question.[107] Nevertheless, if the governing of 'morals' is the aim, it could always be claimed that a lack of results does not prove anything since it would take much longer to study such consequences in order to analyse the society's morals.[108] What is of major concern, however, being the very crux of the matter, is that in practice the burden of proof for the effectiveness at issue seems to be on the limiter rather than the proponent of criminalisation. This appears to be the case even though it is often held in criminal law theory that such a burden of proof should fall on the legislator. There seems to be a similar pattern in the EU context. As will be explained in the next chapter, in the framework of EU legislation such an approach is not in line with conferral of powers nor with the principle of subsidiarity.

To sum up this section on criminalisation, what, if anything can be concluded? More specifically, what is the point of 'effectiveness' as a guiding principle for criminalisation? First, and in extremely general terms, it is often stated that an ineffective provision would undermine the respect for the criminal law system as the prevention in question would lose much of its function. Secondly, if a criminal law is too severe it would render itself ineffective as the citizens would find it unfair.[109] Another argument is, of course, the symbolically influenced idea of the state itself (in an era of secularisation): criminalising certain conduct demonstrates what ought to be regarded as morally wrong. It is submitted that the EU is not yet sufficiently fully formed to take on this symbolic mission, as the definition and use of criminal law – the issue of competence aside – is a role of another calibre than, for example, the creation of citizenship. As will become clear from the following chapters, this apparent 'light' approach by the EU legislator, including the Court, when investigating the real meaning of 'effectiveness', probably stems

[105] A very important reason for distinguishing between criminal and other sanctions, is that the fundamental principle of *nulla poena sine culpa*, stipulated in Art 6.2 ECHR does not apply to administrative offences in its full context and the individual is not guaranteed the right to trial.

[106] Along the same lines, see the interesting discussion in A Ashworth and L Zedner, 'Preventive Orders: A Problem of Undercriminalization?' in Duff et al (above n 92) ch 3.

[107] Lernestedt (above n 93).

[108] ibid.

[109] See J Chalmers and F Leverick, 'Fair Labelling in Criminal Law' (2008) 71 *Modern Law Review* 217.

from the fact that there is a real lack of knowledge of these questions at the EU level. There is, accordingly, as noted in chapter two, an over-reliance on the 'magic' of the criminal law.[110]

V. CONCLUSION

This chapter has been necessarily open-ended in order to paint the broad picture of effectiveness as an enforcement issue and as a principle of criminalisation. As has been shown, the debate ranges from criticising the Court for a lack of consistency or unnecessary interference with national procedural and remedial law in favour of effectiveness of EU law, to pleas for further uniformity to be introduced by, for example, harmonising certain aspects of national procedures and remedies. Others argue that the area of effective enforcement is not suited to harmonisation and therefore requires other solutions. But the chapter attempts to illustrate the many complexities in this area with regard to the AFSJ and EU criminal law. More specifically, the purpose of this chapter is primarily to stress that the area of EU criminal law poses challenges of a kind previously unknown to the EU, and that there is a deficit of knowledge of these issues within the EU's institutions. Equally, the aim was to illuminate the implementation imbalance doctrine and apply it in the context of the third pillar. After all, regardless of the entry into force of the Lisbon Treaty and the end of the third pillar, the main ideological issues of legitimacy, that is, how to reconcile further European action in these matters, are still significant. In addition, the continued use of the Court's 'negative' law power in the area of EU criminal law cooperation runs the particular risk of being far too sharp an instrument when applied in the hugely sensitive area of crime and punishment. Moreover, it seems as if the Court's approach to effective enforcement in the EU is not set in stone either. In other words, the famous 'smorgasbord' approach to enforcement is certainly far from a unique phenomenon in the matters under scrutiny here and constitutes something of a European *déjà vu* for any EU law expert on remedies. After all, within the classical field of the Community, the Court has gone as far as to implicitly suggest that its interpretative strategy of stretching the boundaries of EU law is inherent to the Treaty.[111] Therefore, it seems clear that the question of enforcement in Europe demonstrates the ambiguities in the Court's general approach, which obviously paints an even more complex picture of what is constitutionally happening when one tries to understand it in the context of the former third pillar. Finally, the last section aimed to very briefly illustrate that 'effectiveness' in criminal law is a lot more complex than the mere invocation of 'criminalisation' as such, as criminal law is far from effective per se. It showed that effectiveness as such is a tricky parameter to use when deciding on legislation, despite being one of the principles of criminalisation.

[110] See, however, the Opinion of AG Mazak in C-440/05, delivered on 28 June 2007, for a more nuanced approach.

[111] Case C-397/01 *Pfeiffer* [2004] ECR I-8835.

And yet, one should certainly try to avoid falling into the trap, as one commentator put it, of personalising the Court and attributing to it an underlying policy or hidden agenda.[112] However, the development of EU criminal law through the Court's case law has perhaps cast some doubt on the validity of this statement, as it seems as though the search for effectiveness for EU law continues.

The challenging task is, then, to clarify the intersection of 'effective enforcement', as discussed in this chapter, and competence questions, which is the topic for the next chapter. More specifically, the relationship between enforcement issues and competence matters when they meet may have consequences for how to view the principle of 'effectiveness'. Indeed, before concluding this chapter it should perhaps be recognised that this clash between enforcement issues and legislative competences has, since the early days of the EU, been resolved with the helping hand of the *effet utile* 'paradigm' of EU law. Notoriously, this solution has assisted the EU to expand and develop into a unique legal order without unambiguously answering yes or no to the question of whether we are dealing with academic reasoning and enforcement or competence reasoning in the strict sense. The conundrum that arises in our case is, however, more crucially whether an analogy could be made with the supranational playing field in the present context – or whether such reasoning with respect to the confrontation between enforcement and competence in EU criminal law matters is unwise. Again, this book calls for caution here, not only in the absence of a fully formed system of protection of the individual, but also from the constitutional perspective – legitimacy and legality – and the question of creeping competence, which is generally considered to be harmful to the identity of the EU and as promoting distrust.

Consequently, the following chapter aims to change gear and pace, saddling up a hurdler, and travelling into the constitutional landscape of 'effectiveness' as a question of competence.

[112] Eeckhout (above n 10) at 28.

4

Constitutional Effectiveness: An Exegesis

I. INTRODUCTION

THIS CHAPTER CHARTS the development of the EU principle of effectiveness as a constitutional axiom.[1] It continues the story set out in the previous chapters by exploring the constitutional dimension of the conferral of powers in the EU and the link between this and the concept of effectiveness in the context of criminal law. It provides a short historical account of the general competence provisions under the EU Treaty and discusses the extent to which the Lisbon Treaty has changed this landscape. More specifically, the chapter outlines an argument which runs like a thread throughout this book – that the Court's use of 'effectiveness' as a constitutional principle is dangerously imprecise as a threshold for competence. Although the focus is criminal law, the aim is to construct a broader theoretical framework, or setting, in order to show the underlying concerns permeating this area. In so doing, the chapter seeks to illuminate the wider question of European powers. Arguably, it is necessary to paint such a background picture before looking more specifically at the mosaic of European criminal law and the question of competences. In other words, the aim is simply to place the concept of a supranational criminal law competence in context. Therefore, the chapter runs through the general constitutional issues in the EU, such as the objectives of the Union and the attribution of competences.

While previous chapters outlined the general picture and development of European criminal law as well as the complexities of EU concepts of effective enforcement, this chapter is devoted to the constitutional dimension of effectiveness as a guiding principle for harmonisation of criminal law. However, the question of the need for a better division and definition of competences in the EU is, after all, far from new. For this reason, this chapter starts at the other end of the discussion – that is, by offering an account of the very notion of competence distribution and the question of the objectives of the EU – before introducing some of the broader policy debate in the final part. The primary aim of this chapter is,

[1] I do not think there is any need to define the term 'constitutional' in EU law here, a term that has been around since the early days of the EU legal order. After all, in Case C-294/83, *Les Verts* [1986] ECR 1339 the ECJ declared that the Community had a basic constitutional charter based on the rule of law. In *Kadi* Case C-415/05P [2008] ECR I-6351, it went further and referred to the 'constitutional principles of the EU'. See eg, J Weiler, 'The Transformation of Europe' (1990-91) 100 *Yale Law Journal* 2400; and N MacCormick, *Questioning Sovereignty* (Oxford, Oxford University Press, 1999).

therefore, to explore some of the difficulties of competence monitoring in EU criminal law, by setting out the conundrums of competence allocation in the EU. It is only by doing so that we will fully understand the EU's activity in the field of criminal law. Expressed another way, while previous chapters have looked at the changes brought about by the Lisbon Treaty, as well as explaining what led to the Treaty, this chapter starts and ends with the Lisbon Treaty (but also addresses it throughout) while keeping 'the story' in the middle.

This chapter is structured as follows. Part I offers some introductory reflections on the issue of competence by outlining the different parts of the chapter. In addition, it explains the effectiveness criteria in Article 83 TFEU. Part II clarifies the history of the EU's approach to the supranationalisation of EU criminal law by looking at the objectives of the EU and how they have changed over time. The chapter sets out the main constitutional innovations and charts how 'effectiveness' has been used as a constitutional axiom in this area. Part of this exercise includes a detailed account of ex Article 47 TEU (pre-Lisbon), which guarded the former first pillar from any intrusion by the intergovernmental pillars, and a discussion of what we can learn from the history of this provision. It will become clear that, prior to the entry into force of the Lisbon Treaty, Article 352 TFEU (then Article 308 EC) revealed a similar pattern to ex Article 47 EU and the delimitation of the pillars, although the former was even more indefinite when distributing competences. An analysis of the former Article 47 TEU explains the dynamics of this area and how this helps us to assess the boundaries of the new Article 40 TEU (regarding the delimitation of powers between the Treaties).

Part III explores the question of market construction and the constitutional mystery of Article 114 TFEU in relation to criminal law. It explores the 'federal' boundaries of the establishment and functioning of the internal market. Before embarking upon an analysis of market integration and criminal law, the aim is to offer some general thoughts on Article 114 TFEU, while keeping criminal law as the main theme. Part III starts by setting out the basics of Article 114 TFEU: obstacles to trade and distortion of competition. Thereafter, it investigates the relationship between Articles 114 TFEU and 83 TFEU and the extent to which it would be possible to rely on Article 114 TFEU in the future. This part provides the theoretical basis for the case study on EU financial crimes and the question of preventive harmonisation in criminal law, which will be discussed in chapter five.

Part IV gives an account of subsidiarity and proportionality. Obviously, the intention is not to embark on any deep analysis as these notions have already been discussed in great detail in the legal literature. What seems to have been less well explored is the meaning of subsidiarity and proportionality in the context of EU criminal law. This part attempts to show that criminal law could and should be seen as imbued with 'subsidiarity' and, more specifically, that it could be viewed as expressing the principle of *ultima ratio* – the minimalism approach – in criminal law. This section also tracks the meaning of proportionality and outlines any implications it might have for the notion of EU criminal law as well as the broader question of balancing in the area of freedom, security and justice (AFSJ).

The penultimate part of this chapter, Part V, looks at the new enhanced cooperation mechanisms. Its purpose is to discuss it in the light of the principles of subsidiarity and proportionality and thereby investigate the notion of flexibility with regard to criminal law. This part strikes out from the previous section on subsidiarity and proportionality to illuminate the provision of enhanced cooperation by arguing that it is difficult to imagine that subsidiarity will play any major role here at all, and that this remains true despite its 'alternative to Union action' character.

Finally, Part V concludes by discussing the broad issue of the delimitation of competences and, in particular, the existence of broad competence provisions, in so far as it is relevant from the perspective of criminal law, by briefly mapping out the constitutional path from Laeken to Lisbon. The chapter concludes by supplying a general conclusion.

In other words, this chapter follows up the reasoning presented in the previous chapters by explicitly considering the concept of effectiveness as a difficult parameter when deciding on competences. The starting point is the longstanding effect of the outcome of Case C-176/03[2] discussed in detail above. I will begin this exercise by turning to the competence provision of Article 83(2) TFEU, as it sets the scene of persisting reverberations of effectiveness in this area, before moving on to the broader debate on competences more generally.

A. The Effectiveness Criteria, Article 83(2) TFEU: No Limits to Criminalisation?

As examined in chapter two, before the entry into force of the Lisbon Treaty there was no explicit EU law competence in criminal law matters. Therefore, the EU legislator has, in the absence of legislative competence, relied on the principle of loyalty and effective sanctions of a 'non-criminal law' nature. However, thanks to the outcome of Case C-176/03, EU aspirations to create a supranational criminal law took a step up the ladder towards competence, which resulted in a clash with the principle of attribution of powers in the EU. The Lisbon Treaty opened up a new chapter in the development and creation of EU criminal law by explicitly listing it as a supranational competence.

The AFSJ, like most other EU law policies, now constitutes a shared competence. This is evident from Article 4(2j) TFEU and Article 67 TFEU, as well as Chapter 4 of Title V of the TFEU. This clarification of the EU competence provisions constitutes one of the innovations offered by the Lisbon Treaty as it gives guidance about the nature of the EU's competences (that is, there can be exclusive, shared or supportive/coordinative competences). These categories of competences are set out in Articles 2 to 6 TFEU. Nevertheless, this chapter seeks to demonstrate that despite this clarification of competences in the Lisbon Treaty,

[2] Case C-176/03 *Commission v Council* [2005] ECR I-7879.

the question of the extent to which criminal law could be harmonised for the full effectiveness of EU law remains ambiguous. As explained, the subject of this chapter is the broader reading of effectiveness which covers a wider range of areas such as the criminal law and how it was brought into the core of the EU without any mandate in the Treaty. Therefore, it is important to discuss the constitutional scope of Article 83(2) TFEU more specifically. As noted in chapter two, this provision provides for criminal law legislation in an area which has already been subject to the EU's harmonisation programme if it is essential for the effective implementation of an EU policy. It represents a codification of the Case C-176/03 approach, that criminal law can be harmonised in order to ensure the full effectiveness of EU law. Yet, as noted above, viewing Article 83(2) TFEU as a *carte blanche* would not only render the attribution of powers illusionary, but also be liable to clash with the principle that criminal law should be the last resort as a means of control. Although it is true that Article 83(1) TFEU, which contains a specific list of particularly serious cross-border crimes such as organised crime and illicit drug trafficking that could be harmonised would, be *lex specialis* of criminal law in the absence of any other provisions expressly granting a competence. Thus, it is possible that Article 83(2) TFEU could prove to have significantly wide-ranging constitutional scope as it represents a codification of the effectiveness criteria in Case C-176/03. Moreover, Article 67 TFEU states that the EU shall endeavour to ensure a high level of security through measures to prevent and combat crime and racism, if necessary through the use of criminal laws. So 'necessary' and 'effective' represent extremely important parameters for EU constitutional development in this area.

The aim of the chapter is to outline the broader pattern of the delimitation of powers and thereby to explain why the changes brought about by the Lisbon Treaty are far from new when considering the Court's case law.

II. CONFERRED POWERS AND THE OBJECTIVES OF THE EU

A. Introduction

The EU only has powers which have been specifically allocated to it. This is stipulated in Article 5 TEU and Article 7 TFEU. Article 4 TEU reiterates this by stating that the competences not conferred upon the EU in the Treaties remain with the Member States. As noted by Weatherill:

> Any slippage in EU activity beyond the terms of the mandate that is found in the Treaties is illegitimate in the sense that it is devoid of the authorisation rooted in national ratification of the original Treaties and the subsequent amending texts . . . The principle of conferral, then is tied to legality.[3]

[3] S Weatherill, 'Legality and Concealed Mechanisms behind the Extension of EU Powers' conference presentation, Utrecht, 5 November 2009 (on file with the author).

Therefore, the principle of conferral is reflected in the axiom of legality in criminal law, that any punishment requires prior codification and thus retroactive use of criminal law is prohibited.[4] This is also confirmed by Article 49 of the Charter of Fundamental Rights ('the Charter') as well as in the general principles of EU law as discussed in chapter two.

The significance of the principle of conferral, or attribution, of powers is clearly that the EU does not enjoy unlimited powers to act – it must respect the limits of the powers conferred on it by the Treaty. This means that the EU cannot authorise an increase in the scope of its own competences.[5] It also means that the Treaty has been the target of consistent revision in order to remain in line with the expanding case law of the Court. The *Tobacco Advertising I* case[6] concerning the limits of Article 114 TFEU (explored below in Part II) brought attention to the principle of conferred powers by making it clear that there were limits to EU action which were judicially policed. However, despite the clear wording of Article 114 TFEU, the principle of attributed competences, has not always been respected.[7] Moreover, there has been an apparent connection between the broad boundaries of Articles 114 TFEU and 352 TFEU and ex Article 47 EU which constituted (alongside loyalty in Article 4(3) TEU as discussed in chapter three) the most open-ended provisions in the Treaty. For this reason, they will be frequently cross-referenced.

In any case, it should perhaps be noted that one explanation of the functional expansion of the EU's harmonisation programme lies in the political willingness of the Council to pursue this route. Indeed, such willingness prompted one commentator, in the context of the early jurisprudence on Article 352 TFEU, to assert that 'it [is] hard to take seriously the notion that Community competence is limited by anything other than the need to secure unanimous support in Council'.[8] Another reason for a broad reading of the EU's powers can be found in the case law of the Court. After all, the Court has not always been a faithful follower of the principle of attribution of powers, but has rather chosen to play the role of activist – on some occasions quite aggressively and even passionately – in furtherance of a mission to bring certain particularly attractive areas within the aegis of the EU institutions.

The aim of this first part is to sketch the pattern of the delimitation of powers and thereby to explain why criminal law, although initially not included in the founding EC Treaty, was never exempted from the EU's legislative power. The next section starts by focusing on Article 352 TFEU, the flexibility clause. In doing so, the intention is to shed some light on the importance of identifying what the objectives of the Treaty are and hence whether criminal law – which was not a

[4] See Art 6 ECHR.

[5] To underline this message, Art 7 TFEU, states that the Union shall act within the limits of the powers conferred upon it by the Treaty.

[6] Case C-376/98 *Germany v Parliament and Council* [2000] ECR I-8419.

[7] S Weatherill, 'Better Competence Monitoring' (2005) 30 *EL Rev* 23.

[8] S Weatherill, *Law and Integration in the European Union* (Oxford, Clarendon Press, 1995) 51.

listed objective of the former EC Treaty – could be linked to an objective in the pursuit of greater effectiveness for EU law. I will also discuss the possible significance of Article 352 TFEU in criminal law in the future. It will become clear that Article 352 TFEU reveals a similar pattern to ex Article 47 EU, although the former has been even more ambiguous when distributing competences. This chapter thus seeks to follow up the reasoning presented in the previous chapter by examining the concept of effectiveness as an uncertain parameter when deciding on competences in the framework of the trend towards 'depillarisation' and by considering what we can learn from this for the future.

B. How it all Began

In understanding the constitutional journey of criminal law and the implications of 'effectiveness' it is necessary to place it in context. After all, before the entry into force of the Lisbon Treaty, criminal law was not on the competence list as laid out in ex Articles 2 and 3 EC, which listed core areas such as the establishment of the internal market, including the removal of obstacles to trade and the facilitation of free movement. Although some would have argued that this list was only indicative, until the outcome in Case C-176/03 the EU legislator was fairly cautious with respect to criminal law, and thus sought and found other means to remedy a lack of legislative competence. More specifically, as noted in chapter two, the EU legislator has, in the absence of legislative competence, relied on Article 4(3) TEU (ex Article 10 EC), the principle of loyalty coupled with the notion of effective sanctions of a 'non-criminal law' nature.

When pinning down the objectives of the EU and examining how they have expanded over time, it is useful to start by looking at the history of Article 352 TFEU (ex Article 308 EC) as this provision outlines the objectives of the EU very clearly. Thus, it is universally acknowledged that Article 352 TFEU, or more properly its predecessor, ex Article 308 EC,[9] has always been controversial.[10] This was the article of last resort in carrying out the mission to link objectives to the Treaty that one way or another could be related to the common market. In other words,

[9] Art 308 EC read: 'if action by the Community should prove necessary to attain, in the course of the operation of the common market, one of the objectives of the Community and this Treaty has not provided the necessary powers, the Council shall, acting unanimously on the proposal from the Commission and after consulting the European Parliament, take appropriate measures'.

[10] See eg, J Weiler, 'The Transformation of Europe' (1990–91) 100 *Yale Law Journal* 2400; VM Bungenberg, 'Dynamische Intergration, Art 308 und die Forderung nach dem Kompetenzkatalog', (2002) *Europarecht* 879; R Schtüze, *From Dual to Cooperative Federalism: The Changing Structure of European Law* (Oxford, Oxford University Press, 2009) 132; A Dashwood, 'Article 308 and the Outer Limit of Expressly Conferred Community Competence' in C Barnard and O Odudu *The Outer Limits of European Union Law* (Oxford, Hart Publishing, 2009) 35; T Konstadinides, *Division of Powers in the European Union* (Deventer, Kluwer Law Publishing, 2009) 202; G Conway, 'Conflicts of norms in EU law and the legal reasoning of the ECJ' (2010) 11 *German Law Journal* 966; P Craig, *The Lisbon Treaty, Law, Politics and Treaty Reform* (Oxford, Oxford University Press, 2010) 182; and L Corriras, *The Passivity of Law: Competence and Constitution in the European Court of Justice* (Dordrecht, Springer, 2011).

Article 352 TFEU has always been a 'mopping-up' provision, so that if no other Treaty article granted the desired competence, Article 352 TFEU was often put forward as the legislative solution. Thus, Article 352 TFEU was subsidiary to other specific provisions in the Treaty.[11] Yet the Lisbon Treaty reform also meant a change in this regard. More specifically, the wording of Article 352 TFEU has been amended slightly. To begin with, the reference to the 'common market' has now been deleted. Instead this provision simply refers to the 'policies of the Union'.[12] A second paragraph has also been added to this provision which states that using the procedure for monitoring the subsidiarity principle referred to in Article 5(3) TEU, the Commission shall draw national Parliaments' attention to proposals based on this Article, and that measures based on this Article shall not entail harmonisation of Member States' laws or regulations in cases where the Treaties exclude such harmonisation.[13] Furthermore, the Lisbon Treaty brought another change with regard to the flexibility clause: it now reads that Article 352 TFEU cannot serve as a basis for attaining objectives pertaining to the common foreign and security policy and any acts adopted pursuant to this Article shall respect the limits set out in Article 40 TEU (regarding the non affect obligation between the TFEU and the TEU, respectively).

That said, this chapter aims to do more than simply describe Article 352 TFEU. It explores the implications of 'effectiveness' reasoning for the objectives of the EU. Therefore, in examining this issue, it is arguably necessary to take a short detour via the history of Article 352 TFEU. After all, this provision, like the law on national remedies discussed above, has passed through different stages in the degree of EU intervention. Indeed, as the EU system has developed and matured, Article 352 TFEU's history has been characterised by cycles of integration 'fever' and more autonomy-friendly stages.[14] To briefly run through these phases, the initial foundation period – the so-called first phase – is often said to have started with the Treaty of Rome. Here, Article 352 TFEU was applied in areas such as agricultural policy and customs, but outside of those areas achieved varying degrees of expansion. In particular, in the early 1970s the Paris summit, which had a direct impact on the widening of the EC objectives, was concluded.[15] This period is often referred to as the golden age of Article 352 TFEU (ex Article 308 EC). During this time an array of areas including environmental protection[16] and action to combat poverty – though hardly objectives of the common market –

[11] Case C-8/73 *Massey-Fergusson* [1973] ECR 897.

[12] On this see Conway (above n 10). In view of the *Kadi* case which confirmed a broad interpretation of this concept, discussed below, such a re-wording is perhaps of limited significance as the broad scope of this article had already been confirmed.

[13] This is also reiterated by Declaration 41 attached to the Treaty which states that measures based on this article shall not entail the harmonisation of Member States' laws or regulations in cases where the Treaties exclude such harmonisation.

[14] eg J Weiler, 'The Transformation of Europe' (1990–91) 100 *Yale Law Journal* 2400.

[15] Paris Summit of 1972, Heads of State and Government (predecessor of the European Council). See eg, Schtüze (above n 10) 135.

[16] Case C-240/83 *Proceur de la Republique* [1985] ECR 53; eg Weatherill (above n 7).

were transferred to the supranational level.[17] Subsequently, in 1987 the Single European Act (SEA) entered into force. The SEA and the accompanying introduction of new Treaty provisions – most prominently Article 114 TFEU (ex Article 95 EC) – were expected to draw attention away from Article 352 TFEU. Nevertheless, the use of qualified majority voting (QMV) under Article 114 TFEU did not wipe Article 352 TFEU off the EU's harmonisation programme. In the run-up to the Lisbon Treaty, the controversial *Kadi* judgment[18] (which dramatically expanded the EU's competences to include action against terrorism within the first pillar) demonstrated that the issue of the boundaries of EU competences and the limits of Article 352 TFEU were once again at the centre of the competence debate. Within the framework of Article 352 TFEU more generally, it should, moreover, be recalled – as touched upon in chapter two above – that in *Commission v Germany*[19] (a case concerning the question of whether the EU had the competence to impose administrative sanctions) Article 352 TFEU already figured on the periphery of EC criminal law competence. So whilst AG Jacobs, in his Opinion, argued that sanctions in the agricultural sphere could be harmonised even if such a competence was not one of the EC's objectives, it was not until the *Kadi* case[20] that such a possibility became viable. In other words, even though the objectives of the EC were constantly expanded, criminal law was for a long time exempted from the general expansion model of EU integration.

In any event, when investigating the history of Article 352 TFEU, the principle of conferred competences under Article 5(2) TEU is self-evidently important for any understanding of EU law powers. This was perfectly demonstrated in Opinion 2/94,[21] which concerned the EU's possible accession to the European Convention on Human Rights (ECHR) (pre-Lisbon). In this case, the Court clarified that Article 352 TFEU could not be used to widen the scope of Community powers beyond the framework created by the EC Treaty (former first pillar) as a whole. Neither could it be used as the foundation for the adoption of provisions which would amend the Treaty without following the necessary amendment procedures. Yet it is still the 'pinning down' of these boundaries that remains difficult. The problem is that there is no explicit criterion except in the very idea of the conferral of powers itself, which makes it particularly complex if the effectiveness of EU law, as charted in chapter three, becomes part of the objectives of the EU. There would thus be an uneasy relationship between the need to justify EU action and the implied powers or *effet utile* doctrine. In order to address this somewhat perplexing question it us useful briefly to look at the notion of *effet utile*. The point is

[17] R Schütze, 'Organized Change towards an "Ever Closer Union": Article 308 EC and the Limits to the Community's Legislative Competence' (2003) 22 *Yearbook of European Law* 79.

[18] Case C-402/05P *Kadi* [2008] ECR I-6351discussed below. See also Case T-85/09 *Kadi II* judgment of 30 September 2010 not yet reported, concerning the appropriate standard for judicial review.

[19] Case C-240/90 *Germany v Commission* [1992] ECR I-5383 Opinion of AG Jacobs delivered on 3 June 1992. See also n 19 ch 2.

[20] Case C-402/05P *Kadi* [2008] ECR I-6351.

[21] Opinion 2/94 *Accession to the ECHR* [1996] ECR I-1759; see Konstadinides (above n 10) 214.

that although the flexibility clause does not constitute an instrument for freely implying powers since it has to be tied to the principle of conferral, it nonetheless touches on this issue when defining the objectives of the EU. In this respect not much has changed since the entry into force of the Lisbon Treaty. However, it should also be noted that the unanimity requirement means that it will be more difficult to use this provision in an enlarged EU as Article 352 TFEU also requires the consent of the European Parliament (EP), as opposed to mere consultation as was previously the case under ex Article 308 EC.[22]

i. Are Effet Utile *and 'Effectiveness' the Same Concept?*

In terms of implied powers *effet utile* is often described as an indicator of the objectives of the EU. After all, in the context of external relations, the helping hand of the *effet utile* 'paradigm', as most prominently witnessed by the *ERTA* case, has long been relied upon to resolve the issue of legislative competences.[23] There, the principle of implied powers was linked to Article 4(3) TEU (ex Article 10 EC) and the more general obligation of loyalty which somehow provided a theoretical basis for that principle.[24] Therefore, the very notion of implied powers surely encompasses effectiveness, even though effectiveness itself did not form part of the competence monitoring framework *stricto sensu*, until the Case C-176/03 ruling manifested such a constitutional use of effectiveness. Nevertheless, it is far from clear whether the notion of *effet utile* constitutes the same concept as the principle of effectiveness or whether it is a subtheme of implied powers. Either way, *effet utile* is not only an idiom for the implied powers or the effective enforcement doctrines as discussed above, it is also related to competence matters. Further, this means, (as mentioned in chapter three) that there is no clear-cut distinction between enforcement and competence because vague notions such as necessity and effectiveness make these boundaries particularly imprecise. Equally, it seems as if the old adage that 'there is simply no nucleus of sovereignty that the Member States can invoke as such against the Community' is still true.[25]

So again, arguably not much has been changed by the Lisbon Treaty. Nonetheless, it is true that the new mechanisms provided by the new subsidiarity framework and the national parliaments'[26] participation in the monitoring process, discussed below, means that there are now more visible constraints in place.

[22] Craig (above n 10) at 183.

[23] Case C-22/70 *Commission v Council* [1971] ECR 263.

[24] P Koutrakos, *EU International Relations Law* (Oxford, Hart Publishing, 2006) 82.

[25] K Lenaerts, 'Constitutionalism and the Many Faces of Federalism' (1990) 38 *American Journal of Comparative Law* 205.

[26] The Protocols on the Application of the Principles of Subsidiarity and Proportionality and the Protocol on the Role of the National Parliaments, annexed to the Lisbon Treaty, discussed below in part three, section D.

ii. And 'Necessity'?

In the search for the objectives of the EU, one commentator suggested that the early ruling of *Massey-Fergusson*,[27] where the Court judged that the gap between the EU's objectives and the desired result could be bridged by 'necessity', constituted an 'unconstitutional' use of effectiveness.[28] As already noted, in the context of Case C-176/03, the Court's use of effectiveness is now clearly 'constitutional'. However, it is often suggested that there appears to be a conflict in the very criteria of Article 352 TFEU, as 'necessary' not only forms part of the objectives criteria for deciding on competence but also the subsidiarity check as such.[29] At issue here is not so much a conflict of 'necessity' as such, as the risk of recycling the same legal arguments. Obviously, the danger is that reliance on vague words such as 'necessity' or 'effectiveness' can easily lead to discrepancy. Therefore, the problem is that an effectiveness test from a competence perspective would mean that 'necessity' or 'effectiveness' would have already entered the arena in Article 5 (1 to 2) TEU and not – as it is usually interpreted – as part of the subsidiarity and proportionality monitoring. In other words, 'necessity' as part of an 'effectiveness' test is not a precise threshold for justifying EU action. Again, when looking at Case C-176/03, we have to ask how the Court in that case managed to separate these distinguished yet closely related principles as it did not (explicitly) evaluate the notion of effectiveness. 'Necessity' as formulated in Case C-176/03 and as stipulated in paragraph 48 of this judgment, forms part of the effectiveness criteria in deciding on competence (albeit in the specific context of Article 192 TFEU). Nevertheless, in the *Tobacco Advertising I* case,[30] the Court placed great weight on the notion of 'appreciable' when stating that it was necessary to verify whether there was an appreciable distortion of competition at issue. Indeed, in doing so the Court was rather careful in its reasoning and enumerated several criteria. This appears to be the missing link in judgments such as Case C-176/03: the Court never explained its reasoning yet it allowed the imperative of 'effectiveness' to take precedence. Nonetheless, such a penumbra in legal reasoning is not in line with the principle of conferred powers. After all, as the AG in *Tobacco Advertising I* pointed out, the constitutional division of powers should be drawn on objective criteria.[31] The key point for the present argument is that it is difficult to base the objective criteria in question on vague and subjective concepts such as 'effectiveness' and 'necessity' when distributing competences. As indicated, it confirms the unambiguously broad scope of competences in the EU.

[27] *Massey-Fergusson* (above n 11). See eg, Schütze (above n 15); K St Bradley, 'Powers and Procedures in the EU Constitution: Legal Bases and the Court' in P Craig and G De Burca, *The Evolution of EU Law* (Oxford, Oxford University Press, 2011) 85; and T Konstadinides, 'Between Circumvention and Gap-filling: The conceptual limits around the Treaty's flexibility clause', forthcoming *Yearbook of European Law*.

[28] Schütze (above n 10).

[29] ibid.

[30] Case C-376/98 *Germany v Parliament and Council* [2000] ECR I-8419.

[31] Opinion of AG Fennelly delivered on 15 June 2000, § 4.

The next section aims to explore the pattern of the constitutional use of effectiveness as it has formed part of the necessity requirement of Article 352 TFEU by applying it within the framework of the well-known, albeit controversial, *Kadi* ruling.[32] In doing so, the intention is to show the adaptive, flexible nature of this article and examine it in the light of how effectiveness has been the driving principle in the run-up to the Lisbon Treaty – the so-called 'depillarisation' phenomenon.

C. Article 352 TFEU – How Flexible is 'Flexibility'?

Article 352 TFEU was recently under scrutiny in the aforementioned *Kadi*[33] case concerning the legal basis of a regulation implementing a UN resolution, which ordered the freezing of individuals' funds on the grounds of combating terrorism.[34] In short, the issue that arose was the legal validity of a regulation, initially based on ex Articles 60 EC and 301 EC (now Article 215 TFEU), which allowed measures to be taken against third countries but to which Article 352 TFEU had later been added, presumably to be on the safe 'competence' side when adopting sanctions against individuals rather than state actors.

More specifically, the question raised by *Kadi* was, inter alia, whether the EU had the competence to adopt a regulation freezing the applicants' financial assets within the EU on the basis of an identification and listing made by the Sanctions Committee. In this regard, the General Court (then the Court of First Instance) stated that even though combating international terrorism could not be considered as one of the Community objectives (it being a Common Foreign and Security Policy (CFSP) matter), ex Article 308 EC in conjunction with Articles 301 and 60 EC constituted a possible legal basis for making this goal a Community objective. The General Court held that Article 301 was included in the Treaty for a reason. The purpose was to allow the EU to implement a coherent external policy as a bridge between the Union pillars, which according to ex Article 3 EU (now Article 7 TFEU and Articles 13 and 21 TEU) should in any event constitute a coherent whole in the name of consistency. But why was 'consistency' relevant here at all?[35] Clearly, it is difficult to understand why consistency as such should lead to an expansion of EU powers, without any evaluation of those powers. Thus, it is submitted, we are very close to an effectiveness-based reasoning here as well. More specifically, the point is that effectiveness in its capacity as a constitutional principle does not recognise the traditional division between effectiveness, uniformity and consistency as closely interlinked yet

[32] Case T-315/01 *Kadi* ECR [2005] II-3649; Case 402/05P *Kadi* [2008] ECR I-6351.

[33] ibid.

[34] EC Reg 467/2001 of 6 March 2001 ([2001] OJ L67/1), amended by Commission Reg 2199/2001 of 12 November 2001 ([2001] OJ L 295/16) and repealed by EC Reg 881/2002 of 27 May 2002 ([2002] OJ L139/9).

[35] A question raised by Eeckhout, 'General report External Relations', 22nd FIDE Congress Limassol, Cyprus 1–4 November 2006., available at http://www.fide-europe.eu/index.php/congresses?catid=5&start=10 (accessed 1 April 2008).

separate concepts.[36] In fact, effectiveness as a constitutional idea seems to be a 'catch-all' word, which is why the concept is so dangerously broad and almost impossible to monitor. In practice, the reuse of the same 'necessity/effectiveness' argument at the European level may be questioned. After all, necessity also forms part of the requirement of Article 352 TFEU. Hence, it is difficult to clearly separate this concept especially, as will be explained in Part IV below, as it also forms part of the subsidiarity and proportionality criteria.

Yet there were those who legitimately argued that there was no reason to consider the General Court's interpretation to be inconsistent with the (now former) EC Treaty as the broad interpretation in question could be explained by the logic of the principle of *effet utile*.[37] Nevertheless, even from an international law perspective, the *effet utile* of Treaty law is controversial.[38] Evidently, it is closely connected to the issue of effective enforcement as discussed in chapter three and this poses difficulties when applied in the context of competence since it is a very slippery concept.

In any case, AG Maduro in his Opinion stated that while Articles 301 EC and 60 EC (now Article 215 TFEU) could be seen as a cross-pillar bridge between the Community and the CFSP: 'Article 308 EC surely cannot fulfil that function. Article 308 EC like Article 60(1) EC is strictly an enabling provision: it provides the means but not the objectives.'[39] The Court both agreed and disagreed.[40] The Court pointed out that neither Article 301 EC nor Article 60 EC could independently, or through any bridging function, widen the competences of the EC. Neither could such widening be based on their combination with Article 308 EC (now Article 352 TFEU), as this would extend Community objectives beyond its attributed powers to cover the CFSP field. Therefore, the Court emphasised in paragraphs 199 to 204 of the judgment that: 'The inevitable conclusion is that such a view runs counter to the very wording of Article 308 EC'. Nor could a reference to 'consistency' in ex Article 3 EU remedy such lack of competence. Then, spectacularly, the Court retreated from this position by concluding that the importance of preventing a distortion of competition and allowing the free movement of capital provided a link with the fight against international terrorism and rendered this area an EU objective – hence that there was a competence in the EC. Notably, there was no reference to an 'appreciable' distortion of competition as so

[36] On the classical meaning of consistency, see eg, P Eeckhout, *External Relations of the EU* (Oxford, Oxford University Press, 2004) 148.

[37] C Tomuschat, Annotation (2006) 43 *CML Rev* 537; and in the same vein, M Nettesheim, 'UN Sanctions against Individuals – A Challenge to the Architecture of European Union Governance' (2007) 44 *CML Rev* 567 at 586.

[38] See eg G Fitzmaurice, '*Vae Victis* or Woe to the Negotiators! Your Treaty or Our "Interpretation" of It?' (1971) 65 *American Journal of International Law* 358, 373 stating that 'the principle of effectiveness is all too frequently misunderstood as denoting that agreements should always be given their *maximum possible* effect, whereas its real object is merely . . . to prevent them failing altogether'.

[39] § 15 of the Opinion of AG Maduro, delivered on 16 January 2008, Case C-402/05P *Kadi*.

[40] For an extensive commentary see eg C Eckes, *EU Counter-Terrorist Policies and Fundamental Rights* (Oxford, Oxford University Press, 2009) and K Ziegler 'Strengthening the Rule of Law, but fragmenting international law: the Kadi decision of the ECJ from the perspective of human rights' (2009) 9 *Human Rights Law Review* 288.

famously emphasised in the *Tobacco Advertising I* case.[41] It also appears as if the Court made no distinction between the common market and the internal market and, admittedly, it is very doubtful whether such a distinction mattered anyway. The distinction between the common market and the internal market has now been removed as the term 'common market' was deleted from the Lisbon Treaty. Thus the point is of only historical interest, albeit it still theoretically important. The common market covered a very widely-defined area which is sometimes viewed as broader than the internal market (given that it includes agriculture and competition policies),[42] and although it is true that ex Article 60 EC provided for urgent measures on the movement of capital and on payments with respect to third countries (read with Article 301 EC), the free movement of capital has traditionally been an objective of the internal market in accordance with Articles 3(c), 14 and 56 EC. Looking at the history of Article 114 TFEU, it was not clear, for example, that the prevention of distortion of competition was an objective of the internal market until the Court declared that it was. After all, it was in *Titanium Dioxide*[43] that the Court stated that Article 114 TFEU (ex Article 95 EC) taken in conjunction with Article 26 TFEU (ex Article 14 EC) and the objective of the removal of obstacles (ex Article 2 EC read with ex Article 3 EC) formed the basis of the EC market. Moreover, a precondition for such a market to function effectively was the existence of undistorted competition. Indeed, this has been referred to as an expression of 'market holism' by the EU legislator, that the EU's policy mission extends to virtually anything which could be linked to an obstacle to trade and hence 'cures' the whole market.[44] The point is that the division between these markets was never complete nor was it particularly respected in the art of EU market building.

In paragraph 230 of the *Kadi* judgment the Court stipulated that:

> If economic and financial measures such as those imposed by the contested regulation, consisting of the, in principle generalised, freezing of all the funds and other economic resources of the persons and entities concerned, were imposed unilaterally by every Member State, the multiplication of those national measures might well affect the operation of the common market. Such measures could have a particular effect on trade between Member States, especially with regard to the movement of capital and payments, and on the exercise by economic operators of their right of establishment. In addition, they could create distortions of competition, because any differences between the measures unilaterally taken by the Member States could operate to the advantage or disadvantage of the competitive position of certain economic operators although there were no economic reasons for that advantage or disadvantage.

Furthermore, the Court pointed to the traditional EP argument when deciding on legal basis, an argument that is usually applied when choosing between Article

[41] Case C-376/98 *Germany v Parliament and Council* [2000] ECR I-8419.

[42] P Beaumont and S Weatherill, *EU Law* (London, Penguin, 1999) 34–37.

[43] See Case C-300/89 *Commission v Council* [1991] ECR I-2867; and R Barents, 'The Internal Market Unlimited: Some Observations on the Legal Basis of Community Legislation' (1993) 30 *CML Rev* 85.

[44] A Somek, *Individualism* (Oxford, Oxford University Press, 2008) 134–35.

114 TFEU and Article 352 TFEU, where Article 352 TFEU used to lose out. That was, however, not the case here, as the CFSP nature of action taken under ex Articles 301 and 60 EC led the Court to take the opposite view and it clearly favoured the former first pillar (paragraph 235). It is true that it can be argued that the Court of Justice in *Kadi* nonetheless adopted a fairly restricted reading of Article 352 (then Article 308 EC) and hence an orthodox interpretation of Article 5 TEU.[45] Nevertheless, it is submitted that the invocation of a distortion of competition argument without the appreciably test[46] in particular, as well as the vague concept of 'effects on trade' significantly broadens the scope of Article 352 TFEU in a ground-breaking manner. It is interesting to pause here.

Expressed differently, the concern here is that in the context of a reliance on the distortion of competition as demonstrated in *Kadi*, if there is no 'appreciability' test to the distortion of competition argument when justifying EU action, then somehow there arises a question of whether or not laws vary between Member States. If so, there appears to be a case for prima facie harmonisation. This is not a very high threshold for the EU legislator to reach when deciding on the need to adopt legislation. At issue is whether it should be possible to invoke the full effectiveness of the EU law imperative to justify supranational action per se. However, as explained in chapter three, legal reasoning based on effectiveness in the area of criminal law may not only be counter-productive (the criminal law policy argument) but is also dangerous from the perspective of legitimacy (the legality aspect) and the credibility of EU criminal law.

In any case, it should be observed that pre-*Pupino*,[47] commentators suggested that the *effet utile* concept also applied in the third pillar.[48] For example, Monar has argued that 'while the substantive requirements of the 'necessity test' remain one of the most controversial elements of the implied powers doctrine there can be little doubt that the *effet utile* argument that lies at the heart of the implied powers doctrine also applies to the third pillar area'.[49]

Again, this relates to the previous discussion in chapter three on enforcement. After all, as stated, the old *ERTA* case[50] blurred the boundaries of enforcement and competence by explicitly putting *effet utile* on the constitutional table. Indeed, it appears as if this doctrine is still fully active. However, as noted in chapter three, AG Mengozzi in his Opinion on *Segi* argued that sole reliance on ex Article 352 TFEU could not overcome the jurisdictional shortcomings in the third pillar due to the principle of attributed powers set out in Article 5 EU.[51] Nonetheless, it

[45] M Cremona, 'EC Competence, "Smart Sanctions" and the *Kadi* Case' (2009) 23 *Yearbook of European Law* ch 15.

[46] On the appreciably test see Part III below.

[47] Case C-105/03 *Pupino* [2005] ECR I-5285.

[48] R Wessel, 'The Inside Looking Out: Consistency and Delimitation in EU External Relations' (2000) 37 *CML Rev* 1135.

[49] In contrast, Monar adds that this is particularly obvious in the field of migration and asylum: J Monar, 'The EU as an International Actor in the Domain of Justice and Home Affairs' (2004) 9 *European Foreign Affairs Review* 395 at 398.

[50] Case C-22/70 *Commission v Council* [1971] ECR 263.

[51] Cases C-354/04 and C-355/04P *Segi and others* [2007] ECR I-6157, Opinion of AG Mengozzi

remains unclear why Article 352 TFEU concerning legislative competences was relevant here at all, that is, in a jurisdictional situation. Although it is true that there is no watertight rule, the question of competence should remain distinct from questions of enforcement, not least in order to avoid discrepancy. Moreover, in the *Pupino* case no mention of the flexibility clause – Article 352 TFEU – was at issue; instead there was a reliance on the 'ever closer union' maxim coupled with the principle of effectiveness. Although, as stated, there was no official bridge between the third pillar and the EU domain, the fashion for depillarisation which existed prior to the entry into force of the Lisbon Treaty seemed to have had a potentially far-reaching impact on the Court's case law as an echo of the failed CT and in the run-up to the new Treaty. The significant difference is, however, that the Lisbon Treaty provides for further competences to approximate on legal safeguards for the individual (Article 82 TFEU) in particular, as well as carrying with it the possibility of an emergency brake for the Member States should the proposed legislation be judged to affect fundamental aspects of the national criminal law system.

D. 'Effectiveness' and the History of the *acquis communautaire*

As noted, the impact of effectiveness in the context of the objectives of the EU seems to be particularly far-reaching. Somewhat provocatively, it could be said that it appears as if 'effectiveness' has become an objective in its own right. It should for instance be remembered that in the *PNR* case,[52] AG Léger referred to the General Court's judgment in *Kadi* when pointing out that the General Court had expressly ruled that action to suppress international terrorism did not constitute an objective of the EC.[53] Accordingly, an extremely important question has been the extent to which it was possible to transfer third (and second) pillar competences/reasoning into the EU sphere. Again, in the *Kadi* judgment, the General Court explicitly stated that to seek to use the EU's flexibility clause to achieve Union objectives would be to undermine the constitutional architecture of the pillars, just as Article 47 EU made it clear that EU provisions should not intrude on the *acquis communautaire.* And yet, as explained above there was still considered to be a competence under the former first pillar to adopt sanctions against individuals despite any explicit Treaty-based support. Equally, in the environmental criminal law cases[54] as discussed above, ex Article 47 EU was the EU's trump card and as such was very open-ended, meaning that there were few constitutional limits to the broad use of EU powers if such competence was needed for the full effectiveness of EU law. The history of the depillarisation phenomenon

delivered on 26 October 2006.

[52] Cases C-317/04 and C-318/04 *European Parliament v Council* [2006] ECR I-4721.

[53] ibid, Opinion of AG Léger, delivered on 22 November 2005.

[54] Case C-176/03 *Commission v Council* [2005] ECR I-7879; Case C-440/05 *Commission v Council,* [2007] ECR I-9097.

before the entry into force of the Lisbon Treaty is still of interest not only because of the Transitional Protocol No 36 as mentioned above, in chapter two but also with respect to the relationship between the TEU and the TFEU. In addition, it helps us pin down the newly-won stipulated Treaty powers in criminal law.

Nonetheless, the Court has, admittedly, recently stepped back slightly from its effectiveness line on the subject of whether it was legally possible to delegate legislative power within the Community legal order (ex Articles 63 (now 79 TFEU and 67 EC repealed) and the question of institutional balance.[55] Although it is a pre-Lisbon case it is interesting for its insistence on (possible) limits to effectiveness. Here the Court stated that, the adoption of 'secondary legal bases could not be justified on the basis of considerations relating to the politically sensitive nature of the issue concerned or to a concern to ensure the effectiveness of a Community action'.[56] This is perhaps a sign of a movement away from an all-embracing notion of effectiveness in some areas, even if this movement was more concerned with the issue of protecting the role of the European Parliament than the delimitation of EU powers as such. In any event, it confirms an ad hoc approach to the vigour of 'effectiveness' similar to that demonstrated within the domain of national remedies.

This chapter will now try to tie together the above outlined discussion on the objectives of the Treaty, and its interrelationship with effectiveness in the constitutional development of EU criminal law more specifically. In doing so it is essential to place it in the context of the development of supranational criminal law prior to the entry into force of the Lisbon Treaty. This is best done by turning to the question of competence allocation from the perspective of ex Article 47 EU. The reason for discussing ex Article 47 EU at this point is that this provision involved a similar pattern of competence creep to that of Article 352 TFEU but is in a way even more open-ended. This is the safeguarding of the *acquis communautaire* axis, which provided that no Treaty of the Union activity could affect the competences of the first pillar sphere. Therefore, although ex Article 47 EU was only relevant to policing the boundaries between the former EU Treaties and not the boundaries between the Member States and the EU, the capacity of Article 47 EU to bring new areas into the EC legal sphere was surprisingly broad.[57] In our case, the question that arises is how such links to the former EC Treaty – in the absence of a 'constitutional' document pre-Lisbon granting these powers – were established in the area of criminal law. The question is not merely of historical interest. As noted, this is an area where changes brought by the Lisbon Treaty have been significant but where not all questions have yet been solved.

[55] Case C-133/06 *Parliament v Council* judgment of 6 May 2008 not yet reported. Case Comment by P Craig (2009) 46 *CML Rev* 1265. See also, however, Case C-166/07 *European Parliament v Council* judgment of 3 September 2009 not yet reported.

[56] ibid paragraph 59.

[57] Case C-91/05, *Commission v Council*, Opinion of AG Mengozzi delivered on 19 September 2007.

i. The Curious Case of ex Article 47 TEU

As explained above, before the entry into force of the Lisbon Treaty, the pillar structure was guarded by Article 47 EU, which provided a defence against any intrusion on the *acquis communautaire*.[58] Although the new Article 40 TEU has now taken over this policing function regarding the relationship between the TEU and the TFEU,[59] the history of the boundaries of Article 47 TEU could help us to gauge the scope of Article 40 TEU.

Consequently, the focus of this section is to examine the record of ex Article 47 EU as a competence distributor as well as to question the extent to which this 'pro-Community' stance is reflected in the post-Lisbon architecture. Withn the framework of ex Article 47 EU, the vital question appears to have been not so much whether criminal law was an objective of the EU, but rather whether it could be associated with a Treaty objective that somehow transposed it to the supranational sphere. This was the approach adopted in Case C-176/03 in combination with the pursuit of the full effectiveness of EU law. From a national autonomy point of view, this has been EU legislation through the back door. After all, the intention of the drafters of Treaty was to limit political opportunism by referring such aspirations back to the conferral of powers test, Article 5(1) TEU and the subsequent requirements of this provision (subsidiarity and proportionality). Nevertheless, legal practice painted a different and more ambiguous picture.

Thus, Article 47 EU began life as Article M TEU and was initially on the agenda in the *Airport transit visas* case.[60] In this case the Court concluded that Article 47 EU implicitly assigned to it the task of acting as the watchdog of the boundaries of the pillars. Although this case concerned a question of jurisdiction rather than an issue of legislative competence, somehow the Court used it as a starting point from which to use ex Article 47 EU as a lever of the former first pillar. In connection with this ruling, it was observed that although the Court held that the Council measure in question did not come under Article 100c EC (thereafter Article 65 EC and now Article 81 TFEU), the Commission may nonetheless have felt that it won the case as it found the Court prepared to arbitrate the delimitation of competences between the pillars with an expansive approach to jurisdiction.[61] According to one commentator, this case confirmed the distinct but unified legal discipline of the intergovernmental pillars.[62] Notwithstanding that, it seems as if the question of what was counted as part of the *acquis communautaire* was never solved. Indeed, this frequently-cited benchmark remains unclear.[63]

[58] eg A Dashwood, 'Article 47 EU and the Relationship between First and Second Pillar Competences' in A Dashwood and M Marcesceau, *Law and Practice of EU External Relations* (Cambridge, Cambridge University Press, 2008) 70.

[59] Which, according to Art 1 of each Treaty, should in any event be treated equally.

[60] Case C-170/96 *Commission v Council* [1998] ECR I-2763.

[61] Eeckhout (above n 36).

[62] ibid.

[63] See S Weatherill, 'Safeguarding the *Acquis Communautaire*' in T Heukles et al (eds), *The European Union after Amsterdam* (Amsterdam, European Institute Amsterdam, 1998) 153.

Moreover, ex Article 47 EU was obviously also relevant in Case C-176/03 and the *Ship source pollution* case.[64] As described in chapter three, in these rulings the Court, in deciding whether environmental criminal law belonged to the third or the first pillar, deduced not only from Article 47 EU and the sacred ground of the *acquis communautaire*, but also from the principle of *effectiveness*,[65] that criminal law constituted an 'accessory' to the Community objective of the protection of the environment. Furthermore, AG Mazak in his Opinion in the *Ship source pollution* case pointed out that Article 47 EU was not 'designed merely to ensure that nothing under the EU Treaty affects or runs counter to existing substantive provisions of Community law. Rather, it is intended in a more comprehensive sense to preserve also the powers conferred on the Community as such'.[66] In particular, the AG observed in paragraph 51 of his opinion that not only Article 47 EU but '[now ex] Article 29 EU, expressly provides that Union provisions on police and judicial cooperation in criminal matters are 'without prejudice to the powers of the European Community'. The AG therefore explained that it was necessary to examine whether the provisions in question confirmed this by expressly stipulating that EU provisions on police and judicial cooperation have potentially been adopted on the basis of the EU Treaty and, as outlined in chapter two, he concluded that this was the case. This was also the approach followed by the Court.

Nevertheless, the judgment in *Light weapons and small arms*[67] is arguably even more instructive as it demonstrated the powerfulness, or perhaps sharpness, of ex Article 47 EU as well as the difficulty of dual legal bases in cross-pillar conflicts.[68] Although this case concerned the delimitation of competences between the former first and the second pillars, it illustrates the historical vagueness of Article 47 EU in a remarkable way. For this reason, a brief recap of this case is useful. In this ruling it became clear that the only thing that mattered when discussing the horizontal division of powers in the EU was that the legislative process was pursued by the correct EU pillar as the issue of shared and exclusive competences are only interesting within the core of the Community (vertical) context. AG Mengozzi in his Opinion stressed that the philosophy behind Article 47 EU in its purest sense was not very complicated and could be read as: 'if something could be done by the EC it should have been done by that legislative arena', in other words – not at the intergovernmental third pillar level.[69] More specifically, in the view of AG Mengozzi, Article 47 EU makes no distinction in the protection it confers on the provisions of the EC Treaty according to the distribution of competences between the Member States and the Community, and hence the nature of the competences assigned to the Community. Ex Article 47 EU therefore appears to have rested on

[64] Case C-440/05 *Commission v Council* [2005] ECR I-9097.

[65] Case C-176/03 *Commission v Council* [2005] ECR I-7879.

[66] Case C-440/05 *Commission v Council* [2007] ECR I-9097. Opinion of AG Mazak, delivered on 28 June 2007.

[67] Case C-91/05 *Commission v Council* [2008] ECR I-3651.

[68] This section draws on E Herlin-Karnell, '"Light Weapons" and the Dynamics of Art 47 EU – the EC's Armoury of Ever Expanding Competences' (2008) 71 *MLR* 998.

[69] Opinion of 19 September 2007.

the presumption that all the competences given to the Community, irrespective of the distribution that exists between the Community and the Member States, and irrespective of whether they are concurrent or exclusive, deserve to be protected against any encroachment on the EC. Yet, in this case the Court noted that there was indeed no competence within the first pillar in the area of combating the proliferation of small arms and light weapons, which was accordingly found to be a purely CFSP competence. Therefore, the Court stressed that only in exceptional cases could various corresponding legal bases be accepted. Nevertheless, the Court stated that such a solution – that is, the cross-pillar mix – would be impossible in any case under the heading of Article 47 EU. In particular, the Court concluded that since the contested decision had two components, one falling within the former EC law sphere (development cooperation) and one within the former second pillar (peace and security), *a contrario* this constituted an infringement of Article 47 EU which resulted in an annulment of the second pillar instrument. This was an odd but ambitious approach because it conferred on ex Article 47 EU an almost self-appointed function as the competence distributor. Therefore, what is at issue here is not so much the classic objective and content test (or centre-of-gravity test) – as was notoriously on the agenda in the *Titanium Dioxide* case[70] regarding the choice between Articles 114 and 192 TFEU – but rather the unambiguous question of whether there was a Community link that triggered the use of ex Article 47 EU.

The next subsection aims to cast some light on the blurred boundaries of shared competences and pre-emption because they are highly relevant in the context of ex Article 47 EU. Finally, as pointed out by one commentator, ex Article 47 EU did not regulate the relationship between the second and the third pillars and there was therefore no problem in considering dual legal bases in that sphere.[71]

ii. The Objectives of the EU and Pre-emption

A further issue that needs to be addressed here is the relationship between shared competences and pre-emption when discussing cross-pillar issues. Although the exact contours of the notion of pre-emption are far beyond the scope of this subsection, for the present purposes it is sufficient to note that only once the EU has exercised its shared regulatory powers can the Member States be prevented from adopting additional rules[72] (with the ambiguous exception of minimum harmonisation).[73] The problem is, however, that the Court generally does not

[70] Case C-300/89 *Commission v Council* [1991] ECR I-2867.

[71] R Van Ooik 'Cross-Pillar Litigation Before the ECJ: Community and Union Competences' (2008) 4 *European Constitutional Law Review* 399.

[72] Weatherill (above n 7) 144. More recently, according to Protocol 25 attached to the Lisbon Treaty, shared competence means, 'With reference to Article 2(2) of the TFEU on shared competence, when the Union has taken action in a certain area, the scope of this exercise of competence only covers those elements governed by the Union act in question and therefore does not cover the whole area.' Hence it is possible to make the argument that this is a very simplified description.

[73] See eg, M Dougan, 'Minimum Harmonization and the Internal Market' (2000) 37 *CML Rev* 853.

seem to distinguish between an exclusive competence and a shared one if the latter has been exercised exhaustively that is, 'pre-emption'.[74] Admittedly, such a distinction is largely theoretical and may not have any greater impact in practice. Nevertheless, it appears as if the traditional notion of pre-emption[75] and the familiar issue of when a shared competence ceases to be shared[76] were rather different from ex Article 47 EU and the delimitation of powers between the pillars. More specifically, it is possible to argue that ex Article 47 EU created its own 'pre-emption'. The reason for this is that by not only safeguarding a mysterious area regarded traditionally as the *acquis communautaire* but also by prohibiting the second and third pillars from adopting measures that could be seen – however tentatively connected to a competing EC law measure – as having an objective which could also be linked to the EU law domain, ex Article 47 EU 'pre-empted' the area in question. Thus, the practical consequences of the notion of 'pre-emption' that the supranational level always had priority, were actually – in the context of criminal law highly ambiguous. More especially, it appears as though once a cross-pillar conflict was found, other principles of EU law, critically including conferral, subsidiarity and proportionality, were considered less important. There seems, in other words, to have been such an eagerness to safeguard the *acquis communautaire* that the consequences were not considered. Admittedly, in terms of strict legal reasoning this might have been partially correct. After all, ex Article 47 EU was not an end in itself but rather provided clear-cut guidance in favour of the supranational sphere. This was also recognised by AG Mengozzi, who stressed the complicated regime under Article 47 EU and its unhelpful contribution to the aim and content test by simply being too Community biased as the police of the pillarsand therefore rendering all nuanced object-and-content tests rather meaningless. The problem is that all these cases under Article 47 EU concerned already adopted third and first pillar legislation. As is discussed below in the context of subsidiarity (Part IV), and enhanced cooperation (Part V), the wider implications of Article 47 EU have been considerably more complicated in the context of EU criminal law. In practice, again it seems unwise to leave constitution building in the hands of the Court in this area.

To recap, the point here is that the traditional object and content test – when allocating legal basis – was different in the context of Article 47 EU in that it was less sophisticated and nuanced under this provision. It is also clear that prior to the entry into force of the Lisbon Treaty, the question of whether or not a competence is shared or whether there was a competence at all was less interesting under the ambigious policing function of Article 47 EU. Again, the essential issue under the auspices of Article 47 EU was whether the measure at issue could – in the view

[74] A Von Bogdandy and J Bast, 'The Vertical Order of Competences' in A Bogdandy and J Bast (eds), *Principles of European Constitutional Law* (Oxford, Hart Publishing, 2006) 335.

[75] S Weatherill, 'Beyond Preemption? Shared Competence and Constitutional Change in the European Community', in D O'Keffee (ed), *Legal Issues of the Maastricht Treaty* (London, Chancery Law Publishing, 1994) 13.

[76] ibid.

of the Court – be linked in some way to the supranational level. For this reason, the concept of the objectives of the Union, pre-emption and ex Article 47 EU appears to have constituted a holy trinity for the furtherance of Union objectives. And what is more, knowing the history of ex Article 47 EU might be helpful in understanding the future scope of its successor, Article 40 TEU.

E. The New Article 40 TEU

The successor to Article 47 TEU is Article 40 TEU. As mentioned, this new provision contains a non-affect clause, which states that no activity within the TEU and the TFEU respectively may affect the other according to Articles 1 TEU and TFEU. So the key question is what this means when compared with ex Article 47 EU as explored above. More specifically, the question of the extent to which the Lisbon Treaty has been a major turning point is still highly contested. This question is significant and it might be useful, therefore, to set out the wording of Article 40 TEU in detail:

> The implementation of the common foreign and security policy shall not affect the application of the procedures and the extent of the powers of the institutions laid down by the Treaties for the exercise of the Union competences referred to in Articles 3 to 6 of the Treaty on the Functioning of the European Union. Similarly, the implementation of the policies listed in those Articles shall not affect the application of the procedures and the extent of the powers of the institutions laid down by the Treaties for the exercise of the Union competences under this Chapter.

One commentator has pointed out that while the equal protection clause is politically sound, this creates a legal imbroglio.[77] Others have expressed this as being a matter of 'necessity' rather than one of political preference for the Community as previously guided by Article 47 EU.[78] Accordingly, the exact meaning of Article 40 TEU remains somewhat unclear when compared to ex Article 47 EU (which always pointed in the direction of the first pillar).In particular, it could be questioned whether in future the Court would favour the legal sphere, which ensures greater legitimacy in terms of participation of the EP in the legislative process and the jurisdiction of the Court (over the TFEU area). Moreover, the demarcation problem between the TEU and the TFEU, as guarded by the new Article 40 TEU, is illustrated by the new provisions for the adoption on sanctions within the Lisbon Treaty. After all, under the new Articles 75 TFEU and 215 TFEU it may be difficult to make a distinction between an internal fight against terrorism (Article 75 TFEU) and an external fight against terrorism (Article 215 TFEU) may prove difficult. The delimitation between these two provisions is crucial as recourse to

[77] P van Elsuwege, 'EU External Action after the Collapse of the Pillar Structure. In Search of a New Balance between Delimitation and Consistency' (2010) 47 *CML Rev* 987.

[78] M Klamert, 'Conflicts of Legal Basis: No Legality and Basis but a Bright Future under the Lisbon Treaty?' (2010) 35 *EL Rev* 497.

Article 75 TFEU would guarantee what prior to the Lisbon Treaty was called the 'Community' method, that is, it would ensure a greater role for the European Parliament in the legislative process. But while the normal rule is that the Court does not have jurisdiction with regard to CFSP issues, this is subject to exceptions under the Lisbon Treaty as the Court will always have jurisdiction to review the legality of restrictive measures (made under Article 215 TFEU and Chapter 2 of Title V of the TEU) according to Article 275 TFEU. From this perspective, it does not really matter what legal basis is used. Nevertheless, the fine line between these provisions is demonstrated by the fact that the EP has recently sued the Council on the grounds that amendment of Council Regulation 881/2002, which imposed certain specific restrictive measures directed against a particular persons and entities associated with the Al-Qaida network was based on the wrong legal basis.[79] It goes without saying that the outcome of this case will offer some clarification on the scope of Articles 75 TFEU and 215 TFEU as well as the relationship between the TFEU and the TEU.

i. Centre of Gravity Post Lisbon

A further question of interest is the centre of gravity debate or, perhaps more properly, the confusion surrounding it. As indicated at the outset of this chapter, there has been a lot of discussion concerning the delimitation of powers between the pillars before the entry into force of the Lisbon Treaty. Expressed in somewhat simplified terms, there have been two camps here: those who have analysed the former third pillar and the AFSJ criminal law area;[80] and those who have focused on the former second pillar and the delimitation of powers in this area.[81] Both camps have been united in their judgement of the importance of ex Article 47 EU and the question of the delimitation of powers between the pillars as explored above. However, as indicated, these Article 47 cases were different from the classic case law on choice of the correct legal basis and the *Titanium Dioxide*[82] string of cases (centre of gravity) in relation to the choice between Articles 114 TFEU (ex Article 95 EC) and 192 TFEU (ex Article 175 EC). Rather the main question appears to have been whether there was a Community link that triggered the use of ex Article 47 EU. After all, as stated, prior to the entry into force of the Lisbon Treaty, the argument was not really about any centre of gravity but about establishing some kind of effects on EU law that could be linked to the first pillar, and then Article 47 did the rest of the job. In other words, the only thing that needed to be demonstrated was a Community link, which is arguably a lot weaker than

[79] Case C-130/10 *EP v Council*, pending case concerning the amendment of No 1286/2009, action brought 11 March 2010.

[80] eg the author as well as O Lynsky and A Dawnes, 'The Ever Longer Arm of EC Law: The Extension of Community Law into the Field of Criminal Law' (2008) 45 *CML Rev* 131. N Neagu, 'Entrapment between Two Pillars: The European Court of Justice Rulings in Criminal Law' (2009) 15 *European Law Journal* 536.

[81] eg Dashwood (above n 58).

[82] Case C-300/89, *Commission v Council* [1991] ECR I-2867, discussed more fully in Part III below.

anything a 'centre of gravity test' could offer. The situation has been changed dramatically by the Lisbon Treaty. Within this new structure, the AFSJ is incorporated into the '*acquis*'. The real centre of gravity questions will, therefore, arguably be to demarcate the specific provision of Article 83 TFEU concerning the harmonisation of substantive law from other areas where the criminal law could be brought in. Article 67 TFEU is one candidate here, discussed below, which provides for a more general legislative power for the creation of an AFSJ.[83] Clearly, it seems as if Article 67 TFEU offers a more general framework for the prevention of crime.

ii. Articles 67 and 75 TFEU: Setting the Scene of Crime Prevention in the EU[84]

As explained in chapter two, Article 67 TFEU (in Chapter 1 of Title V of the TFEU), paints the broad picture of crime prevention at the EU level. It poses interesting questions as regards the relationship between Chapters 1 and 4 in Title V of the TFEU. As for competence allocation it may be argued that it is unclear to what extent criminal law could be harmonised outside the *lex specialis* provisions, Articles 82 and 83 TFEU as drawn out in chapter two above. The key point is simply that Article 67 TFEU – the portal provision of the AFSJ – should be read in conjunction with the specific provisions on criminal law as discussed above. Accordingly, Article 67 TFEU sets the scene and outlines the values the Union seeks to guarantee – freedom, security and justice and respect for fundamental rights. Moreover, as explained, Article 75 TFEU provides for the competence to adopt restrictive measures in the fight against terrorism. Therefore, a further question arises as to which cases concerning the fight against terrorism are to be considered as falling within the scope of Article 75 TFEU as opposed to Article 83 TFEU (which it includes in its list) and the criminal law grid, or whether these articles are intended to complement each other. It seems as if the dividing line here is between administrative sanctions (freezing of funds) and criminal law, where the former is part of Article 75 TFEU and the latter forms part of Chapter 4 and Article 83 TFEU. In any case, and to further muddy the water: Article 75 TFEU stipulates 'where necessary to achieve the objectives set out in Article 67 TFEU'. It also refers to the possible harmonisation of 'related activities', which begs the question of what 'related activities' means. Would it, for example, be possible to bring in money laundering legislation and the financing of terrorism under Article 75 TFEU too? In other words, although substantive criminal law is dealt with in Article 83 TFEU, it is far from clear how much of (what remains of national) criminal law could be also be transferred through Articles 67 and 75 TFEU. Clearly, it confers on the Union a more general aim of fighting crime and protecting security within the Union, although it is true that the third pillar

[83] Discussed in E Herlin-Karnell, 'The Lisbon Treaty and the Criminal Law: Anything New Under the Sun? (2008) 10 *European Journal of Law Reform* 321.

[84] This section draws on E Herlin-Karnell, 'EU Competence in Criminal Law after Lisbon' in A Biondi et al (eds) *EU Law After Lisbon* (Oxford, Oxford University Press forthcoming) ch 16.

similarly emphasised the importance of creating a genuinely crime-free EU. The difference is that this crime prevention agenda will now take place at the supranational level. Accordingly, it appears obvious that the above-mentioned reference in Article 67 TFEU to 'measures to prevent and combat crime and, if necessary, through the approximation of criminal laws' constitutes a broadly defined outline. In particular it highlights the strong emphasis on security as being particularly important in this area.

iii. (In)Security as the New Acquis Communautaire?

As explained, much of the history of EU criminal law concerned the contours of the *acquis communautaire* and the boundaries of the full effectiveness of EU law. Viewed in the context of the Lisbon Treaty and against the background of an increased focus on security matters such as combating the financing of terrorism and money laundering, it would be possible to refer to issues of 'internal' and 'external' security as issues of 'TFEU security' and 'TEU security'. In addition, national security remains the competence of the Member States (Article 4(2) TEU as well as Article 73 TFEU). More specifically, the question that needs to be asked is whether it is possible to clearly distinguish between internal, external and national security in light of the fact that there is clearly an external dimension to the AFSJ. This issue is important as it has implications for the question of the Court's jurisdiction, which is largely excluded from the TEU. The point here is that 'security' is as ambiguous as the catchword 'effectiveness'. Cautiously expressed, a blind focus on security risks not only rendering the Union's proclamation of humanist values meaningless, but also risks undermining the legitimacy of any action taken. It goes without saying that such a focus on security in combination with the effectiveness mantra constitutes a particularly dangerous combination. It could perhaps be asked, somewhat provocatively, if the new *acquis communautaire* – in the post Lisbon era – will be the question of Union security coupled with the more general pursuance of the full effectiveness of EU law. Such a securitisation of criminal law would lead to a dangerous trend pointing in the direction of preventive criminalisation and this is scrutinised in further detail in chapter five.

F. The Final Word goes to Article 13 TEU: Institutional Balance and the Effectiveness of EU Law

Article 13 TEU is one of the innovations introduced by the Lisbon Treaty, as briefly mentioned above. It stipulates not only that each institution shall act within the limits of the powers as stated by the Treaties but also that the EU shall have an institutional framework which aims to promote its values, advance its objectives, serve the interests of its citizens and of its Member States, and ensure the consistency, effectiveness and continuity of its policies and actions. In addition, Article 7 TFEU makes it clear that the Union shall provide consistency between its activities. This links us back to chapter three, where it was argued that the quest for consistency and uniformity are closely linked with the search for 'effectiveness' at the EU level. As was argued in that chapter, it seems as though 'effectiveness', involving consistency and uniformity, has become one big legal cluster.

Nevertheless, it is significant that the EU places the individual at the centre of this debate by stipulating that the EU shall serve the interests of its citizens and those of the Member States. Yet the assurance that the EU shall ensure the consistency, effectiveness and continuity of its policies appears to be an extremely broadly defined mission. As we have seen in chapter two the Stockholm programme also claims to be driving citizens' rights as part of the goal of making European policies more effective. However, there may be an inherent contradiction here. It is the promise of establishing a consistent and effective as well as a continuing EU policy, while at the same time serving its citizens and respecting Member States' preferences and EU law values, most importantly, the respect for human rights. This poses difficulties when applied in EU legal practice. It is obvious that in the area of criminal law and issues touching upon national sovereignty this seems to be a job still not fully accomplished and where the EU is aiming for a consistent framework. The danger is if 'consistent' is always taken to mean 'effective', without any real evaluation of what it means when applied to the area of EU criminal law.

G. Conclusion

The purpose of this part was to explain that the question of competence monitoring in the EU, despite the drastic changes in terms of the abolition of the previous pillar structure as introduced by the Lisbon Treaty, is still active. In particular, provisions such as Article 352 TFEU reveal the difficulty, and the importance, of pinning down what the objectives of the EU really are when deciding whether a question falls within or outside the EU's powers. An important part of this thesis was to show the road to the Lisbon Treaty and what we could learn from the broad use and scope of the now dead but not totally buried ex Article 47 EU.

It has also been argued that the narrative of Article 352 TFEU and ex Article 47 TEU demonstrated a similar pattern, although ex Article 47 EU has been even more elusive. As explained above, the capacity of these provisions to bring new competences under the wings of the EU legislator is surprisingly broad. In combination with the effectiveness slogan, it appears as though there were not many constitutional obstacles left to an over-ambitious reading of EU law. However, as always, there are modifications to all statements. On the one hand the abolition of the reference to the common market in Article 352 TFEU extends this provision to all areas of Union law regardless of any market link. On the other hand, the sector-specific competences and the requirement of the consent of the EP to use

Article 352 TFEU, as well as the clear statement that it cannot extend the EU's competences, severely limits this. As does the new monitoring procedure of subsidiarity by the national parliaments which is explicitly referred to in this provision. In addition, Article 352 TFEU now includes a final paragraph which states that measures based on this Article shall not entail the harmonisation of Member States' laws or regulations in cases where the Treaties exclude such harmonisation.[85] And yet, as history often repeats itself, we know from Article 352 TFEU that this link to the Treaty has been far too easy for the legislator to break when justifying EU action and achieving new EU objectives. Although it is true that the creation of the AFSJ and criminal law will now constitute one of the EU's objectives, it is difficult to rely on Article 352 TFEU in this area, given the specific provisions in Title V (in particular Article 83 TFEU discussed above). Nevertheless, the reason for having dissected the breadth of Article 352 TFEU was to demonstrate the difficulties with the pinning down of competences. Moreover this part of the chapter argued that the principle of effectiveness could be reflected in the necessity requirement in Article 352 TFEU. For this reason, the question of the expansion and widening of EU powers is closely related to the very issue of clarifying the EU's objectives. There is thus a difficulty in monitoring these objectives and reconciling them with the principle of conferral, when viewed in the light of general effectiveness concerns in the EU.

Yet this is not in line with the principle of conferral powers. It is thus not in line with the imperative of legality in criminal law either. Furthermore, there is still more to come. Consequently, the next part of this chapter embarks on a tour of Article 114 TFEU and examines this provision from the perspective of criminal law. In doing so, it will become clear that the internal market provision of Article 114 TFEU reveals a constitutional ambiguity which is dangerously open-ended. Moreover, it shows an over-reliance on the principle of effectiveness as the main navigator for EU legislation.

III. CRIMINAL LAW AND MARKET INTEGRATION

A. Introduction

This part covers the constitutional uncertainty of Article 114 TFEU – and the 'federal' boundaries of the establishment and functioning of the internal market. Whilst the previous part of the chapter examined the limits of Article 352 TFEU and the broader objectives of the EU, this Part looks at criminal law within the framework of market integration. This chapter explores whether the EU legislator could (still) harmonise criminal law pursuant to Article 114 TFEU by using the same arguments as pioneered in Case C-176/03. It then investigates the extent to which Article 83 TFEU is 'exclusive' *lex specialis* in this area and also focuses on

[85] See also Declaration 41 attached to the Lisbon Treaty.

the EU legislator's use of effectiveness and confidence in the market as justification for harmonisation. The purpose of so doing, is to examine how it could be applied in the context of EU financial crimes legislation. So, while Part II of this chapter charted the constitutional terrain of EU competences and the notion of constitutional effectiveness, this Part looks more specifically at the internal market provision and Article 114 TFEU, and thereby asks whether it is possible to harmonise criminal law under the auspices of this provision. As explained in chapter two, the Lisbon Treaty has essentially restructured this landscape. The question is no longer whether or not there is a criminal law competence but to the extent to which criminal law could be harmonised. Article 83 TFEU provides us with the basic roadmap for EU substantive criminalisation, but the extent to which criminal law could be harmonised outside this provision, that is, outside *lex specialis*, is still unclear. In EU law in general, this is of course where Article 114 TFEU has previously stepped in, when no other Treaty base has been found. Yet this is not the whole story, as it has not simply been a question of 'stepping in'; Article 114 TFEU requires more than that, namely that the measure at stake contributes to market-making by genuinely removing obstacles to trade or competition. The point is important because there is no opportunity to use an 'emergency brake' outside Chapter 4 of Title V and the specific criminal law provisions as provided in Articles 82 and 83 TFEU.[86]

As discussed above, Case C-176/03[87] has developed the principle of effectiveness into something more than an enforcement mechanism. Thus the concept of 'effectiveness' is given priority in the direct allocation of competences, rather than being a minor consideration within the subsidiarity or proportionality test. As seen in chapter two, in the wake of the outcome of Case C-176/03 the Commission presented a communication on the possibility of further harmonisation of criminal law[88] This initiative was bold in linking this case with a whole range of criminal law offences going far beyond the limited arena of environmental protection. In particular, it connected the principle of effectiveness with Article 114 TFEU and the functioning and establishment of the internal market. Consequently, the purpose of this section is to scrutinise the constitutional validity of the Commission's reading of Article 114 TFEU and give 'effectiveness' as a reason for legislation. In doing so, the section not only outlines the market creation test of Article 114 TFEU and examines the distinctive and well-documented vagueness of this article, but also reviews its relationship with ex Article 47 EU and the distribution of powers between the pillars to illustrate the different avenues for the emergence of EU criminal law. It perhaps goes without saying that if the *Tobacco Advertising I* case[89], which operated as a brake to EU competences, is not strictly applied, the communication was revolutionary in the wideness of its scope.

[86] S Peers, *EU Justice and Home Affairs* (Oxford, Oxford University Press, 2011) 765.

[87] Case C-176/03, *Commission v Council* [2005] ECR I-7879.

[88] Commission on the implications of the Court's judgment of 13 September 2005 (Case C-176/03 *Commission v Council*). (Communication) COM (2005) 583 final.

[89] Case C-376/98 *Germany v Parliament and Council* [2000] ECR I-8419.

More specifically, the purpose of this part is to track the ambiguities of Article 114 TFEU in the context of European criminal law. In doing so it dissects the constitutional parameters of Article 114 TFEU by exploring the meaning of obstacles to trade and 'disparities' of laws between the Member States as well as the concept of an EU market. The notion of distortion of competition will then be briefly examined, together with the possible impact of the object and content test, commonly referred to as the centre-of-gravity assessment, in the framework of Article 114 TFEU, as well as the relationship between Article 114 TFEU and ex Article 47 EU.[90] This section also looks at the notion of 'non-market values' in the context of Article 114 TFEU insofar as it is of relevance to criminal law.

This part of the chapter looks more deeply into the justifications of harmonisation in the field of criminal law. To do so it is first necessary to clarify the law on market integration by focusing on the internal market provisions of Articles 114 and 26 TFEU. Consequently, this part serves as a background, or theoretical foundation, for the case study on financial crimes in relation to Article 114 TFEU and the notion of precautionary criminalisation, discussed below in chapter five.

B. The Establishment and Functioning of the Internal Market

The internal market is defined in Article 26 TFEU as an area without internal frontiers in which the free movement of goods, persons, services and capital is ensured in accordance with the provisions of the Treaties. It states that the Community shall adopt measures with the aim of progressively establishing the internal market. It is here that Article 114 TFEU enters the picture. This article grants the EU the power to adopt 'measures for the approximation of the provisions laid down by law, regulation or administrative action in Member States which have as their object the establishment and functioning of the internal market'. Moreover, this provision cross-refers back to Article 26 TFEU in setting out the removal of obstacles as the objective of the internal market. Although the time limit for the completion of the internal market passed decades ago, it is commonly accepted that this mission has still not been accomplished.[91] This raises a further issue, namely that one needs to establish how direct and concrete the barriers to trade must be in order to qualify as an 'obstacle'.[92] Clearly, there is some ambiguity in Article 26 TFEU which makes it more difficult to interpret in the context of Article 114 TFEU and the question of harmonisation. Indeed, Article 114 TFEU is the subject of heated debate – regarded with scepticism by some as easily overriding the concerns of Member States by the use of QMV in the

[90] Opinion of AG Fennelly delivered on 15 June 2000.

[91] The DG internal market website is instructive in stating that the single market is not yet complete. See ec.europa.eu/internal_market/top_layer/index_3_en.htm (last accessed January 2012). See also S Weatherill, 'The Common Market – Mission Accomplished?' in Heiskanen and Kulovesi (eds), *Function and Future of European Law* (Helsinki, Helsinki University Press, 1999) 33.

[92] P Nebbia, 'Internal Market and Harmonization of European Contract Law', in P Nebbia and T Tridimas (eds), *European Law for the Twenty-First Century* (Oxford, Hart Publishing, 2004) 89.

Council,[93] and with admiration by others for its functional character.[94] Clearly, there has always been constitutional uncertainty about Article 114 TFEU. In the context of criminal law, this issue has been particularly tricky as, despite the lack of Treaty-based support and the clear wording of the constitutional limits set out in Article 5 TEU (then Article 5 EC), Article 114 TFEU has always been relevant to this area, especially in the fight against money laundering. More crucially still, this chapter argues that criminal law – in general – does not suit the European pattern of market creation. Despite this, there has been a clear willingness in the EU's institutions to see criminal law as akin to any other area of law, capable of being transferred to the supranational level as a component of market creation. It raises the issue of whether, strictly speaking, criminal law could be linked to market creation at all as well as the consequences of such a policy choice.

As mentioned in Part II, Article 114 TFEU was introduced in connection with the SEA in 1987.[95] The purpose of Article 114 TFEU was to enable the EU to be more effective in promoting market integration through the use of QMV. After all, Article 114 TFEU is horizontal in character which means that it is very open-ended, restricted only by paragraph 2 of the same provision, which states that EU powers are limited in the field of fiscal provisions to those relating to the free movement of persons or to the rights and interest of employed persons. Obviously, this is the core of the 'dynamics' or 'ambiguity' of Article 114 TFEU. However, regarding the 'dynamics', it has been argued that the description of Article 114 TFEU as being 'dynamic' is a fatal misunderstanding of this provision, since it has to be tied to Article 5(1) TEU, and moreover, that Article 114 TFEU is imprecise by its nature.[96] Nevertheless, the paradoxical nature of competence allocation in the EU lies precisely in that it is limited by conferred powers yet is very difficult to define. Given that, there is a tension between the message of Article 5(1) TEU, which requires the legality of EU action on the one hand, and the broad scope of Articles 2 and 3 TEU and 26 TFEU – which state the goals of the EU, including the elimination of obstacles to trade – on the other hand. There is thus a connection between the notion of legislative harmonisation and the construction of the internal market, and the Court appears to take a rather broad view of the context in which that connection may be established.[97] Moreover, the classic crucial free movement element to Article 114 TFEU has arguably been somewhat weakened and replaced by the more freestanding aim of creating a 'market space', encompassing not only the removal of obstacles but also the prevention of distortion of competition, as explained above. After all, in cases such as *Rundfunk*[98] and

[93] eg D Wyatt, 'Community Competence to Regulate the Internal Market', Oxford Legal Working Paper No 9/2007, July 2007.

[94] Especially the Commission, eg The Commission's communication on Case C-176/03 (above n 2).

[95] eg S Weatherill, *Law and Integration in the European Union* (Oxford, Clarendon Press, 1995) 14–15 and T Konstadinides, *Division of Powers in the European Union* (Deventer, Kluwer Law Publishing, 2009) ch 6.

[96] A Von Bogdandy and J Bast, 'The Vertical Order of Competences' (2002) 39 *CML Rev* 227.

[97] S Weatherill, 'Recent Developments on the Free Movement of Goods' (2006) 55 *ICLQ* 457.

[98] Joined Cases C-465/00, C-138/01 and C-139/01 *Rundfunk and others* [2003] ECR I-4989.

Lindquist[99] the Court stated that recourse to Article 114 TFEU as a legal basis does not presuppose the existence of an actual link with free movement between Member States in every situation referred to by the measure in question founded on that basis. Accordingly, while the Court is not explicit about what makes a market, it has ruled that a contrary interpretation could render the limits of the field of application of a certain directive particularly unsure.[100]

In any event, it has been suggested that the mission of the new Constitutional era is to identify the ultimate objective of the internal market.[101] Looking at the EU constitutional debate more broadly, however, it becomes clear that the crucial issue is actually the importance of 'clarification' of these objectives.[102] Nevertheless, the argument that, if not an 'ultimate' objective, then at least an appropriate objective needs to be identified, appears to suit criminal law, since in this area we do not only need to know what the EU is aiming for, but we need a clearer division of powers as well. The reason for this is twofold. First the citizens of Europe need to know who the legislator is. Secondly, the principle of legality requires maximum certainty in criminal law. The Lisbon Treaty addresses these issues, indeed Chapter 4 of Title V of the TFEU endeavours to clarify the issues and the legally binding status of the Charter emphasises the principle of legality.

The following section will outline the depiction of the market concept and thereby investigate past and future possibilities of relying on the internal market provision of Article 114 TFEU in criminal law.

C. The Market Concept: Obstacles to Trade and Distortion of Competition

When exploring the boundaries of Article 114 TFEU, the *Tobacco Advertising I* judgment[103] is crucial to any understanding of the scope of EU powers. The precise question asked in this case was whether Article 114 TFEU was a valid legal basis for a Directive concerning the regulation of advertising for cigarettes and snuff.[104]At this point, forming a part of EU legal history, the Court ruled that the effects of a directive must serve the genuine aim of creating an internal market and not just have a sweeping general aim. The problem with the Directive in question was that scrutiny of its actual provisions revealed the internal market aims to be, at best, marginal or tenuous.[105] The measure at issue must genuinely

[99] Case C-101/01 *Lindquist* [2003] ECR I-12971.

[100] ibid, para 41.

[101] Nebbia (above n 92).

[102] S Weatherill, 'Better Competence Monitoring' (2005) 30 *EL Rev* 23; P Craig, 'Competence, Containment, Conferral and Consideration' (2004) 29 *EL Rev* 323.

[103] Case C-376/98 *Germany v Parliament and Council* [2000] ECR I-8419.

[104] Directive 1998/43/EC on the approximation of the laws, regulations and administrative provisions of the Member States relating to the advertising and sponsorship of tobacco products [1998] OJ L213/9.

[105] G de Burca, 'Setting Constitutional limits to EU Competence?' Francisco Lucas Pires Working Papers Series on European Constitutionalism, 2001/02.

contribute to forming a market; mere regulation is not enough. However, the distinction between facilitating or contributing and regulating remains a rather tricky one to draw. For this reason, it is helpful to set out some points about the market concept itself.

Underlying the debate on what makes a market is the evasiveness found in the Treaty itself. The crux of the matter is how much market creation is required in order to legitimise the use of Article 114 TFEU. The EU is still searching for the boundaries of this task. In any event, as has already been touched upon, the classic question has been whether there was a difference between the goals of the common market and the aims of the internal market. The answer here varied with some arguing that there was a difference[106] while others argued that the two notions should be treated interchangeably.[107] Suffice it to say that while the Treaty definition of the internal market was narrower than the common market – as it did not embrace a completed external trade policy, a system of fair competition and the harmonisation or coordination of legislation for reasons other than the elimination of barriers between national markets – the Court seems to have treated these 'markets' indistinguishably.[108] In any case, as noted above, the Lisbon Treaty has now solved this issue by simply abolishing the common market. The question is whether there is a difference between the 'functioning', 'facilitating' and 'establishment' of the market. There appears to be no clear-cut answer here, although the mere 'establishing' exercise seems not to be 'enough' according to the *Tobacco Advertising I* formula. After all, Article 114 TFEU refers to both establishing and functioning, thus requiring the assumption that they have to be read in conjunction with each other. Furthermore, as mentioned in part II of this chapter, in *Titanium Dioxide*[109] the Court recognised that the establishment and functioning of the internal market requires not only the elimination of obstacles to trade but also the removal of certain distortions of competition.[110] Indeed, in *Tobacco Advertising I* itself the Court considered both 'obstacles' and 'distortion' in deciding whether the directive fulfilled the criteria of facilitating the market. In this respect, AG Leger has noted that by carrying out this twofold examination in *Tobacco Advertising I*, the Court merely verified that recourse to Article 114 for the adoption of the directive in question could not be justified by merely having recourse to one of the objectives on which the creation of the internal market is based.[111] Nonetheless, the Court has subsequently held, as in the *BAT* judgment,[112] that once an obstacle to trade is established, it is not necessary to prove distortion

[106] R Barents, 'The Internal Market Unlimited: Some Observations on the Legal Basis of Community Legislation' (1993) 30 *CML Rev* 85.

[107] K Lenaert and K Nuffel, *Constitutional Law of the European Union* (London, Sweet & Maxwell, 2005) 139.

[108] L Gormley, 'Competition and Free Movement: Is the Internal Market the Same as a Common Market?' (2002) 13 *European Business Law Review* 517.

[109] Case C-300/89 *Commission v Council* [1991] ECR I-2867.

[110] ibid.

[111] Case C-380/03 *Germany v Parliament and Council* [2006] ECR I-11573, Opinion of AG Léger on 13 June 2006.

[112] Case C-491/01 *ex p BAT and Imperial Tobacco* [2002] ECR I-11543.

of competition in order to legitimise the use of Article 114 TFEU. Looking back at the *Kadi* case,[113] the Court referred to 'effects on trade' in addition to the distortion of competition argument. Nevertheless, if 'effects' on trade are to be regarded as equivalent to the establishing and functioning of the market, then that is not a very high threshold to be reached when justifying EU action. There is also a risk that the search for 'effects' on trade will overshadow the need to show a genuine market element when deciding on legislation under Article 114 TFEU. The point is that 'effects' on trade is a very subjective notion. Hence, it is submitted that the 'effects on trade' maxim reveals a similar pattern to the effectiveness principle. It is simply very difficult to pin down its exact meaning.

In addition, the precise contours of a 'measure for the approximation' requirement as stipulated in Article 114 TFEU also needs to be clarified. This question was considered in the *Smoke flavourings*[114] judgment.[115] AG Kokott in her Opinion argued that as long as 'a measure merely serves as a whole for the approximation of the law of the Member States, it can provide for procedures which do not bring about approximation directly but only in a multi level stage model with intermediate steps'.[116] The Court concluded that by using the words 'measure for the approximation', the authors of the Treaty intended to confer a wide discretion depending on the general context and the specific circumstances, which could be used to choose the most appropriate harmonisation technique, potentially involving a multi-stage approach. Nevertheless, it should be noted that the 'general context' in the *Smoke flavourings* case was the scientific field, which could justify a multi-stage approach. It is less clear how direct or indirect each step needs to be in such a multi-level approach in order to contribute to market creation at the EU level. As will be shown in the case study on money laundering in chapter five, such a tactic of complementary measures confirms a dual legislative approach to money laundering in the framework of Article 114 TFEU. Furthermore, as will be demonstrated, the Commission seems to assume that divergent criminal laws constitute obstacles which would affect confidence in the market.[117] For this reason, it is useful to look at the meaning of 'disparities' between the Member States in further detail.

D. Disparities between Laws of Member States as Obstacles

Variations between the laws of Member States are often portrayed as impeding the smooth functioning of the market and therefore such variations often constitute the main component or *ratio* for proposed legislation.[118] Nevertheless, the

[113] Case C-402/05 P *Kadi* [2008] ECR I-6351.

[114] Case C-66/04 *UK v Council and Parliament* [2005] ECR I-10553.

[115] K Gutman, 'Case comment' (2006–2007) 12 *Columbia Journal of European Law* 147.

[116] Opinion delivered on 8 September 2005.

[117] Commission ' on criminal measures aimed at ensuring the enforcement of intellectual property rights' (Communication) COM (2006) 168 final, 26 April 2006.

[118] See eg, B Kurcz, 'Harmonisation by Means of Directives – Never-ending Story?' (2001) 12 *European Business Law Review* 287.

Court has confirmed that heterogeneity between Member State laws does not in itself justify harmonisation.[119] Therefore, the Court has also stated that while mere disparities between national rules is not sufficient to justify recourse to Article 114 TFEU, it is sufficient where there are differences between the laws, regulations or administrative provisions of the Member States which could obstruct fundamental freedoms and thus have a direct effect on the functioning and establishment of the internal market.[120] The main issue seems to be how much diversity the Community can cope with before it ceases to be a properly functioning market.[121] For example, in the *PNR* case,[122] the Commission argued that due to a 'conflict of laws' – in the context of public international law – between US legislation and Community rules, it was necessary to act under Article 114 TFEU because of an obstacle in the form of 'disparities'. Although this argument was rejected by the Court, in criminal law there seems to be a clear risk that any diversity – such as the levels of punishment in the various Member States – could be argued as constituting a barrier to trade. There must be some criteria to trigger the 'disparities' test to come into play but it remains unclear just what this criteria entails.

Another closely related question is about the relationship between obstacles and disparities and whether such 'disparities' are merely obstacles to trade. Therefore we will next examine what 'obstacles' or 'barriers' mean in practice.

E. Obstacles and Market Access

As noted above, Articles 26 TFEU and 3 TEU require the abolition of any obstacle to the establishment and functioning of the EU market. Therefore, it is often said that the severity of an obstacle or a distortion is a functional idea. A related matter in the framework of Article 114 TFEU and obstacles to trade is how to view this provision in relation to Article 34 TFEU (ex Article 28 EC) and the free movement of goods. After all, the landmark ruling of *Keck*[123] shifted the trend from market expansion to market maintenance by stipulating that rules affecting selling arrangements fall outside the ambit of Article 34 TFEU.[124] Although it is true that Article 34 TFEU does not concern EU criminal law, it nonetheless highlights the wider constitutional debate on Article 114 TFEU. The core of the question is whether the EU can still harmonise selling arrangements that are not within the scope of Article 34 TFEU under Article 114 TFEU.[125] At issue here is the question of whether market access arguments should apply to Article 34 TFEU at all, in line

[119] See eg, Case C-210/03 *Swedish Match* [2004] ECR I-11893.

[120] ibid, para 29.

[121] Kurcz (above n 177).

[122] Joined Cases C-317/04 and C-318/04 *European Parliament v Council* [2006] ECR I-4721.

[123] Case C-267/91 *Keck* [1993] ECR I-6097.

[124] S Weatherill, 'After *Keck*: Some Thoughts on How to Clarify the Clarification' (1996) 33 *CML Rev* 885.

[125] G Davies, 'Can Selling Arrangements Be Harmonised?' (2005) 30 *EL Rev* 371.

with the other Treaty freedoms.[126] This question is also relevant in the context of Article 114 TFEU. After all, the concept of market access could be viewed – in a broad sense – as already forming part of the removal of obstacles or significant distortions of competition doctorine and hence could be regarded as an implicit part of Article 26 TFEU. Therefore, there is an obvious risk that woolly notions such as 'effects' or removal of 'appreciable' distortion of competition do not amount to any limitation on the EU legal mandate at all. More specifically, it appears as if market access arguments in the context of Article 114 TFEU would lower the market-creation threshold, as any effect on trade would be sufficient to justify harmonisation. For example, in the context of the *PNR* case it has been suggested that it is desirable to look not only at the objectives of the instrument at issue but also at its effects: if the effects contribute to achieving the Treaty objective then, arguably, that should be sufficient.[127] As regards criminal law, it appears very unclear how such 'effects' could possibly be measured.[128] Furthermore, such a reliance on effects on trade as a possible justification for legislation without any evaluation is not in line with effectiveness as a principle of criminalisation. The point is that in the criminal law field, effectiveness should be seen as a restrictive axiom. Moreover, the problem is to decide when an obstacle exists, and this is especially tricky in the area of criminal law, as we are left without much guidance. For example, it could be questioned whether disparities in sentencing levels are enough to trigger the use of Articles 26 and 114 TFEU. Indeed, from the perspective of Article 114 TFEU, anything could be harmonised if it contributes to market creation. Nonetheless, what really constitutes an obstacle to trade seems unclear although there is a tendency to treat disparities as obstacles per se. This is particularly significant in the context of future obstacles to trade.

F. Preventive Market Creation

Admittedly, considering future obstacles is not a ground-breaking idea but a template that has already been applied in, for example, the *Swedish Match* case.[129] After all, the Court has consistently held that while recourse to Article 114 TFEU as a legal basis is possible if the aim is to prevent future obstacles to trade resulting from

[126] For a breakthrough judgment on the mentioning of 'market access' in connection with Art 28 EC, see Case C-110/05 *Commission v Italy*, judgment of 10 February 2009. On market access, eg G Davies 'Understanding Market Access: Exploring the Economic Rationality of Different Conceptions of Free Movement Law' (2010) 11 *German Law Journal* 671.

[127] M Cremona, 'External Relations of the EU and the Member States: Competences, Mixed Agreements, International Responsibility and Effects of International Law' EUI Working paper LAW No 2006/22.

[128] See ch 3 and Part IV of this chapter.

[129] Case C-210/03 *Swedish Match* [2004] ECR I-11893, §§ 30–33. On the concept of preventive harmonisation see M Seidel, 'Präventive Rechtangleichung im Bereich des Gemeinsamen Markets' (2006) *Europarecht* 26. As for harmonisation via negative integration via the Courts case law see already the famous *Dassonville* case, Case C-8/74 *Procureur du Roi v Benoit and Gustave Dassonville* [1974] ECR 837 where a merely hypothetical impediment to free trade was enough to strike down a national rule.

the heterogeneous development of national laws, it is likely that such obstacles will emerge and measures must be brought in to prevent them. Moreover, in *Tobacco Advertising II*,[130] the Court stipulated that Article 114 TFEU can also be relied on if the aim is to prevent the emergence of future obstacles to trade resulting from developments of national laws as new Member States join the EU, if there is an appreciable risk that such disparities would increase (the 'likeliness' test). Accordingly, a slightly different pattern seems to be emerging here, since recognising that barriers increase with the enlargement of the EU has helped to justify recourse to Article 114 TFEU. In the context of criminal law, this raises some intriguing issues. After all, organised crime is clearly a problem for the EU and particularly for some of the new Member States. Nevertheless, if we accept the consequences of the enlargement of the EU as a future obstacle to trade then, in the broader context of organised crime, the notion of 'disparities' is a very low threshold to be crossed when justifying legislative action in the area of criminal law.

It goes without saying that if the mere fact that divergent national approaches to organised crime could create obstacles to trade capable of constituting a justification for harmonisation, then this would constitute a kind of *carte blanche*, even though the next steps to be taken in checking the measures' validity are subsidiarity and proportionality. However, if one considers that the principle of conferred powers requires more analytical arguments and concrete reasons in defining 'obstacles', the crucial point then becomes whether the measure at issue actually contributes to removing appreciable distortions of competition, which again, is a question of degree. Furthermore, despite the difficulties of gathering empirical data, some evidence of the possible effects would probably be desirable when judging the adequacy of a directive, although it is true that no such data was available to the Court in *Tobacco Advertising I*.[131] Furthermore, as will be demonstrated in the case study below, the Court almost seems to be influenced by self-defence reasoning – of a preventive character – which is hardly in line with the requirement for a concrete market-making investigation but rather constitutes a touchstone of risk regulation without assessment.[132]

More recently, in the *Vodafone* case[133] the Court seems to have followed the continuing movement towards preventive market creation. This case concerned the Roaming regulation 717/2007 aimed at regulating the price of public mobile phone networks across Member States. What was actually being harmonised was the bad behaviour of companies, that is, it was addressed at private practices and not the laws of Member States themselves. This was a new development under Article 114 TFEU, and as such a very significant stretch of its application,[134] even

[130] Case C-380/03 *Germany v Parliament and Council* [2006] ECR I-11573.

[131] G Tridimas and T Tridimas, 'The European Court of Justice and the Annulment of the Tobacco Advertisement Directive' (2002) 14 *European Journal of Law & Economics* 171.

[132] Cf in a different context Somek, *Individualism* (Oxford, Oxford University Press, 2008) ch 5–6.

[133] Case 58/08 *Vodafone*, judgment of 8 June 2010 not yet reported, concerning Roaming regulation 717/2007, OJ L171/32.

[134] S Weatherill, 'The Limits of Legislative Harmonisation Ten Years after Tobacco Advertising: How the Court's Case Law has become a "drafting guide"' (2011) 12 *German Law Journal* 827.

though such an effect on private parties had been the case in practice as a result of free movement laws in general. AG Maduro in his Opinion advocated such a view by suggesting the horizontal application of this provision.[135] The Court did not touch upon this issue but again focused on the preventive aspect of the likeliness of future obstacles to trade. On the one hand it confirmed the preventive aspect of the Article, as the Court treated it uncritically as orthodox 'preventive harmonisation'.[136] Therefore, it could be argued that *Vodafone*[137] is in line with *Alliance for Natural Health*[138] and *Tobacco Advertising II*[139] which confirms the relative ease with which the EU legislator could cross the threshold. On the other hand, there is something new in the *Vodafone* case: a more nuanced approach to the notion of preventive market-making can be found in the attention given to impact assessments. In examining the proposed measures in relation to proportionality the Court pointed out that:

> In this respect, it must be recalled, first, that, before it drafted the proposal for the regulation, the Commission carried out an exhaustive study, the result of which is summarised in the impact assessment mentioned in paragraph 5 of this judgment. It follows that the Commission examined various options including, inter alia, the option of regulating retail charges only, or wholesale charges only, or both, and that it assessed the economic impact of those various types of regulation and the effects of different charging structures.

Some commentators have chosen to view this as a hugely exciting development and a move away from blind harmonisation.[140] However, as will be explained in Part IV this is far from straightforward as impact assessments often point in the direction of more legislation albeit in a slightly more complicated way.

This chapter will now briefly turn to the other major competence component of Article 114 TFEU, namely the regulatory element of the prevention of distortion of competition. The purpose here is to illuminate the adaptive nature of Article 114 TFEU.

G. Distortion of (Appreciable) Competition

The concept of 'appreciable distortion' seems to constitute a similarly fuzzy test to the 'functioning' of the market template. It is often suggested that in *Tobacco*

[135] Opinion of AG Maduro delivered on 1 October 2009. Interestingly though, in his opinion AG Maduro suggested that private actors could be regulated by Art 114 TFEU for the functioning of the market. In this regard AG Maduro argued that Art 114 TFEU could be relied upon for a different reason (ie not only because of removal of obstacles or appreciable distortion of competition due to MS's 'bad' behaviour) namely to the removal of restrictions to free movement arising from the behaviour of private parties which disfavour cross boarder economic activities. According to the AG's view a horizontal application of Art 114 TFEU was legitimate.

[136] S Weatherill (above n 50).

[137] Case 58/08 *Vodafone*, judgment of 8 June 2010 not yet reported.

[138] Cases C-154/04 and C-155/04 *Alliance for Natural Health* [2005] ECR I-6451.

[139] Case C-380/03 *Germany v Parliament and Council* [2006] ECR I-11573.

[140] See the interesting account by D Keyaerts 'Ex ante Evaluation of EU Legislation Intertwined with Judicial Review? Case comment' (2010) 35 *EL Rev* 869.

Advertising I the Court appeared to have introduced a *de minimis*[141] requirement by placing a lot of weight on the 'appreciable' distortion of competition. It was in the *Titanium Dioxide* judgement,[142] however, that the Court first touched on the appreciable criterion in relation to the amount of competition that could be distorted. It later developed it into an internal market criterion in the *Tobacco Advertising I* judgment. Indeed, it should be recalled that in *Tobacco Advertising I*, the Court stated (paragraphs 106–115) that in the absence of such a requirement, the powers of the Community legislator would be almost unlimited. Therefore, the point is that if the EU could rely on a small distortion of competition in order to justify recourse to Article 114 TFEU, then this would again contradict the principle of conferred powers.[143] And yet there is a problem in the very attempt to draw a line between an 'appreciable' and 'non-appreciable' distortion of competition, as these are very imprecise words which seem to constitute key passages in the Court's reasoning. As noted in connection with the *Kadi* case and Article 352 TFEU in Part II above, there was no such 'appreciable' test in the context of the distortion of competition argument. More shocking still, the absence of such criteria has more recently also been true in the context of Article 114 TFEU.[144] This is alarming, though it is true, as Wyatt observed, that it appears as if the threshold for an appreciable distortion of competition to justify harmonisation measures is to be assessed somewhat 'impressionistically'.[145] After all, as in the context of disparities, in the criminal law context one could ask whether distortion will arise if the criminal laws in one Member State are so lenient that moral standards in the Member State will fall. Such a statement presupposes that criminal law determines moral standards, which, as explained in chapter three, may not always be the assumption. Clearly, this is an issue beyond the scope of this chapter but it is nonetheless an issue that should be kept in mind when discussing criminalisation at the EU level.

More recently, in the *Vodafone* case[146] the Court appears to have gone back to using the language of significant distortion of competition. This is interesting in the light of the fact that the Lisbon Treaty has delegated the distortion of competition object to a protocol. Protocol No 27 is attached to the Treaty indicating that the reference to the internal market in Article 3 includes a system for ensuring undistorted competition.[147] Although protocols have the same value as Treaties it remains to be seen whether this will have an impact on the EU aim of market construction.[148]

[141] D Wyatt et al, *European Union Law* (London, Sweet & Maxwell, 2006) 85–89.

[142] Case C-300/89 *Commission v Council* [1991] ECR I-2867.

[143] P Craig, *EU Administrative Law* (Oxford, Oxford University Press, 2006) ch 12.

[144] Case C-301/06 *Ireland v Parliament and Council* judgment of 10 February 2009 not yet reported. On this case see T Konstadinides, 'Wavering between Centres of Gravity: Comment on *Ireland v Parliament and Council*' (2010) 35 *EL Rev* 88; and M Dougan, 'Legal Developments' (2010) 48 *Journal of Common Market Studies* 163.

[145] Wyatt (above n 93).

[146] Case 58/08 *Vodafone*, judgment of 8 June 2010 not yet reported.

[147] Protocol 27 TEU.

[148] D Chalmers, G Davies and G Monti, *EU Law* (Cambridge, Cambridge University Press 2010) ch 1.

In any case, it has been argued that the Court may simply have been wrong in justifying EU regulatory intervention in terms of preventing 'distortion of competition'.[149] According to this view, the Court is misguided in focusing on distortion of competition at all. It has been suggested that the Court considers that distortion of competition exists whenever different economic costs or opportunities result from regulatory choices with regard to which jurisdictions have an incentive to regulate strategically in order to gain a competitive advantage or preclude another jurisdiction from gaining a competitive advantage.[150] Therefore, it has been stated that the answer to successful market creation is found in more aggressive attention being paid to proportionality, rather than relying on distortion of competition.[151] It has also been suggested that the best understanding of 'distortion of competition' is that it is deemed 'not appreciable' when the beneficial effects of any federal intervention are clearly outweighed by the costs connected to the loss of Member States' regulatory autonomy. Conversely, a distortion of competition is deemed to be 'appreciable' when the benefits are not outweighed by the costs of intervention.[152] This presupposes that everything has a price. In any case, the all too familiar 'balancing' act seems once again to be the norm. Then again, is that 'competence' or 'subsidiarity' or 'proportionality'? Back to square one.

H. Normative Concerns or Why Article 114 TFEU is Difficult to Reconcile with the Attribution of Powers Axiom

As explained, hypothetical market creation is not enough to take precedence over the attribution of powers, as was demonstrated by the *Tobacco Advertising I* ruling.[153] It is worth repeating that this case put the notion of legality in terms of the conferral of powers back onto the constitutional agenda. In fact, as one commentator put it

> the Court has made irrelevant not just market liberalism (where the Union would have legal power to harmonize only if such harmonization would result in greater volume of trade) but a whole host of approaches for resolving competence allocation such as the use of proportionality and subsidiarity.[154]

It is true that the Court in the *Tobacco Advertising I* judgment never reached the subsidiarity and proportionality stage *stricto sensu*. However, this is only logical

[149] M Kumm, 'Constitutionalising Subsidiarity in Integrated Markets: The Case of Tobacco Regulation' (2006) 12 *ELJ* 503.

[150] ibid.

[151] The principle of proportionality will be discussed below in Part VI of this chapter and is therefore not dealt with here.

[152] Kumm (above n 149).

[153] Case C-376/98 *Germany v Parliament and Council* [2000] ECR I-8419.

[154] Somek (above n 134) 90–91 in the context of economics and trade, citing J Trachtman, 'Trade and Problems, Cost Benefit Analysis and Subsidiarity' (1998) 9 *European Journal of International Law* 32.

as Article 5(1–2) TEU – conferralprecedes subsidiarity (3) and proportionality (4).[155]

The post-*Tobacco Advertising I* cases appear to pay less attention to constitutional concerns as drawn up by the Treaty.[156] It is true that the *PNR* case made clear that Article 114 TFEU could not be used as a means of remedying a lack of competence in the former third pillar area.[157] Nevertheless, the facts in this case were quite unusual. In this ruling the Court first annulled a Council Decision[158] on the conclusion of an Agreement between the EC and the US on the processing and transfer of passenger name record (PNR) data by air carriers and, secondly, annulled a Commission Decision[159] on the adequate protection of personal data contained in the PNR of air passengers transferred to the US.[160] Regarding the legality of the Council Decision, the Court held that Article 114 TFEU, read in conjunction with Article 25 of Directive 95/46, could not justify a Community competence to conclude the Agreement with the US. In support of that finding, the Court held that the Agreement related to the same transfer of data as the Commission Decision and therefore to data-processing operations that were excluded from the scope of the Directive. It concluded from this that the Council Decision on the conclusion of the Agreement between the EC and the US could not have been validly adopted on the basis of Article 114 TFEU.[161] The Court annulled both Decisions. The *PNR* ruling was clear-cut and therefore does not provide much guidance. In other words, it would simply have been too difficult to link the fight against international terrorism with the internal market, even for the most eager advocate of harmonisation, and explain in legal terms how or why the Directive in question contributed to market creation and was able to pass the narrow test set out in Articles 5 TEU and 114 TFEU.

Despite this, it has been suggested that it is in Article 26 TFEU that we should seek the answer to the breadth of Article 114 TFEU, since the former has a very straightforward message: it states that the internal market shall be an area without frontiers, and that Article 114 TFEU is helping to achieving it.[162] According to this view, there is a competence within Article 26 TFEU which can be allocated to the Member States by use of subsidiarity and proportionality. Taken to a different level, and applied in the context of criminal law, this could create difficulties if

[155] Weatherill (above n 102).

[156] eg Case C-210/03 *Swedish Match* [2004] ECR I-11893.

[157] Cases C-317/04 and C-318/04 *European Parliament v Council* [2006] ECR I-4721.

[158] Council Decision 2004/496/EC [2004] OJ L183.

[159] Commission Decision 2004/535/EC [2004] OJ L183.

[160] A clarifying summery of the facts of the case is provided by AG Leger, Opinion delivered on 22 November 2005. See also eg H Hijmans and A Scirocco, (2009) 'Shortcomings in EU Data Protection in the Third and Second Pillars. Can the Lisbon Treaty be Expected to Help?' 46 *CML Rev* 1443. See also more generally on data protection E De Busser (2010) 'Transatlantic Adequacy and a Certain Degree of Perplexity' 1 *Eucrim* 31.

[161] AG Leger was more specific and argued that the main aim of the Agreement with the US was the fight against terrorism, which could not be based on Art 95 EC. Opinion of AG Leger delivered on 22 November 2005.

[162] Davies (above n 125).

there was judged to be a dormant competence in every policy field, including criminal law. The reason for this is that the requirements of Article 5(1–4) TEU are different though closely interlinked. It would be dangerous not to uphold the distinction between the principle of conferred powers and the principle of subsidiarity and proportionality in Article 5 TEU as this would facilitate competence creep. This is not to deny that it is important to pay attention to Article 5 TEU as a whole. What is at issue here is not only legitimacy issues of EU action, but also how to ensure that fundamental principles of criminal law – most importantly legality and fair trial guarantees – are respected at the EU level, and how such actions are linked to the principles of criminalisation. Clearly, there is an uneasy relationship between, on the one hand the attribution of powers, and on the other the open-ended character of Article 114 TFEU. There seems to be a tendency to recycle the same legal arguments when distributing competences in the EU.

As will be explained in the context of the relationship between Article 114 TFEU and ex Article 47 EU, the market-creation test threshold was lowered in *Ireland v Parliament and Council*[163] to include any effects on the first pillar. Hence such reading of Article 114 TFEU in conjunction with ex Article 47 EU had a direct impact on the possibilities of harmonising criminal law within the former first pillar.

i. Centre of Gravity and Article 114 TFEU

As discussed in Part I of this chapter, the centre-of-gravity element, or object and content template, in choosing the right legal basis is often discussed in connection with the choice between Articles 114 and 352 TEU. As regards Article 114 TFEU, there is no real centre-of-gravity test available; instead the question rests on whether the measure in issue contributes to market creation at all. Indeed, AG Fennelly in his Opinion in *Tobacco Advertising I* dismissed the centre-of-gravity test as irrelevant:

> I do not view it as appropriate to seek to determine the lawfulness of the Directive by reference to the question whether its centre of gravity lies in the pursuit of health protection rather than of internal-market objectives. This approach is only relevant where there is a dispute as to whether a measure should have been adopted by reference to one or other of two possible legal bases.[164]

Nevertheless, such an approach has been criticised. Somek has argued that:

> He [AG Fennelly] denied the relevance of centre of gravity where one legal basis alone is concerned and the question is thus whether the Union has jurisdiction at all. But I do not see any good reason for drawing a distinction here. Why shouldn't centre of gravity considerations be relevant to this type of case also? In both cases the question also comes down to whether the Union has chosen the right basis for its action.[165]

[163] Case C-301/06 *Ireland v Parliament and Council* [2009] ECR I-00593, discussed below.

[164] Opinion of AG Fennelly delivered on 15 June 2000, para 68.

[165] See the impressive work by Somek (above n 132) fn 50 at 118.

I disagree with this view. As pointed out in the context of the *Tobacco Advertising II* ruling, the Court did not consider the centre-of-gravity test here: 'Rather, the only question posed when examining the conferral of competences is whether a competence of the Community can be identified [in relation to market creation] or not'.[166]

Thus, it is here that the argument for taking non-market values, and by implication the 'centre-of-gravity' debate, into consideration enters the discussion. More specifically, how much market creation is 'enough' to activate the use of Article 114 TFEU? As shown, the *Tobacco Advertising I* case clarified that the threshold that has to be crossed is quite high. Later cases paint a less clear picture. It is submitted that what is under consideration here is not the usual 'centre-of-gravity' test as pioneered by *Titanium Dioxide.*[167] Nonetheless, it should be noted that the object and content test or the centre-of-gravity assessment in cross-pillar conflicts had a somewhat academic renaissance in connection with the above-stated *PNR* case and the possible impact of ex Article 47 EU as a competence booster for Article 114 TFEU.[168] Therefore, as explained in Part II, the centre-of-gravity test was somewhat biased in the context of ex Article 47 EU and the safeguarding of the EC against the EU pillars, as the central question in connection with that provision was a – albeit tenuous – Community aspect which triggered the use of Article 47 EU. However, the *PNR* case did not concern the scope of ex Article 47 EU, but rather the scope of Article 114 TFEU and whether a directive which explicitly excluded the former third pillar could be circumvented by a decision regulating that area based on Article 114 TFEU. Therefore, the next subsection examines the possible relationship between Article 114 TFEU and ex Article 47 EU by focusing on the judgment in *Ireland v Parliament and Council.*[169]

ii. Article 114 TFEU in Relation to ex Article 47 EU

The relationship between ex Article 47 EU and Article 114 TFEU has been largely unexamined in legal doctrine. It is appropriate to look at the case of *Ireland v Parliament and Council* in further detail.[170] This ruling is of particular interest since it is the first judgment to specifically deal with the link between Article 114 TFEU and ex Article 47 EU in the first pillar/third pillar grey area[171] and follows

[166] Case C-380/03 *Germany v Parliament and Council* [2006] ECR I-11573, M Ludwigs, Annotation C-380/03 (2007) 44 *CML Rev* 1159.

[167] Case C-300/89 *Commission v Council* [1991] ECR I-2867. See also Case C-377/98 *Netherlands v Parliament and Council* [2001] ECR I-7079. More recently, in Case C-166/07 *European Parliament v Council* judgment of 3 September 2009 not yet reported, the Court held that when no Treaty provision provides on its own a sufficient legal basis, the EU legislator can have recourse to two legal basis. See T Konstadinides, 'Between Circumvention and Gap-filling: The Conceptual Limits around the Treaty's Flexibility Clause' *Yearbook of European Law* (forthcoming; on file with the author).

[168] Case C-317/04, C-318/04, *European Parliament v Council* [2006] ECR I-4721, eg G Gilmore and J Rijpma 'Case Note' (2007) 44 *CML Rev* 1092; V Mitsilegas, 'The External Dimension of EU Action in Criminal Matters' (2007) 12 *European Foreign Affairs Review* 457.

[169] Case C-301/06 *Ireland v Parliament and Council* judgment of 10 February 2009 not yet reported.

[170] ibid.

[171] E Herlin-Karnell, Annotation, Case C-301/06 (2009) 46 *CML Rev* 1667.

on from the aforementioned *PNR* ruling. The case concerns Directive 2006/24/EC,[172] amending Directive 2002/58/EC[173] (which excluded the third pillar from its ambit) on the retention of data. This Directive 2006/24 was based on Article 114 TFEU on the grounds that Member States had adopted varied legislation providing for the retention of data. The background to this case is that Ireland brought an action against the Council and the EP, arguing that Directive 2006/24 on the retention of data with the purpose of fighting serious crime was incorrectly adopted under Article 114 TFEU, as it should have been based on the third pillar.[174] Therefore, at issue here was Article 47 EU in reverse. As explained in Part II above and as observed by AG Maduro in *Kadi*[175] and AG Mengozzi in the *Segi* case,[176] ex Article 47 EU worked in both directions even if it favoured the first pillar.

AG Bot in his Opinion concluded that it was clear from the recital in the preamble to the directive in question that there were legislative and technical disparities between the national provisions relating to data retention by service providers.[177] The AG emphasised that the mere fact that the directive referred to the objective of the protection of privacy as well as the retention of data as a means of combating serious crime and facilitating prosecutions and investigation, did not preclude Article 114 TFEU from being its legal basis. The reason for this was, in the view of the AG, the question of security more generally. More specifically, he stated that there are certain overriding requirements of public interest that must be taken into account and that such concerns could include the requirement for security. Moreover, a measure such as the directive in question which harmonises the conditions on the retention of certain data for the purposes of crime prevention contributes to the requirement that a high level of security be guaranteed within the internal market in accordance with Article 114(3) TFEU. This is astonishing. First, Article 114(3) TFEU does not mention security but 'safety', and secondly it requires scientific evidence. There seems to have been no such risk assessment analysis available in this case. Nevertheless, AG Bot concluded his Opinion by stating that even if it was possible to contemplate a dual component covering both the establishment and functioning of the internal market and judicial and police cooperation as covered by the third pillar, ex Article 47 EU stood in the way by unambiguously favouring the first pillar.

The Court's judgment was brief. It simply concluded that Article 114 TFEU constituted the correct legal basis for the directive in question as such recourse may be justified where disparities exist between national rules which obstruct the fundamental freedoms or to distort competition. As seen in *Kadi*, the 'appreciable' test is not used for the degree of distortion of competition. However, the

[172] OJ L105/54.

[173] OJ L201.

[174] ibid.

[175] AG Maduro, Opinion delivered on 16 January 2008, Case C-415/05P [2008] ECR I-6351.

[176] Case C-354/04, C-355/04P *Segi and others* ECR [2007] I-6157, Opinion of AG Mengozzi delivered on 26 October 2006.

[177] Opinion of AG Bot delivered on 14 October 2008.

Court stated that it was clear that the directive had significant economic implications for service providers possibly involving substantial investment and operating costs. For this reason, the Court pointed out that differences between the various national rules adopted on the retention of data relating to electronic communications were liable to impact directly on the functioning of the internal market and that it was foreseeable that such impact would become more serious with the passage of time. Significantly, the Court did not refer to the establishing requirement in the context of constructing a market. It is not clear whether the Court considers such a market to have already been established or whether the Court simply did not explain its reasoning in this regard.[178] Arguably, and in the broader EU governance context, the case law on Article 114 TFEU touches upon what has been referred to as a shift from market creation to market maintenance.[179] In any case, the Court stated that the outcome in that case was not comparable to the outcome in the *PNR* case discussed above, as the latter concerned the governance of personal data and enforcement questions, while the case under consideration concerned the activities of service providers. Nonetheless, it seems as if the market element is rather tenuous, it being sufficient to find an economic link to service providers. In contrast with the *Tobacco Advertising I* Directive,[180] which was also based on Articles 53 TFEU and 62 TFEU governing the services sector, there is no such additional link with services in this directive. Therefore, the Court read Article 114 TFEU as including services without the need to specifically refer to the existence of an additional free movement basis within the meaning of Article 26 TFEU. The point is that this confirms a trend of relying on Article 114 TFEU as being capable of doing the whole job without the help of any additional free movement clause.[181] It also appears as though this is the position taken by the EU legislator.

In any event, and more importantly from the perspective of the present work, it is hard to see why the prevention of serious organised crime was an objective of the EU when it was an explicit objective of the third pillar – ex Article 31 EU. Clearly, this confirms the concern that prevention – in terms of future disparities – will lead to a very low threshold for justifying EU action. Consequently, it seems as if the question of market creation under Article 114 TFEU will become ancillary to ex Article 47 EU and the safeguarding of the *acquis communautaire*. It seems that what was at issue in the context of Article 114 TFEU, until *Ireland v Parliament and Council*, is not really the classic 'centre-of-gravity test'. Instead, the core of the question is whether there is a market element within the scope of Article 114 TFEU at all. In other words, it is not only about the 'centre' or aim and content, but there must also be a genuine need to harmonise pursuant to Article

[178] See also para 81 *Tobacco Advertising II* Case C-380/03 *Germany v Parliament and Council* [2006] ECR I-11573.

[179] M Egan, *Constructing a European Market* (Oxford, Oxford University Press, 2001).

[180] Directive 98/43 (above n 103).

[181] See also in the area of consumer law legislation where Art 114 TFEU is often used as the sole legal basis, S Weatherill, *EC Consumer Law* (Cheltenham, Edward Elgar, 2007).

114 TFEU. Nevertheless, as highlighted in the *Ireland v Parliament and Council* judgment, Article 47 EU read with Article 114 TFEU demonstrated a very low threshold and appear to resemble a centre-of-gravity test more than the market creation criterion. In other words, and more provocatively, it seems as if it does not matter how much non-market purpose or non-first pillar purpose there is, as long as there is some market purpose and (an appreciable) market effect, or some first pillar purpose. This is hardly in line the golden rule for harmonisation but confirms the ambiguous nature of the internal market.

As noted, AG Bot's Opinion is an interesting example of attention being paid to the notion of 'security' – without risk assessment – as a justification for harmonisation. However, the issue is even more significant. The matter also turns on the more general question of the role of non-market values such as combating serious crime or terrorism in the context of market building. The next subsection addresses this issue in further detail. In doing so, the intention is to provide a context for the case study on financial crimes in the EU under Article 114 TFEU, particularly money laundering, as will be explored in chapters 5 and 6.

iii. Non-market Values as Reasons for Harmonisation

Increasingly, there is a debate on the possibility of invoking non-market values as justification for harmonisation under Article 114 TFEU.[182] In particular, it has been suggested that the opportunity to pursue non-market values does not depend on whether a particular value is expressly recognised by the text of the Treaty or whether it is seen as a general principle of EU law.[183] In this respect De Witte has noted that: 'internal market legislation is always about something else and that something else may, in fact, be the main reason why the internal market legislation was adopted in the first place'. According to this view, there is an EU competence to *regulate* the internal market, as any other conclusion would give a distorted picture of what is at stake, that is, a balance between market integration and policy integration more broadly.[184] A recent example and confirmation of this view is, perhaps, the pending case concerning the validity of Regulation 1007/2009[185] regarding the harmonisation of the market for seal products.[186] This instrument requires seal products to be permitted in the EU market only where the seal products in question result from hunts traditionally conducted by Inuit and other indigenous communities and contribute to their subsistence.[187] With

[182] B De Witte, 'Non-market Values in Internal Market Legislation' in N NicShuibne (ed), *Regulating the Internal Market* (Cheltenham, Edward Elgar, 2006) ch 3. See also presentation by De Witte, 'A Competence to Protect: The Pursuit of Non-Market Aims through Internal Market Legislation' paper delivered in Antwerp 8–9 March 2010 (on file with the author).

[183] ibid.

[184] ibid at 63.

[185] [2009] OJ L286, 36

[186] Case T-18/10R *Inuit Tapiriit Kanatami* pending, order brought on 30 April 2010.

[187] For an analysis, see Weatherill (above n 134).

narrow exceptions, no other seal products were allowed on the EU market.[188] Accordingly, it was clear that animal welfare was the main objective of this measure. So, the internal market is a market with values.[189] Nevertheless, most commentators would agree that a market element has to be present in order to activate the use of Article 114 TFEU. Only then could other values enter the stage, such considerations therefore being secondary with respect to Article 114 TFEU.[190] However, again, measuring the 'market element' in question remains difficult, as it simply boils down to a very abstract test. And that market element has proved to be very weak in practice. More crucially though, we are also confronting the question of whether we are dealing with paternalistic legislation, enacted beyond the explicit powers of the Treaty to ensure a high level of protection, in the sense that this power pre-supposes that the EU can in fact make such moral choices,[191] or whether this is simply a question of market failure. As will be seen in chapter five, the matter of paternalistic legislation is a very heated topic in criminal law as it highlights a wider philosophical debate on criminal law policy and legislation.

The next section discusses cases described above and examines them from the 'confident in the market' perspective and highlights the question: why does the confidence-building introduce harmonised criminal laws?

I. Confidence in the Market is as Slippery as Effectiveness[192]

The concept of 'confidence in the market' has for a long time been a hot topic in EU law.[193] Nonetheless, it is generally considered that although it is crucial to breed trust in the Union, the confidence framework can be overworked and is sometimes used as a general goal without any clear destination.[194] For example, in the more familiar EU domain of consumer law, the EU has long been referring to 'confidence' as justification for harmonisation. This section looks more closely at what happens when one moves beyond this sphere into the area of penal law, thereby introducing the conundrums described in chapter five. Accordingly, the aim of this section is to examine the notion of 'confidence in the market' from a criminal law perspective. Here, the core of the argument seems to be that without 'confidence', the functioning of the market will be jeopardised by the efforts of criminal organisations which hinder consumers in their conduct of cross-border activities and hamper the full effectiveness of EU law. As indicated, the question of non-market values in the context of Article 114 TFEU is multifaceted. One

[188] ibid.

[189] See also Davies (above n 125).

[190] ibid.

[191] Somek (above n 132).

[192] This section draws on E Herlin-Karnell, 'Is there more to it than the fight against Dirty Money? Article 95 EC and the Criminal Law' (2008) 19 *European Business Law Review* 558.

[193] T Wilhelmsson, 'The Abuse of the Confident Consumer' (2004) 27 *Journal of Consumer Policy* 317.

[194] S Weatherill, 'Why Object to Harmonization of Private Law by the EC?' (2004) 5 *European Review of Public Law* 663.

issue – or extra dimension of Article 114 TFEU – being the 'confidence-in-the-market' *ratio* used to justify harmonisation. Nevertheless, it is often argued that the broad contours of 'confidence' as a justification for harmonisation was excluded by the *Tobacco Advertising I* case.[195] For example, linguistic variations and impeded access to justice may be much more serious impediments than a more or less 'hypothetical' lack of confidence in the market caused by legal diversity. On the other hand, it could also be argued that the broader 'confidence building' view was simply not an issue in *Tobacco Advertising* and was therefore not ruled out by this judgment.[196] In other words, this is a classic dispute about whether there is one way (market creation) or two ways (market creation and confidence building) to assess the validity of harmonisation measures.[197] The problem is not only that the scope of 'confidence in the market' reasoning is very broad and difficult to reconcile with the limits of Article 5(2) TFEU, but also that it is not clear whether it actually has any impact on the market at all. For example, it has been pointed out that, as regards capital markets in general, 'confidence' alone would not be a stable basis for the EU market, as a number of criteria would be required including, most importantly, investor awareness and investor protection across the EU.[198] The aspiration of generating confidence in the operation of the market using criminal law sheds light not merely on the principles of criminalisation and the adequacy of 'confidence', but also on some intriguing questions about the adequacy of 'confidence in the market'. The problem is, moreover, that the 'burden of proof' seems to be on the limiter rather than on the legislator in the pursuit of the general effectiveness of EU law. More specifically, action in this area appears to a great extent to be based on speculation – which is not necessarily wrong but is not really in tune with the requirement of attributed competences. The whole question can be reduced to what makes a market. However, the problem for this thesis is that such market orientation is especially difficult when applied in the context of criminal law. Criminal law plainly does not fit into the EU pattern of market creation.[199]

It is useful to briefly consider the Market Abuse Directive.[200] This Directive is particularly instructive when exploring the logic of the 'confidence in the market' paradigm. Here, the prohibition against manipulating the market aims to protect market efficiency in general.[201] It has been argued that there are alternatives, such

[195] ibid.

[196] S Weatherill, 'Reflections on the EC's Competence to Develop a European Contract Law' (2005) 13 *European Review of Public Law* 405.

[197] ibid.

[198] N Moloney, 'Confidence and Competence: The Conundrum of EC Capital Market Law' (2004) 4 *Journal of Corporate Law Studies* 44.

[199] See G Corstens, 'Criminal Law in the First Pillar?' (2003) 11 *European Journal of Crime, Criminal law and Criminal Justice* 131.

[200] Directive 2004/72/EC [2004] OJ L162 implementing the Market Abuse Directive 2003/6/EC, [2003] OJ L96/16. See for an overview of this landscape N Moloney, *EC Securities Regulation* (Oxford, Oxford University Press, 2002) ch 13.

[201] G Ferrarini, 'The Market Abuse Directive' (2004) 41 *CML Rev* 711.

as an information strategy, that could be more useful.[202] Indeed, in connection with the creation of the Market Abuse Directive, it was stressed that it should not be enough for the EU legislator simply to state that the prevention of the market abuse in question could not be sufficiently achieved by the individual Member States due to scale and effects of the abuse.[203] Obviously, this relates to the discussion outlined above on how to distinguish between competences, and the principles of subsidiarity and proportionality. It is submitted that in the area of criminal law and sanctions in general, competence based on a confidence concept causes even greater alarm than the 'usual' abuse of the 'confident consumer' when justifying harmonisation. In that respect, it should not be forgotten that in practice it is rare, or at least very difficult, to decriminalise,[204] and at worst this could cause a backlash against the whole idea of confidence promotion and the effectiveness of EU law. For this reason, the main issue is that more analytical and sophisticated arguments are needed to explain why the measures at issue are needed. Despite that, there seems to be a stubborn unwillingness by the EU legislator to engage in such investigations. There appears to be a belief that the mystique surrounding criminal law will ensure its effectiveness automatically. It might be disappointing news for the EU legislator in this regard that criminal law scholars insist that it should be used as the last resort, not only because it can have drastic consequences, but also because it is far from always 'effective'. The issue here is that the application of Article 114 TFEU should be based on a realistic understanding of the merits of invoking criminal law at the supranational level. In particular, it should not be held to contribute to market creation without any real assessment. In any event, one conclusion can be drawn: in combination with the general aim of effectiveness, the confidence argument seems almost indefinite and blind to constitutional concerns.

J. Conclusion

It is tempting to conclude by once again stressing the importance of legality. As noted in previous chapters, legality is the *sine qua non* for all discussions of criminal law, both procedural and substantive. In the context of legislative competence under the auspice of Article 114 TFEU, legality interacts not only with the conferral of powers (Article 5(1–2) TEU) but, as will be examined in the next part, also with subsidiarity and proportionality. Furthermore, legality enhances 'trust' in the Union project and remedies the accusation of competence creep. Most importantly, this chapter has shown the vagueness of Article 114 TFEU. The obvious exception is the *Tobacco Advertising I* case, and to some extent the *PNR* case, and they are – or at least should be – more significant than merely judicial drops in the ocean. Clearly, the message sent by these cases confirms that the limits set by the

[202] ibid.
[203] ibid.
[204] eg P Asp, *EU & Straffrätten* (Uppsala, Iustus, 2002) ch 2.

principle of the attribution of powers are to be taken seriously, but this leaves a good deal of uncertainty about the exact meaning of the Court's policing of this object through notions such as the 'appreciable' distortion of competition and the 'functioning' of the internal market. Specifically, the concept of effects on trade in the context of Article 114 TFEU reveals a similar pattern to the market access doctrine in the internal market. This is particularly true if there is no need to show 'appreciable' distortion of competition in order to rely on Article 114 TFEU, and this is arguably the case despite the somewhat unclear meaning of 'appreciable'. Moreover, this part of the chapter points to the previous policing function of Article 47 EU and argued that this provision, in combination with Article 114 TFEU, made the market-making less strict. Indeed, it seems as if it does not matter how much non-market purpose, or non-first pillar purpose, there is as long as there was some market-purpose and a market effect, or some first pillar purpose or effect which triggered use of ex Article 47 EU. It is true that the situation has changed as the Lisbon Treaty now provides for a specific competence as given by Article 83 TFEU which will remain *lex specialis.* Nonetheless, given the history of the broad interpretations of Article 114 TFEU and the current preventive approach to harmonisation which, as will be examined in chapter five, we are justified in speaking about a precautionary approach to criminal law at the EU level. After all, there are strong reasons to believe that Article 114 TFEU has not been wiped off the EU criminal law agenda. Obviously such a demarcation is important as measures taken within the framework of Article 83 TFEU would allow for the emergency brake to be pulled. There is however no such brake to be put on in relation to Article 114 TFEU.

The whole question comes down to what makes a market. The problem is that this market orientation is especially difficult when applied in the context of criminal law. Forthcoming rulings will clarify the possible scope of Article 114 TFEU in the criminal law area. Yet it is not with any ease that one welcomes constitution building based on judicial activism in an area closely related to legitimacy and legality – especially if the construction of such action rests on legal grounds as shaky as the effectiveness of EU law and confidence in the market.

It was recently stated that a sea of ink has been spilled on the subject of subsidiarity.[205] This chapter does not attempt to swim in it, but nonetheless tries to provide some new ideas on the principles of subsidiarity and proportionality from the perspective of EU criminal law. It aims to provide some general thoughts from the perspective of effectiveness and criminal law. The next part examines subsidiarity and proportionality before considering the fourth constitutional question in this chapter, namely the phenomenon of enhanced cooperation and its inherent complexities.

[205] Von Bogdandy and Bast (above n 96).

IV. SUBSIDIARITY AND PROPORTIONALITY

A. Introduction

This part of this chapter aims to explain the basics of subsidiarity and proportionality, and assess them in the light of EU criminal law. The intention is not to undertake a deep analysis as these concepts have already been examined in the EU legal doctrine. Therefore, this part will only touch upon the essential aspects of subsidiarity and proportionality as important institutional principles. What seems to be less closely examined, however, is the meaning of subsidiarity and proportionality in the AFSJ and EU criminal law in particular. In exploring these issues, this chapter tries to show that criminal law could and should be seen as imbued with subsidiarity/proportionality and, more specifically, that it could be viewed as an expression of the principle of *ultima ratio* – a minimalism approach – in criminal law. The chapter examines the changing landscape of the AFSJ and EU criminal law in particular and touches upon the Stockholm programme[206] in relation to the use of more nuanced regulation tools such as impact assessments. Paying attention to subsidiarity and proportionality is especially important in criminal law in order to avoid excessive criminalisation. Although the specific focus of this part of the chapter is the application of subsidiarity and proportionality within the areas of the AFSJ and EU criminal law more broadly, this section outlines the basics of subsidiarity and proportionality, including the wide theoretical questions.

B. Subsidiarity and Proportionality: The Basics

Bermann once wrote that his chapter on 'proportionality and subsidiarity' was concerned with proportionality[207] and very 'subsidiarily, about subsidiarity', but this exercise serves the opposite purpose: its main object is to explore the meaning of subsidiarity in the context of EU criminal law. Yet proportionality will also be investigated. This is so although, as will be explained, the principle of proportionality has more lately been celebrated as the solution for a more successful allocation of powers within the EU. Indeed, it should be noted that one of the main proponents of proportionality is Davies, who has rather forcefully argued that subsidiarity is the wrong idea, in the wrong place at the wrong time.[208] Although there may be practical merits in addressing proportionality rather than the

[206] The Stockholm programme – An open and secure Europe serving and protecting the citizen (Council of the European Union Brussels, 2 December 2009) available at http://register.consilium.europa.eu/pdf/en/09/st17/st17024.en09.pdf (last accessed January 2012).

[207] G Bermann, 'Proportionality and Subsidiarity' in C Barnard and J Scott (eds), *The Law of the Single European Market* (Oxford, Hart Publishing, 2002) 75.

[208] G Davies, 'Subsidiarity: The Wrong Idea, in the Wrong Place, at the Wrong Time' (2006) 43 *CML Rev* 63.

obscure concept of subsidiarity, this section aims to be provocative in stating that it is far too easy to rely on proportionality as the ideal solution to the question of multilevel governance in Europe, as there are difficulties in clarifying exactly what proportionality means. The point is that it is very difficult to separate these principles. Nonetheless, according to Schütze 'subsidiarity', properly understood, is 'federal proportionality'.[209] The subsidiarity principle would then examine whether the European law in issue disproportionally restricts national autonomy and the principle of proportionality would thereafter tell us whether the European law unnecessarily interfered with liberal values.[210] What then are these values? As is clear from the Lisbon Treaty, the Union sets out to be a key player in this area. The Lisbon Treaty makes it clear in Article 2 TEU that 'the Union is founded on the values of respect for human dignity, freedom, democracy, equality, the rule of law and respect for human rights. These values are common to the Member States in a society in which pluralism, non-discrimination, tolerance, justice, solidarity and equality between women and men prevail'. In addition, Article 3 TEU stipulates that the EU shall also offer its citizens an area AFSJ. Nevertheless, the aspiration of creating an AFSJ poses challenging questions of just what values the EU seeks to protect when scrutinised in detail. After all, the safeguarding of one person's security might constitute a restriction of someone else's freedom. The crucial question is perhaps what 'justice' means in a transnational setting. It will be argued that while the justice paradigm – which is also connected to fairness – is best understood in the context of proportionality, the *ultima ratio* of criminal law in the context of criminalisation is best reflected in the notion of subsidiarity at the EU level.

As indicated in Parts II and III of this chapter, there has recently been a tendency among EU scholars to view the assessment of subsidiarity and proportionality as the crucial concern and as more important than the abstract question of 'competence'.[211] However, it is submitted that this is to take too simplified a view, particularly in the context of criminal law where competence is interlinked with legality. After all, subsidiarity and proportionality *stricto sensu* are not about determining or defining the competences of the EU, but about providing some kind of guide to the exercise of the EU's existing powers.[212] A further complexity in this context lies in distinguishing between a Court pursuing a legal interpretation and 'activism' when ruling on subsidiarity. This is clearly a difficult question and, moreover, it is a question that is strongly connected to the phenomenon of 'competence creep' in the context of subsidiarity. Thus, the tension underlying subsidiarity was once captured by De Búrca, who observed that

> Even if it is accepted that the deeply political nature of the questions underlying subsidiarity make them inappropriate for the Court rather than the political institutions

[209] R Schütze, 'Subsidiarity after Lisbon: reinforcing the safeguards of federalism?' (2009) 58 *CLJ* 525.
[210] ibid.
[211] Bermann (above n 207).
[212] This is now stated in Art 5 TEU. For earlier statements see N Bernard, 'The Future of European Economic Law in the Light of the Principle of Subsidiarity' (1996) 33 *CML Rev* 633.

> ultimately to decide, it must surely be the case that if subsidiarity is a justiciable principle of judicial review, the institutions must be obliged to provide something more substantial by way of justification than a simple assertion that they consider the legislation to be compatible with the principle.[213]

Under discussion here is the question of whether it is enough that the EU's institutions simply declare in their legislation's preambles that the subject matter is not in breach of subsidiarity. On the other hand, an objection that has been voiced, is that a substantive discussion of subsidiarity would turn judges into explicit politicians. This 'catch 22' dilemma of how to monitor subsidiarity is well recognised in legal doctrine.[214] After all, the usual accusation is that the essence of subsidiarity is too vague to have merit as a legal principle.[215] So – *summa summarum* – the starting point when considering subsidiarity is that the EU's institutions are currently not applying it. As noted, the argument is that subsidiarity involves a political decision, which only political institutions should take.[216] The crux is that the principle of subsidiarity suffers the same shortcomingsthat is, it is treated lightly – whether applied by the Commission, the European Parliament or the Council. On the other hand, the Court has not refrained from making political choices in other areas, so from this perspective we could question why subsidiarity would be any different.[217]

Accordingly, we will begin this section by examining the principles of subsidiarity and proportionality as they form parts of Article 5 TEU and thereafter address it in the light of EU criminal law. The leading theme is again the increasingly active effectiveness principle. It is appropriate to begin the present exercise by briefly setting out the traditional 'effectiveness test'.

i. The Classic Effectiveness Criteria

When discussing the concept of subsidiarity there are clearly a number of 'better criteria' available. This is reflected in the so-called efficiency check of proposed legislation, which requires a comparative evaluation of the costs and benefits of action at the Community and national level.[218] This 'better criteria' analysis is thus commonly described as the comparative efficiency test,[219] where EU action must be, to put it simply, more effective than action at the national level. More specifically, the Community should act only if the action in question cannot be achieved

[213] G de Búrca, 'The Principle of Subsidiarity and the Court of Justice as an Institutional Actor' (1998) 36 *Journal of Common Market Studies* 217.

[214] eg G de Búrca, 'Reappraising Subsidiarity's Significance after Amsterdam', Jean Monnet paper 7/1999. www.jeanmonnetprogram.org/papers/99/990701.html (last accessed January 2012).

[215] eg D Wyatt, 'Is Subsidiarity too Vague as a Legal Principle' in K Nicolaidis and S Weatherill (eds), *Whose Europe? National Models and the Constitution of the European Union* (European Studies at Oxford, 2003) 86 available at www.europeanstudies.ox.ac.uk/ (last accessed January 2012).

[216] eg De Búrca (above n 213).

[217] Cf De Búrca (above n 214).

[218] L Senden, *Soft Law in the European Union* (Oxford, Hart Publishing, 2004) 83–84.

[219] P Craig, *EU Administrative Law* (Oxford, Oxford University Press 2006) 422.

by the individual Member States and the EU can better achieve the desired result because of its effects or scale.[220] The problem, however, is how to interpret these criteria in practice. One difficulty is that the notion of effectiveness suggests in itself various other criteria, such as whether a given level of government is in the best position geographically or in terms of access to information.[221] However, part of the difficulty appears to be that there will be many areas in which the comparative efficiency test comes out in favour of EU action, as the very *raison d'être* of the EU will often demand supranational action to ensure the 'effectiveness' of EU law.[222] In other words, it will always be possible to argue that EU action is necessary and that the efficiency test would favour the supranational arena.

Although the efficiency test as a component of subsidiarity connects to the familiar concept of 'better regulation' and more lately 'smart regulation',[223] for structural reasons the notions of impact assessment and better regulation will be dealt with in the case study provided below in chapter five and will therefore not be examined here. Nevertheless, this part will dip into the Stockholm programme as an example of a regulatory document, in the context of the balancing mechanisms within the AFSJ and EU criminal law in particular.

ii. The Concept of Subsidiarity Proper

The notion of subsidiarity viewed from a historical perspective derives originally from Roman Catholic philosophy. Here, in theological terms and for the benefit of the organisation of society, the view was that responsibility for state action is better undertaken by small groups.[224] Therefore, the purpose of subsidiarity is to avoid rigid centralisation and in the context of EU law is not only found in Article 5 (1 and 3) TEU. Further, as noted, Article 1 TEU encompasses the idea of subsidiarity by stating that decisions shall be taken as closely as possible to the individual citizen. A change introduced in the Lisbon Treaty, apart from the participation of national parliaments discussed below, is that subsidiarity has its own place in Article 69 TFEU within the AFSJ. Moreover, it could be said that the concept of subsidiarity is reflected in Article 4(1) TEU which stipulates that the Union shall respect the Member States' national identities and have an institutional framework that shall serve the interests of its citizens and the Member States. Nevertheless, the idea of subsidiarity was active long before the entry into force of the Lisbon Treaty and goes back to before the Maastricht Treaty. In short, subsidiarity as a legal concept can be traced back to the adoption of legal instruments, such as the philosophy underpinning directives, but it may also be

[220] ibid.

[221] De Búrca (above n 214).

[222] Craig (above n 219).

[223] Commission, 'Smart regulation in the European Union' (Communication), COM/2010/0543 final. The Commission believes that it is now time to step up a gear. 'Better regulation must become smart regulation and be further embedded in the Commission's working culture'.

[224] eg N Emiliou, 'Subsdiarity: An Effective Barrier against "the Enterprise of Ambition"' (1992) 17 *EL Rev* 383; C Henkel, 'Allocation of Powers in the European Union' (2002) 20 *Berkeley Journal of International Law Journal* 359.

identified in the so-called 'new' approach to harmonisation initiated in the SEA era, which involves minimum approximation.[225] As already explained, despite such a codification, the subsidiarity principle has remained a rather hazy concept. In an attempt to remedy this lack of clarity, the first Protocol No 30 (forerunner to the Lisbon Protocol) on the application of subsidiarity and proportionality was agreed and was attached to the Amsterdam Treaty in the late 1990s. However, there seems to be a consensus that the very notion of subsidiarity is very fluid and/or vague and consequently that subsidiarity identifies the debate about EU competences rather than resolving it.[226]

In any event, any discussion of subsidiarity must start with a short note on the new Protocol No 2 on the Application of the Principles of Subsidiarity and Proportionality as attached to the Lisbon Treaty, which replaces Protocol No 30 as previously attached to the Amsterdam Treaty. Briefly, this important protocol declares that the Commission must consult widely when proposing on legislation and that it must furnish reasons as to why an objective is better achieved at the EU level which are supported by qualitative and, wherever possible, quantitative indicators.[227] Furthermore, the protocol makes it clear that subsidiarity applies when checking whether a measure is still needed.

Looking more closely at Protocol No 2, Article 5 reveals that:

> Draft legislative acts shall be justified with regard to the principles of subsidiarity and proportionality. Any draft legislative act should contain a detailed statement making it possible to appraise compliance with the principles of subsidiarity and proportionality. This statement should contain some assessment of the proposal's financial impact and, in the case of a directive, of its implications for the rules to be put in place by Member States, including, where necessary, the regional legislation. The reasons for concluding that a Union objective can be better achieved at Union level shall be substantiated by qualitative and, wherever possible, quantitative indicators.[228]

It is difficult to pin down exactly what the aspects in question mean: that is, how concrete do they need to be?[229] In any event, it confirms what Dehousse once referred to as the 'double-edged sword of subsidiarity',[230] in that it could be used to both expand and restrict action. Nevertheless, it seems as if the Court will not lightly overturn EU action for non-compliance with subsidiarity. Indeed, AG Geelhoed's approach in the *BAT*[231] case is illuminating in determinating the cur-

[225] eg De Búrca (above n 214).

[226] S Weatherill, 'Better Competence Monitoring' (2005) 30 *EL Rev* 23.

[227] Moreover, the Commission must submit an annual report to the Council, the European Council and the EP.

[228] However, when viewed against the old wording of Art 5 of the now repealed Amsterdam Protocol is it interesting that the transnational aspect has been deleted. More specifically, the old protocol stated that: 'for Community action to be justified the following guidelines should be used in examining whether the subsidiarity condition is fulfilled: the issue under consideration has transnational aspects which cannot be satisfactorily regulated by action by Member States'.

[229] ibid.

[230] R Dehousse, *The European Court of Justice* (London, Macmillan, 1998) 161.

[231] Case C-491/01 *ex p BAT and Imperial Tobacco* [2002] ECR I-11543, Opinion delivered on 10 September 2002.

rent attitude to subsidiarity. It should be recalled that he rather dismissively stated that: 'The issue of subsidiarity may, in my view, be easily disposed of . . . the Court can, without going into unduly detailed reasoning, confirm that the principle of subsidiarity has not been infringed.' So why then aspire towards subsidiarity at all?

iii. Why Subsidiarity?

It seems clear that there is no exact limit to the Union's competence in the context of subsidiarity and any formal legal boundary that we make will be constantly changing.[232] Therefore, it should be observed that EU scholars have long distinguished between the procedural and substantive sides of this coin.[233] Briefly, the principle of substantive subsidiarity gives the EU institutions guidance as to whether or not the EU should act – that is, whether it is appropriate – which links with proportionality. An example of substantive subsidiarity reasoning is provided in the *Biotechnology* case.[234] In paragraph 32 of this ruling the Court held that:

> The objective pursued by the Directive . . . could not be achieved by action taken by the Member States alone. As the scope of that protection has immediate effects on trade, and, accordingly, on intra-Community trade, it is clear that, given the scale and effects of the proposed action, the objective in question could be better achieved by the Community.

Again, the lightness of the review of subsidiarity is striking. There is no real test but simply an assumption that the supranational arena is the correct forum. The notion of procedural subsidiarity, however, involves a number of conditions that the EU institutions have to fulfil. Generally, the common view is that the Court ought to be tougher when considering whether the procedural principle has been taken into account. Nonetheless, the dividing line between substantive and procedural subsidiarity is quite narrow.[235]

Nevertheless, as noted, most EU law scholars in the current EU legal debate seem to be of the view that subsidiarity as a legal notion is too vague to be reviewable by the Court and furthermore it is a political question. Many commentators have celebrated the concept of procedural subsidiarity as having greater potential than that of a substantive notion.[236] In any case, the Lisbon Treaty explicitly says in Article 8 of Protocol No 2 that the Court has jurisdiction to consider infringement of subsidiarity under Article 263 TFEU as brought by the Member States or as notified by them in accordance with the their legal order on behalf of their national parliament or a chamber of it. This has always been the case although this is the first time it has been so explicit.

[232] De Búrca (above n 214).

[233] eg T Tridimas, *General Principles of EU Law* (Oxford, Oxford University Press, 2006) ch 9.

[234] Case C-377/98 *Netherlands v Parliament and Council* [2001] ECR I-7079.

[235] A Estella, *The EU Principle of Subisidiarity and its Critique* (Oxford, Oxford University Press, 2002) 157.

[236] Tridimas (above n 233).

iv. National Identity as the New 'Safeguard Clause'

A further novelty offered by the Lisbon Treaty is the national (and constitutional) identity clause as set out in Article 4 (2) TEU. Arguably, this national identity clause is connected to the subsidiarity principle, as it insists on respecting Member State values. Yet however appealing this new Article 4 TEU may look at first sight, it is submitted that this provision is one of the most schizophrenic articles in the Lisbon Treaty. In its first paragraph it stipulates the principle of conferral. Thereafter it states that the Union shall respect the national identity clause.[237] It also states that national security remains the sole responsibility of the Member States. Interestingly, paragraph 3 of this provision subsequently sets out the famous loyalty obligation. As was seen in chapter three, the loyalty obligation has been one of the strongest and most forceful principles in the history of the Lisbon Treaty and is closely connected to the issue of effectiveness and consistency. It is, therefore, unclear what national identity means in the context of effectiveness. It is also unclear as to whether 'national identity' is the same as 'constitutional identity' as referred to by the German Constitutional Court in its Lisbon judgment where the criminal law was extensively discussed. We will return to this judgment in Part VI.[238] The aim here was simply to point out the multifacited function of 'subsidiarity'. So the EU's aspiration to respect subsidiarity is also mirrored in the EU's desire to respect Member State values (to the *extent* that these values can actually be separated from EU values).

C. The Concept of Proportionality

The principle of proportionality is as complex as the principle of subsidiarity. As with most EU law principles it also has a European background, but is not, as subsidiarity, derived from Catholic values but rather from German hard core administrative law.[239] It is often said that the concept of proportionality constitutes the doctrinal core of any transnational constitutionalism.[240] The Lisbon Treaty introduces something new on this subject. Article 7 TEU states that the Union shall ensure consistency between its policies and activities. 'Consistency' in this book has been taken to mean 'effectiveness', but it has, surely, a proportionality element to it too. Generally, proportionality in EU law is taken to mean balancing means and ends where the notion of 'appropriateness' constitutes the

[237] Case C-208/09 *Ilonka Sayn-Wittgenstein v Landeshauptmann von Wien* judgment of 22 December 2010 not yet reported.

[238] We will briefly return to this issue in Part V on the constitutional debate in the EU and implications it might have for the constitutional dimension of criminal law. BVerfG 2 BvE 2/08 from 30 June 2009, discussed below.

[239] eg N Emiliou, *The Principle of Proportionality in European Law* (The Hague, Kluwer Law Publishing, 1996).

[240] A Stone Sweet, 'All Things in Proportion? American Rights Doctrine and the Problem of Balancing' available at works.bepress.com/cgi/viewcontent.cgi?article=1034&context=alec_stone_sweet (last accessed January 2012).

golden thread for deciding on EU action. Although, as mentioned, this principle has been considered to be a better legal tool than the abstract notion of subsidiarity,[241] here too the Court has been criticised for not understanding what proportionality means in the context of law making.[242] As noted above, it is often suggested that the principle of proportionality should be regarded as a wider principle than subsidiarity, even if there is a clear overlap between them.[243] The difference is that proportionality also applies to areas under the exclusive competence of the Union as stipulated in Article 5 TEU. Nevertheless, these principles are sometimes fused together as one concept, which makes it difficult to discern each one separately. The accusation is that the Court's analysis of proportionality remains peculiarly abstract with general invocations of the limits of judicial review and the, political nature of social and economic choices.[244] Despite this, it is commonly held, first that the exercise of competence has to be appropriate or suitable – it must be reasonably effective to achieve the aim for which the competence has been granted; secondly, that the exercise of competence must be indispensable; and thirdly that such exercise of competence must be proportionate in the strict sense – the adverse effect on other interests must be weighed against the positive effect that the exercised competence entails for the objective pursued by it.[245] This is the 'manifestly inappropriate' template as applied by the Court.

i. The Court and Proportionality

Kumm has argued that the Court does not understand proportionality and confuses it with the general proportionality framework as traditionally applied within the general area of free movement.[246] More specifically, he argues that while 'proportionality' is about the balancing of interests, jurisdictional concerns are about assessing the means/ends relationship, and that the latter needs to be distinguished from the context of fundamental rights and substantive policy concerns. Nevertheless, it has been pointed out that the Court allows the authority concerned a wide discretion and only considers whether the EU legislator has made an obvious error – to which the answer is rarely yes.[247] According to some commentators, action is indispensable where it cannot be replaced by an alternative action that would have equal effectiveness having regard to the intended aim and would be less detrimental to another aim or interest protected by Union law.[248] Tridimas has pointed out that the principle of proportionality in the Court has

[241] Davies (above n 208).

[242] M Kumm, 'Constitutionalising Subsidiarity in Integrated Markets: The Case of Tobacco Regulation' (2006) 12 *ELJ* 503.

[243] C Timermanns, 'Subsidiarity and Transparency' (1999) 22 *Fordham International Law Journal* 106.

[244] Estella (above n 235).

[245] Senden (above n 218) 88.

[246] Kumm (above n 242).

[247] ibid.

[248] K Lenaerts and P Van Nuffel, *Constitutional Law of the European Union* (London, Sweet & Maxwell, 2005) 112.

become an unreliable basis on which to question economic and social policies and tame Community competences.[249] Moreover, he holds that proportionality should not be considered in isolation but in the context of Article 5 TEU as a whole, as examining these separately may be misleading. However, in practice, this has not been the case. As explained, the Court and the EU legislator use the same reasoning. It is submitted that although it is highly desirable to pay attention to Article 5 TEU as a whole, there is a risk that blurring of the boundaries between these principles could lead to discrepancies.

This chapter now addresses the question of to the extent to which the Lisbon Treaty will make these principles more visible in practice, before looking at their meaning in the specific context of EU criminal law.

D. Will the National Parliaments do the Trick?

According to Article 12 TEU, the national parliaments shall contribute actively to the efficient functioning of the Union. Indeed, one of the most important innovations in the Lisbon Treaty regarding subsidiarity is that the Treaty imposes an obligation on the Commission to send legislative initiatives to the national parliaments at the same time as to the EU institutions.[250] Thereafter, the national parliaments have eight weeks to draft a statement of any objection as to why the proposed legislation does not comply with subsidiarity. If the national parliaments expressing concern about non-compliance represents one-third of the votes – or one-quarter for proposals in the AFSJ allocated to these parliaments, there is a duty to review the proposal. This is the 'yellow card system', as in football, where if an EU measure appears to go beyond its constitutional limits it is deemed unfair and incurs a warning.[251] The Commission may then maintain, amend or withdraw the draft giving reason for its decision. As observed by one commentator, the big mistake with this Protocol has been the decoupling of subsidiarity and proportionality.[252] So proportionality is excluded in the monitoring process in the national parliaments despite the artificial distinction, as examined above, between these principles that makes such distinction difficult to uphold in practice.

[249] Tridimas (above n 233).

[250] P Craig, *The Lisbon Treaty, Law, Politics and Treaty Reform* (Oxford, Oxford University Press, 2010) 184–86; P Kiiver, 'The Treaty of Lisbon: the National Parliaments and the Principle of Subsidiarity' (2008) 15 *Maastrict Journal of European and Comparative Law* 77.

[251] S Weatherill, 'Competence and Legitimacy' in C Barnard and O Odudu (eds) *The Outer Limits of EU Law* (Oxford, Hart Publishing, 2009) 1; Craig (ibid), House of Lords EU Committee 'Strengthening national parliamentary scrutiny of the EU – the Constitution's subsidiarity early warning mechanism' available at www.publications.parliament.uk/pa/ld200405/ldselect/ldeucom/101/10102.htm (last accessed January 2012); M Gennert, 'Les Parlements Nationaux dans le Traité de Lisbonne: Evolution ou Révolution' (2010) 17 *Cahiers de droit Europeen* 46/1–2; and A von Bogdandy and J Bast, 'The Federal Order of Competences' in A von Bogdandy and J Bast, *Principles of European Constitutional Law* (Oxford/ Munich, Hart/Beck/Nomos, 2010) 275. I Cooper, 'The Watchdogs of Subsidiarity: National Parliaments and the Logic of Arguing in the EU' (2006) 44 *Journal of Common Market Studies* 281.

[252] Weatherill, ibid.

The reasoned opinion procedure mechanism in national parliaments is only available for actions taken under Article 352 TFEU and not for actions taken under Article 114 TFEU, which is highly regrettable.[253] More specifically, under Article 352(2) TFEU the Commission must draw national parliaments' attention to proposals made under the flexibility clause, using the new procedure for monitoring the subsidiarity principle.[254] Thus, the national parliaments could then monitor Article 352 TFEU as a whole, that is, also on the grounds of proportionality and competence. This is different from Article 114 TFEU where they would only be competent to monitor subsidiarity.[255] Moreover, the point is that it is unclear whether this provision is intended to act with reference to the 'yellow card' system or whether it is meant to materially extend the national parliaments' power to issue reasoned opinions so as also to cover proposals for the adoption of non-legislative measures under Article 352 TFEU, which would otherwise fall outside the scope of the 'yellow card' system.[256] In any case, the reasoned opinion procedure could at least provoke a more open political/constitutional debate about when resort to Article 352 TFEU is justified.[257]

Furthermore, as noted above, Article 8 of Protocol No 2 on the application of the principles of subsidiarity and proportionality refers to Article 263 TFEU, which means that the Court has jurisdiction to consider infringements of subsidiarity. This has always been the case even though the crux of the matter has been the political sensitivity of the issue.[258] However, it is remarkable that there is no direct access to Court for national parliaments but rather an action is dependent on Article 263 TFEU and the normal requirements for action for annulment.[259]

It is, of course, an open question as to how thorough-going such a review by the Court could and ought to be in terms of substantive reasoning. Nonetheless, there is reason to believe – again as observed by Weatherill,[260] that the use of the new *ex ante* monitoring system will provide the basis for a slightly more intensive *ex post* control by the Court. It could also be argued that in future the Court will refrain from such intervention if the Member States had already approved the proposed legislation in question during the rather extensive *ex ante* monitoring process should the situation arise where only one Member State brought an action. There is one exception to this however. Article 4 of Protocol No 1 on the Role of National Parliaments in the EU grants exceptions to the eight-week monitoring process rule in urgent cases. This is of particular relevance in the area of criminal law and

253 ibid.

254 M Dougan, 'The Treaty of Lisbon 2007: Winning Minds, Not Hearts' (2008) 45 *CML Rev* 617.

255 For a slightly different view see P Craig (above n 250) at 184–85.

256 ibid. The latter interpretation seems to be more in keeping with the restrictive spirit of the new 'flexibility clause', but this is not obvious from the actual wording of Art 352 TFEU.

257 D Wyatt, 'Could a Yellow Card for National Parliaments Strengthen Judicial as well as Political Policing of Subsidiarity?' (2006) 2 *Croatian Yearbook of European Law & Policy* 1.

258 On the changes brought by Lisbon, see S Weatherill, 'The Limits of Legislative Harmonisation Ten Years after Tobacco Advertising: How the Court's Case Law has become a "Drafting Guide"' (2011) 12 *German Law Journal* 827.

259 A von Bogdandy and J Bast (above n 251).

260 Weatherill (above n 258).

the fight against terrorism, and could become a good testing ground for more vigorous scrutiny in the Court. Thus, it is plausible that the Court will act as a more aggressive watchdog of subsidiarity in this area.

Therefore, the framework provided by the Lisbon Treaty could serve an important function in striking a balance between political assessment and judicial control.[261] However, it is not clear how useful a monitoring system by the national parliaments would be in practice,[262] as many national parliaments are likely to adopt the position adopted by the Member State in Council.[263]

Moreover, within the field of the AFSJ, there are special mechanisms for monitoring EU legislation.[264] Apart from the emergency brake procedure and the enhanced cooperation mechanisms discussed in chapter two which will be examined in Part IV, there are further, more specific roles for the national parliaments outside the realm of law making.[265] More specifically, Article 70 TFEU makes it clear that the national parliaments should take part in the evaluation of EU policies in the AFSJ. This article states that:

> Without prejudice to Articles 258, 259 and 260, the Council may, on a proposal from the Commission, adopt measures laying down the arrangements whereby Member States, in collaboration with the Commission, conduct objective and impartial evaluation of the implementation of the Union policies referred to in this Title by Member States' authorities, in particular in order to facilitate full application of the principle of mutual recognition. The European Parliament and National Parliaments shall be informed of the content and results of the evaluation.

As pointed out by Peers, these evaluation measures are non-legislative acts to be adopted by QMV in the Council on a proposal from the Commission with no direct involvement of the European Parliament.[266] This evaluation process is also reflected in the Stockholm programme, discussed in further detail below.

Article 69 TFEU is an additional safeguard of subsidiarity as it makes it clear that subsidiarity has an important or privileged status in EU criminal law to which we will now turn.

[261] Wyatt (above n 257).

[262] G Davies, 'The Post-Laeken Division of Competences' (2003) 28 *EL Rev* 686; Weatherill (above n 251).

[263] See eg, K Auel, 'Democratic Accountability and National Parliaments: Redefining the Impact of Parliamentary Scrutiny in EU Affairs' (2007) 13 *ELJ* 487. P Kiiver, 'The Early Warning System for the Principle of Subsidiarity: The National Parliament as a Conseil d'Etat for Europe' (2011) 36 *EL Rev* 98; Cooper (above n 251).

[264] For an overview see J-C Piris, *The Lisbon Treaty, A Legal and Political Analysis* (Cambridge, Cambridge University Press, 2010).

[265] M Fletcher, 'EU Criminal Law Justice: Beyond Lisbon' in C Eckes and T Konstantinides, *Crime within the AFSJ* (Cambridge, Cambridge University Press, 2011) 10.

[266] S Peers, *EU Justice and Home Affairs Law* (Oxford, Oxford University Press, 2011) ch 2.

E. Subsidiarity and Proportionality in EU Criminal Law

As explained above, while the principle of proportionality is exempted in the monitoring process in Protocol No 1 on the Role of National Parliaments, there first appears to be a similarly biased approach within the AFSJ. Thus, Article 69 TFEU singles out the importance of respect for subsidiarity in this area. This provision states that national parliaments shall ensure that the proposals and legislative initiatives submitted under chapters 4 and 5 comply with the principle of subsidiarity, in accordance with the arrangements laid down by the Protocol on the application of the principles of subsidiarity and proportionality. Thus, it is interesting that here too, under a literal reading, national parliaments are exempted from scrutinising proportionality. The exact meaning of this provision is unclear as this area is also subject to the 'normal' proportionality requirement stipulated in the Protocol on subsidiarity and proportionality. Obviously, attention to subsidiarity and proportionality is especially important in criminal law in order to avoid excessive criminalisation. Indeed, the need for delegation away from centralisation appears particularly important in the sensitive area of criminal law. After all, criminal law has its own principle of subsidiarity embedded in the idea of *ultima ratio*.[267] Briefly, this means that criminal law should be the last resort as a means of control. Although it is true that the concept of *ultima ratio* may be more of an ethical than a constitutional principle,[268] the basic idea is that criminal law should be reserved for the most serious invasion of interests. The reason for this is that less serious misconduct is more appropriately dealt with by civil law or administrative regulation.[269] When discussing criminalisation one has to ask whether there is an intelligible reason to undertake action: that is, whether the consequences of legislative action in the area in question are sufficiently clear, effective and precise.[270]

Nevertheless, the Lisbon Treaty appears unclear in its minimalistic approach to the use of criminal law (as an *ultima ratio*). It is true that it intensifies the national parliaments' participation in the monitoring process of subsidiarity.[271] The problem is that even if a competence could be established it seems as if the will to exercise that competence is stronger than the will to restrain action at the EU level. Admittedly, this problem is not unique to the EU as the debate on criminal law as an *ultima ratio* is readily transferable to the national level where more

[267] Opinion of AG Mazak in C-440/05, delivered on 28 June 2007, where he states that in the classic liberal tradition the subsidiarity principle indicates that a minimal sanction is at the same time optimal. On Subsidiarity in EU criminal law. This part draws on E Herlin-Karnell 'Subsidiarity in the Area of EU Justice and Home Affairs – A Lost Cause?' (2009) 15 *ELJ* 351. On subsidiarity in criminal law see also L Gröning, *EU staten och rätten att straffa* (Stockholm, Sandeus, 2008).

[268] N Jareborg, 'Criminalization as Last Resort (*ultima ratio*)' (2005) 2 *Ohio State Journal of Criminal Law* 531.

[269] See generally, A Ashworth, *Principles of Criminal Law* (Oxford, Oxford University Press, 2006).

[270] ibid.

[271] The Protocols on the Application of the Principles of Subsidiarity and Proportionality and the Protocol on the Role of the National Parliaments, annexed to the Lisbon Treaty.

criminal law is often seen to be a good criminal law policy.[272] Yet, the Commission's recent communication on the Stockholm programme, which sets up goals to be achieved within the next five years within the AFSJ as mentioned in chapter two, stresses the need to respect subsidiarity.[273] More specifically, the Commission states that criminal cooperation should be pursued in close cooperation with European Parliament, national parliaments and the Council and acknowledges that the focus will primarily remain on mutual recognition, and the harmonisation of offences and sanctions will be pursued for selected cases. This is to be welcomed because it recognises the sensitive nature of criminal law. The Commission's recent evaluation of subsidiarity and proportionality could also serve as an example of a document in which the Stockholm programme is listed as an example of an EU document which at least contains the 'words' subsidiarity or proportionality.[274]

In order to understand the problems in this area it might be useful outline the (short) history of the application of subsidiarity and proportionality in the area of criminal law. Under the previous third pillar regime, the principles of subsidiarity and proportionality were almost unnoticed. Indeed, the previous Protocol No 30 did not refer to the third pillar at all. However, ex Articles 1, 2 and 5 EU referred to subsidiarity and proportionality as European principles and so did the Twelfth Recital of the Preamble of the former TEU. For this reason, it has been suggested that the explanation for the lighter touch applied to the intergovernmental sphere was that it was already governed by a much softer form of cooperation.[275] After all, unanimity in the Council remedied some of this 'deficit'. Thus the Member States in Council were responsible for the light approach, not only to competence questions but also to the application of subsidiarity. Nonetheless, there is a real need to bring subsidiarity out of obscurity in this area. More specificly, from the perspective of this chapter there is a risk that should the suppression of terrorism in the EU following the attacks of 9/11, 'calm down', a rush towards general criminalisation could lead to a future backlash against the whole phenomenon of European criminal law. There are thus some common features with the EU financial crises regulation; even though this is a very different area the approach illustrates the current eagerness for doing 'something' which tends to result in rush legislation.[276] This is the same problem as for over-criminalisation; because it is often difficult to 'de-criminalise' or 'de-legislate', any action must rest on sound reasoning.[277] The present part of the chapter will explain why it is important to recognise subsidiarity in this area.

[272] Jareborg (above n 268).

[273] Commission, Delivering an area of freedom, security and justice for Europe's citizens Action plan implementing the Stockholm programme. (Communication) COM (2010) 171 at 5.

[274] COM (2010) 547 final, Report from the Commission on subsidiarity and proportionality, 12.

[275] P de Hert, 'Division of competences between National and European levels with regards to Justice and Home Affairs' in J Apap (ed), *EU Justice & Home Affairs* (Cheltenham, Edward Elgar, 2004) ch 4.

[276] I draw this parallel from a talk given by Prof Ellis Ferran, 'Financial Crises as a Driver of Law Reform: Where is it taking the EU?' Oxford Said Business School, 10 March 2011.

[277] See also (n 268).

An interesting example of subsidiarity outside its traditional playing field is provided by the General Court (then the CFI) in the *Ayadi* case.[278] Although this judgment concerned the second /first pillar distinction and the issue of the boundaries of Article 352 TFEU (as discussed in Part II), it is nonetheless useful – in the absence of concrete AFSJ examples – to look at this ruling in further detail. The *Kadi* case introduced a conjunctive reading of ex Articles 60, 301 (now Article 215 TEU) and 308 EC (now Article 352 TFEU) in order to move competence between the previous pillars. The case of *Ayadi* concerned, among other things, the issue of whether such competence reasoning was a breach of subsidiarity when applied to justify sanctions against individuals at EU level. The reasoning of the General Court (then the CFI) is so interesting that it deserves to be set out by paragraph:

> 108 The Court of First Instance considers, however, that this general principle [subsidiarity] cannot be relied on in the sphere of application of Articles 60 EC and 301 EC, even on the assumption that it does not fall within the exclusive competence of the Community (see, in this connection, Article 60(2) EC).
>
> 109 In fact, with regard to the interruption or reduction of economic relations with third countries, those very articles provide for action by the Community when that is 'deemed necessary
>
> . . .
>
> 111 Moreover, since the Court has accepted, in Kadi . . .. that the sphere of application of Articles 60 EC and 301 EC [now Article 215 TFEU] could be extended, by having recourse to the additional legal basis of Article 308 EC, to the adoption of economic and financial sanctions imposed on individuals in the battle against international terrorism even when no connection with third countries has been established, it must follow that the lawfulness of Community measures adopted on that basis in accordance with a CFSP common position or joint action of the Union cannot be challenged by individuals in the light of the principle of subsidiarity either.
>
> 112 In any event, even assuming that the principle of subsidiarity finds application in circumstances such as those of this case, it is plain that the uniform implementation in the Member States of Security Council resolutions, which are binding on all members of the United Nations without distinction, can be better achieved at Community level than at national level.

Indeed, this expresses the concerns outlined in Part II, that the use of 'necessary' appears very discretionary. When considering the proportionality requirement, the General Court concluded that the measure in question was 'necessary'. Here the General Court treated proportionality as a free movement/human rights concept, that is, as a balancing of interests. As noted above, it has been suggested by Kumm,[279] for example, that such an approach is wrong as proportionality in terms of legislative competence monitoring is slightly different – though exactly how it differs from competence remains somewhat ambiguous. In any case, this brings

[278] Case T-253/02 *Ayadi v Council* ECR [2006] II-2139, now pending Case C-403/06 P.

[279] Kumm above (n 242).

us to what subsidiarity and proportionality mean in the context of 'pure' criminal law. Before dissecting the notion of subsidiarity in the AFSJ setting in particular, it may be useful briefly to sketch out what it means to speak of subsidiarity in the area of criminal law.

i. The ultima ratio *of Criminal Law and the Principle of Subsidiarity*

As explained in the introduction to this work, criminal law is often considered as reflecting the principles at the core of a nation state (the right to punish its citizens and the power to decide on what ought to be criminalised) where a democratically-elected legislator is a precondition for the legitimacy of enacted legislation.[280] Accordingly, going beyond the so-called core crimes (*mala in se*, that is, crimes that will always be considered punishable),[281] De Sade's (pre-EU era) description: 'What is defined as a crime in France ceases to be such a few hundred miles away . . . it is all just matter of geography and opinion'[282] illustrates the cultural and philosophical underpinnings of why some acts are criminalised and others are not. More recently, it has been recommended that one way of preserving the political function of national borders in criminal law in the European context is the adoption of the principle of subsidiarity.[283] In order to understand why subsidiarity is important, a few points about criminal law should be examined.

Criminal law has its own principle of subsidiarity embedded in the *ultima ratio* concept.[284] Briefly, this means that criminal law should be the last resort as a means of control. Of course this issue is closely connected to what definition of a crime is adopted and it should consequently be remembered that the European Court of Human Rights has given a statement of what is to be regarded as a 'crime'.[285]The definition of a crime is important because only criminal law procedures can guarantee the presumption of innocence (Article 6 ECHR) requirement. Up to now the EU law debate has focused on the primary character of the first pillar. As explained earlier, there is clearly an overestimation of the deterrent effect of criminal law at the European level. It is submitted that criminal law should not be regarded as just another instrument in the EU legal toolbox and this is so regardless of the failings of the former third pillar with minimum transparency and the general 'democratic deficit' as well as the limited jurisdiction of the Court that characterised this area. At issue here, is the special character of crimi-

[280] See generally, eg G Corstens and J Pradel, *European Criminal Law* (The Hague, Kluwer Law Publishing, 2002).

[281] eg murder as opposed to, for instance, speed limit regulations. For example, C Clarkson and H Keating, *Criminal Law* (London, Sweet & Maxwell, 2003); A Norrie, *Crime, Reason and History* (London, Butterworths, 2001).

[282] D De Sade, *Justine or the Misfortunes of Virtue* (Ware, Wordsworth Editions, 1996) cited in C Lernested, *Kriminalisering* (Uppsala, Iustus, 2002) ch 1.

[283] De Hert above (n 275).

[284] ibid, where he states that in the classic liberal tradition the subsidiarity principle indicates that a minimal sanction is at the same time optimal.

[285] eg *Engel and others v Netherlands*, Series A, No 22; [1979–80] and *Orzuk v Germany*, Series A, No 73; [1984] 6 EHRR 365, 21 February 1984.

nal law, which can have dramatic consequences such as imprisonment and social stigma. However, as touched upon above, the question is wider still – and this is how it connects to subsidiarity in the traditional sense – in that the issue also concerns whether a supranational EU legislator would be too 'far from the people' to legislate in criminal law. In other words, it is not clear that the supranational level is automatically 'closest' to the people when operating in the criminal law. Expressed differently, EU citizens need to know what actions are criminal and who the legislator is. This may sound self-evident but in fact is not if, for example, we consider EU regulations, which merely refer to other regulations and thus render it impossible for non-lawyers to know which acts are permitted and which are not.[286] Therefore, it is once again to the history of ex Article 47 EU that this section now turns. The purpose of doing so is to examine is the relationship between the former Article 47 EU and subsidiarity in the context of EU criminal law and what implications it could have for the future of subsidiarity within the AFSJ and criminal law in particular.

ii. Subsidiarity and EU Criminal Law: The Paradoxes of Efficiency and Legitimacy

As discussed in Part II, the history of ex Article 47 EU shows us that the EC supranational stage took precedence in cross pillar conflicts and thereby overshadowed the EU intergovernmental terrain. Yet in fact, the principle of ex Article 47 EU was not in harmony with EU criminal law. It could even be suggested that the reliance on Article 47 EU in criminal law matters was not in line with Article 1 EU which famously stated not only the 'ever closer Union' maxim but also that decisions should be taken as openly as possible and as closely as possible to the citizen. The reason for this accusation is the difficulty of legitimising a supranational legislator in criminal law.

Looking in detail at Chapter 4 of Title V in the TFEU, it is evident that Article 82 TFEU sets out the principle of mutual recognition to constitute the main rule in EU criminal law cooperation.[287] This would certainly preserve much of the nation state 'feeling' in criminal law matters, and would therefore encompass a touch of 'subsidiarity', although there will be extensive opportunities to introduce accompanying legislation on procedural safeguards. Nevertheless, mutual recognition presupposes a common framework of underlying regulation in the name of foreseeability in criminal law which is itself complicated. There is thus a tension here between the concept of mutual recognition as better recognising subsidiarity in EU criminal law cooperation than the harmonisation of criminal law, and the need to fully respect the rights to defence and the protection of the individual. It brings us back to the previous discussion concerning the complex issue of supranational criminal law. Indeed, it should be added here that the ruling by the

[286] See the discussion in the context of criminal law and legality in Asp (n 204) ch 5 stating that so-called cross-referring between EU regulations regarding sanctions in, eg the area of agriculture is not in line with the principle of maximum certainty in criminal law.

[287] Arts III-270–272 CT.

Federal Constitutional Court in Germany, the BVerfG, on the conformity of the Lisbon Treaty with German constitutional law underlines the complexity of the issue.[288] The BVerfG held that although the criminal law (or, more properly, the right to 'punish') is in principle not amenable to integration, establishment of minimum rules not covering the substantive part of an offence could save the national autonomy in this area. It also stated that the principle of guilt or the subjective element (*mens rea*) of an offence is not reconcilable with a supranational legislator. Regardless of whether it is possible to successfully adopt a supranational model in this area, could the principle of subsidiarity serve as the intermediary in supranational criminal law? It is at least very interesting to note that AG Mazák in his Opinion in the *Ship source pollution* case[289] stated – and thereby attempted to revive subsidiarity from obscurity in these matters – that the Member States are generally better placed than the Community to 'translate' the requirement of 'effective, proportionate and dissuasive' criminal law penalties into their legal systems and social contexts.[290] Although the Court in this case did not explicitly spell out the word 'subsidiarity', it nonetheless nodded in its direction by concluding that it is for the Member States to decide on the level and type of the punishment. For this reason, AG Mazák's Opinion should serve as an important guideline in the debate on subsidiarity in EU criminal law in the future. This could also be said to be in line with the new national identity clause, as mentioned above, as provided by the Lisbon Treaty. It should be recalled that Article 4(2) TEU states that the Union shall respect the equality of Member States before the Treaties as well as their national identity inherent in their fundamental structures, political and constitutional, including regional and local self-government. Moreover, this provision states that 'national security' remains the sole responsibility of each Member State. Nonetheless, there may also be conceptual difficulties here in pinning down the exact meaning of national security in the context of criminal law. After all, is this not what criminal law, to a large extent, is about (that is, security aspects)?

Of course, embracing subsidiarity as the solution to EU criminal law in general would probably constitute a theoretical shortcut (the need for a 'democratically elected legislator in criminal law' argument). However, this chapter should not be read as 'if you can't beat them, join them'. What is at issue is how to link a supranational legislator with the principles of criminalisation and we will briefly return to this in chapter eight.

Finally, and regardless of the difficulty for the Court to enter into a discussion of substantive subsidiarity and thus the need for the EU's institutions to be more attentive in order to avoid the problem, the closely related notion of proportionality in EU criminal law needs to be addressed.

[288] *Lisbon*, BVerfG 2 BvE 2/08 from 30 June 2009.

[289] Case C-440/05 *Commission v Council* [2007] ECR I-9097.

[290] Opinion of AG Mazák delivered on 28 June 2007.

iii. The Impact of Proportionality in EU Criminal Law

The principle of proportionality in criminal law traditionally forms part of the sentencing process.[291] As observed by Ashworth, while the ECHR poses few constraints in this regard, other than the general message of Article 7 ECHR and the ban on retroactive criminal law, Article 49 of the Charter makes it clear that the severity of a penalty must not be disproportionate to the criminal offence. Although, as noted in chapter two and as stipulated in Article 51, the Charter is addressed to the EU institutions and the Member States when they are implementing Union law[292], there is good reason to believe that the Charter will have a wider impact in the area of EU criminal law.

So when it comes to sentencing the principle of proportionality is most significant in this area. Here, proportionality means that the punishment for an offence should be proportionate to the seriousness of the offence, taking into account the harm, wrongdoing and culpability involved. It is related to the issue of a fair trial because it insists that that appropriate legal safeguards have been respected.[293] Furthermore, it could be argued that the principle of non-discrimination in EU law forms part of proportionality in the context of EU criminal law as it is related to the very concept of 'fairness'. As the Court has frequently pointed out, the principle of non-discrimination requires that comparable situations must not be treated differently and that different situations must not be treated in the same way unless such treatment is objectively justified.[294] It is perhaps the most fundamental principle of Union law for it accounts for the very authority of supranational law. Hence, it is obvious that the notion of non-discrimination is also of utmost importance in criminal law as forming part of the broad concept of a fair trial. In this way, it is also connected to proportionality and the broader notion of fairness (and fair trial).

As was argued above, the principle of subsidiarity in EU law is reflected in the notion of criminal law as an *ultima ratio*. Similarly, it could be argued that the principle of proportionality is also, generally speaking, connected to the *ultimo ratio* principle. Nevertheless, even if linked with the last resort requirement, it could be argued that the principle of proportionality is better reflected in the very notion of justice. Moreover, the issue of whether something should be criminalised is linked to the 'appropriateness and necessity test'.[295] Thus, the question of the extent to which the *ultima ratio* principle has an independent normative func-

[291] 'Ask any American criminal law writer or analyst about proportionality, and her first thought will be sentencing, followed by the death penalty, some aspects of substantive criminal law, and, as a possible final afterthought, criminal procedure.' R Singer, 'Proportionate Thoughts about Proportionality' (2010) 8 *Ohio State Journal of Criminal Law* 217.

[292] For an overview see M Dougan, 'The Treaty of Lisbon 2007: Winning Minds, Not Hearts' (2008) 45 *CML Rev* 617.

[293] A Ashworth, 'Criminal Law, Human Rights and Preventive Justice' in A Norrie et al (eds), *Regulating Deviance* (Oxford, Hart Publishing, 2009) 87.

[294] See eg Case C-303/05 *Advocaten voor de Wereld* ECR [2007] I-3633.

[295] L Gröning, *EU, Staten och rätten att straffa* (Stockholm, Sandeus, 2008) 224.

tion rather than being derived (solely) from the proportionality principle is beyond the scope of this section. Proportionality in criminal law is concerned with the widely-felt distinctions between different kinds of offences and degrees of wrongdoing that are labelled so as to represent fairly the nature and magnitude of the law breaking.[296] Therefore, there is a link between proportionality, 'fair labelling' and maximum certainty in criminal law.

To complicate matters further, there are, generally speaking, two different aspects of proportionality in criminal law.[297] The first aspect concerns the link between the penal value of some conduct, ie the seriousness of such conduct and the severity of the penalty in question. The second matter concerns the relationship between means and goal. According to this view, the proportionality principle is breached if the legislation at stake is too severe or too lenient.[298] But proportionality in criminal law could be a question of self-defence, that is, whether an act carried out in order to avoid a crime being committed was proportionate to the harm caused.[299] Moreover, as mentioned in chapter two, the principle of proportionality is generally speaking different from the traditional administrative principle within EU law.[300] The reason for this is that the administrative principle can take into account future-oriented aspects and its broader impact on EU law while the principle of proportionality is restricted to the facts at hand. Consequently, the administrative principle is prospective and therefore different from the criminal law principle of proportionality, which is retrospective, that is, it requires that the penalty be proportionate to the seriousness of the infringement in question. Of course, these issues demonstrate the very complex nature of the supranational involvement in criminal law where the same principles have different meanings.

Finally, it is necessary to clarify the meaning of proportionality and subsidiarity within the AFSJ more generally. In other words, what does it mean to refer to a balancing exercise in the context of the AFSJ?

iv. The Bigger Question of Balancing in the AFSJ

It would be useful to briefly clarify the meaning of proportionality within the AFSJ more broadly. Such a clarification is particularly important in relation to the adequate protection of human rights at EU level. The question that needs asking, is what it means to refer to a balancing exercise in the AFSJ? Any discussion of balancing usually starts with a reference to the work of Alexy and the notion of

[296] See Ashworth, (above n 271) at 89; see also J Chalmers and F Leverick, 'Fair Labelling in Criminal Law' (2008) 71 *MLR* 217.

[297] N Jareborg, 'Criminalization as Last Resort (*ultima ratio*)' (2005) 2 *Ohio State Journal of Criminal Law* 53.

[298] ibid.

[299] eg A von Hirch and N Jareborg, 'Gauging Criminal Harm: A Living Standard Analysis' (1991) 11 *OJLS* 1.

[300] See, P Asp, 'Two Notions of Proportionality' in K Nuotio (ed) *Festschrift in honour of Raimo Lathi* (Helsinki, Helsinki University Press, 2007) 207.

rights-based proportionality review.[301] Such a discussion is often connected to the actual application of proportionality and balancing in courts where the discussion has been centred on 'rights' and to what extent rights could be adequately balanced.[302] However, our concern here is with the legislative arena. Indeed, the Lisbon Treaty was (to some extent) a child of political negotiations. This is what makes EU law challenging when searching for a general regime or balance in this area. After all, and to return to the issue of national identity, how could the EU live up to the consistency requirement as stipulated in Articles 7 TEU and 13 TEU while at the same time convincing the Member States that the EU does not undermine national identity in criminal law? Obviously, much will depend on the willingness of the Member States to pursue further integration in the AFSJ.

As already noted, the Charter plays an important role as it explicitly puts the ideas of legality and a proportionate penalty on the table. According to Article 51, the Charter applies when the Member States are implementing EU law. But it is exactly in this balancing exercise of new legislation that the Charter has a huge impact when deciding on the content of new criminalisation. Thus, as stipulated, Articles 47 to 49 of the Charter give strong guidance, as already noted in chapter two, by stipulating the legality and proportionality requirements.

Therefore, the central question is perhaps whether the new subsidiarity system with the national parliaments' participation will change the 'impact assessment' mechanisms and the need for them. Surely such impact assessments must become more politically structured, as one of their functions will now be to influence national parliaments. In this respect too, it appears to constitute something of a balancing exercise between the EU and the Member States. The effect of impact assessments will be discussed in further detail in chapter five; in the meantime it might be useful to address possible problems raised by the participation of national parliaments. In other words, although the assertion is that the national parliaments participation is a much warranted change, and therefore highly desirable as making the EU more democratic, there may in practice be some less desirable aspects to the EU federal architecture which could conceivably point in the direction of a harsher EU criminal law regime.

v. Will the Participation of National Parliaments in Subsidiarity Monitoring increase Penal Populism?[303]

The above subheading is intended to cause controversy. After all, a familiar argument by proponents for action at the EU level, in relation to criminal law policy

[301] R Alexy, *A Theory of Constitutional Rights* (Oxford, Oxford University Press, 2002), M Kumm, 'The Idea of Socratic Contestation and the Right to Justification: The Point of Rights-based Proportionality Review' (2010) 4 *Law & Ethics of Human Rights* 141.

[302] K Möller, 'Balancing and the Structure of Constitutional Rights' (2007) 5 *International Journal of Constitutional Law* 453.

[303] This section draws on E Herlin-Karnell, 'EU Competence in Criminal Law After Lisbon' ch 16 in A Biondi et al (eds), *European Union Law after the Treaty of Lisbon* (Oxford, Oxford University Press, forthcoming).

issues, is the fact that the citizens of Europe want the EU to be more actively involved in criminal law matters, especially in the fight against terrorism. It is true that public support is an important element in gaining approval of the EU project. And the EU should obviously be a democratic project. It should, nevertheless, be emphasised that the legitimacy of criminal law legislation requires much more than public approval.[304] The facilitation of penal populism at the EU level by relying on uncontextualised public opinion is unwise.[305] In other words, there are some fundamental rights and some crucial axioms in criminal law theory including the imperative of legality and the right to fair trial – as discussed above – which are absolute rights and hence not negotiable rights. But when dealing with criminal law and human rights protection it is necessary to adopt a critical stance and ask what concepts we are really dealing with and what it means for the development of an EU criminal law policy to rely on them. Looking at criminal law in the national arena, history tells us that the public often tend favour a more severe criminal law system (the tough-on-crime argument) despite the fact that further legislation does not always make the system more effective. Sound empirical research plays an important function here, but should be far from the only concern. Thus, it is important to move beyond mere opinion polling.[306] In other words, any empirical research needs to be very carefully examined and collected.[307]

F. Conclusion

As explained above, the protocols on subsidiarity and proportionality have attempted to reify the rather abstract concepts of subsidiarity and proportionality and to move away from 'blind' centralisation. As has also been shown, legal praxis paints a darker picture where the notions of subsidiarity and proportionality are not fully considered in EU law making. Yet the concepts of 'better law making', consultation and the philosophy underpinning directives indicate that the principles of subsidiarity and proportionality are still alive. This part of the chapter has highlighted the difficulty the Court has had in striking down legislation on the basis of subsidiarity without acting as the legislator.

This chapter has pointed to the importance of recognising subsidiarity and proportionality in EU criminal law. This part has attempted to show that the concepts of subsidiarity and proportionality in the AFSJ could – and should – be an aspiration closely connected to a minimalist approach to criminal law. One problem is that there seems to be an acute deficit in the knowledge of the criminal law within the EU institutions and this, for the time being, appears to render subsid-

[304] M Nolan, 'Law Reform, Beyond mere Opinion Polling and Penal Populism' in A Norrie et al (eds) *Regulating Device* (Oxford, Hart Publishing, 2009) 165.

[305] ibid.

[306] ibid.

[307] It is important to consider how one frames the questions, ibid.

iarity in EU criminal law a lost cause. Indeed, though 'impact assessments' and other evaluation exercises are steps in the right direction towards a more sophisticated attitude to EU legislation,[308] it does not help much if their outcomes are not sufficiently explained or analysed. It is, of course, true that for the emergence of a European criminal legal space, the protection of the individual should be at the top of the agenda insofar as the issue concerns where such legislation is best undertaken. As for criminalisation, an accompanying rule of thumb should be the principle of subsidiarity, as reflected in the *ultima ratio* of criminal law. The point is that excessive criminalisation is far from effective and therefore turns the traditional efficiency test in the EU upside down. Moreover, the value of justice is one of the objectives the EU seeks to safeguard. This mission is best reflected in a proportionate approach to criminal law at EU level.

The next Part of this chapter considers enhanced cooperation. Its purpose is to show how the notions of subsidiarity and enhanced cooperation are interrelated.

V. ENHANCED COOPERATION AND LOYALTY

A. Introduction

The purpose of this Part of the chapter is to go back to the specific question of EU criminal law, while at the same time continuing the discussion of EU competences more broadly, following on from the previous sections. Accordingly this Part seeks to map the EU constitutional terrain with regard to criminal law. The aim is to provide a brief overview of the architecture of 'flexibility' in terms of enhanced cooperation, and more specifically to show how such a phenomenon relates to the wider discussion of the scope of the constitutional powers in the EU. In short, the notion of enhanced cooperation opens up the possibility of flexibility whereby some Member States can go further towards integration than other less integration-minded States. Before the Lisbon Treaty, the mechanisms for enhanced cooperation were set out in ex Article 11 EC and Articles 40 EU and 43 EU. These provisions stipulated that no cooperation between the Member States may intrude on the competences of the EU, or distort competition.[309] Here, Article 43 EU acted as an executive provision, which governed the criteria as set out in Articles 11 EC and 40 EU governing the former first and the third pillars respectively. In doing so, this Article excluded cooperation which affected the competences, rights, obligations and interests of non-participants. Thus, in the context of enhanced cooperation, the whole question has been what to count in the *acquis communautaire* (as in the history of the vague ex Article 47 EU discussed above) as well as how to

[308] See, A Meuwese, *Impact Assessment in EU Lawmaking* (The Hague, Kluwer Law Publishing, 2008) 126–29.

[309] On the detail of these provisions, see T Konstadinides, *Division of Powers in the European Union* (Deventer, Kluwer Law Practice, 2009) ch 8.

apply the notion of loyalty towards the EU more broadly.[310] Therefore, the concept of enhanced cooperation and the history surrounding ex Article 47 TEU were united in their insistence on safeguarding the *acquis communautaire.*

More specifically, the section seeks to examine what is meant by the *acquis communautaire* in the context of EU criminal law after Lisbon and to consider whether the Lisbon Treaty offers anything new here. Finally, this part discusses the vague notion of loyalty in relation to the principle of subsidiarity in this regard and consider how such a concept relates to enhanced cooperation as an 'alternative to Union action'. It moves away from the matters discussed in the previous part on subsidiarity and proportionality to highlight the provision of enhanced cooperation. It will become clear that the establishment of enhanced cooperation reveals much of the same pattern as the question of judicial review in the area of subsidiarity monitoring discussed above, that is, that the Court's function and powers in this area are far from undisputed. However, this part does not deal with the Schengen *acquis*[311] nor the complexities of the Prüm Treaty,[312] which are beyond its scope.

B. The Concept of Enhanced Cooperation

As a result of the entry into force of the Lisbon Treaty,[313] the possibility of pursuing enhanced cooperation in the area of criminal law has increased dramatically. For example, should a Member State decide to use the emergency brake provision, as discussed in chapter two, which would permit a State to 'opt out' of criminal law legislation, the Lisbon Treaty is clear that the other States (nine or more) could still proceed by establishing enhanced cooperation. It is difficult to imagine how subsidiarity, discussed in Part IV, could play a major role here despite the 'alternative to Union action' character of enhanced cooperation and despite criminal law as the *ultima ratio.* In any event, it should be noted that prior to the Lisbon Treaty the EU Treaty regulation of enhanced cooperation has never been used, since, owing to its very high procedural thresholds in the form of restrictions regulating such cooperation, almost nothing has ever met the criteria.[314] Still, the very notion of enhanced cooperation lies in the same pathway as subsidiarity, because of its character as an alternative to Union action.[315] Indeed, it has

[310] S Weatherill, 'If I'd wanted you to understand I would have explained it better: What is the Purpose of the Provisions on Closer Co-operation introduced by the Treaty of Amsterdam?', in D O'Keeffe and P Twomey (eds), *Legal Issues of the Amsterdam Treaty* (Oxford, Hart Publishing, 1999) 21.

[311] See S Peers, *EU Justice and Home Affairs* (Oxford, Oxford University Press, 2011) ch 1.

[312] Convention between Belgium, Germany, Spain, France, Luxembourg, the Netherlands and Austria, signed in Prüm Germany on 27 May 2005.

[313] Treaty of Lisbon amending the Treaty on European Union and the Treaty establishing the European Community, signed at Lisbon, 13 December 2007, OJ C306 of 17 December 2007.

[314] M Dougan, 'The Unfinished Business of Enhanced Cooperation: Some Institutional Questions and their Constitutional Implications' in A Ott A and E Vos (eds), *50 Years of European Integration: Foundations and Perspectives* (The Hague, TMC Asser Press, 2009) 157.

[315] ibid.

been described as reflecting the anxiety among the Member States about the expansion of Community powers and therefore as representing a way for States to 'tap' on the brake.[316] As will be explained, however, the brake in question is rather imprecise. So the concept of enhanced cooperation is an expression of flexible integration as it accepts that there is room for action outside the 'traditional' EU model. Therefore, as expressed by one Advocate General, the notion of enhanced cooperation is a legal expression of the balancing exercise between 'making the Union wider and making it deeper'.[317]

As noted, however, prior to the entry into force of the Lisbon Treaty, the concept of 'enhanced cooperation' had never been used since very little has met the criteria since such cooperation could always be considered to fall within the ambit of the *acquis communautaire* or as distorting competition. In any case, the first ever use of the Treaty was recorded in 2010 regarding the law applicable to divorce and legal separation.[318] The second was concluded soon after in the area of unitary patent protection.[319] Still, enhanced cooperation in the area of criminal law has not been used so far. In spite of this, it seems as if fighting crime and terrorism are high priorities for the EU and Member States so there is strong reason to believe that cooperation will now become a legal reality. In spite of this, there is still a significant risk that cooperation within the area of the suppression of terrorism could touch on security questions and common foreign policy issues and therefore fall within the *acquis* of the Treaty of the EU, and moreover could be hard to reconcile with the spirit of loyalty to the EU. It appears as if the previously dormant character of the establishment of enhanced cooperation will come to an end, as the importance of combating crime and terrorism are currently high on the agenda for the EU and the Member States. In other words, there seems to be a willingness to move forward.

C. Emergency Brakes and Accelerators

It could be argued that the notion of 'enhanced cooperation' accepts that there is room for action outside the traditional EU model and that it is therefore

[316] Weatherill (above n 310).

[317] Case C-77/05 *United Kingdom v Council* [2007] ECR I-11459 and § 83 of the Opinion of AG Tristenjak delivered on 10 July 2007. See also A Faber, 'Theoretical approaches to EU Deepening and Widening A Multi-disciplinary Overview and Some Tentative (Hypo)theses', EU-CONSENT Project Publications, 2006, available at www.eu-consent.net/library/brx061012/WP%20II%20III%20Paper redefiningconcepts.pdf (accessed June 2011).

[318] December 2010/405 [2010] OJ L189/12. For a commentary, see S Peers, 'Divorce, European Style: The First Authorization of Enhanced Cooperation' (2010) 6 *European Constitutional Law Review* 339.

[319] Council Decision 2011/167/EU of 10 March 2011 authorising enhanced cooperation in the area of the creation of unitary patent protection There is currently a case pending for the annulment of this decision: Case C-295/11 *Italian Republic v Council of the European Union* [2011] OJ L 76/53. Italy argues, inter alia, that the enhanced cooperation procedure was authorised by the Council outside the limits provided for in the first subparagraph of Article 20 (1) TEU, according to which such a procedure is to be allowed only within the framework of the European Union's non-exclusive competences.

connected with the concept of subsidiarity. In the context of EU criminal law, the question of enhanced cooperation is also closely connected to the emergency brake provision, as mentioned above. In short, the Lisbon Treaty contains an emergency brake that permits Member States to apply a brake if the legislation in question would affect fundamental aspects of criminal law legislation.[320] Whether or not a single Member State pulls the emergency brake, the Lisbon Treaty provides for the possibility of enhanced cooperation for the remaining Member States. Articles 82 and 83 TFEU of the Lisbon Treaty respectively, state:

> In case of disagreement, and if at least nine Member States wish to establish enhanced cooperation on the basis of the draft directive concerned, they shall notify the European Parliament, the Council and the Commission accordingly. In such a case, the authorisation to proceed with enhanced cooperation referred to in Article 20(2) of the Treaty on European Union and Article 329 of this Treaty shall be deemed to be granted and the provisions on enhanced cooperation shall apply.[321]

Briefly, this means that there is no obligation as set out in Article 329 TFEU of the Lisbon Treaty to address a request to the Commission, specifying the scope and objectives of the enhanced cooperation in question. Neither is there an obligation (as Article 20(2) TFEU of the Lisbon Treaty reads) that the Council as a last resort shall adopt the decision at issue. In addition, there is no obligation to consult the European Parliament. This raises two questions. First, it is possible to argue that the mere fact that the Member States do not need to show the last resort requirement as stated in Article 20(2) TFEU can be regarded as being in disharmony with the sensitive character of criminal law as the *ultimo ratio*. Secondly, there is a risk that such cooperation could result in varying views on what exactly it means to refer to freedom, security and justice in multi-speed Europe.[322]

Moreover, it seems clear that the Court will face a number of difficulties in this area in particular around the problem of justicability.[323] For example, one could legitimately ask whether the Court's jurisdiction will only cover the establishment of enhanced cooperation or if it also covers the actual exercise of such cooperation (which it probably will as long as the cooperation in question is Treaty-based).[324] This will not only be the case with the initial decision to establish enhanced cooperation but also in the observance of the conditions to the admission of an existing enhanced cooperation regime. Yet, it could be argued that the Court will consider such a ruling too political and therefore choose not to inter-

[320] This issue will be explored in ch 7 on the Lisbon Treaty and therefore is not dwelt upon in this section.

[321] S Kurpas et al, 'The Treaty of Lisbon: Implementing the Institutional Innovations' (2007) available at www.ceps.eu/files/book/1554.pdf (last accessed January 2012).

[322] S Carrero and F Geyer, The Reform Treaty and Justice and Home Affairs (2007), available at www.libertysecurity.org/IMG/pdf_The_Reform_Treaty_Justice_and_Home_Affairs.pdf (last accessed January 2012).

[323] F Amtenbrink and D Kochenov, 'Towards a More Flexible Approach to Enhanced Cooperation' in A Ott and E Vos (eds) *50 Years of European Integration: Foundations and Perspectives* (The Hague, TMC Asser, 2009) 181.

[324] cf C Lyons, 'Closer Co-operation and the Court of Justice' in G de Búrca and J Scott (eds), *Constitutional Change in the EU, From Uniformity to Flexibility?* (Oxford, Hart Publishing, 2000) 95.

vene in much the same way as with the sensitive question of whether the Court should – and could – strike down EU law measures for incompliance with substantive subsidiarity.[325]

The UK and Ireland opt-outs create further complexity. These Member States' 'ergonomically-designed-mini-brakes' are set out in Protocol No 21 as well as Protocol No 36 on transitional provisions whereby the UK and Ireland have the opportunity not to participate in future AFSJ legislation. This is a highly convoluted area and concerns the phenomenon of a multi-speed AFSJ. The opt-out/opt-in system and how it will work in future is beyond the scope of this chapter.[326] Nevertheless, it should be noted that it remains unclear how, for example, mutual recognition will function in this regard if not all the Member States are participating. The same goes for the emergency brake. After all, Article 82 TFEU stipulates that as regards the very concept of mutual recognition there is no opportunity for the Member States to pull an emergency brake. There is, however, an opportunity with respect to the enactment of legislation to the extent necessary to facilitate mutual recognition in criminal law cooperation matters having a cross-border dimension such as the rights of individuals in criminal law procedure. In conclusion, it remains unclear to what extent the concept of mutual recognition could function adequately here without the participation of all the Member States.

In any case, it is sometimes pointed out[327] that a way of avoiding the difficult question of cross-border crime in an enlarged Union is to emphasise regional forms of enhanced cooperation, as such flexibility may provide tailor-made responses to region-specific criminal activities instead of the 'one size fits all' template provided by a programme of harmonisation. In addition, the phenomenon of enhanced cooperation may constitute a more effective solution than the 'lowest common dominator' agreements provided for by the Treaty.[328] A further dimension can be added here, as the possibility of enhanced cooperation in criminal law in emergency brake situations also begs the question of what such cooperation means – from the perspective of the Member State that pulled the brake. This may sound paradoxical as under the previous Treaty structure it was generally accepted that it is the Member States pursuing enhanced cooperation that are under a loyalty obligation and not the other way round. Furthermore, the establishment of enhanced cooperation is traditionally felt to lie in the same pathway as EU subsidiarity as it accepts that there is room for action outside the EU model.[329] However, in the setting of EU criminal law, the picture is less clear.

[325] Dougan (above n 314) 157.

[326] E Fahey, 'Swimming in a Sea of Law: Reflections on Water Borders, Irish (- British)- Euro Relations and Opting Out and Opting In After the Lisbon Treaty' (2010) *CML Rev* 673.

[327] M den Boer, 'Crime and the Constitution: A Brief Chronology of Choices and Circumventions' (2004) 11 *Maastrict Journal of European and Comparative Law* 143.

[328] ibid; G Majone, 'One Market, One Law, One Money? Unintended Consequences of EMU, Enlargement and Eurocentricity', LSE Law, Society and Economy Working Papers 1/2007, available at www.lse.ac.uk/collections/law/wps/wps.htm (last accessed January 2011).

[329] S Weatherill, 'Finding Space for Closer Cooperation in the Field of Culture' in De Búrca and J Scott (eds) (above n 323) 237.

D. Loyalty, Yes but in What *Direction*?

In fact, the establishment of enhanced cooperation particularly under the regime provided by the Lisbon Treaty, appears to be ambiguous if we consider the general principle of loyalty, which has become universally codified with the Treaty of Lisbon. Consequently, the loyalty principle is now also explicitly applicable in the former third pillar field. As stated, the 'last resort' solution requirement as set out in Article 20(2) TEU of the Lisbon Treaty does not need to be complied with in criminal law if a Member State has pulled the emergency brake. This would confront it with principles of criminal law policy. At issue here is the fact that it may not always be in the EU's interest to move forward and in this regard the possible disharmony with subsidiarity comes to the fore as well as the criminal law principle that any criminalisation must be the last resort as means of control.

The core of the issue in the present context is the obligation of loyalty as set out in Article 4(3) TEU. To repeat from previous chapters, it seems as if loyalty via the *Pupino* judgment[330] has transformed itself into a European axiom. Accordingly, one may ask – in the framework of the Lisbon Treaty and as already implied above – whether it would be the Member State that pulled the emergency brake in criminal law that would be under a loyalty obligation rather than the other Member States. As indicated, this would be in contrast to enhanced cooperation under, for example, ex Article 11 EC where it would be the Member States pursuing closer cooperation that would be under a loyalty requirement towards the Community. This poses two immediate questions: first, whether 'moving forward' is always the best alternative. Secondly, and as already outlined in the previous chapters, whether it really is feasible to treat criminal law as one EU policy among others. It is once again submitted that criminal law does not suit the traditional pattern of EU law making as law making requires a more sophisticated approach in which the aspiration of uniformity or consistency is not enough to take precedence over fundamental principles of criminal law. Indeed, the whole question links to the wider debate on subsidiarity and its function in the AFSJ and EU criminal law.

The point is that the emergency brake as invented in the ill-fated Constitutional Treaty (CT) and maintained in the Lisbon Treaty, is far from a solution, as it raises as many issues as it attempts to solve. Furthermore, although the Lisbon Treaty abolishes the pillar structure, it provides for two Treaties (TFEU and TEU) where all issues on external relations are confined to the TEU. In the context of EU criminal law cooperation, this raises some interesting issues. In the field of anti-terrorist financing, for example, there is no clear dividing line between internal and external security, despite the Lisbon Treaty's attempt to draw one, which makes it difficult to pin down just what the *acquis communautaire* – post Lisbon – entails and hence where the boundaries of enhanced cooperation lie.

So imagine the following scenario: nine Member States wish to go further by establishing enhanced cooperation despite the fact that the emergency brake has

[330] Case C-105/03 *Pupino* [2005] ECR I-5285.

been pulled. If the proposed legislation concerns the fight against terrorism the problem seems to be one of how to demarcate internal and external security. More specifically, the question arises of how to view the relationship between loyalty obligations and the non-affect clause as stipulated in Article 40 TEU. We know from Articles 1 TFEU and TEU respectively that the Treaties are to be treated equally, as discussed in Part II of this chapter. This is important because the Court is largely excluded from jurisdiction over the external sphere of the Union's activities but will nonetheless be asked to monitor its own jurisdiction under Article 40 TEU.

This brings us back to the 'renaissance of the implementation imbalance' theory discussed in chapter three. The point is that paying insufficient attention to accompanying regulation regarding the adequate protection of the individual in criminal law proceedings, as well as respect for the principles of criminalisation, risks making the current pursuit of effectiveness (as both a competence and an enforcement issue) and the development of criminal law within the EU, counterproductive. Obviously, this connects to the argument set out in Part II of this chapter, namely the ambiguous function of effectiveness as a constitutional parameter in EU law when discussing the objectives of the Union.

It is also necessary for the EU to consider the principle of proportionality here. As explained, the concept of loyalty has previously dictated the exercise and establishment of enhanced cooperation in this area, which meant that it was never used in practice. It is likely, therefore, that what will emerge in this area is something similar to a proportionality test: a balancing act between the Member States and the EU. Arguably, such a proportionality assessment would better recognise the sensitivity of the use of the emergency brake in criminal law than the loyalty precept. In particular, it would make the emergency brake more meaningful in practice.

E. Conclusion

This short section has highlighted the multifaceted notion of 'flexibility' from the perspective of EU criminal law. This part sought to demonstrate the link between ex Article 47 EU and the delimitation of competences and the notion of enhanced cooperation as it all came down to what to count as the *acquis communautaire*. Moreover, this part examined the relationship between the phenomenon of enhanced cooperation and the principle of subsidiarity and concluded that in the context of EU criminal law it is difficult to imagine how subsidiarity will play a major role in the current EU focus on moving forward. Some of the issues that have been discussed will be elaborated upon in chapter seven in the more specific discussion of the Lisbon Treaty. Therefore, the intention here has been to highlight the complex matter of 'loyalty' (involving 'effectiveness') and how it connects to wider competence concerns in EU criminal law and thus to explain its ambiguous nature – that is, that the very notion of loyalty in the EU criminal law is not a blessing per se. There may be sensitive principles such as the broad concepts of fair trial and legality that are overridden too easily. Proportionality could arguably offer a more attractive solution than a loyalty obligation. But (as always) it depends on what this concept is taken to mean when applied in EU law practice.

VI. THE CONSTITUTIONAL DEBATE IN BRIEF

A. Introduction

This final part will supply some thoughts on the EU constitutional dialogue as initiated by the Laeken Declaration[331] and taken further in the debate[332] on the drafting of the CT[333] and the Lisbon Treaty.[334] After all, the question of the division of competences between the EU and Member States has been at the top of the European agenda for a long time. Indeed, the Laeken Declaration has already asked how to establish and monitor a more precise delimitation of competences between the EU and the Member States, which would reflect the principle of subsidiarity.[335] Moreover, it is often noted that Laeken, by referring to the 'Union' rather than the 'EC', intended to include the intergovernmental pillars in the discussion of competences. It may sound trite, but the issue of depillarisation (or an integrated but separate legal order) was at the fore of the integration programme in the run-up to the Lisbon Treaty. While the issue of depillarisation now belongs to EU legal history, it is surely the case that the issue of legitimacy of EU action is still a burning question.

The purpose of this section is not to go through the constitutional debate on the Lisbon Treaty in detail as any such exegesis would be beyond its scope. Instead, it seeks to provide some reflections on the wider debate on the question of competences in the EU. In particular, it focuses on the very existence of broad provisions such as Articles 352 TFEU and 114 TFEU as discussed in the previous parts of this chapter.

[331] European Council at Laeken, 2001.

[332] P Craig, 'Competence, Clarity, Conferral, Containment and Consideration' (2004) 29 *EL Rev* 323; G Davies, 'The Post-Laeken Division of Competences' (2003) 28 *EL Rev* 686; S Weatherill, 'Is Constitutional Finality Feasible or Fesirable? On the case for European constitutionalism and the European Constitution' (2002) available at www.wiso.uni hamburg.de/fileadmin/sowi/politik/governance/ConWeb_Papers/conweb7-2002.pdf (last accessed 1 June 2011); B De Witte (ed), *Ten Reflections on the Constitutional Treaty of Europe*' (EUI, booklet, Florence 2003), Dougan (above n 254) 613; P Craig, 'The Lisbon Treaty, Process, Architecture and Substance' (2008) 33 *EL Rev* 137.

[333] Treaty Establishing a Constitution for Europe [2004] OJ C316/1.

[334] Treaty of Lisbon amending the Treaty on European Union and the Treaty establishing the European Community, signed at Lisbon, 13 December 2007, OJ C 306 of 17 December 2007.

[335] eg G De Burca and B De Witte 'Delimitation of Powers' in A Arnull and D Wincott (eds), *Accountability and Legitimacy in the European Union* (Oxford, Oxford University Press, 2002) 201.

B. On the Preservation of Broad Competence Provisions

The classic example of a clash between the institutional desire to extend the objectives of Article 352 TFEU and the scepticism of the national courts is the Maastricht decision, where the German BVerfG reminded the Court of the boundaries of EU law.[336] Nevertheless, it has been argued that the German 'warning'[337] was actually superfluous as the Court's dynamic approach to integration had already been replaced by a more static, although difficult, notion of subsidiarity.[338] Nevertheless, in its ruling on the constitutionality of the Lisbon Treaty it insisted on the primacy of the principle of conferral as a buffer against the EU asserting *Kompetenz-Kompetenz* or violating a State's constitutional identity.[339] Interestingly, the BVerfG focused solely on this provision while it seems to have ignored the even broader contours of Article 114 TFEU.[340] Also as noted above, the BVerfG stipulated that criminal law is in principle not amenable to supranational integration. Thus, the BVerfG held that Article 83 TFEU must be interpreted in a limited fashion. It further held that the broadly drafted Article 83(2) TFEU – referred to as the dynamic blanket empowerment[341] – was tantamount to an extension of codified powers of the Union and therefore subject to the enactment of a statute under the German Basic Law. It remains to be seen to what extent this will represent a 'Solange'[342] – as long as – approach in criminal law.

Moreover, in the Lisbon Treaty judgment the BVerfG referred to the notion of constitutional identity as a shield against overly intrusive influence of EU law on German constitutional values. Yet, in principle the BVerfG confirmed the validity of the German Act approving the Lisbon Treaty, albeit in a very guarded manner. It should be noted that while the Lisbon judgment has been widely seen as a clear signal from the BVerfG that European integration is going too far, more recent

[336] Judgment of 12 October 1993, 2 BvR 2134 and 2159/92, BVerfGE 89, 155. eg, S Boom, The European Union after the Maastricht Decision: Will Germany be the Virginia of Europe' (1995) 43 *American Journal of Comparative Law* 177.

[337] In 2009 the BVerfG delivered a ruling that, in principle, approved the Lisbon Treaty. Lisbon case, BVerfG 2 BvE 2/08 from 30 June 2009. See eg P Kiiver, 'The Lisbon Judgement of the German Constitutional Court: a Court-Ordered Strengthening of the National Legislature in the EU' (2010) 16 *ELJ* 578 as well as several important papers in the special issue in the *German Law Journal* in 2009 'The Federal Constitutional Court's Lisbon Case' (2009) 10 *German Law Journal* 1169 as well as D Thym, 'In the Name of Sovereign Statehood: A Critical Introduction to the Lisbon Judgment of the German Constitutional Court' (2009) 46 *CML Rev* 1795.

[338] K Meessen, 'Hedging European Integration: The Maastricht Judgment of the Federal Constitutional Court of Germany' (1994) 17 *Fordham International Law Journal* 511, cited in G de Burca, 'The European Court of Justice and the Evolution of EU Law' in T Börzel and R Cichowski, *Law, Politics and Society* (Oxford, Oxford University Press, 2003) 48.

[339] Weatherill, (above n 258) 827.

[340] ibid.

[341] Para 363.

[342] BVerfGE 37, 271; BVerfGE 73, 339. See eg C Grabenwarter, 'National Constitutional Law Relating to the European Union' in A von Bogdandy and J Bast *Principles of European Constitutional Law* (Oxford/Munich, Hart/Beck, Nomos, 2010) 83.

cases such as the *Data retention* case,[343] concerning the constitutional validity of the storage of data, and the *Honeywell* case regarding the constitutional implications of the *Mangold* decision,[344] have been considered as representing a more cautious approach on the German side.[345] In the former case the BVerfG declared that it is part of the constitutional identity of Germany that the citizens' enjoyment of freedom means that any storage of data must be the exception rather than the rule. In the *Honeywell* case, the BVerfG rejected the claim that the *Mangold* decision,[346] which extended the reach of the non-discrimination principle to cover age discrimination, was ultra vires.[347] Thus, it seems as if the BVerfG are particularly concerned that criminal law should be protected from the overly intrusive influence of EU law. The protection of criminal law is, according to the BVerfG, closely connected with constitutional identity.

In any event, as regards the existence of Article 352 TFEU, as charted in Part II, it is sometimes pointed out that the whole purpose of Article 352 TFEU is that it can be used in a gap-filling capacity.[348] The reason for this is that there will always be unforeseen cases where Article 352 TFEU constitutes the only possible legal ground, if such action appears 'necessary' to carry out one of the objectives of the EU. According to this view, labelling Article 352 TFEU as a normal concurrent competence misses the point of the special character of this provision, which resembles that of a *kompetenz kompetenz* mechanism. And yet, as explained, Article 352 TFEU does not constitute a *kompetenz kompetenz*, at least not in its true meaning, even though the very notion of implied powers (or *effet utile*) encompasses a degree of self-imposed *kompetenz*. As seen in Part II, there is no universally true definition of *effet utile* at the EU level, and as already explained, there is no watertight division between enforcement and competence either. Indeed, the Laeken Declaration had targeted this problem by linking Articles 114 TFEU and 352 TFEU as both representing dangerously broad provisions. As explained, Article 83(2) TFEU should be added to the list as it seems as if this provision could have a very broad scope for the effective implementation of an EU law policy.

Yet, many commentators have pointed out that an inflexible set of rules would damage the efficient functioning of the Union.[349] For this reason, during the crafting of the CT and the Lisbon Treaty it was considered that the strongest argument in favour of the preservation of Articles 352 TFEU and 114 TFEU was that it would give flexibility, which would be crucial for the Union to be able to act in a

[343] Data retention case, Decision of 2 March 2010, 1 BvR 256/08, 1 BvR 568/08 (concerning Directive 2006/24/EC).

[344] Decision of 6 July 2010, 2 BvR 2661/06, not yet reported *Honeywell*.

[345] M Payandeh, 'Constitutional Review of EU Law after Honywell: Contextualizing the Relationship between the German Constitutional Court and the EU Court of Justice' (2011) 48 *CML Rev* 9.

[346] Case C-144/04 *Mangold v Helm* [2005] ECR I-9981, discussed in ch 3.

[347] ibid.

[348] Meessen (above n 338).

[349] See the discussion in W Swenden, 'Is the European Union in need of a Competence Catalogue? (2004) 42 *Journal of Common Market Studies* 381; S Weatherill, 'Competence and Legitimacy' in C Barnard and O Odudu (eds), *The Outer Limits of EU Law* (Oxford, Hart Publishing, 2009) 1.

dynamic manner and as a problem solver.[350] It was also observed that some protection against an over-generous use of broad competences was highly desirable and that this could, for example, could rest on an insistence on unanimity in the Council plus parliamentary approval.[351] Therefore, 'adjustability' was considered as invaluable. However, reins that are too loose result in excessive competence creep and conversely – to continue the analogy with equestrian sport – reins that are too short result in disharmony or in the worst case an explosion of powers. Obviously, there is a delicate balancing act here between inflexible rules and the phenomenon of creeping competence in the EU. The intention is merely to demonstrate that the debate on the degree of EU integration remains alive. After all, the CT did not attempt to provide an answer to the big issue of the purpose and reach of European integration (the 'is the European process an end in itself?' dispute). On the other hand, it is equally often suggested that had the CT – and now the Lisbon Treaty – attempted to answer this question, it would probably have fallen apart.[352] According to this view, the essence of multi-level governance is exactly its evolving character.[353]

Given that, it has been correctly observed that the appropriate way forward is to embrace the intertwining of State and Union competence as a constructively cooperative feature of the EU system of governance, while bearing in mind that it is desirable to draw the constitutional contours more clearly to improve legitimacy.[354] But how is this possible? Would it not be like having your cake (that creeping competence is bad) and eating it (no definitive list please)? There are no easy answers here and the legitimacy of the EU is clearly a work in progress. Thus, there seem to be a consensus that the failed CT and its successor, the Lisbon Treaty, are of great importance in their attempt to address these issues. Moreover, a constitutional debate on how to handle these questions is important in the future shaping of the European project.[355]

As for criminal law, it could be argued that it was the very failure of the CT which led to the creation of a whole new dimension to the discussion of EU criminal law. After all, in the absence of a CT and in the run-up to the Lisbon Treaty, the Court had already begun to erase the division of powers between the Union pillars. Accordingly, in the view of the Court, the AFSJ and criminal law in general were already legal areas fit for the supranational legislator. Nevertheless, the Lisbon Treaty has now legitimately abandoned the pillars and hence supranationalised

[350] S Weatherill, 'Competence Creep and Competence Control' (2004) 23 *Yearbook of European Law* 1.

[351] ibid. See, however, G Conway, 'Conflicts of norms in EU law and the legal reasoning of the ECJ' (2010) 11 *German Law Journal* 966, arguing that 'Applying *lex specialis* much more fully reflects the idea of conferral as *lex speciali* logically reflects the will of the constituent power.'

[352] See the interesting account by U Haltern, 'On Finality' in A von Bogdandy and J Bast (eds), *Principles of European Constitutional Law* (Oxford/Munich, Hart/Beck/Nomos, 2010) 205.

[353] See the discussion in P Craig 'Integration, Democracy and Legitimacy' in Craig and De Burca, *The Evolution of EU Law* (Oxford, Oxford University Press, 2011) 14; S Weatherill and A Menon, 'Legitimacy, Accountability and Delegation in the European Union' in Arnull and Wincott (above n 334) 113.

[354] Craig (above n 332, 2008).

[355] See eg, JC Piris, *The Constitution for Europe – A Legal Analysis* (Cambridge, Cambridge University Press, 2006).

criminal law. Therefore, we could ask whether this constitutes anything new with respect to competences, or whether such restructuring – given the new powers of the EU's institutions – concerns rather the question of capacity of Union action. As will be explained in chapter seven, it is not possible to separate capacity and competence so distinctly. After all, the Lisbon Treaty provides not only for the constitutionalisation of criminal law but for new specific areas of EU criminal law, such as combating money laundering at the supranational level. From a legitimacy perspective, this is a major departure from the previous supranationalisation of the criminal law as witnessed by the Court's case law.

C. The Beginning of *de lege feranda*

In spite of concerns not to bring the Union process to a halt through rigid rules, it could be argued that some areas of the law, such as criminal law, are not appropriate for 'one size fits all' reasoning. It is true that prominent commentators such as Weiler have said that one should worry less about judicial statements of sovereignty and competence matters and focus more on the fact that the enforcement of European law continues to be in the hands of Member States.[356] Be that as it may, it is is not a sufficient solution for European criminal law. The reason for this is that in this area we need a clear delimitation of powers in the name of the principle of legality. As noted in previous chapters, traditionally, only an elected legislator could legitimise criminal law. The citizens of Europe need to know who their legislator is. Admittedly, such a problem may be more theoretical than practical as most EU law is implemented into national law and of course the vast majority of Europeans are non-criminals. However, this is hardly the point here, as the principle of legality is an imperative for any criminalisation. Furthermore, the principle of legality is also a fundamental principle of European law and is proclaimed in the Charter. The danger arises when broad competence provisions such as Articles 114 TFEU and 352 TFEU are boosted with constitutional use of effectiveness where the threshold for competence is manipulated to extend the EU into criminal law. As stated in chapter two it is possible to argue that showing the 'effectiveness' of an EU rule is a precondition to establishing the EU's competence to act in the first place.

The good news is that even in the current trend for treating more criminalisation as good law per se, it seems as if there has never been a better opportunity to influence the discussion of EU criminal law. Indeed, the era of impact assessments, consultations and 'better and smarter regulation' if taken seriously – promises at least a healthy debate on the development of European criminal law. Chapters five and six demonstrate how this evaluation scheme works in practice.

[356] J Weiler, *The Constitution of Europe* (Cambridge, Cambridge University Press, 1999).

D. Conclusion

Notwithstanding the 'fear' of Articles 352 TFEU and 114 TFEU as the engines of competence creep, the temptation to remove this type of functionally broad competences from the agenda was, as indicated above, resisted by the Convention and subsequently the crafters of the Lisbon Treaty, in order to preserve the adaptable nature of the Union's powers. Clearly, the broad contours of Article 83(2) TFEU could be added to this 'black list' of provisions that are prone to competence creep.

However, these broad competence provisions in the Treaty combined with effectiveness reasoning mean that there are not many hurdles left for an over-ambitious reading of EU competences. This is unwise: if the EU wishes to be involved in criminal law matters then the reasoning for such involvement should be based on more convincing arguments than a flawed exercise in effectiveness. There was, after all, no Treaty-based support for criminal law prior to the Lisbon Treaty. Indeed, this chapter has singled out Article 114 TFEU as easily overriding Member State concerns, thus constituting a self-appointed competence distributor. However, the Lisbon Treaty represents both an expansion in the extent to which criminal law is brought within the official realm of European law and, at the same time, a limit on European competences to a number of specific requirements in chapter four of title V of the TFEU.

As shown – and as will be examined further – this is not the most important aspect, however. What matters is the key role played by effectiveness in this area.

VII. GENERAL CONCLUSION

This long chapter only needs a short conclusion. It has endeavoured to track the development of the principle of effectiveness in EU law as a constitutional principle. In particular, the aim of this chapter has been to look more closely at Case C-176/03 and how the Court's reading of effectiveness pertained to more fundamental questions of the phenomenon of competence allocations in the EU. In doing so the aim of the chapter was to continue the story of the force of effectiveness in this area. In other words, it sought to explore the meaning of effectiveness as a constitutional axiom, as developed in the landmark ruling of Case C-176/03 and examine how a broader reading of effectiveness has eroded the attention being paid to the principle of conferral. In testing these propositions, the chapter set out to conceptualise the principle of effectiveness in the context of the principle of attributed competences. Specifically, the focus of this chapter has been on how the broad competence provisions of Articles 352 TFEU and 114 TFEU concerning the limits of the Treaty, and the history of ex Article 47 EU regarding the delimitation of power between the pillars, were already built into bases for the development of an EC criminal law prior to the entry into force of the Lisbon Treaty. In investigating these issues the chapter looked closely at the *acquis communautaire* concept. In addition, it explored the narrative of ex Article 47 EU and its similarities with Article 352 TFEU in unequivocally favouring an expansive reading of the Union objectives. In doing so the chapter explained why this (still) deserves critical attention, by discussing how much of this reasoning could be readily transferred to the post Lisbon era.

This chapter has also examined Article 114 TFEU in detail, and thereby set out to look at the market concept. In doing so, the study focused particularly on the 'effects on trade' catchphrase. The starting point for this discussion was the new *lex specialis* function of Article 83 TFEU and the scope of the concept of EU criminal law, particularly with regard to the extent to which it would be possible to rely on Article 114 TFEU in the future. The chapter also sought to demonstrate that the classic centre of gravity test has always been different in the context of Article 114 TFEU as being a question of market-making regardless of the gravity at stake. Moreover, this chapter has looked at the emerging trend of preventive market-making and its relevance for the phenomenon of preventive criminalisation in the Article 114 TFEU context. It was argued that this represents a dangerous trend, as it appears as if there are no hurdles left to an expansive reading of EU law powers undermining other values that the EU wants to protect, such as the due process in criminal law.

Thereafter, Part IV scrutinised the wide EU law issues of subsidiarity and proportionality and discussed them within the framework of European criminal law. The purpose of doing so was to show that these principles appear to play an insignificant role not only in mainstream EU constitutional law but also, more specifically, in EU criminal law. This is so despite the fact that EU notions of subsidiarity and proportionality are reflected in the *ultima ratio* of criminal law. This chapter has also investigated the new function of the national parliaments in this area as well as problems with penal populism. It also touched on the bigger issue of balancing in the AFSJ and the extent to which criminal law is different from other areas.

Part V of this chapter embarked on a short exposé of the enhanced cooperation mechanisms in EU criminal law, and how the EU notion of flexibility could become a testing ground in the criminal law area. The purpose of doing so was to point to the dangers in advancing the EU criminal law cooperation project at the expense of adequate attention to what such cooperation means from the perspective of the emergency brake. This part investigated the emergency brakes mechanisms. This part also discussed the meaning of the imperative of loyalty in this area and to the extent to which the proportionality principle could play a future role as better recognising the sensitive nature of criminal law cooperation in the present area.

Finally, Part VI endeavoured to highlight the wider question of the allocation of powers in the EU and addressed the eternal question of to what extent competences need to be 'fixed', or whether the Member States are 'better off' preserving the pliable nature of EU competences. This section cautioned against such an approach in EU criminal law as it does not sit easily with the principle of legality unless the approach to the use of effectiveness as a constitutional parameter – and as now part of Article 83 TFEU – is carefully analysed and evaluated. This section also looked at the recent BVerfG Lisbon judgment, which confirms the likelihood of continued national worries in this area, at least on the German side, as the German highest court made it clear that criminal law remains inexorably linked to (what was once the prerogative of) the core nation state.

5

Case Study I: EU Financial Crimes

I. INTRODUCTION

THIS CHAPTER LOOKS more closely at recent legislative developments in the area of financial crime, and, more specifically, in the fields of money laundering, piracy and counterfeiting as the major test cases in the wake of Case C-176/03, by providing a detailed case study. Whilst chapter four explored the meaning of EU 'effectiveness' as a constitutional catchphrase, this chapter looks at the difficulties with such an approach in the area of EU financial crime. In other words, the purpose is to continue the discussion started in chapter four by investigating and thereby contextualising legislative initiatives in this area and examining how they actually contribute to market creation under Article 114 TFEU. This chapter explores the underlying ratio behind the EU's legislative activity in the area of financial crimes by asking three fundamental questions. The first concerns the EU anti-money laundering legal framework itself, the concept of a risk-based approach to money laundering and how this overlaps with national systems; and the strong focus of security and risk in this area. As will be shown there is a strong interrelationship between these principles and the notion of effectiveness that tends to lead to precautionary criminalisation at the EU level. The second issue concerns the proposed Counterfeiting and Piracy Directive. In both these areas, Article 114 TFEU constitutes the main legal component in tandem with the broader impact of the judgment in Case C-176/03 and the 'full effectiveness' mantra. The third issue under scrutiny goes beyond concrete legislative measures in this field to investigate the wider protective regime at the supranational level, and also considers whether the EU should be involved in these issues at all. In doing so, this chapter will discuss whether the EU's approach is appropriate and examine the issues through the lens of EU constitutional (criminal) law.

This chapter is divided into three further parts, with the first dealing with the EU's anti-money laundering agenda, including the umbrella label of 'organised crime' and the notion of terrorist finance as part of the Money Laundering Directive. The next part examines the EU counterfeiting and piracy framework from the perspective of national criminal law in particular. The final part links back to chapter four Part III by supplying some reflections on what the usual EU reliance on the 'confident consumer' maxim and a protective regime means in the context of EU criminal law.

II. MONEY LAUNDERING

A. Introduction

This section addresses the justification of the Third Money Laundering Directive under Article 114 TFEU. It is a-historical (or a-Lisbon) in the sense that it takes a step back and discusses money laundering in the context of Article 114 TFEU which is the legal basis of this measure. As noted however, the entry into force of the Lisbon Treaty means that Article 83 TFEU now lists money laundering as an explicit EU law crime. As explained in chapter four, Article 83 TFEU is *lex specialis*, but the market provision of Article 114 TFEU will still be relevant to the extent that the suppression of money laundering and terrorist financing would be necessary for the establishing and functioning of the internal market. In any case, there is no sign that the Money Laundering Directive[1] would be repealed because of this new legal basis.[2]

This the chapter starts by recapping the history of the EU's measures to combat money laundering and the proceeds of crime, moving to discuss the inclusion of the financing of terrorism in the anti-money laundering framework as well as how such a system relates to existing third pillar legislation. The chapter also locks at the issue of adopting a risk-based approach and the notion of risk as introduced by the Third Money Laundering Directive. Consequently, this section examines whether different notions of 'risk' exist, specifically within the traditional context of EU risk regulation and the sphere of money laundering and terrorism financing, respectively.

B. Tainted Money

'Money laundering is at the very heart of organized crime. It should be rooted out wherever it occurs.' These are the words of the Tampere conclusions as proclaimed in 1999.[3] Indeed, the combating of tainted money has been a high priority for the EU for a long time. Much has been written about the history of this European struggle.[4] Therefore, it should be sufficient to make a few general

[1] Directive 2005/60/EC on the prevention of the use of the financial system for the purpose of money laundering and terrorist financing [2005] OJ L309.

[2] However, the Commission has suggested in its communication 'The EU internal security strategy in action', that the EU should consider revising the EU Anti-Money Laundering legislation by 2013 to enhance the transparency of legal persons and legal arrangements, but there was no mention of legal basis. The EU Internal Security Strategy in Action, Objective 1, 5 available at ec.europa.eu/commission_2010-2014/malmstrom/archive/internal_security_strategy_in_action_en.pdf (last accessed January 2012).

[3] Tampere conclusions European Council October 1999.

[4] eg V Mitsilegas, 'International Regulation of Money Laundering and Terrorist Finance' in I Bantekas and G Keramides (eds), *International and European Financial Criminal Law* (London, Butterworths, 2006) 305.

observations here before looking at how the EU's harmonisation programme affects criminal law. In this field, legislation has usually been adopted because of the classic Community fear that without 'common rules for a common market', obstacles to trade will occur *but* with the additional argument that without a joint fight against crime, criminals will take advantage of free movement. So, the same old EU law ratio appears to apply in all policy areas. It is the all-embracing EU theory that without EU rules Member States will adopt measures inconsistent with the internal market, which could seriously jeopardise free movement and would result in the loss of public trust and thus enable money launderers to take advantage of a 'distorted' market.[5]

The first Directive on money laundering was adopted in 1991.[6] Subsequently, this Directive was amended in 2001[7] and then superseded by yet another Directive in 2005.[8] These legal instruments have been largely based on existing measures taken by the UN and the Council of Europe. For example, the 1988 Vienna Convention on drug trafficking provided for the criminalisation of drug-related money laundering. The Council of Europe has been an active legislator in this area. In 1980 it adopted recommendations for action against the transfer and safekeeping of funds of criminal origin and in 1990 it adopted a Convention on laundering, search, seizure and confiscation of the proceeds of crime.[9] It should also be mentioned that in 2000 and 2003[10] the UN agreed on a Convention against transnational organised crime and a Resolution against corruption and for the criminalisation of the laundering of proceeds of crime.[11] Obviously, these international steps have largely influenced the EU legal framework. A particularly significant actor in the global war against money laundering and an important trendsetter for the EU in these matters is the Financial Action Task Force (FATF) and its 40 Recommendations on Money Laundering.[12] Briefly, the FATF was set up by the 1989 G7 summit. Its original mandate concerned the war against chiefly drug-related money laundering but was, in the aftermath of the terrorist attacks of 9/11, expanded to cover the financing of terrorism. As will be explained,

[5] Recital (2) of Directive 2005/60/EC 25 November 2005 on the prevention of the use of the financial system for the purpose of money laundering and terrorist financing [2005] OJ L309/15.

[6] Directive 91/308/EEC of 10 June 1991 on the prevention of the use of the financial system for the purpose of money laundering [1991] OJ L166/77.

[7] Directive 2001/97/EC of the EP and of the Council amending Directive 91/308/EEC on the prevention of the use of the financial system for the purpose of money laundering [2004] OJ L344.

[8] Directive 2005/60/EC OJ L309 (above n 1). The Commission's own website is instructive: ec.europa.eu/internal_market/company/financial-crime/index_en.htm (last accessed January 2012).

[9] W Gilmore, *Dirty Money: The Evolution of Money Laundering Counter-Measures* (Strasbourg, Council of Europe Publishing, 2004) 161.

[10] GA Res 55/25 of 15 November 2000 and GA Res 58/4 31 October 2003.

[11] J Handoll, *Capital Payments and Money Laundering in the European Union* (London, Richmond, 2006) 112.

[12] FATF is an intergovernmental group with a mandate 'to assess the results of co-operation already undertaken in order to prevent the utilisation of the banking system and financial institutions for the purpose of money laundering and to consider additional preventive efforts in this area'. V Mitsilegas, *Money Laundering Counter-Measures in the EU: A New Paradigm of Security Governance versus Fundamental Legal Principles* (The Hague, Kluwer Law Publishing, 2003).

this is now the approach taken by the Third Money Laundering Directive as well. It may be helpful to begin this section by briefly clarifying what constitutes 'money laundering'.

Money laundering is by definition based on another crime termed a predicate offence, which gives rise to the laundering in question. In this respect, it should, however, be observed that there is an on-going debate in legal doctrine about the need to have a general definition of predicate offences in order to meet the legality requirement of strict construction in criminal law.[13] It has been suggested that a problem with the 1991 and 2001 Money Laundering Directives was that they did not provide a definite list of predicate offences or the definition of a serious crime as the threshold for criminal activity. The 2005 Directive on the other hand, aims to clarify this issue by stipulating that a serious crime is one for which the sentence is a minimum of six months imprisonment, but still leaves the exact definition of predicate offences somewhat blurred. An additional complication is that the reporting of suspicious transactions does not depend on the identification of the predicate offence but rather on a subjective fault element – that is, the *mens rea* requirement. In any case, the term 'money laundering' is rather misleading as it not only concerns money, but also 'grey' property of virtually any kind, which is covered and embraces a continuum of economic activity where the moral culpability associated with money laundering activity varies as one moves along this scale.[14] The main problem in this respect has been that the criminalised area at issue has been rather imprecise.[15] For example, the UK includes a prohibition on insider dealing in its anti-money laundering legislation while most other Member States do not.[16]

The 2005 Directive attempts to solve the problem of ill-defined legislation. Article 1 states that the following conduct, when committed intentionally, shall be regarded as money laundering:

> (a) the conversion or transfer of property, knowing that such property is derived from criminal activity or from an act of participation in such activity, for the purpose of concealing or disguising the illicit origin of the property or of assisting any person who is involved in the commission of such activity to evade the legal consequences of his action;
>
> (b) the concealment or disguise of the true nature, source, location, disposition, movement, rights with respect to, or ownership of property, knowing that such property is derived from criminal activity or from an act of participation in such activity;
>
> (c) the acquisition, possession or use of property, knowing, at the time of receipt, that such property was derived from criminal activity or from an act of participation in such activity.

[13] eg Handoll (above n 11).

[14] K Hinterseer, *Criminal Finance, The Political Economy of Money Laundering in a Comparative Legal Context* (The Hague, Kluwer Law Publishing, 2002) 101.

[15] R Alexander, *Insider Dealing and Money Laundering in the EU: Law and Regulation* (Aldershot, Ashgate, 2007) 145.

[16] ibid.

i. The History of Anti-money Laundering Legislation

Throughout the history of the EU's anti-money laundering agenda, European tactics have been dominated by a twofold approach: namely, performing a preventive role and adopting a strategy based on the notion of control by combining regulatory measures within the financial system through the use of criminal law.[17] However, as already explained, prior to the outcome of Case C-176/03 there was no explicit EU supranational legislative competence in the area of criminal law. For this reason, it is interesting to note that a Commission communication COM (1995) 54 in connection with the 1991 Directive stipulated that despite the lack of EU criminal powers, the word 'prohibition' of money laundering had to be interpreted as requiring criminalisation as a precondition for the Directive working 'effectively'. Nevertheless, a number of Member States wanted to go further than the 1991 Directive and agreed on so-called 'all crime legislation' which resulted about a decade later in an amended Directive. The legislative process towards the adoption of this Directive was additionally accelerated in the aftermath of the attacks of 9/11.[18] This Directive, 2001/97/EC, known as the Second Money Laundering Directive 2001, extended the number of crimes to which the provisions applied and widened the range of professions who received reporting obligations under its main anti-money laundering instrument. This included professionals and non-financial businesses such as legal professionals acting in any financial or real estate transactions, auditors, external accountants and tax advisors, real estate agents, money transfer agents, dealers in high-value goods, auctioneers, and casinos believed to be vulnerable to money laundering. The 2001 Directive applied to a range of serious crimes including drug trafficking, various activities of criminal organisations and certain categories of fraud and corruption. It also imposed a system of mandatory reporting of suspicious transactions including duties on customs identification (Article 3), record keeping (Article 4) and due diligence (Article 5). The Directive also required credit and financial institutions to provide internal control and anti-money laundering training to staff.[19]

Essentially, the 2001 Directive had two major areas of influence. The first was the range of originating offences covered by the definition of money laundering, and the second was the range of institutions that are now required to implement measures to combat money laundering. Therefore, the scope of this Directive was rather far-reaching and covered serious fraud against the EU budget, corruption, any other offence committed by a criminal organisation, and offences that could generate substantial proceeds punishable by a severe custodial sentence in accordance with Member State penal law. There was no guidance, however, regarding

[17] Mitsilegas (above n 12).

[18] Alexander (above n 15) at 146–47.

[19] Certain exemptions were provided for legal professionals, accountants, auditors and tax advisors with regard to information obtained from their clients in the course of ascertaining the legal position of the client or in relation to judicial proceedings.

the meaning of 'substantial proceeds' or the definition of a 'severe sentence' in the Directive. As already implied, it has been argued that the aim of the fight against dirty money at the EU level has been fuelled by a more general and wider aspiration to create an 'honest' single market space meriting specific protection since its early days. This message was recognised in the 2001 Directive, which explicitly emphasised the importance of confidence in the market. Since then, this importance of boosting confidence in the market, as discussed in chapter four Part III, has constituted the leading theme in the EU's fight against dirty money. Nevertheless, it could be concluded that money laundering is a 'chameleonic' threat: it must be fought since it is perceived to foster organised crime while obscuring the target.[20] The question is, therefore, one of all-encompassing regulation, where money laundering is separated from its initial aim of suppressing, in particular, 'drug trafficking' to facilitate the more general fight against organised crime, including the war on terrorism. It seems that the EU has been 'shooting from the hip'[21] and in so doing is hoping to hit some of the crimes, or criminals, capable of sabotaging the smooth running of the market. In other words, 'remote harm' rather than 'direct harm' is at hand. This is nothing new though, as it has been observed and criticised since the First Directive was adopted in 1991.[22] Nonetheless, issues of 'causation' are clearly still under fire and the complexities at hand should not be underestimated. The reason for this is that defining causation is self-evidently important when discussing criminalisation.[23] Without doubt, it appears quite difficult to draw any clear distinction between money laundering, terrorism and organised crime as individual European threats.

Moreover, it has been pointed out that it is necessary to partially 'de-securitise' the money-laundering phenomenon, as its expansion to cover broader categories of offences, people and policing structures in the name of 'security' jeopardises issues of legality and legal certainty.[24] Nevertheless, the 2005 Directive, examined below, increases rather than decreases the focus on security aspects in this respect. As noted in chapter four Part III, AG Bot recently highlighted the security aspect in the context of combating serious organised crime as a justification for harmonisation in the framework of Article 114 TFEU.[25] Clearly, the security focus appears to play an important role not only as part of the area of freedom, security and justice (AFSJ) paradigm, but also at the supranational level as such.

In any case, the Third Money Laundering Directive is the latest step by the EU in combating tainted money, now with the more specific aim of also fighting the

[20] V Mitsilegas, 'Countering the Chameleon Threat of Dirty Money: "Hard" and "Soft" Law in the Emergence of a Global Regime against Money Laundering and Terrorist Finance' in A Edwards and P Gill, *Transnational Organised Crime* (London, Routledge, 2003) 195.

[21] To borrow an expression from R Lööf, 'Shooting from the Hip: Proposed Minimum Rights in Criminal Proceedings throughout the EU' (2006) 12 *European Law Journal* 421.

[22] See Mitsilegas (above n 12) 56.

[23] See eg, A Norrie, *Crime, Reason and History* (London, Butterworths, 2003).

[24] V Mitsilegas and B Gilmore, 'The EU Legislative Framework against Money Laundering and Terrorist Finance: A Critical Analysis in the Light of evolving Global Standards' (2007) 56 *ICLQ* 119.

[25] Case 301/06 *Ireland v Parliament and Council*, Opinion of AG Bot delivered on 14 October 2008.

financing of terrorism. However, the definition of terrorism in this Directive is similar, though not identical, to that found in the UN's 1999 Convention. Instead, the concept of 'terrorism' is formulated in accordance with the relevant EU Framework Decision in this area.[26]

C. Directive 2005/60/EC[27]

The Third Money Laundering Directive 2005 offers an interesting case study as it not only introduces a risk-based approach to the struggle against tainted money but also includes the financing of terrorism within its scope. This Directive is based on Articles 114 TFEU and 53 TFEU (ex Article 47 EC) and was to be implemented by 15 December 2007.

Although this measure does not explicitly require criminalisation but states rather that effective, proportionate and dissuasive sanctions must be imposed, it could nonetheless be argued, as explained in chapter two, that it implicitly requires criminalisation in order to meet the requirement of effective sanctions. This section explores the implications of the apparent combination of an administrative and criminal law approach and the potential difficulties of including actions against the financing of terrorism in the Money Laundering Directive.

The 2005 Directive calls upon Member States to extend the definition of 'criminal activity' to any kind of criminal involvement in the commission of 'serious crime'. The concept of a serious crime is defined in Article 3(5) (a–f), which stipulates that all acts defined in Articles 1 to 4 of Framework Decision 2002/475 JHA on terrorism constitute serious crimes.[28] Further categories amounting to serious crime are the participation in a criminal organisation as defined in 98/733/JHA of 21 December 1998 and serious fraud as defined in Articles 1 to 2 of the Convention on the protection of the EU's financial interests. The Directive also states that all offences which are punishable by deprivation of liberty or a detention order for a minimum of six months constitute serious crime. In summary, serious crime in the 2005 Directive means at least:

- —acts defined in Articles 1 to 4 of Framework Decision 2002/475/JHA on combating terrorism;
- —any of the offences defined in Article 3(1)(a) of the Vienna Convention;
- —activities of criminal organisations as defined in Article 1 Council Joint Action 98/733/JHA of 21 December 1998;
- —'fraud' at least as serious as that defined in Article 1(1) and (2) of the Convention on the EC's Financial Interests;[29]
- —corruption (but no definition is given); and

[26] Council Framework Decision 2002/475/JHA of 13 June 2002 OJ L164 amending Framework Decision 2008/919/JHA of 28 November 2008 OJ L320/21.

[27] Directive 2005/60/EC The Third Money Laundering Directive , 25 November 2005, OJ L309/15.

[28] Council Framework Decision (above n 26).

[29] [1995] OJ C316, 49.

— all offences which may generate substantial proceeds and which are punishable by severe sentences such as the deprivation of liberty or, as regards those States which have a minimum threshold for offences in their legal system, all offences punishable by deprivation of liberty or a detention order for a minimum of six months.

As previously explained, the post 9/11 era and the subsequent amendments of the FATF recommendations constitute the main reason for an increased need to combat the financing of terrorism at the EU level.[30] It has been pointed out that since sentencing policy varies considerably between Member States, such a move has only a limited effect in establishing an EU-wide policy against money laundering.[31]

The 2005 Directive stresses the need for a risk-based approach and states that there has been a trend in recent years towards much wider definitions of money laundering based on a range of predicate offences.[32] According to the Directive, it is important to keep pace with such a movement.[33] However, many commentators have stated that this strong focus on prevention is especially problematic from a human rights perspective as it could undermine the values it seeks to protect.[34] One issue is the fact that the Directive includes the legal profession in the targeted group making them a bigger part of the preventive strategy than in the 2001 measure by imposing on them the duty to report irregularities.[35] It has been suggested that such an obligation could breach the right to fair trial as guaranteed by Article 6 European Convention on Human Rights (ECHR) and Article 48(2) of the Charter of Fundamental Rights, in which the principles of independence and professional secrecy are considered intrinsic.[36] However, in the judgment of *Ordre des barreaux francophones*[37] the Court ruled that an inclusion of members of the legal profession within the scope of the 2001 Directive did not infringe the right to fair hearing as contained in Article 6 ECHR. The reason for this is that there is no obligation to report irregularities when the activities in question have a direct link to judicial proceedings. However, the Court went further and stated:

> § 36 . . .it must be recognised that the requirements relating to the right to a fair trial do not preclude the obligations of information and cooperation laid down in Article 6(1) of Directive 91/308 [as amended by the 2001 Directive] from being imposed on lawyers acting specifically in connection with the activities listed . . . where those obligations are justified by the need . . . to combat money laundering effectively, in view of its evident influence on the rise of organised crime, which itself is a particular threat to society in the Member States.

[30] Gilmore (above n 9) 133.

[31] Alexander (above n 15) 146–47.

[32] A further controversial matter beyond the scope of this chapter is the fact that the Directive introduces increased use of comitology.

[33] It is held that the definition of serious crime should be brought into line with the definitions in Framework Decision 2001/500/JHA (OJ L182 5 July 2001).

[34] A Odeby, 'The European Union and Money Laundering' in Bantekas and Keramides (above n 4).

[35] ibid.

[36] Mitsilegas and Gilmore (above n 24).

[37] Case C-305/05 *Ordre des barreaux francophones and others v Council* [2007] ECR I-5305.

It is difficult to know exactly what the Court means herethe paragraph appears to be an extremely broad statement and raises the question of whether the effectiveness criteria render the guarantee of fair trial as enshrined in Article 6 ECHR a mere formality. It also highlights the tricky relationship between money laundering and organised crime, as well as the difficulties with a preventative strategy from a human rights perspective. Moreover, it should be noted that the recitals in the 2005 Directive state that although the Directive cannot interfere with Member States' judicial procedures, it nonetheless recognises that it is crucial for the effectiveness of the instrument that Member States do what they can to protect employees who report their suspicions of money laundering from being subjected to threats or hostile action. Arguably, this could be read as an implicit recognition of the potential impact on the national system.[38] Again, we see the possible effects of the spill-over phenomenon and the obligation of loyal cooperation as discussed in chapters two and three.

As mentioned, the Directive follows the 'confidence' path by stating that the market could be seriously jeopardised by the efforts of criminals and their associations.[39] The Directive is clear that Member States shall provide penalties (on natural and legal persons) in line with the EU requirements of effectiveness, proportionality and dissuasiveness. Therefore, although it does not explicitly require the use of criminal law – it does so implicitly by making it compulsory for the Member States to provide such sanctions. Furthermore, the Directive stipulates a subjective fault requirement when stating that Member States may only prohibit offences 'when committed intentionally', which, both in theory and practice, means criminal law as opposed to administrative sanctions with strict liability.[40] The Directive does not stop here though. It goes on to state that without prejudice to the right of Member States to adopt criminal penalties, they shall ensure that the appropriate administrative measure or sanctions can also be imposed against credit and financial institutions.[41] It should also be remembered that all Member States have already criminalised money laundering in order to meet the effectiveness criteria.[42] However, the Commission did not consider this to be enough in the fight against tainted money. Consequently, it also included money laundering in the notorious Communication delivered in the wake of Case C-176/03, as discussed in chapter two.[43] A difficulty with such an approach, however, is that there

[38] Mitsilegas and Gilmore (above n 24).

[39] The previous criticism based on the of lack of underlying empirical data is considered this time: there is an obligation (stated in the Directive) for the Commission to produce a report on the implementation by 2009 and the Member States are required to maintain comprehensive statistics on the effectiveness of their preventative systems.

[40] A Ashworth, *Principles of Criminal Law* (Oxford, Oxford University Press, 2006).

[41] However, the Court has explicitly stated that strict liability is no impediment as long as there are genuine and sufficient safeguards for exculpation, in accordance with the principle of proportionality (in this connection, a balancing of interests). Cf *Salabiaku v France ECHR* Ser A No 141 A 1988; Case C-326/88 *Anklagemyndigheten v Hansen & Son* [1990] ECR I-2911.

[42] Mitsilegas (above n 12).

[43] Commission to the European Parliament and the Council on the implications of the Court's judgment of 13 September 2005, (Communication) COM (2005) 583 final 2, 24 November 2005.

may be a risk of so-called double procedures, resulting in criminal and administrative sanctions. This remains the case despite it being true that the general requirement of proportionality would apply to this area which, in practice, would probably remedy such a double sanction.[44] Admittedly, the Commission has adopted a Communication on *ne bis in idem* throughout Europe, but this does not automatically apply to administrative sanctions.[45] The Court has emphasised the principle of fairness, for example, in the area of competition fines but the fact remains that 'administrative' sanctions do not, strictly speaking, constitute criminal law proceedings.[46] In any case, the Directive further stipulates in Article 5 that Member States may adopt or retain in force, stricter provisions in the field covered by this Directive to prevent money laundering and terrorist financing. Moreover, 'corruption' is included among the punishable list of crimes although, as noted, the notion of corruption is not defined – it is simply stated in Article 3(5)(e) that 'corruption' constitutes a serious crime.

Finally, Member States are required to prohibit their credit and financial institutions from keeping anonymous accounts or passbooks (Articles 6 to 9). This is the so-called customer due diligence requirement and forms part of the risk-based confidence and transparency policy. Customer due diligence is to be applied in four cases. First, when establishing a 'business relationship'; second, when carrying out larger transactions; third, regardless of any derogation, exemption or threshold, where there is a suspicion of money laundering or terrorist financing; and fourth, where there are doubts about the veracity or adequacy of previously obtained customer identification data. Furthermore, there are several cases where Member States are required to adopt, on a risk-sensitive basis, enhanced customer due diligence in addition to the above outlined.[47] Clearly, the web of EU anti-money laundering legislation is not simple and this chapter seeks to demonstrate just how complex and confusing it can be.

i. Regulation No 1889/2005

There is a complementary Regulation (1889/2005)[48] concerning the control of cash entering and leaving the Community. This regulation is based on Articles

[44] Another question, beyond the scope of this chapter, is whether the Court's inconsistent use of proportionality within the EC (administrative) principle makes the boundaries any clearer.

[45] COM (2005) 696 final. Green paper on Conflicts of Jurisdiction and the Principle of *ne bis in idem* in Criminal Proceedings. Cf the definition: 'a decision in criminal matters which has either been taken by a judicial authority or which has been subject to an appeal to such an authority'.

[46] See generally, GM Corstens and J Pradel, *European Criminal Law* (The Hague, Kluwer Law Publishing, 2002).

[47] Handoll (above n 11) 153–62.

[48] Reg 1889/2005 of the EP and the Council of 26 October 2005 on controls on cash entering or leaving the Community. Based on a Proposal from the Commission OJ C227 E 24 September 2002. See also Commission 'On the application of Regulation (EC) No 1889/2005 of the European Parliament and of the Council of 26 October 2005 on controls of cash entering or leaving the Community pursuant to article 10 of this Regulation; (Communication) COM (2010) 429 for an evaluation of the Member States.

114 TEFU and 33 TFEU (ex Article 135 EC) and is intended to supplement the Directive. However, it remains unclear why ex Article 135 EC was chosen as an additional legal basis.[49] It should be recalled that ex Article 135 EC dealt with customs operation and explicitly stated that EU measures in this area should not concern the application of national criminal law or the administration of justice (this has now been deleted from its successor Article 33 TFEU). It has also been observed that this regulation involves action at the external border of the Community and that the EU provisions which specifically deal with this area involved persons and not capital (ex Article 62 EC now Article 77 TFEU).[50] It could also be questioned whether a regulation was necessary here, as it is not clear how the regulation contributes to market creation. More specifically, it is difficult to see how cash entering or leaving the Community would jeopardise the soundness of the financial system as a whole and thus hamper the establishment and functioning of the internal market.[51]

This Regulation is intended to be a complementary measure. Why then this dual approach to anti-money laundering? Could such an approach qualify as 'measures for the approximation' under Article 114 TFEU and hence fit the so-called 'smoke flavouring' overlapping legislative pattern as discussed in chapter four Part III?[52] As mentioned in that chapter, AG Kokott in her Opinion in the *Smoke flavouring* case argued that as long as a measure serves to approximate the laws of Member States, it can provide for procedures which do not bring about approximation directly but by multi-level stages with intermediate steps.[53] The Court agreed and stated that the authors of the Treaty intended to give the Community legislature discretion, depending on the general context and the specific circumstances of the matter, to be harmonised, using the most appropriate technique to achieve the desired result. Clearly, such an approach widens the constitutional scope significantly, but it should also be stressed, as explained in the previous chapter, that the *Smoke flavouring* case concerned scientific evidence which may have explained the need for a 'multi-level' regime.

We will now turn to look at the Money Laundering Directive from the perspective of the financing of terrorism. As already mentioned, the inclusion of the financing of terrorism in the anti-money laundering instrument constitutes a radical change. In particular, it constitutes a challenge to the relationship between EU market integration and the national criminal law system. The purpose here is to outline EU financial crimes and thus provide a background to the second case study discussed in chapter six.

[49] Mitsilegas and Gilmore (above n 24).

[50] ibid.

[51] ibid.

[52] Case C-66/04 *UK v Parliament and Council* [2005] ECR I-10553.

[53] Case C-66/04 *UK v Parliament and Council* [2005] ECR I-10553. Opinion of AG Kokott delivered on 8 September 2005, paras 26–40.

D. The Financing of Terrorism and the Link with Money Laundering

The fight against terrorism became a global priority in the aftermath of the terrorist attacks that began with 9/11. Following these events, the FATF mandate was extended to cover not only money laundering but also terrorist finance. In particular, the FATF has adopted a series of special recommendations specific to terrorist financing which are largely mirrored in the EU's approach. The EU's mandate was also extended to cover not only money laundering but also terrorist finance, owing to the adoption of nine special recommendations at the FATF level.[54] The main justification for this proposal has again been the need to update EU law in the light of the FATF.[55] While some of these recommendations simply reflect the UN framework, others represent a 'unique' European approach specifically targeting cross-border cash movements.[56] However, as noted, the definition of terrorism in the Money Laundering Directive is similar but not identical to the classical definition found in the 1999 UN Convention, but is in line with the EU Framework Decision on the suppression of terrorism.[57]

The terrorist-related laundering process is sometimes known as 'reverse money laundering', which refers to the use of 'clean' money for 'dirty' ends.[58] It is, therefore, much harder for a financial institution to identify terrorist-related money laundering, and it is extremely difficult to trace or prove the proceeds of crime before a crime is committed. Therefore, the financing of terrorism and countering the financing of terrorism presupposes a different risk perception than that of classic anti-money laundering.[59] What makes it difficult for laws to prevent terrorism financing is that many terrorist cells are self-financing.[60] Nevertheless, the financing of terrorism is now included in the 2005 Directive. Recital 8 of the Directive is instructive and states:

> the misuse of the financial system to channel criminal or even clean money to terrorist purposes poses a clear risk to the integrity, proper functioning, reputation and stability of the financial system. Accordingly, the preventive measures of this Directive should cover not only the manipulation of money derived from crime but also the collection of money or property for terrorist purposes.

Furthermore, Article 1(4) of the Directive clarifies the meaning of terrorism financing by stipulating that:

> For the purposes of this Directive terrorist financing means the provision or collection of funds by any means, directly or indirectly, with the intention that they should be

[54] Mitsilegas and Gilmore (above n 24).

[55] ibid.

[56] eg S Peers, 'EU Responses to Terrorism' (2003) 52 *ICLQ* 227.

[57] Amending Framework Decision 2008/919/JHA [2008] OJ L300/42.

[58] A Kersten, 'Financing of Terrorism – A Predicate Offence to Money Laundering?' in M Pieth (ed), *Financing Terrorism* (The Hague, Kluwer Law Publishing, 2002) 49.

[59] ibid.

[60] N Ryder, 'A false Sense of Security? An Analysis of Legislative Approaches towards the Prevention of Terrorist Finance in the United States and the United Kingdom' (2007) *Journal of Business Law* 821.

> used, in full or in part, in order to carry out any of the offences within the meaning of Articles 1 to 4 of Council framework decision 2002/475JHA on combating terrorism.[61]

It should be noted that there was no universal definition of terrorism until the abovementioned Framework Decision was adopted. Consequently, the EU has been highly innovative in at least providing a definition. Nonetheless, a common claim is that the definitions of terrorism in this measure are too broad. For instance, the offence 'destruction of social structures of a country' hardly meets the strict construction requirement encompassed in the principle of legality.[62]

Another well-known problem with the EU's fight against terrorism and terrorist financing – and without entering the domain of criminal law in general – has been the increased focus on subjectivism, that is on the subjective element, amounting to excessive *mens rea*.[63] It should be noted that the *mens rea* requirement is traditionally only of interest once *actus reus* has already been established (the subjective and objective requirement).[64] The offence of terrorism, however, erases these distinctions and goes straight to the delicate question of intent by focusing only on the motive in question.[65] Accordingly, this issue connects with the principle of legality as discussed in chapter two. For example, and as will be discussed in the next chapter, the UK has enacted anti-terrorism legislation with an extremely broad ambit, such as the Terrorism Act of 2006, which poses difficulties from the perspective of maximum certainty.

Moreover, as explained, the Third Money Laundering Directive is based on Article 114 TFEU (and Article 53 TFEU and ex Article 47 EC) yet it remains unclear how the combating of the financing of terrorism connects to market-making at all. After all, combating international terrorism is not within the EU's competence *stricto sensu*, although it is true that the *Kadi* ruling[66] as explained in chapter four, has found ways of remedying such a lack of legislative powers by relying on a conjunctive reading of ex Articles 60, 301 EC (now Article 215 TFEU) and 308 EC (now Article 352 TFEU). It should also be noted that the suppression of 'European' terrorism was explicitly on the list in ex Article 31(e) EU and the freezing of funds is now an objective of the Lisbon Treaty as set out in Article 75 TFEU.[67] The key point, however, is whether combining the suppression of money laundering and the financing of terrorism in the same instrument, would cause

[61] Council Framework Decision (above n 26). Amending Framework Decision 919/JHA [2008] OJ L330 added the offences of 'public provocation', 'training' and 'recruitment' to the definition of terrorism provided in the Council of Europe Convention on the Prevention of Terrorism.

[62] J Husabo, 'The Implementation of New Rules on Terrorism through the Pillars of the European Union' in J Husabo and A Strandbakken, *Harmonization of Criminal Law in Europe* (Antwerp, Intersentia, 2005) 58.

[63] ibid.

[64] As should be clear from any criminal law textbook eg, A Ashworth, *Principles of EU Criminal Law* (Oxford, Oxford University Press, 2006).

[65] It should be observed here that in English criminal law, *mens rea* covers part of what would constitute *actus reus* in civilian traditions, which means that the exact distinction between these two sides of the construction of a crime is far from clear. Ashworth (ibid) ch 2.

[66] Case C-402/05P [2008] *Kadi* ECR I-6351.

[67] See ch 4 Part II.

any problems, and how effective such a combination would be. This question is relevant because, for example, it has been pointed out that while money is the *raison d'être* of organised crime, this is not the case with terrorism.[68] The reason for this is often held to be that unlike organised crime, terrorism is not geared towards generating economic benefits. In other words, money is a means rather than an end for terrorism networks.[69] According to one commentator, it is in this respect that the traditional definition of money laundering breaks down.[70] More specifically, although it is true that supporters or financers are obviously a very important source of funds, they do not necessarily commit criminal offences in acquiring the property they give to the organisation in question.[71] Therefore, it has been emphasised that with terrorist funding, the focus should not be on where the property has come from but on where it is directed, that is, its ultimate purpose. Hence, the problems outlined here are far from new and constitute some of the main difficulties with combating terrorism – that is, it has a clear psychological dimension rendering traditional criminological templates inadequate. Consequently, simply removing financial means or specific finance channels cannot remove the original danger, namely the commission of further acts of terror. Nevertheless, the EU follows the pattern set out in the European Union Counter-Terrorism Strategy, which stresses the need to prevent, protect, pursue and respond (adopted in December 2005 by the Justice and Home Affairs Council).[72] As noted, this is also in line with the UN and FATF approaches.[73] The problem is that focusing on the financial aspects of terrorism is a useful weapon but is no panacea.[74]

Finally, in addition to Framework Decision 2002/475/JHA, the Commission issued a Proposal for an amendment of the Framework Decision which has now been transposed as Framework Decision 2008/919.[75] Briefly, this measure states that the 'old' Framework Decision needs to be updated in order to keep pace with the increasingly growing phenomenon of internet crimes, specifically to cover public incitement to commit terrorist offences and recruitment for terrorism. Clearly, this is highly dynamic territory and has had a strong cross-pillar dimension.

[68] M Kliching, 'Financial Counterterrorism initiatives in Europe' in C Fijnaut et al (eds), *Legal Instruments in the Fight against International Terrorism* (Leiden, Brill Publishing, 2004) 203.

[69] ibid. As the expression goes: 'organized criminals seek to earn money, terrorists spend it'.

[70] Alexander (above n 15).

[71] ibid.

[72] Available at register.consilium.europa.eu/pdf/en/05/st14/st14469-re04.en05.pdf (last accessed January 2012).

[73] I Bantekas and S Nash, *International Criminal Law* (London, Cavendish 2003) ch 3.

[74] W Gilmore, 'International Financial Counterterrorism Initiatives' in C Fijnaut et al (above n 68) 189.

[75] Amending Framework Decision on combating terrorism (above n 57). See also Commission 'amending Framework Decision 2002/475/JHA on combating terrorism' (Communication) COM (2007) 650 final.

i. Short Comment on the Former Third Pillar Dimension

It should be noted that the 2005 Directive may also have an important impact on how EU policies develop in the area of criminal confiscation, which was previously a third pillar issue,[76] since for the first time the Directive requires Member States to ensure they are able to review the effectiveness of their systems to combat money laundering or terrorist financing by maintaining comprehensive statistics on any matters relevant to the effectiveness of these systems. Such statistics, as a minimum, must cover 'how much property has been frozen, seized or confiscated by competent authorities'. In this respect, it could be argued that the future availability of such comparable statistical information should allow important inferences to be drawn regarding the effectiveness of the Member States' different approaches to the confiscation of criminal assets.[77]

After all, it has been suggested that the main achievements of the EU in combating money laundering and terrorism should be sought in the former intergovernmental sphere and moreover that they are to be found in related areas such as that of the confiscation of criminal proceeds and not in the money laundering/terrorism instruments themselves. The measures in question are the Framework Decision on the freezing of property and evidence,[78] the Framework Decision on confiscation of crime-related proceeds, instrumentalities and property[79], and the Framework Decision on the application of the principle of mutual recognition to confiscation orders.[80] One could question the need for further legislation in connection with money laundering given that there was already a Framework Decision regulating the same area.

E. The Multifaceted Threat of Organised Crime and its Relationship with Money Laundering

As indicated, the somewhat broad securitisation of the EU's fight against crime poses challenges for criminal law.[81] In particular, there seems to be no clear dividing line between organised crime and Union efforts to combat dirty money. Moreover, any attempt to measure the occurrence of organised crime is affected by a number of factors including the diversity of what is actually being measured.[82] The reason for devoting a separate section to organised crime is to illustrate that, as already mentioned, there is an overlap between terrorism, money

[76] Note that the Transitional protocol stipulates a five-year transition period before former third pillar instruments will be treated in the same way as Community instruments.

[77] N Kaye, 'Freezing and Confiscation of Criminal Proceeds' (2006) 77 *Revue Internationale de Droit Penal* 326.

[78] Framework Decision 2003/22/JHA OJ L196/45.

[79] Framework Decision 2005/212 JHA OJ L68/49.

[80] Framework Decision 2006/783/JHA OJ L328.

[81] eg Mitsilegas (above n 12) at 8–9.

[82] ibid.

laundering and organised crime. Regardless of whether one could separate organised crime from other more specific forms of organised criminality, it is often argued that money laundering constitutes a means of furthering the interests of organised crime by attributing quasi-lawfulness to the latter's criminal proceeds, which are subsequently used in their unlawful activities.[83] Organised crime thus appears to constitute a varied security threat but it seems less clear whose security it imperils, strictly speaking. However, it is generally accepted that the definition of organised crime at the EU level is largely influenced by Italian anti-mafia regulation.[84]

In any event, the penalisation of 'organised crime' entered the Union arena with the entry into force of the Maastricht Treaty as part of the wider concept of 'international crime'.[85] As in the case of the suppression of terrorism, it should be pointed out that the EU's path towards the criminalisation of organised crime essentially follows the UN approach. Looking back at the EU history of organised crime, the first move towards fighting organised crime was the Treaty of Amsterdam (see Articles 29 to 31 EU) although there had been specific references to the phenomenon of 'organised crime' as early as the Europol Convention[86] of 1995.[87] Another example of an early reference to the concept of organised crime is to be found in the third pillar convention on extradition.[88] However, the first explicit EU instrument in the fight against organised crime was adopted in the 1997 Action Plan to combat organised crime.[89]

Moreover, in 2006 the Council agreed on a Framework Decision,[90] which slightly modified the definition of a 'criminal organisation'. More specifically, this measure stipulated that participation in such an organisation consisted of either taking part in an organisation's criminal or other activities, or agreeing with other persons to pursue activities that would amount to the commission of serious offences.[91] More recently, in October 2008 the Council adopted the new 2008/841/JHA Framework Decision on the fight against organised crime.[92] Nevertheless, it has been observed that the Commission's increased focus on a general expansion

[83] ibid.

[84] Gilmore, *Dirty Money* (above n 9).

[85] V Mitsilegas, 'Defining Organized Crime in the European Union' (2001) 26 *EL Rev* 565. See also M Fichera, 'Organized Crime: Developments and Challenges for an Enlarged European Union' in C Eckes and T Konstadinides, *Crime within the Area of Freedom, Security and Justice* (Cambridge, Cambridge University Press, 2011) 159.

[86] Europol Convention [1995] OJ C316.

[87] Thereafter, a European Council resolution made specific reference to 'the fight against international organised crime' although it did not provide a definition of what really constituted organised crime. V Mitsilegas, 'The Ambivalent Concept of Transnational Organized Crime' in M Beare (ed), *Critical Reflections on Transnational Organized Crime: Money Laundering and Corruption* (Toronto, Toronto University Press, 2003) 72.

[88] Extradition Convention [2006] OJ C313/1.

[89] 1997 Action Plan to combat organised crime, OJ C251/1.

[90] Proposal for a Council Framework decision on the fight against organised crime, COM (2005) 6, final 19 January 2005.

[91] eg, see generally S Peers, *EU Justice and Home Affairs* (Oxford, Oxford University Press, 2011) ch 9.

[92] 2008/841/JHA Framework Decision on the fight against organised crime, [2008] OJ L300/42.

of the expected sentences is not in line with legality; in some cases it constitutes a double assessment of the same elements and as such violates the proportionality principle.[93] Admittedly however, many of the broadly-defined offences, such as the definition of 'participation in criminal law organisation', have simply been copied from UN measures in this area. Nevertheless, it has been pointed out that the EU seems to equate organised crime with terrorism more generally and that making a parallel with terrorism is inappropriate, as the wrongfulness of acts of terrorism is quite different from that of organised (economic) crimes.[94] What is more, such an approach will inevitably lead to an undue expansion of organised crime as a true umbrella label.[95]

In summing up this short analysis of organised crime: it seems clear that the EU's attempt to adopt a broad global instrument against organised crime faces the challenge of accommodating divergent legal and empirical realities. The problem is that we are dealing with an area which is notoriously difficult to defineand it has resulted in all-encompassing and vague provisions at the EU level. For this reason, it has been suggested that any new EU proposal for a legal instrument in this area should – apart from the constituent element of the criminal organisation already in use – include some reference to an 'entrepreneurial' and not merely 'structured' group.[96] More specifically, such a classification should be characterised by the following: (a) an allocation of specific roles between its members; (b) possession of an abundance of technical and – notably – financial means that it uses for the fulfilment of its criminal objectives, or involvement in legitimate financial structures that yield high profits; and (c) the aim of the acquisition of wealth on a massive scale.[97] It has also been proposed that the main criminal activity from which illegal profits are accrued should arguably only be identified with crimes committed by a criminal organisation with an entrepreneurial structure, as such a demarcation of organised crime would mean that at least those onerous measures which do not have a clear preventive character may be confined to actions of increased harmfulness in line with the principle of proportionality, which would in turn facilitate the fight against organised crime.[98]

i. The Tangled Web of EU Anti-corruption Policy

It is necessary to touch upon the question of corruption and the notion of white-collar crime more generally. As noted above, 'corruption' is included in Article 3(5)(e) in the 2005 Directive, but no definition is given. The Commission's own website is instructive when seeking to understand the EU's policy on corruption.

[93] M Kaiafa-Gbandi, 'Towards a New Approach of Organized Crime in the EU: New Challenges for Human Tights' (2007) 3 *Zeitschrift für Internationale Strafrechtsdogmatik* 537.

[94] ibid.

[95] ibid.

[96] E Symeonidou-Kastanidou, 'Towards a Definition of Organized Crime in the European Union' (2007) 16 *European Journal of Crime, Criminal Law and Criminal Justice* 83.

[97] ibid.

[98] ibid.

Here 'corruption' is singled out as hampering trust and democracy.[99] In 1997 the EU adopted the Convention on the fight against corruption, which distinguished between 'passive' (the deliberate action of an official directly or through an intermediary) and active corruption (the deliberate action of whoever promises or gives directly or through an intermediary).[100] Although there is a link between corruption and organised crime, they have been dealt with separately within the EU, in contrast to the UN where they have been dealt with in tandem.[101] However, even though the EU has fought corruption through civil law means, the Commission recently presented a working document, which stressed the importance of criminalisation.[102] Here, 'corruption' is defined as an abuse of power for private gain.[103]

In any case, it has been argued that one of the problems with the fight against white-collar crime is the excessive use of the criminal law to regulate such irregularities. The point is that while the offences are drafted in draconian terms, the enforcement of the punishments imposed tend to be weak, which undermines the credibility of the legislation in question.[104] The EU's approach here is often described as consisting of three parts.[105] Initially, the policy was directed at protecting Community finances from corruption from within the EU's own institutions. The second objective was to provide EU citizens with a high level of safety in the AFSJ, devoid of criminal activity. The third rationale for EU anti-corruption measures relates to the internal market and, more specifically, to linking the elimination of corruption to market integration. There is also a clear link between the EU anti-corruption policies and public procurement.[106] For example, Directives 2004/17 and 2004/18[107] on public procurement require mandatory exclusion on the ground of corruption, the participation in criminal organisations and the occurrence of fraud and money laundering (Articles 54 and 45 respectively). Clearly, the EU's anti-corruption network is difficult to grasp but it deserves mention as it is interlinked with the more general effort to combat organised crime at the EU level.[108] In addition, the third Anti-Money Laundering Directive lists corruption as one of the predicate offences for money laundering. Finally, it should be noted that the Commission has recently launched a communication on Fighting Corruption in the EU.[109]

[99] ec.europa.eu/dgs/olaf/mission/index_en.html (last accessed January 2012).

[100] Convention against Corruption [1997] OJ C195/1.

[101] Commission staff working document, an examination of the links between organized crime and corruption Sec (2008) 196, 8 February 2008.

[102] ibid.

[103] For a recent analysis, P Sazarek-Mason, 'EU Policy against Corruption' in C Eckes and T Konstadinides (above n 85) 43.

[104] Hinterseer (above n 14) ch 4.

[105] ibid.

[106] S Williams, 'The Mandatory Exclusions for Corruption in the New EC Procurement Directives' (2006) 31 *EL Rev* 711.

[107] OJ L134, 30 April 2004, 1–113, 114–240.

[108] Green Paper on the modernisation of EU public procurement policy, Towards a more efficient European Public Procurement Market, COM (2011) 15 final.

[109] Commission 'Fighting Corruption in the EU' (Communication), COM (2011) 308 final. See Council Document 17024/09, adopted by the European Council on 10/11 December 2009. (OJ C115,

After outlining EU anti money laundering legislation and the concept of 'organised crime' and the vague concept of 'corruption' it is appropriate to examine the 2005 Money Laundering Directive in further detail. After all, the 2005 Money Laundering Directive is ground-breaking in the sense that it introduces for the first time the concept of a 'risk based' approach in EU criminal law. Indeed, within EU criminal law the use of risk as a legal concept was first introduced in the context of anti-money laundering legislation. For this reason it is worth looking at how risk has been used and understood in this particular context. It could be argued that the word 'risk' has been used not only to justify EU action but also as a way of imposing a harsher criminal law regime. Hence, the next section sheds some light on the question of EU risk regulation and more specifically, addresses it in the framework of EU criminal law.

F. Why is 'Risk' Important in EU Anti-money Laundering? Beyond Suspicious Reporting

The Third Money Laundering Directive is innovative in its emphasis on a risk-based approach.[110] Within such a risk-based approach to money laundering, private actors, such as lawyers and banks, are expected to make risk assessments of their customers and divide them into low and high-risk.[111] The rationale for actively engaging the private sector in the anti-money laundering process is to ensure that they collect the appropriate information.[112] This is commonly referred to as a 'risk-based approach' because private actors are required to pass on sensitive information based on a risk assessment of their clients. However, the risk-based approach could also be seen in a broader governing context of risk regulation at the EU (criminal law) level. Therefore, the question of the governing of risk connects to the justification of EU legislative action under Article 114 TFEU.

i. Risk-based Approach to Money Laundering and Terrorist Financing

When discussing the risk-based approach it is tempting to wonder whether a risk-based approach is the same as a 'preventive' approach. This is interesting at least

1). See also the Resolution of the Council 6902/05, adopted on 14 May 2005, which called upon the Commission to also consider the development of a mutual evaluation and monitoring mechanism.

[110] Directive 2005/60/EC of 25 November 2005 [2005] OJ L309.

[111] This is the so-called customer due diligence requirement (know-your-customer) and forms part of the risk-based confidence and transparency policy. In short, customer due diligence is to be applied in four cases. First, when establishing a 'business relationship'; secondly, when carrying out larger transactions; thirdly, regardless of any derogation, exemption or threshold, where there is a suspicion of money laundering or terrorist financing; and fourthly, where there are doubts about the veracity or adequacy of previously obtained customer identification data.

[112] For an interesting discussion on how these private actors can be held accountable, see M Bergstrom et al, 'A New Role for Profit Actors? The Case of Anti-money Laundering and Risk Management' (2011) 49 *Journal of Common Market Studies* 5, 1043.

from the perspective of criminal law, as the increased attention to risk assessment at the EU level is mirrored in the literature on criminology, which focuses on the cause and prevention of crime.[113] Therefore, the Money Laundering Directive promotes the risk-based approach both in customer due diligence standards and in the approach that supervisory authorities take in order to monitor firms.[114] However, little attention has been paid to how the private sector responds to the notion of 'risk'.[115] There is, moreover, an obvious lack of criminological research in this area.[116] For example, it has been pointed out that although the 2005 Directive is said to be risk-based, it is not based on 'risk' in the sense that underground banking transactions are (completely) forbidden.[117]

Nevertheless, there seems to be a tendency in EU institutions to treat risk assessment as 'risk elimination'.[118] The point remains, as pointed out by other commentators, that the apparent 'less' versus 'more' dichotomy which seem to dominate 'better regulation' is unhelpful when discussing regulatory choices, as 'better' is not only a very fuzzy word but is also highly subjective.[119] It is true that the notion of impact assessment has found its way into this area as demonstrated, for example, by the proposal for the amending Framework Decision[120] on combating terrorism, mentioned above. There is a willingness to engage in the perception of 'better' law making, and yet – and herein lies the main problem – there seems to be a clear lack of experience in dealing with these kind of 'crime' issues. In the context of the third pillar sphere, a further complexity is that such inexperience originates partly from the fact that there has been another decision-making procedure within the former third pillar.[121] It has thus been argued that the third pillar illustrates how impact assessment should *not* be carried out, because of the political sensitivity of these kinds of issues which tend to become the focus of attention.[122] Another explanation, apart from a lack of time and resources, has been that within the third pillar the proposed measure was often on the table prior to the relevant impact assessment.[123] One could argue, therefore, that the very notion of impact assessment in EU criminal law has revealed a similarly vague picture as the principle of subsidiarity (discussed in chapter four part IV),

[113] H Albrecht and M Kilchling, 'Crime Risk Assessment, Legislation, and the Prevention of Serious Crime – Comparative Perspectives' (2002) 10 *European Journal of Crime, Criminal Law and Criminal Justice* 23.

[114] See eg, UK HM Treasury report (implementing the Third Money Laundering Directive: A consultation Document) available at www.hm-treasury.gov.uk/media/E/D/moneylaundering310706.pdf (last accessed January 2012).

[115] H Albrecht and M Kilchling (above n 113).

[116] ibid.

[117] M Borgers, 'Regulating and combating underground banking' (2009) 22 *Criminal Law Forum* 97.

[118] S Weatherill, 'The Challenges of Better Regulation' in Weatherill (ed), *Better Regulation* (Oxford, Hart Publishing, 2007) 7.

[119] JB Wiener, 'Better Regulation' (2006) 59 *Current Legal Problems* 447.

[120] COM (2007) 650 final, 6 November 2007.

[121] A Meuwese, *Impact Assessment in EU Lawmaking* (The Hague, Kluwer Law Publishing, 2008) ch 7.

[122] ibid.

[123] ibid.

in being infrequently considered by the EU's institutions.[124] However, it seems as if the Lisbon Treaty offers a more attractive framework in this respect. As explained in chapter four, Article 69 TFEU stresses the importance of subsidiarity in the AFSJ sphere. The Commission's yearly evaluation of its own approach to subsidiarity and proportionality is less enthusiastic albeit instructive: although things are becoming considerably more sophisticated in this field, the AFSJ sphere is merely listed in the annex as a reference to the Stockholm programme and as an example of where attention was being paid to subsidiarity and proportionality in an impact assessment.[125]

More generally, it should be noted – as briefly discussed in chapter four Part IV above – that Article 70 TFEU provides for evaluation measures to be taken within the AFSJ. These evaluations are non-legislative acts adopted by qualified majority voting in the Council on a proposal from the Commission and with no involvement from the European Parliament (EP).[126] The purpose is to ensure the correct implementation of AFSJ measures into national law. The focus is thereby limited to the implementation of AFSJ policies which are intended to facilitate mutual recognition. Indeed, the Stockholm programme[127] calls for regular evaluation of the AFSJ policies and for the Commission to make proposals to implement Article 70 TFEU.[128] Accordingly, the Stockholm programme endorses the need for a more evidence-based approach in this area.[129] In addition, this agenda highlights the need for more effective regulation as well as a strong security focus.[130] The Stockholm programme is an example of such focus as it frequently emphasises the need for more effective policies and better regulation, implying a need to better address certain risks. Article 71 TFEU also stipulates that a standing committee should be set up to ensure that operational cooperation on internal security is promoted and strengthened within the Union. Such a committee was established by the Council shortly after the entry into force of the Lisbon Treaty.[131] Thus, there seems to be a close link between a risk-based approach and the concept of security in this area.

It is therefore useful to set out some basic EU concepts of risk.

[124] For an interesting discussion of the quality of EU impact assessments more generally, see J Torriti, 'The unsustainable rationality of impact assessment' (2011) 31 *European Journal of Law and Economics* 307

[125] Report from the Commission on subsidiarity and proportionality, COM (2010) 547, see ch 4 Part IV.

[126] On accountability see S Peers, *EU Justice and Home Affairs* (Oxford, Oxford University Press, 2011) 51–52.

[127] The Stockholm programme – An open and secure Europe serving and protecting the citizen (Council of the European Union Brussels, 2 December 2009), available at http://register.consilium.europa.eu/pdf/en/09/st17/st17024.en09.pdf (last accessed January 2012).

[128] Commission, 'Delivering an area of freedom, security and justice for Europe's citizens' COM (2010) 171.

[129] M Fletcher, 'EU Criminal Law Justice beyond Lisbon' in T Konstadinides and C Eckes (above n 85) 40–41.

[130] COM (2010) 171 (above n 128).

[131] [2010] OJ L52/50. See Peers n 93 at 53. The Commission's communication sets out 'Five steps towards a more secure Europe': the disruption of international crime networks, the prevention of terrorism, security in cyberspace, improved border management, and increased resilience to crises and disasters. See www.statewatch.org/news/2011/may/eu-internal-security-uk-hol-report.pdf (last accessed January 2012).

ii. What is Risk in EU Law?

The idea of 'risk' regulation in EU law has, of course, developed within the framework of environmental law and the question of scientific uncertainty.[132] It is equally well known that the starting point when discussing 'risk' at the EU level is the precautionary principle, although the birth of such a principle and the evolution of the EU's risk regulation regime have occurred in tandem.[133] Of course, the precautionary principle in the EU context was developed into a general principle by the Court of First Instance (CFI) in the cases of *Pfizer* and *Artegodan*.[134] These cases are crucial and made clear – among other things – that the burden of proof in relation to the need to take precautionary measures was on the EU institutions. More generally, it should be recalled that the precautionary principle can be used by either the EU legislator (as cause to take action if the 'risk' prompts action taken before the danger has occurred) or by Member States (as a way of derogation from EU law).[135] Nevertheless, the Commission in its famous communication on risk regulation stated that a revised burden of proof might be necessary if substances were deemed a priori hazardous.[136] In any case, there seems to be very little examination of the interrelationship between notions of risk regulation and the precautionary principle and the latter is being applied in many different, though interrelated, contexts.[137] More to the point, there seems to be no fixed understanding of 'risk'.

Certainly, the precautionary principle seems highly complex and its wider implications are beyond the scope of this chapter. In any event, the precautionary principle is mostly on the agenda in connection with environmental protection and is especially important in relation to risk management that regulates understandings of reasonable administrative discretion in circumstances of scientific uncertainty.[138] The relationship between EU risk regulation and the precautionary principle seems rather imprecise as there is a considerable amount of overlap.[139] Despite this, it could be argued that although the precautionary principle has so far dominated the EU law scene, its application may be seen as too costly and that in future the EU regulator will prefer greater use of 'impact assessments'.[140] Others have argued that the precautionary principle has already been included in the

[132] eg M Lee, *EU Environmental Law* (Oxford, Hart Publishing, 2005). Some of this section draws on E Herlin-Karnell, 'The EU's Anti Money Laundering Agenda: Built on Risk?' in T Konstadinides and C Eckes (above n 85).

[133] L Fisher, *Risk Regulation and Administrative Constitutionalism* (Oxford, Hart Publishing, 2007) ch 6.

[134] Case T-13/99 *Pfizer* [2002] ECR II-3305, T-141/00 *Artegodan* [2002] ECR II-4945.

[135] P Craig, *EU Administrative Law* (Oxford, Oxford University Press, 2006) 721.

[136] Commission on the precautionary principle (Communication) COM (2000)1 final.

[137] J Torriti, 'Impact Assessment in the EU: A Tool for Better Regulation, Less Regulation or Less Bad Regulation' (2007) 10 *Journal of Risk Research* 239.

[138] Fisher (above n 133).

[139] Meuwese (above n 121).

[140] J Torriti (above n 137).

concept of 'impact assessment'.[141] More generally however, risk analysis is said to be composed of risk assessment, risk management and risk communication where risk assessment constitutes a scientific process entailing four stages set out in the Commission's communication (hazard identification, hazard characterisation, exposure assessment and risk characterisation).[142] Thus, 'risk management' means a process distinct from risk assessment where policy alternatives are weighed in consultation with interested parties, considering risk assessment and other legitimate factors, and if necessary, selecting appropriate prevention and control options. Finally, risk communication is about exchange of information at all stages of risk analysis between all interested parties.[143]

The question arises, nevertheless, as to whether the precautionary principle, as a tool of risk analysis intended for risk control, belongs under 'risk assessment' or 'risk management'.[144] At least the Commission seems to be of the view that 'measures applying the precautionary principle belong to the general framework of risk analysis, and in particular risk management'.[145] Risk management, in contrast to risk assessment, is the public process of deciding how safe is safe when making political decisions.[146] However, any such decision must comply with the principle of proportionality. As has been noted by commentators, there seems to be no fixed understanding of risk assessment.[147] Moreover, as will be shown, these concepts of management, assessment and communication appear somewhat blurred in the framework of the EU's anti-money laundering and crime agendas, as it is far from clear that one could adopt the same understanding of 'risk' in EU criminal law.

Thus, the subject we will explore in further detail is what the reliance on 'risk' means in the context of the 2005 Directive. For example, it could be suggested that even though the text of this Directive refers to hazardous aspects of risk, the notion of risk can also present itself as opportunity.[148] The reason for this, the argument goes, is that in taking a risk, 'hazard' and 'opportunity' are two sides of the same coin, whereas 'being at risk' emphasises hazard alone. However, looking at the precautionary principle, it has been noted that the CFI distinguished between 'risk', on the one hand, and 'hazard' or 'danger', on the other.[149] More specifically, the CFI in the *Pfizer* case indicated that the precautionary principle can apply (paragraph 146) 'only in situations where there is a risk, notably to human health, which, although it has not yet been fully demonstrated, is not founded on mere hypothesis that have not been scientifically confirmed'. The

[141] Meuwese (above n 121).
[142] eg Lee (above n 132) 80–81.
[143] ibid.
[144] J da Cruz Vilaca, 'The Precautionary Principle in EC Law' (2004) 10 *European Public Law* 369.
[145] COM (2000) 1 final (above n 90).
[146] N de Sadeleer, 'The Precautionary Principle in EC Health and Environmental Law' (2006) 12 *ELJ* 139.
[147] eg G Majone, 'What price safety?' (2002) 40 *Journal of Common Market Studies* 89.
[148] D Demetis and O Angell, 'The Risk-based Approach to AML: Representation, Paradox and the 3rd Directive' (2007) 10 *Journal of Money Laundering Control* 412.
[149] Fisher (above n 133).

Commission has also stated that the precautionary principle should not be used for arbitrary decision-making.[150] However, it still leaves the definition of risk largely undefined.

It is true that the 2005 Directive distinguishes between high and low risk; the Directive is implies that risk can be quantified.[151] Nevertheless, the delineation of low and high risk in the FATF and 2005 Directive is problematic. It singles out all cash intensive business as being subject to manipulation by launderers, but also as risk hybrids (both low and high risk). Furthermore, as regards the attribution of 'risk sensitivity', it has been pointed out that it quickly becomes evident that such a concept of risk sensitivity is even more elusive than the risk itself. More specifically, '[since] there is a widespread misunderstanding of the way risk is perceived, represented and handled; we choose not to refer to managing or controlling risk because these are inappropriate oversimplifications'.[152] Thus, it could be suggested that it is not the handling of risk itself that is crucial but its communication (risk assessment) between stakeholders. It seems easy to get involved in metaphysics here, as the whole concept of 'risk' becomes questionable as 'each individual, despite using the same categorical labels, will make different decisions'.[153] But in fact, the question of the risk-based strategy is also related to the idea of confidence as a justification for harmonisation and is particularly relevant to the discussion on competence in chapter four Part III. At issue here is the fact that the EU legislator relies on arguments that are far from clear (for example, what is risk?). It also illustrates that there are many different meanings of 'risk' in the EU's fight against money laundering and the financing of terrorism. The policy question which thus arises is whether the EU's suppression of the money laundering agenda constitutes an effective approach to dealing with 'dirty' money. Indeed, it was recently stressed in an international survey that after almost 20 years the results of money-laundering prevention have been disappointing and organised crime and drug trafficking continue to prosper.[154] In short, this survey concluded that:

— Measures taken to prevent money laundering in the financial system should be judged on their effectiveness to achieve their stated goal and the benefits should be defined in terms of predicate crimes.
— As a general rule, a measure should be deployed only if the benefits achieved exceed its costs. It is not feasible to place a high burden on society and the economy without corresponding results.

In relation to the first requirement, the 2005 Directive now focuses on this kind of tactics by broadening the list of predicate offences. The principle of legality in

[150] COM (2000)1 final.
[151] Demetis Angell (above n 148).
[152] ibid.
[153] ibid.
[154] H Geiger and O Wuensh, 'The Fight against Money Laundering: An Economic Analysis of a Cost-benefit Paradoxon' (2007) 10 *Journal of Money Laundering Control* 91.

criminal law should nonetheless not be forgotten or underestimated. The point is that any expansion of predicate offences needs to comply with the axioms of legality, such as maximum certainty, in criminal law. The second requirement reflects the EU principle of proportionality. However, the reason for the limited success of anti-money laundering regulation was, according to commentators, that the attractiveness of criminal ventures is determined by many factors, and that the aim of combating money laundering has achieved a life of its own, where the objective of preventing predicate crime has been replaced by other goals. Thus, we may ask whether these goals, apart from the apparent general will to constitutionalise criminal law, could stem from ignorance – that is, taking the positive results for granted. As noted, the risk-based strategy as 'traditionally' interpreted is related to the concept of justification for harmonisation in the first place. In other words, the attention to risk often constitutes the main explanation for the adoption of the legislation in question, as most prominently witnessed in the post-9/11 era and the many instruments adopted in aftermath of the terrorist attacks. After all, the Commission has adopted yet another instrument in the current fight against money laundering and terrorist financing. This is Directive 2006/70/EC,[155] which lays down implementing measures for Directive 2005/60/EC and stipulates that Member States shall establish risk-based monitoring activities or take any other adequate measures to ensure that the above-mentioned exemption granted by Directive 2005/60/EC is not abused by money launderers or financers of terrorism. Indeed, we could ask whether anything could be considered 'low risk' under such a definition. Finally, the question arises whether crime prevention or crime risk assessment is the same as the risk-based approach. In what follows, I will try to show how the notion of 'risk' has been translated to the EU criminal law context. Consequently, the next section outlines the meaning of risk in the area of criminal law. The reason for doing so is to show that 'risk' in EU law might not necessarily be the same in criminal law.

iii. Risk Assessment from an EU Criminal Law Perspective

The notion of 'risk' in criminal law is perhaps even more difficult than that of scientific uncertainty. It could be argued that a risk-based approach is reflected in the very idea of crime prevention. In this respect, it should be noted that the concept of financial or white-collar crime is different from the 'street crime' phenomenon when it comes to gauging risk.[156] In criminal law policy, or perhaps to some extent criminology, risk is linked to perceptions of seriousness, as well as future predictions, as not every negative consequence is considered, but only those effects which are serious enough to justify planning and prevention.[157] As in the

[155] Directive 2006/70/EC, laying down implementing measures for Directive 2005/60/EC [2006] OJ 214/29.

[156] M Maguire et al, *The Oxford Handbook of Criminology* (Oxford, Oxford University Press, 2007).

[157] ibid.

EU context, it is context that is the important factor in criminal law.[158] The central question seems to be whether it is possible to predict crime within a complex set of variables and how crime prevention should be weighed against other legitimate goals. In other words, what does it mean from the perspective of sound EU criminal law justice and the construction of the AFSJ more broadly, to justify measures based on 'risk'? It could be argued that risk is fundamentally ill-suited as a normative foundation in this area. More specifically, risk as applied in EU law (traditional scientific context) and criminal law not only illustrates the difficulty of the application of risk but also that there is a danger that it might be used as a justification to impose harsher criminal law. The problem in criminological research is – as all students of criminology know – never to trust empirical data crime rates. Crime rates can vary depending on the level of reported crime and do not necessarily reflect the number of instances of criminal activity.[159] The Scandinavian countries are often mentioned as an example of successful crime prevention with a focus on selected problems areas,[160] and this is also what the EU has done within the framework of the former third pillar.

As indicated, there is already a similar discussion in the terms of prevention in criminal law and criminology theory. After all, the notion of 'risk' in criminal law is as multifaceted as within the EU context. In short, and expressed in very simplified terms, it could be said that 'risk' in substantive criminal law theory is often a question of culpability.[161] Alternatively, it can also be a question of anti-social behaviour and criminal law policy more generally.[162] Indeed, the so-called *Corpus Juris* project on the protection of the financial interests of the Community seemed to announce a risk-based approach in EU criminal law.[163] It has been suggested that it is evident that the extent and the nature of thinking about and organising risk assessment within the framework of legislation are also dependant on the existence of crime prevention activities as well as political approaches to crime research. However, herein lie the main differences between the Member States.[164] Moreover, it could be argued that an explanation for such differences may lie in investments made in and experiences drawn from procedures within the environmental and technological spheres, where the Scandinavian countries and Germany have been 'pioneer states'.[165]

It is true that the so-called Dublin declaration called for the development of common European crime statistics to assist with the assessment of crime trends and the benchmarking of policy effectiveness, and to facilitate valid comparisons.[166] The

158 Albrecht and Kilchling (above n 113).

159 Maguire et al (above n 156).

160 ibid.

161 N Jareborg, *Allmän kriminalrätt* (Uppsala, Iustus, 2001).

162 N Lacey et al, *Reconstructing Criminal Law* (London, Butterworths, 2003) ch 3.

163 On the Corpus Juris, see M Delmas-Marty and J Vervaele, *The Implementation of Corpus Juris in the Member States*, vol 1 (Antwerp, Intersentia, 2000).

164 ibid.

165 ibid.

166 Dublin declaration on tackling organized crime (Doc 16302/03 CRIMORG 95, 19.12.2003).

Hague programme,[167] and more recently the Stockholm programme,[168] stress the importance of empirical data for developing a strategic concept on tackling organised crime. The Stockholm programme stipulates (p 43) that:

> Adequate, reliable and comparable statistics (both over time and between Member States and regions) are a necessary prerequisite, inter alia, for evidence-based decisions on the need for action, on the implementation of decisions and on the effectiveness of action.

It should also be noted that there is a Commission decision on the setting up of an expert group on the policy needs for data on crime and criminal justice.[169] The Commission has also introduced an action plan for the period 2006 to 2010 to prepare a comprehensive European strategy to measure crime and criminal justice as well as a Green Paper on detention including statistics on the prison populations in Europe.[170] Furthermore, the 2005 Directive obliges Member States to collect data. Although it is very important that the EU's institutions recognise the need to create a sophisticated system of criminal law statistics, in practice this goal has not been achieved although a system will probably develop rapidly with the force of EU criminal law.

There appears to be a connection between the notion of risk and the concept of security in EU criminal law. After all, it seems as if these ideas are fused into one concept[171] which makes it difficult to pin down what exactly the EU is referring to when using the language of 'risk'. In other words, although the Third Money Laundering introduces the notion of a 'risk-based' approach, it could be argued that what really is at stake is an emphasis on *security*. Hence, the underlying question is the link between risk and security in this regard.

G. Risk as Security

As explained, ever since the events of 9/11 there has been a growing securitisation of the AFSJ.[172] After all, it is stated in Article 67 TFEU that the Union shall not only constitute an AFSJ (as promised by Title V of the TFEU) but that it shall endeavour to ensure a high level of security. This shall be done through measures to prevent and combat crime, racism and xenophobia, and through measures for coordination and cooperation between police and judicial authorities and other

[167] The Hague programme: Strengthening Freedom, Security and Justice in the EU [2005] OJ C53/1.

[168] The Stockholm programme (above n 127).

[169] 2006/581/EC Commission Decision of 7 August 2006 setting up a group of experts on the policy needs for data on crime and criminal justice [2006] OJ L234.

[170] Developing a comprehensive and coherent EU strategy to measure crime and criminal justice: an EU Action Plan 2006–2010 COM (2006) 437 final. See also Strengthening mutual trust in the European judicial area – A Green Paper on the application of EU criminal justice legislation in the field of detention, with annex on prison population in Europe 2009–2010 COM (2011) 327 final.

[171] L Zedner, 'The Concept of Security: An Agenda for Comparative Analysis' (2003) *Legal Studies* 153.

[172] eg J Monar, 'The Area of Freedom, Security and Justice' in A Von Bogdandy and J Bast (eds), *Principles of European Constitutional Law* 2nd edn (Oxford/Munich, Hart/Beck/Nomos, 2010) 551.

competent authorities, as well as through the mutual recognition of judgments in criminal matters and, if necessary, through the approximation of criminal laws.

It would seem natural to begin this section with a definition of 'security'. However, security is rarely defined in EU law.[173] It is, of course, true that the question of security in EU law has traditionally been an external relations matter (defence concerns) or an issue of the internal market as a means of derogation from EU law (public policy, public security and so on).[174] After all, in EU law there are various provisions allowing Member States to derogate from its rules on security grounds, subject – of course – to proportionality.[175] More fundamentally, the notion of security in EU law has evolved as part of the peace mission but has expanded far beyond the desire to avoid state violence.[176] So 'security' has had a dual dimension here: on the one hand the external dimension of security under the framework of the CFSP, and on the other hand is the internal dimension of security within the AFSJ.[177]

Consequently, it is necessary to return to the recent Stockholm programme.[178] In section four of this programme, the security agenda for the next five years is clearly set out. It states that the Union should define a comprehensive EU internal security strategy based on the clarity of the division of tasks between the EU and Member States, reflecting a shared vision of today's challenges. It also states that such an agenda shall respect fundamental rights, international protection and the rule of law as well as solidarity between Member States. Moreover, it points out that 'security' requires an integrated approach. In this respect the internal security mission, as proclaimed by Stockholm, is tied to making the AFSJ agenda more effective. As will be discussed further, however, it is difficult to get a true sense of what such a focus on security involves. In fact, it could be argued that the Stockholm programme is highly ambiguous in its emphasis on 'security' whilst claiming to protect and serve the citizen. Indeed, it is interesting how much the focus on security within AFSJ area of law has increased from the Tampere conclusions to the recent Stockholm programme. Yet security is not simply a question of enforcement of EU law. Furthermore, particularly in the context of legislative competences and data retention, as already mentioned at the outset of this chapter, it should be recalled that AG Bot has justified reliance on Article 114 TFEU (ex Article 95 EC) for the establishment and functioning of the internal market in

[173] It is rather to be found in political science literature, see eg, S Lavenex and W Wagner, 'Which European Security? Sources of Imbalance in the European Area of Freedom, Security and Justice' *European Security* 16 (2007) 225 and special issue in *Journal of European Integration* 31 (2009) 'The External Dimension of Justice and Home Affairs: A Different Security Agenda for the EU?' 83.

[174] eg Art 45(3) and (4) TFEU.

[175] For a recent example, see Case C-145/09 *Tsakouridis* judgment of 23 November 2010. In this case the Court held that an expulsion measure must be based on an individual examination of the specific case and can be justified on imperative grounds of public security within the meaning of Article 28(3) of Directive 2004/38 only if, having regard to the exceptional seriousness of the threat.

[176] On the peace mission in relation to security, see A Williams, *The Ethos of Europe* (Cambridge, Cambridge University Press, 2010) 60–61.

[177] ibid.

[178] The Stockholm programme (above n 128).

this area from the perspective of 'security'. Yet as explained in chapter four there is a rather tenuous link to such consideration under Article 114 TFEU which refers to the notion of safety rather than security and requires scientific evidence as justification for EU action.[179]

The problem is that the security agenda has been pursued at the expense of the concept of freedom and justice. This means that the EU concentrates almost exclusively on the prevention aspect. It could be said that there is a clear tendency for an almost *in blanco* use of 'security' as justifying action. This is dangerous as security is a very capacious concept, perilously capable of meaning all things to all comers.[180] Admittedly, this is not unique to the EU, as the global combat on terror has demonstrated; security has had a very wide-ranging and dangerously broad potential for justifying action. The key point is that although it is necessary to maintain a secure society, the security agenda can be easily manipulated. Furthermore, the Commission's communication in relation to the Stockholm programme, COM (2009) 262/4 and its title: 'An area of freedom, security and justice serving the citizen' is instructive. In particular, the communication states that the main focus for the future is building a Europe for citizens. The citizen is at the heart of this cooperation. In order to make real such a claim, the Commission highlights the importance of strengthening mutual trust in EU criminal law cooperation in the security context as well. According to the Commission, the internal security strategy must be constructed around three complementary and now inseparable fields of activity which are: stronger police cooperation; a suitably adapted criminal justice system; and more effective management of access to EU territory. Yet how does 'trust' relate to the focus on security? It could be argued that the Commission equates the notion of trust with security. After all, who would be against trust or security?[181] For this reason, it could be argued that the focus on security and the thin line between the EU internal agenda as manifested by the AFSJ and the EU's external dimension to security, is also about risk regulation. 'Risk' is, therefore, also about security.

In the following sections, this chapter seeks to confront the principles of effectiveness, security and risk by arguing that a combination of these principles could lead to the phenomenon of precautionary criminalisation at the EU level.

[179] Case C-301/06 AG Bot Opinion delivered on 14 October 2008 and judgment of the Court 10 February 2009 discussed above.

[180] Zedner (above n 171).

[181] Along the same lines, see S Weatherill, 'The Challenges of Better Regulation' in Weatherill (ed), *Better Regulation* (Oxford, Hart Publishing, 2007) 7, who give the example of 'worse regulation'. See also Somek, *Engineering Equality* (Oxford, Oxford University Press, 2011) for the example of 'non-discrimination' as something which is impossible to be against.

H. The Intersection of Risk, Security and Effectiveness: The Development of Precautionary Criminal Law at the EU Level[182]

The contention presented here is that linking the concepts of risk and effectiveness to the idea of security may be problematic. The problem is that such a conjunctive reading sheds light on not only the constitutional dimension of what it means to refer to these concepts (their slippery nature as explored earlier) but also highlights the fact that such an approach may harm other interests which the Union seeks to protect – the adequate protection of human rights at the EU level. There is an apparent connection between the concept of 'risk' and the principle of effectiveness (discussed in earlier chapters) in EU criminal law in the way in which these principles are invoked as being self-evident. Moreover, these principles appear to play a significant constitutional function as part of the constitutionalisation process of justifying EU action in the first place.

A question worth asking is whether the EU precautionary principle, as mentioned above, is of any interest in this area at all. After all, the CFI has developed this principle into a general principle of EU law.[183] In examining this issue it is important to look more closely at the Commission's communication on the precautionary principle. Accordingly, this communication states:

> At Community level the only explicit reference to the precautionary principle is to be found in the environment title of the EC Treaty, and more specifically Article 174. However, one cannot conclude from this that the principle applies only to the environment . . . In other words, the scope of the precautionary principle also depends on trends in case law, which to some degree are influenced by prevailing social and political values. [184]

The most controversial example of such a trend is the possibility of using this principle in the aftermath of the attacks of 9/11 and the need to combat terrorism on an emergency basis. Obviously, this is an exercise in 'speculation', but taking into consideration the current legislation eagerly pursued by EU's institutions, it is a rather important and somewhat alarming issue. The point is that it is the recognition of such danger that calls for close attention to what is meant when the concept is invoked as a justification for public policy decisions. We are concerned not only by the criminological dimension as to why it is dangerous to place an over-reliance on risk, but also the constitutional concern about what the EU is and is about to become. It is a matter of the effectiveness and meaningfulness of the emergent phenomenon of EU crime control in a broad sense.

Admittedly, as explained, the Commission has also stated that the precautionary principle should not be used for arbitrary decision-making.[185] And yet the

[182] This section draws on E Herlin-Karnell, 'The Development of EU Precautionary Criminalization' (2011) 1 *European Criminal Law Review* 149.

[183] eg Case T-141/00 *Artegodan* [2002] ECR II-4945.

[184] Commission, on the precautionary principle (Communication) COM (2000) 1 final.

[185] ibid.

whole area is imbued with subjective definitions of risk, security and effectiveness and is therefore prone to arbitrariness. There is a very close relationship between the notion of risk regulation and the aspiration of a high level of security within the AFSJ. It seems as if, when read together, they point in the direction of stricter criminal law and more prevention. As pointed out by Ashworth, a preventive regime is problematic as it might lead to an extended use of strict liability to increase the efficiency of criminal law process, which undermines the fundamental right of due process.[186] More provocatively, and taking the preventive model one step further, we might ask why it is necessary to wait until the crime has already been committed (the why wait for a crime argument)? This has some echoes of the 1960s where general prevention, in terms of incarceration, was seen as the ultimate answer to a successful criminal law policy.[187]

As explained in chapter four the *ultima ratio* notion means that criminal law should be avoided as far as possible as means of control. The classic question is then whether to rely instead on, for example, administrative sanctions with strict liability. The crux of the matter is that extended use of strict liability does not sit well with ECHR case law[188] on an autonomous concept of criminal law, that is, criminal law would guarantee a fair trial but may impose greater punishment such as imprisonment as well as the moral stigma associated with crime. And yet the problem is deeper. There is a general concern that at the EU level the debate is taking place elsewhere, namely on the preventive character of criminal law.

Moreover, as implied, the idea of a precautionary crime fighting agenda highlights the bigger issue of what kind of criminal law policy the EU should aim to achieve. There are at least two reasons for this. First, a preventive system has dangers of its own as it could lead to a more repressive criminal law system which undermines the guarantee of due process and respect for fundamental rights. Secondly, the facilitation of penal populism – and as briefly discussed in chapter four Part IV – at the EU level by relying on (often uncontextualised) public opinion is unwise.[189] Sound empirical research obviously has an important function here, but data needs to be collected carefully and should not be the only concern. In other words, there is a need for a normative debate in EU criminal law about what kind of criminal law the EU wants to create. This is all work-in-progress and the Commission deserves 'credit' for being active and for doing something.[190] But when dealing with criminal law and human rights protection it is necessary to adopt a critical stance and ask what concepts we are really dealing with and what it means for the development of an EU criminal law policy to rely on them.

[186] A Ashworth, 'Criminal Law, Human Rights and Preventive Justice' in S Bronitt et al (eds) *'Regulating Deviance'* (Oxford, Hart Publishing, 2009) 87.

[187] On this see, eg N Christe, *Crime Control as Industry* (London, Routledge, 2001).

[188] *Engel and others v Netherlands* Series A, No 22; [1979–80]. See Ashworth (above n 186).

[189] M Nolan, 'Law Reform, Beyond mere opinion polling and penal populism', in S Bronitt et al (above n 186) 165.

[190] For earlier comments on the Commission's legislative activity in other areas of law such as EU private law, S Weatherill, 'European Contract Law: Taking the Heat Out of Questions of Competence' (2004) 16 *European Business Law Review* 23.

Interestingly, it was recently suggested that engaging with the value of security in criminal law could prove an important instrument in the critique of the phenomenon of over-criminalisation.[191] More specifically, the problem is not only that the politicians take security more seriously than they should, underplaying the importance of other values, but also that the important aspects of security can be eroded through badly researched and hastily enacted criminal offences.[192] In other words, according to this view, there is a lack of concern with security itself. Indeed, it has been observed that the fact that a proposed criminal sanction would enhance security if complied with, could be a good reason to enact it.[193] But whilst this rationale is in principle plausible, in practice, it leads to a range of too broadly constructed offences. The problem is that this is in disharmony with the principle of legality (and thereby the principle of strict construction of penal provisions) as also guaranteed by Article 49 of the Charter of Fundamental Rights.

In any case, the Lisbon Treaty strengthens the EU's preventive focus. After all, Article 84 TFEU states that the EP and the Council may establish measures to promote and support the action of Member States in the field of crime prevention, excluding any harmonisation of the laws and regulations of Member States. It is difficult to estimate the importance of this statement, however, since Article 83 TFEU provides for a rather sweeping competence for the EU in criminal matters not only for a list of crimes including money laundering, organised crime and drug trafficking, but also for any other crime policy area that would be needed for the effective implementation of existing Union policies. Surely this has a preventive aspect added to it. Alternatively, Article 84 TFEU simply means that the EU shall have its own crime prevention programme – if such a programme can in fact be distinguished from national laws and regulation.

The next subsection will look at recent initiatives where the preventive aspect is striking. It links back to chapter two, where the fundamentals of EU criminal law where outlined, but takes it a step further by analysing the preventive aspect of criminal law.

i. Recent Initiatives: Final Test Case

The recent initiative for a European Investigation Order,[194] based on the idea of mutual recognition, would repeal (the politically sensitive and therefore long debated[195]) European Evidence Warrant (EEW)[196] framework decision by proposing

[191] V Tadros, 'Crimes and Security' (2008) 71 *MLR* 940.

[192] ibid.

[193] ibid.

[194] See Council of the European Union, Note on an Initiative for a Directive of the European Parliament and of the Council regarding the European Investigation Order in criminal matters, 9145/10, Brussels, 29 April 2010(b).

[195] For a detailed account, V Mitsilegas, 'The Third Wave of Third Pillar Law. Which Direction for EU Criminal Justice?' (2009) 43 *EL Rev* 523.

[196] Framework Decision 2008/978 on the European evidence warrant. See eg, C Murphy, 'The European Evidence Warrant: Mutual Recognition and Mutual (Dis)Trust?' in C Eckes and T Konstadinides (above n 85) 224.

an initiative for a new Directive on the basis of Article 82(2) TFEU. In its preamble, the proposed Directive stresses that in order to ensure the effectiveness of cooperation in the area of criminal law, the opportunities for recognising or executing an investigation order, as well as grounds for postponing such an order, should be limited. Indeed, this instrument is influenced by efficiency thinking. This measure introduces the concept of 'deadlines' where the investigation into serious offences have a shorter deadline (Article 11) and should take place as soon as possible or in any case within 30 days.[197]

Furthermore, interestingly, the sacred notion of *ne bis in idem* is abolished, as is the role of territoriality, where Member States have had the option to investigate and punish crimes committed on its territory. Moreover, in the initial proposal to the investigation order, the dual criminality rule was completely abolished. It should perhaps be recalled, and as explained in chapter two, that the European Arrest Warrant (EAW) framework decision had infamously abolished this requirement for a list of 32 crimes, but the proposed investigation order went further by initially suggesting that the dual criminality rule be completely abolished. Even though this was changed in the latest draft[198] to cover only the 32 crimes previously listed in the EAW, it tells us something about the general willingness for preventive action at the EU level. Although the Directive ensures in Article 1 that it complies with fundamental rights and that it would not require Member States to breach fundamental rights, there is a risk that the general focus on efficiency will have a negative impact in this respect and would undermine rights without serving the effectiveness of EU law. As pointed out by Peers, these reassurances of human rights protection are too vague to be taken seriously.[199]

Another recent example worth mentioning in this context is the Communication on the EU Counter-Terrorism Policy.[200] This communication is to be read in conjunction with a Commission staff working paper, 'Taking Stock of EU Counter-Terrorism Measures'[201] and the Stockholm programme. The Commission staff working paper includes a table showing concrete achievements and future challenges to be achieved by focusing on four words: 'prevent, protect, pursue and respond'. This Communication points at the success with the current instrument, such as the EAW[202] and the Third Money Laundering Directive[203] as well as a whole range of legislative measures for the prevention of the use of internet for

[197] Briefly, this means that the executing authority must reject the request in question within 30 days, or take possession of the evidence requested within 60 days of receipt. For an overview of this instrument, see A Ferris, 'The European Investigation Order: Stepping Forward with Care' (2011) 2 *New Journal of European Criminal Law* 426.

[198] www.statewatch.org/analyses/no-112-eu-eio-update.pdf (last accessed January 2012).

[199] Analysis by S Peers, 'The proposed European Investigation Order: Assault on human rights and national sovereignty' available at www.statewatch.org/analyses/no-96-european-investigation-order.pdf (last accessed January 2012).

[200] Commission, 'The EU Counter-Terrorism Policy: main achievements and future challenges' (Communication), COM (2010) 386 final.

[201] SEC (2010) 911.

[202] [2002] OJ L190/1, on the EAW.

[203] Directive 2005/60/EC of 25 November 2005 [2005] OJ L309.

terrorist purposes,[204] all of which have, however, been criticised from the human rights perspective.[205] For this reason, the Commission points out that the relationship between the many interacting instruments and the mechanism for information exchange needs to be evaluated. The argument is centred on effectiveness concerns coupled with the need to prevent, pursue and protect. Admittedly, there are also good aspects of this communication such as the explicit recognition of the need to respect fundamental rights, and it also highlights the priority of ensuring that any measure complies with the Charter of Fundamental Rights. Yet in the light of the EU history on the fight against terrorism since 9/11, it is easy to get the impression that such a reassurance is vague.[206] At least it remains to be seen in practice. The danger, as discussed above, is that the emphasis on prevention easily leads to measures that are too precautionary. After all, it remains the case that both Articles 67 TFEU and 75 TFEU provide for a legal basis for the prevention of and fight against terrorism and related activities, and none of these provisions entail the emergency brake provision, which is otherwise granted in Article 82 (2) TFEU and Article 83 TFEU.[207]

The next part of this chapter turns to the other major EU criminal law area – in the history of the EU's aspirations to colonise criminal law at the supranational level – namely the area of counterfeiting and piracy. As will be described in the next part, the EU legislator clearly has the ambition of creating an honest, crime-free market.

III. THE COUNTERFEITING AND PIRACY DIRECTIVE

A. An Aspiration to Create EC Criminal Law prior to the Lisbon Treaty

One of the hottest areas in the longstanding aspiration to create an EC criminal law is without doubt the area of intellectual property rights. Criminal law has long been figuring in the periphery of this field. For example, in 2004 the Commission presented a Directive[208] which initially referred to the use of criminal law, but this reference was later amended.[209] Thereafter, the Commission adopted a new proposal (replacing COM (2005) 276) for a Directive (COM (2006) 168 final)[210] to

[204] Such as amending Framework Decision 2002/475/JHA on combating terrorism.

[205] Peers (above n 199).

[206] See eg, C Eckes, *EU Counter-Terrorist Policies and Fundamental Rights* (Oxford, Oxford University Press, 2009).

[207] Articles 82(2) TFEU and 83 TFEU allow for the possibility for the Member States to use an emergency brake if a proposed legislation is considered to be particularly sensitive from the perspective of a Member State's criminal justice system.

[208] Directive 2004/48/EC of 30 April 2004 [2004] OJ L157 on the enforcement of intellectual property rights.

[209] Revised proposal 6376/04 (codec), 2003/0024 (COD) 16 February 2004.

[210] Directive (COM (2006) 168 final), on criminal measures aimed at ensuring the enforcement of intellectual property rights 2005/0127 (COD).

combat intellectual property offences.[211] The underlying ratio again was the Case C-176/03 judgment and the 'aura' of effectiveness. Although this proposal was later withdrawn, it is nonetheless interesting to examine since it was one of the first proposals for supranational criminal law as presented by the Commission in the wake of the outcome in Case C-176/03.[212] In particular, this proposal highlighted the ambitious reading of Case C-176/03 to cover a very broad area. It also highlights the sensitive issues that confront the EU in this area particularly with regard to criminal liability for legal persons. According to the preamble of this proposed Directive, the effective approximation of Member State criminal legislation in this field is the minimum requirement to pursue a major campaign aimed at eradicating counterfeiting and piracy. The measure thus claimed to be 'designed to bring Member States' criminal legislation more closely into alignment. And thereby to improve European cooperation so as to combat more effectively counterfeiting and piracy, which are frequently committed by criminal organizations, often pose a risk to health and safety and consumer protection which seriously harm the interests of many sectors in the European economy.' Clearly, in this instance the Commission is 'borrowing' arguments from the EU private law field.[213] The reference to 'health and safety', 'many sectors' and 'European economy' seem indicate very broadly defined areas covering almost anything within the scope of the internal market. The Directive also argues that the disparities in question between the national systems regarding penalties, as well as hampering the proper functioning of the internal market, make it difficult to combat counterfeiting and piracy effectively. Nonetheless, it states that counterfeiting and piracy are increasingly linked to the phenomenon of organised crime. The occurrence of organised crime is thereby painted as 'the enemy', justifying legislative action in itself.[214] This is not to deny the fact that organised crime, and counterfeiting and piracy are related, or that organised crime is a problem in Europe. Instead, as noted in the previous section, the purpose here is simply to make the point that organised crime is an umbrella label that is increasingly invoked when dealing with the constitutional basis for law-making in the area of combating crime at the EU level – and this is, to put it mildly, a frighteningly imprecise basis. In any case, the emphasis on the fight against organised crime has probably resulted in subsidiarity being taken lightly: the measure simply states that 'the Community may take measures in accordance with the principle of subsidiarity as set out in Article 5 TEU. Proportionality was not even considered.[215]

[211] During the legislative process of this instrument, Members of the Legal Affairs Committee backed the overall aim of the Directive and amended some of its provisions. They excluded patent rights from its scope and decided that criminal sanctions should only apply to those infringements deliberately carried out to obtain commercial advantage available at ec.europa.eu/internal_market/iprenforcement/index_en.htm (last accessed January 2012).

[212] Later withdrawn by the Commission, see OJ C252, 18 September 2010, 7 for no clear reason.

[213] S Weatherill, 'The Commission's Options for Developing EC Consumer Protection and Contract Law: Assessing the Constitutional Basis'(2002) 13 *European Business Law Review* 497.

[214] V Mitsilegas, 'Defining Organized Crime in the European Union' (2001) 26 *EL Rev* 565.

[215] Cf ch 4 part VI.

The proposed Directive also provided that Member States shall ensure that all intentional infringements (including attempting, aiding or abetting and inciting such infringements) are treated as criminal offences. It also declared that Member States should provide custodial sentences of a minimum of four years for crimes committed under the aegis of a criminal organisation. This is controversial as this is clearly a sphere where the laws of Member States vary considerably. The explanation lies in the need to underline the seriousness of these kinds of crime.[216] Furthermore, this measure stipulated that Member States may also provide for criminal procedures and penalties to be applied in cases not covered by the Directive 'in particular where they are committed wilfully and on a commercial scale'. One may wonder whether such a statement, applied in the context of Article 4(3) TEU (the principle of loyalty is discussed in chapters two and three), in practice covers other intellectual property-related crimes under the auspices of the Directive.

The proposed Directive also covered attempts, aiding or abetting and inciting the offences in question. This is interesting, as aiding and abetting are among the most controversial criminal law concepts that highlight the question of causation. Thus, when making a foray into the regulation of 'aiding and abetting', there is a general requirement that the defendant should be not only be aware of his or her own act (as stated in the Directive), but also of the intentions of the principal (that is, there is a dual fault requirement).[217] Another delicate area is that of complicity: suffice it to say that this is an area where the laws of Member States vary.[218] As for the subjective (fault) requirement, here again sensitive criminal law matters are dealt with in a worryingly light fashion. The proposed Directive stated that an infringement must be intentional whether it is an actual infringement, an attempt at infringement or the aiding and abetting or inciting of such an offence.[219] It should be noted that the question of intent had previously been left to the discretion of the Member States when deciding what kind of subjective element to invoke.[220] It is beyond the scope of this section to penetrate the general principles of criminal law, but obviously the requirement of intention means that *mens rea* must be established. Nevertheless, it is here that the proposed Directive dived into deep waters. The problem is that the theories concerning the concept of attempt are ambiguous and complicated.[221] Certainly, the law of attempts is fascinating, from a normative point of view, with the so-called 'subjective vs objective' theory. According to the latter, attempts are 'punished' only if they constitute a possible

[216] It is also stipulated that in appropriate cases, the remedies available shall include the seizure, forfeiture and destruction of the infringing goods.

[217] eg CMV Clarkson and HM Keating, *Criminal Law, Text and Materials* (London, Sweet & Maxwell, 2003).

[218] S Peers *EU Justice and Home Affairs* (Oxford, Oxford University Press, 2011) ch 8.

[219] Proposed Directive (COM (2006) 168 final), on criminal measures aimed at ensuring the enforcement of intellectual property rights 2005/0127 (COD). The Directive states, however, that the subjective fault requirement does not affect specific liability systems such as the system set out for internet service providers in Arts 12–15 of Directive 2000/31/EC on electronic commerce.

[220] Peers (above n 11).

[221] A Duff, *Criminal Attempts* (Oxford, Clarendon Press, 1996).

attempt, that is, a feasible crime. Conversely, according to the former theory, an attempt can be punished even if the attempt was an impossible attempt, that is, impossible to carry out, but where the offender thought that he or she was committing a crime.[222] However, there are various degrees of 'subjectivity'. The questions here are obviously, what is the aim of criminal law?; what are we punishing?; and so on. More significantly, this highlights how difficult it is to superimpose a single 'European' approach in such philosophical diversity.

Another interesting question – more or less dismissed by the Commission in its proposed Directive – is the regulation of corporate liability or criminal liability for legal persons. Nonetheless, the Court has so far recognised this sensitivity by stating that Member States are free to choose whether to enforce liability on legal persons as long as effective, proportionate and dissuasive sanctions are imposed on someone.[223]

i. Criminal Liability for Legal Persons

The issue of criminal liability for legal persons has already been touched upon. The purpose of this section is to provide some additional thoughts, as the question of criminal liability or corporate liability is a hugely sensitive matter in some Member States. Accordingly, and as indicated in the discussion on effective sanctions in chapter two, Member States have so far been free to choose whether to impose criminal and non-criminal sanctions on legal persons as long as the relevant legal response is 'effective' from an EU law perspective.[224] However, as always, there are exceptions: criminal liability of legal persons *stricto sensu* was introduced by the third pillar Fraud Convention.[225] Therefore, EU involvement in criminal law may result in constitutional clashes between the national criminal law and EU law norms as increased involvement by the EU in these matters impacts on the national system as it demands that it makes a choice about the content of a harmonised regime. Another good example here is the EU's current trend of insisting on corporate criminal liability. For instance, the Commission's proposal (now adopted) for an amendment of the Framework Decision on the combat of terrorism stressed the importance of criminalising conduct by legal persons.[226] So although it is true that the Court has been reluctant to explicitly rule on criminal liability for legal persons it remains less certain whether in practice, Member States have much choice when asked to comply with effective sanctions. This poses potential difficulties for Member States that do not recognise criminal liability for legal persons.

[222] ibid.

[223] Case C-7/90 *Vandevenne* [1991] ECR 1-4371. Peers (above n 11).

[224] ibid.

[225] Second Protocol of the Convention on the protection of the European Communities Financial Interests [1997] OJ 221/11.

[226] Framework decision COM (2007) 650 proposal for an amending framework decision 2002/475/JHA on combating terrorism.

It has also been observed that there are a number of examples in secondary legislation where Member States are required to impose penalties on both natural and legal persons.[227] There are, however, differences between Member States when it comes to the issue of criminal liability for legal persons. Suffice it to say in this context that EU law usually recognises this tension and hence leaves it to Member States to decide what sanctions to impose. One may wonder however, whether this is still true if we consider the effectiveness criteria. For example, the aforementioned Framework Decision on the fight against terrorism stipulates in Article 8 that:

> Each Member State shall take the necessary measures to ensure that a legal person held liable pursuant to Article 7 is punishable by effective, proportionate and dissuasive penalties, which shall include criminal or non-criminal fines and may include other penalties.

Furthermore, as pointed out by Peers, Article 2 of the Market Abuse Directive, discussed above, states that Member States 'must pierce the veil' and prohibits a natural person from using inside information even when a legal person is de jure the possessor of the information.[228] However, there are measures which go even further. For example, the Convention on the protection of the European Communities' financial interests (PIF),[229] in combating fraud, required Member States to impose criminal liability on the heads of legal business. This was later transposed into the First PIF Protocol along with the Convention on national corruption law which, however, leaves it to the Member States to choose the nature of the relevant sanction.[230] In short, the Protocol stipulates that legal persons must be punished by effective, proportionate and dissuasive sanctions which shall include criminal or non-criminal fines and other measures such as temporary or permanent disqualification.

As shown, third pillar measures have not followed the golden rule of permitting but not requiring criminal liability for legal persons. After all, the Joint Action Plan on organised crime specifically states that legal persons must be held criminally liable, or failing that otherwise liable, in accordance with the procedure laid down in national law. There was no definition of 'legal persons' in this Protocol. Nevertheless, the recent Framework Decision on organised crime defines a 'legal person' as any entity having legal personality under the applicable law, except for States or public bodies in the exercise of State authority and for public international organisations.[231] It should be observed that as regards money laundering, neither the Vienna nor the Strasbourg Convention contain any such liability, although the latter emphasised the advantage of such a system in cases where money laundering is pursued through them. Therefore, the Second Fraud

[227] Peers (above n 218) ch 8.

[228] ibid at 411.

[229] OJ C316 of 27 November 1995, 48.

[230] Reg 2988/95 of 18 December 1995 on the protection of the European Communities financial interests [1995] OJ L312.

[231] Framework Decision 2008/841/JHA.

Protocol[232] also provided in Article 3 that each Member State should take the necessary measures to ensure that legal persons can be held liable for fraud, corruption and money laundering, as well as for involvement of such fraud, active corruption or money laundering, or for the attempted commission of fraud. In this respect there appears to be no national rationale for whether or not to impose criminal liability on legal persons. Moreover, the FATF 40 recommendations have emphasised the importance of criminal liability for legal persons.[233] Furthermore, the Framework Decision on combating terrorism stressed the importance of criminalising conduct by legal persons.[234]

Another recent example of EU legislation concerning liability for legal persons is the proposal for a Directive on sanctions against employers of illegally staying third-country nationals, based on Article 79 TFEU (ex Article 63(3)(b) EC), which establishes an obligation to impose criminal sanctions on natural and legal employers.[235] Other examples of criminal liability for legal persons are the Directives on environmental crimes and ship-source pollution, respectively which contain the standard rule on liability for legal persons but no rules on the specific sanctions for legal persons except the effective, proportionate and dissuasive requirement.[236] Finally, a recent example of criminal liability for legal persons is the proposed Directive on cyber crime.[237] Article 11 of the Directive stipulates that Member States shall take the necessary measures to ensure that legal persons can be held liable for offences committed for their benefit by any person, acting either individually or as part of an organ of the legal person, and holding a leading position within the legal person. Moreover, it is held that Member States shall take the necessary measures to ensure that legal persons can be held liable where the lack of supervision or control by a person referred to in paragraph 1 has allowed a person under its authority to commit of any of the offences referred to in Articles 3 to 8 for the benefit of that legal person.

Although the Court has been reluctant to explicitly rule on criminal liability for legal persons, as discussed in chapter two, it remains less certain whether Member States in practice have much choice when asked to comply with effective sanctions.

[232] Second Protocol of the convention on the protection of the EC financial interests OJ C221 1997, 11, cited in Mitsilegas (above n 71).

[233] www.fatf-gafi.org/document/28/0,3343,en_32250379_32236930_33658140_1_1_1_1,00.html (last accessed January 2012).

[234] Framework Decision 2008/919/JHA [2008] OJ L300/42 amending Framework Decision 2002/475/JHA on combating terrorism. On these provisions, V Mitsilegas, 'The Third Wave of Third Pillar Law. Which Direction for EU Criminal Justice?' (2009) 34 *EL Rev* 52.

[235] 'Proposal for a Directive of the European Parliament and of the Council providing for sanctions against employers of illegally staying third-country nationals' COM(2007)249 final. See O Lynsky and A Dawnes, 'The Ever-longer Arm of EC law: The Extension of Community Law into the Field of Criminal Law' (2008) 45 *CML Rev* 131.

[236] Directive 2008/99 [2008] OJ L328/28 on the protection of the environment through criminal law and Directive 2009/52 [2009] OJ L168/24 providing for minimum standards on sanctions and measures against employers of illegally staying third-country nationals. See S Peers, *EU Justice and Home Affairs* (Oxford, Oxford University Press, 2011) ch 10.

[237] Commission, 'on attacks against information systems and repealing Council Framework Decision 2005/222/JHA(Communication) COM (2010) 517 final.

As will be explained in chapter six, this poses potential difficulties for countries such as Sweden that do not in principle recognise criminal liability for legal persons.

This brings us to the final part of this chapter and the question of a protective regime in EU criminal law.

IV. THE CONFIDENCE PATH – SUPRANATIONAL CRIMINAL LAW

A. Paternalism and Market Failure

As discussed in chapter four, Part III, the confidence argument in EU law is often invoked as a justification for EU action under Article 114 TFEU. As noted at the beginning of this chapter, the intention here is to look more closely at such reasoning in the context of criminal law as a tool for market integration. More generally, this chapter has sought to demonstrate such a link between the 'confidence' ratio and the EU's measures against financial crimes coupled with effectiveness, security and risk concerns. However, there is certainly an uneasy dynamic between liberalisation (no barriers to trade) and regulation (investor protection).[238] More specifically, regulation in this area is often composed of a combination of paternalistic and market-failure based measures.[239] However, the issue of confidence as a justification for harmonisation connects not only to the competence question but also to the issue of who – in criminological terms – the regime is trying to safeguard as well as whether such a regulation is actually an aspect of market failure theory rather than an instrument for the protection of the citizen. Furthermore, it seems as if the notion of paternalism in combination with market failure theories and the extent to which these govern the EU's characterisation of 'risk' has a bearing on whether the regulatory regime is coherent.[240]

The problem in this argument is that there is no obvious connection between criminal law and 'confidence' in the market. More specifically, there is no clear relationship between the confidence in the market argument and the need to criminalise in order to boost such confidence. Yet academic opinion seems divided here, with criminal law theorists being mostly sceptical of any such occurrence, while comparative lawyers[241] seeming more positive. EU law discourse has yet to take place in this area. There seems to be a general consensus that in relation to market abuse and insider dealing, there is no support for the idea that such activity hampers confidence in the market.[242] On the other hand, it is commonly

[238] N Moloney, 'Investor protection and the Treaty' in G Ferrarini et al (eds), *Capital Markets in the Age of the Euro* (The Hague, Kluwer Law Publishing, 2003) 17.

[239] ibid.

[240] For a recent account see A Somek, *Individualism* (Oxford, Oxford University Press, 2008) at 107, discussing the notion of paternalism at the EC level in the context of anti-smoking legislation.

[241] K Hinterseer, *Criminal Finance, The Political Economy of Money Laundering in a Comparative Legal Context* (The Hague, Kluwer Law Publishing, 2002) ch 2.

[242] ibid. Not according to the Commission, see 'Commission reinforcing sanctioning regimes in the financial services sector, (Communication) COM (2010) 716 final.

accepted that money laundering should be fought.[243] The question then, is how this should be done. It should be stressed that there seems to be no equivalent aspect to the EU law 'confidence in the market' principle in criminal law theory when discussing the need for criminalisation. There seems to be no general justification of 'confidence', but rather the issue becomes a question of whether one could envisage or legitimise paternalistic legislation, and to what extent the effectiveness requirement in terms of the 'general good', should prevail over the autonomy of the individual. In short, we are required to decide whether an offence is sufficiently serious to justify criminalisation while also considering the empirical dimension and the so-called over-criminalisation phenomenon.[244]

This part dissects the confidence argument from the perspective of financial crime. For this reason, the present analysis should be read in the light of the general outline of confidence as a competence-enhancing factor as developed in Part III of chapter four. The famous, alleged need to introduce confidence in the market in order to establish the internal market is under consideration.

i. Protective Regulation, for Whom?

The notion of market confidence at EU level is often viewed as a matter of public interest and as essential for the proper functioning of the market.[245] As noted, in the area of EU securities law, investor protection is connected with the promotion of investor confidence. Although such protection could be driven by more paternalistic concerns, investor protection regulation seeks primarily to address market failures that hinder the attainment of investor protection.[246] Notwithstanding this, it is arguably useful to consider the notion of paternalistic legislation in more detail. In this respect, since the justification behind EU intervention in this area seems to be that EU-investors should be protected from themselves, it reveals similar characteristics to those of criminal law theory and paternalistic legislation as a justification for criminalisation. Paternalistic regulation thus takes a broad view of the extent to which the citizen should be protected. In this way the EU legislator could be said to intervene beyond the simple correction of market failures.[247]

At the core of the matter is whether financial crimes such as money laundering undermine the confidence of the market at all. This may sound controversial (that is, outside the sphere of EU consumer policy), but as Moloney has pointed out, the Court has already accepted a link between investor confidence and the smooth operation of securities markets – for the first time *Alpine Investment*.[248] Indeed, it should be recalled that in this case the Court held that:

[243] ibid.

[244] See eg, D Husak, *Overcriminalization* (Oxford, Oxford University Press, 2009). See also RA Duff et al (eds), *The Boundaries of the Criminal Law* (Oxford, Oxford University Press, 2011). And see ch 3, section III and the discussion on effectiveness as a general principle of criminal law.

[245] Moloney (above n 238).

[246] ibid.

[247] N Moloney, *EC Securities Regulation* (Oxford, Oxford University Press, 2002) 510.

[248] Case C-384/93 *Alpine Investment* [1997] ECR I-1141.

> Paragraph 42 Financial markets play an important role in the financing of economic operators and, given the speculative nature and the complexity of commodities futures contracts, the smooth operation of financial markets is largely contingent on the confidence they inspire in investors. That confidence depends in particular on the existence of professional regulations serving to ensure the competence and trustworthiness of the financial intermediaries on whom investors are particularly reliant.

Again, this takes us back to chapter four and the discussion on Article 114 TFEU. In fact, it should be clear from the above discussion that there is more to Article 114 TFEU than the mere removal of obstacles to trade and the distortion of competition. This additional element is the 'confidence' argument as a reason for harmonisation/criminalisation. This poses challenges not only from the perspective of the conferral of powers but also from the point of view of where the dividing line between national sovereignty, personal autonomy and the need to protect the general good lies. It should be stressed that the very issue of criminalisation is the subject of a protracted and heated debate in criminal law, where theories of criminalisation range from moralist views, law and economic theories, and utilitarianism, to minimalist approaches.[249] The question here is the legitimacy of the confidence maxim. In other words, what is the EU's mandate here? It appears as if the Union has subscribed to a market failure theory of criminal law coupled to effectiveness concerns and more paternalistic aspirations in terms of 'confidence' in the market. The point here is simply to emphasise that the question of confidence as a justification for criminalisation is largely undefined. It is also unclear to what extent it actually connects with market integration, unless we define this market in a more sophisticated way. Obviously, the EU is promoting a 'clean' market (which is clear from Article 3 TEU). Interestingly, however, it has recently been suggested that since the global approach to the fight against money laundering and financial crimes in general has not been very effective it might be necessary to adopt a more nuanced approach to market integration by clarifying what 'market' we are referring to.[250] Such an approach should take into account economic and criminological questions.

In any case, it should also be noted, as touched upon above, that the relationship between the EU's fight against dirty money and the free movement imperative remains unclear.[251] After all, it appears less clear how the EU could fight money laundering effectively but at the simultaneously ensure that the free movement of

[249] See the classic work of J Mill, *On Liberty* (London, Routledge, 1991) also summarised in J Feinberg, *Harm to Others* (Oxford, Oxford University Press, 1981). See also the introductory chapter to RA Duff et al (eds), *The Boundaries of the Criminal Law* (Oxford, Oxford University Press, 2011).

[250] M Nardo, 'Economic Crime and Illegal Markets Integration: A Platform for Analysis' (2011) 18 *Journal of Financial Crime* 47.

[251] Cases C-358/93 and C-416/93 *Bordessa and others* ECR [1995] I-00361, Opinion of AG Tesauro delivered on 17 November 1994: 'In short, I believe that a system of compulsory authorization applied generally to the transfer of banknotes constitutes an impermissible restriction on the free movement of capital. A restriction of that nature is not absolutely necessary for the attainment of the objectives of the Directive, which may also be pursued by means of other measures, equally effective, which hinder to a lesser degree the movement of capital within the common market.'

capital is not hampered.[252] Indeed, it somehow resembles the so-called EU abuse of law doctrine, according to which Member States should fight the abuse of EU law but at the same time not hinder the its intelligent use.[253] In any case, it does not challenge the basic point at which this section is directed, namely the wider debate on how much morals should or could be governed at EU level. Perhaps the notion of paternalistic legislation at EU level can be regarded as an expression of the very concept of Union citizenship and the exercise of European authority in a broad sense.[254] The EU should accordingly seek to be involved, but criminal law lags behind and it is questionable whether it will ever catch up.

As indicated, it is the distinctive character of criminal law which makes it fundamentally ill-suited for clear-cut analogies with private law. As has been frequently argued throughout this book, criminal law is far more complex than can be understood by such comparisons with the single market. After all, as already explained, the EU might not have the necessary expertise. At a more theoretical level, it remains unclear how one could possibly explain the legitimacy of a supranational legislator here and why effectiveness really could legitimise such a shift to the EU level in the absence of a fully-formed regime of procedural safeguards. As noted in chapter three, the principle of effectiveness is, moreover, a very tricky parameter when deciding on criminalisation. More crucially, there is no evidence that the imperative of effectiveness must point in the direction of criminalisation and eventual over-criminalisation.

Could one, for example, make a comparison with current scholarship in European private law and thus argue that the constitutional dimension of EU criminal law was right to have been left pending as it was? In other words, was it right for the EU to 'partially' set competence questions aside because of the possibility of Treaty amendment (which became a reality) or because issues of legitimacy 'have to be tackled anyway'?[255] There is no doubt that these problems will have to be tackled. However, there is a major problem with such a view in the context of European criminal law After all, as has already been explained, the EU might not have the necessary expertise. At a more theoretical level, and if for one moment we disregard the political dimension of why criminal law is included in the Lisbon Treaty, it remains unclear how one could possibly explain the legitimacy of a supranational legislator here and why effectiveness really could legitimise such a shift to the supranational level in the absence of a fully formed regime of procedural safeguards.

[252] GW Smith, 'Competition in the European Financial Services Industry: The Free Movement of Capital versus the regulation of Money laundering' (1992) *University of Pennsylvania Journal of International Business Law* 101. See also G Stessens, 'Money Laundering' (2006) 77 *International Association of Penal Law* 201.

[253] Case C-212/97 *Centros* [1999] ECR I-1459, Case C-127/08 *Metock and others*, judgement delivered on 25 July 2008, Case C-109/01 *Akrich* [2003] ECR I-9607.

[254] A Somek, *Individualism* (Oxford, Oxford University Press, 2008) chs 9–12.

[255] Compare S Weatherill, Constitutional Issues – How much is Best left Unsaid? in S Vogenauer and S Weatherill (eds), *The Harmonisation of European Contract Law: Implications for European Private Laws, Business and Legal Practice* (Oxford, Hart Publishing, 2006) 89.

V. CONCLUSION

This chapter has identified the inherent difficulties in the field of EU financial crime by looking at the EU's anti-money laundering harmonisation programme. Specifically, the chapter has sought to examine the existing 'woolliness' of the definition of money laundering. As explained, the Third Money Laundering Directive sought to remedy this lack of clarity by providing a clearer definition of money laundering and focusing on a risk-based approach. Thus, the problem is that there may be different notions of risk, at the EU level and the national criminal law level. At the same time, this measure includes the financing of terrorism within its scope, despite the absence of any clear evidence of the appropriateness of combining these two offences; except in simply following the FATF approach. In crude terms, there is a lot of ambiguity hidden in the approach to dirty money and terrorism financing, and the link to Article 114 TFEU and the notion of market creation remains largely unclear. In particular, this part of the chapter investigated the difficult concepts of risk and security and how these concepts, in the light of the effectiveness principle, could lead to precautionary criminalisation at the EU level. This chapter also described the now abandoned proposal for a counterfeiting and piracy instrument, as an example of an early aspiration to create EC criminal law. In this way, this chapter pointed at problems from a criminal law perspective, as well as highlighting the legislation being brought out in the wake of Case C-176/03. Finally, the chapter offered a glimpse at the ambiguous, limitless justification of confidence in the market, by offering an account of the question of 'non-market' values in the context of Article 114 TFEU from the perspective of supranational criminal law. In doing so it examined how such thinking could be linked not only to market-failure theories but also to the traditional paternalism debate within criminal law theory, as well as the difficult role played by the effectiveness principle. The conclusion here was that the confidence ratio is far too vague to justify harmonisation or criminalisation, as it leaves too much uncertainty about what the EU is trying to achieve and why.

6

Case Study II: What Happens in Practice? The Implementation of the Third Money Laundering Directive in the UK and Sweden

I. INTRODUCTION

THIS CHAPTER APPLIES the conclusions from chapter five in the context of the implementation of the Third Money Laundering Directive in the UK and Sweden. But why Sweden, a small Member State, instead of examining the UK and the traditional comparative law giants of France or Germany? The reason for this is that the Swedish regime on money laundering is largely unexplored.[1] It presents particular challenges for the question of liability for legal persons. The UK and Sweden also have very different approaches to the function of private actors in this area, with the UK relying to a greater extent on private parties, while Sweden takes a more traditional public actor standpoint.[2] Consequently, this case study aims to provide some reflections on the implementation of the 2005 Directive in the UK and Sweden and thereby investigate the EU law influence on the national systems.

This chapter starts by discussing the implications of the EU's anti-money laundering regime on the UK legislation (part II). Thereafter, it examines the EU law impact on the Swedish anti-money laundering framework (part III). The chapter concludes with general conclusion.

[1] See, however, M Bergstrom, 'EU Anti-money Laundering Regulation: Multilevel Cooperation of Public and Private Actors' in C Eckes and T Konstadinides, *Crime within the Area of Freedom, Security and Justice* (Cambridge, Cambridge University Press, 2011) 97; and D Magnusson, 'The Costs of Implementing the Anti-money Laundering Regulations in Sweden' (2009) 12 *Journal of Money Laundering Control* 101.

[2] For a study on this specific aspect see Bergstrom (ibid).

II. THE UK'S IMPLEMENTATION OF THE EU MONEY LAUNDERING DIRECTIVES

A. Introduction

To begin with, it should be clarified that the UK is a political union made up of four countries: England, Wales, Northern Ireland and Scotland. While the former three are common law jurisdictions, Scotland operates a hybrid system based on both common law and civil law principles.[3] For the purposes of simplification, this study focuses primarily on England, Wales and Northern Ireland but refers nonetheless to the UK. It should be stressed, however, that the purpose here is not to provide a general overview of the British legislative system and its interaction with EU law – our focus is solely on the anti-money laundering laws.

When conducting a case study on money laundering in the UK, it is axiomatically important to turn to Financial Action Task Force's (FATF) country evaluation report.[4] According to this study, the overall threat to the UK from serious organised crime and contingent money laundering is particularly high; the economic and social costs of serious organised crime in the UK is £20 billion a year.[5]

The anti-money laundering architecture in the UK involves criminal law, the civil law and regulatory law.[6] At present, the UK regime consists of a number of related instruments including the Proceeds of Crime Act 2002 (PoCA), the Serious Organised Crime Act, the Money Laundering Regulations, industry and professional guidance, and Financial Services Authority (FSA) rules and supervision.[7] Whilst the Money Laundering Regulations implement the Money Laundering Directives, the substantive money laundering offences are found in the PoCA and supplemented by separate provisions relating to terrorist property under the Terrorism Act 2000, as amended by the Anti-Terrorism, Crime and Security Act 2001, and more recently, the 2006 Act of the same name. It has been argued that the UK legislative framework is over-complicated and consequently that the UK would benefit from a single money laundering act.[8]

The next section provides a short outline of the history of the UK anti-money laundering regime. It is, of course, true that the Lisbon Treaty has somewhat

[3] eg AW Bradley and KD Ewing, *Constitutional and Administrative Law* (Harlow, Longman, 2007) ch 3.

[4] Financial Action Task Force, Third mutual evaluation report 29 June 2007 available at www.fatf-gafi.org/dataoecd/55/29/39064399.pdf (last accessed January 2012). See also mutual evaluation fourth follow-up report, anti-money laundering and combating the financing of terrorism 16 October 2009, available at www.oecd.org/dataoecd/44/8/44048060.pdf (last accessed January 2012).

[5] ibid.

[6] A Veng Mei Leong, 'Chasing Dirty Money: Domestic and International Measures against Money Laundering' (2007) 10 *Journal of Money Laundering Control* 140.

[7] The Financial Services Authority is an independent non-governmental body, given statutory powers by the Financial Services and Markets Act 2000. P Sproat, 'The UK's Anti Money Laundering and Asset Recovery Regime' (2007) 47 *Crime Law and Social Change* 169.

[8] N Ryder, 'The Financial Services Authority and Money Laundering a Game of Cat and Mouse' (2008) 67 *CLJ* 635.

changed the framework since money laundering is now listed in Article 83 TFEU, as explained in the previous chapter, as part of Title V of the TFEU. This means that the UK would have the opportunity to opt out of criminal law cooperation provisions as provided by the Lisbon Treaty and Protocols Numbers 21 and 36. Nevertheless, it appears less likely that the UK would opt out, given that it is not only the EU which lies behind these initiatives (that is, the FATF compliance 'threat' would remain) and that the UK has been one of the leading proponents of further cooperation against money laundering across the EU.

B. A Brief History of the EU's Anti-money laundering Rules in the UK

Prior to the 1980s, the financial sector in the UK was essentially self-regulated.[9] However, the Drugs Trafficking Offences Act was passed in 1986 in order to strip from drug traffickers as many of the fruits of their trade as possible, primarily by inviting judges to make assumptions about the provenance of all assets shown to be in the possession of a defendant.[10] Thus, UK legislation on anti-money laundering initially focused on drug-related criminality. This was extended to cover other crimes by the 1991 Directive. At the same time an array of legislative initiatives was introduced to implement international treaty obligations, such as the Vienna Convention.[11] Nevertheless, the UK's war on drug-money laundering originates much earlier than EU and international involvement and stems from the mid-nineteenth century and the trade in opium.[12] However, it was as not until the late 1980s and early 1990s in connection with the 1991 Directive that the legislative carousel began to turn.[13]

Until 2002 the UK relied on three different laws that stipulated money laundering offences: the Drug Trafficking Act 1994, the Prevention of Terrorism Act 1989 and the Criminal Justice Act 1988, as amended by the Criminal Justice Act 1993. These measures did not cover the proceeds of all offences but only indictable offences.[14] Thereafter, the PoCA entered into force and superseded previous instruments in this area. Contrary to previous legislation, this Act includes all 'criminal conduct', that is, any offence is covered.[15] Therefore, even though the UK regime on money laundering was self regulated prior to the 1980s, the regulated sector has consistently expanded and now includes banks and building soci-

[9] *R v Cuthbertson* [1981] AC 470.

[10] D Bedingfield and C Sallon 'Drugs, Money and the Law' (1993) *Crim LR* 165.

[11] P Marshall, 'Part 7 of the Proceeds of Crime Act 2002: Double Criminality, Legal Certainty, Proportionality and Trouble Ahead' (2003) 11 *Journal of Financial Crime* 111.

[12] eg K Hinterseer, *Criminal Finance, The Political Economy of Money Laundering in a Comparative Legal Context* (The Hague, Kluwer Law Publishing, 2002).

[13] eg Money Laundering Regs, 1993 UK SI No 3075.

[14] ie offences either triable on indictment or triable either way. So-called summery offences were, in principle, not included.

[15] In connection with the 2002 Act, it has been pointed out that persons in Scotland could be found guilty of money laundering when they carry out transactions with respect to the proceeds of an act which was legal in Scotland but not in England. R Alexander, *Insider Dealing and Money Laundering in the EU: Law and Regulation* (Aldershot, Ashgate, 2007).

eties, accountants, lawyers, estate agents, casinos, money exchange services and dealers in high value goods. Particularly because of the 2005 Directive the UK's anti-money laundering net has been widened to include trust and company service providers too.

Moreover, in English law there has traditionally been an relationship between anti-money laundering regulations and the fight against insider dealing.[16] In fact, no other Member State in 2007 covered the proceeds of insider dealing in their money laundering legislation.[17] This is interesting and the question is, obviously, whether insider dealing as such constitutes a predicate offence in relation to money laundering. In any case, it also illustrates a change of attitude in the UK legislator. After all, the case of *Oxford v Moss* made clear that under English law, information does not constitute property.[18] Nonetheless, it is unclear whether it also constitutes a predicate offence of money laundering.[19]

It is often argued that the main changes introduced in English law by the 2001 Directive was the extension of the 2003 Regulation to cover auditors, accountancy firms and tax advisors, estate agents, solicitors or other professionals, auctioneers (where payment is made in cash over €15,000), casinos and bureaux de change.[20] It has been observed that this Regulation was deliberately left open in order to cover limited liability partnership (LLP)[21] cases as well. Indeed, the 2001 Directive and the 2005 Directive imposed an obligation of identification of customers and the reporting of suspicious transactions, plus the training of staff. In the UK, this meant drafting new guidance notes for previously unregulated industries.[22]

Apart from the UK's anti-money laundering legislation itself, a complementary actor on the British anti-money laundering scene has been the more general confiscation regime. Prior to the 1980s, English criminal courts did not have any specific power to confiscate crime-linked property. Indeed, in *R v Cuthbertson*[23] the House of Lords (now the Supreme Court) refused to recognise the confiscation of the proceeds of crime. The inadequacy of such a system became the subject of inquiry in the so-called Hodgson Committee.[24] Their report advocated the need to introduce an increased power of confiscation and forfeiture for the courts.[25]

[16] ibid.

[17] ibid.

[18] *Oxford v Moss* (1978) 68 CR AppR 183.

[19] Directive 2003/6/EC [2003] On insider dealing and market manipulation (market abuse) OJ L96/16.

[20] N Padfield, 'Country Report: Anti-money Laundering Rules in the United Kingdom' in M Pieth and G Aiolfi (eds), *A Comparative Guide to Anti-Money Laundering* (Cheltenham, Edward Elgar, 2004) ch 6.

[21] The LLP retains the essential features of partnership – ie the partners have a considerable joint stake in the running of the firm in a way that company directors do not – but introduces some of the exemptions from personal liability for the firm's obligations and debts that are found in company law.

[22] Alexander (above n 15).

[23] *R v Cuthbertson* [1981] AC 470.

[24] ibid.

[25] M Wasik, 'The Hodgson Committee Report on the Profits of Crime and their Recovery' (1984) *Criminal Law Review* 708, cited in V Mitsilegas, 'Global Standards in Domestic Legal Cultures: The Money Laundering Offences in English Law' in S Braum (ed), *Droit Pénal Européen des Affairs* (Berliner, Wissenschaftsverlag, 2009) 1.

However, there has been much debate as to whether this confiscation regime constitutes criminal law or civil law,[26] which is a question beyond the scope of this case study. In any case, the PoCA is probably one of the most controversial as well as most important legal developments in the UK's effort to combat money laundering. Accordingly, the next section will shed some light on the PoCA.

C. The PoCA 2002

> It was precisely because we believe it is important to rebalance the system that we introduced, for example, the Proceeds of Crime Act 2002, which allowed us to take money of those suspected . . . Yes; we will make sure that our human rights legislation does not get in the way of common sense legislation to protect our country.[27]

The PoCA came into force in early 2003 and has been described as a very extensive piece of law-making with its prime object 'turning those engaged in financial and related services (including bankers, accountants and lawyers) into unofficial policemen of financial transactions'.[28] The general structure of the Act is derived from the Vienna Convention, although the Act is intended to reflect the requirements imposed by the second Directive. Part VII of the Act deals with money laundering. Briefly, the Act expands, reforms and consolidates the UK's anti-money laundering offences.[29] It defines money laundering as including not only traditional money laundering by third parties on the basis of a predicate offence but also the possession by criminals of the proceeds of their own criminal activities (self-laundering). A crucial element of the PoCA is furthermore the fact that it imposes a legal obligation – as opposed to simply a moral one – on lawyers and the gatekeepers of the commercial or banking systems to report suspicious transactions to the financial intelligence unit of the Serious Organised Crime Agency.[30] Most of the offences under the Act apply to all individuals and businesses in the UK, although some apply only to those doing business in the 'regulated sector' as defined in Schedule 9 of the Act. In any case, the interesting point here is that Parliament went considerably beyond the requirements of the Second Directive, as money laundering under the Act covered the proceeds from any criminal activity, meaning that the predicate offence need have no connection with the UK or be within its jurisdiction. The explanation for this was, according to one commentator, that the Government wanted to ensure that those at the forefront of those sectors more vulnerable to money laundering report transactions that any reasonable person would regard as suspicious.[31] It has, however, been pointed out that the

[26] M Gallant, *Money Laundering and Proceeds of Crime* (Cheltenham, Edward Elgar, 2005) 33.

[27] Citation of former Prime Minister A Blair in response to a question by D Cameron, 17 May 2006, cited in Sproat (above n 7).

[28] P Marshall, 'Part 7 of the Proceeds of Crime Act 2002: Double Criminality, Legal Certainty, Proportionality and Trouble Ahead' (2003) 11 *Journal of Financial Crime* 111.

[29] M Gely, 'Tax Offences: The Hidden Face of Money Laundering?' (2003) 10 *Intertax* 328.

[30] www.soca.gov.uk/financialIntel/suspectActivity.html (last accessed January 2012).

[31] Marshall (above n 28).

PoCA is disproportionate in relation to the requirements presented in the 2001 Directive, and as such is arguably in disharmony with the principle of legality and 'fair labelling' in criminal law.[32] There is, furthermore, the competitiveness element at issue here – that a more restrictive regime in the UK could harm a business in another Member State. In addition, it is argued that such far-reaching legislation was not needed in order to meet the demands of the Community legislation in question.[33] As implied, however, it is not easy to pin down the criminalised area in question, the PoCA notwithstanding. After all, this Act should be viewed in conjunction with the provisions of Section 1 Criminal Law Act 1977 (chapter 45), Section 1 Criminal Attempts Act 1981 (chapter 47) and Section 8 Accessories and Abettors Act 1861 (chapter 94), which together make it an offence to conspire to commit, to attempt to commit, and to aid, abet, counsel or procure the commission of any offence indictable in the UK.[34] It remains unclear whether such cross-referring is in line with the principle of maximum certainty in the interests of the public understanding of what is criminalised. In any event, the next section will explain the main features of the 2005 Directive and its implementation in the UK.

D. The 2005 Directive and the UK

The 2005 Directive was implemented in the UK by the Money Laundering Regulations 2007.[35] Thus, the UK Treasury report on the implementation of the 2005 Directive is instructive.[36] This report emphasises effectiveness, proportionality and engagement as the key principles for success in combating money laundering. As noted, the UK is a strong supporter of the FATF and the development of international standards. It states that the UK welcomes an 'all-crimes' approach 'allowing money laundering legislation to be as flexible and dynamic as the criminals themselves and that the UK's business reputation and competitive position depends upon its reputation for integrity and honest dealing'.[37] It also states that the UK's priority during its presidency in 2005 was the adoption of a risk-based approach. In particular, HM Treasury stressed the importance of 'better money laundering regulation', as the risk of money laundering and financing of terrorist activities varies across customers, jurisdictions, products and delivery channels over time. Therefore, it stipulates that firms are better placed than the legislator to assess and mitigate the particular money laundering and terrorist financing risks they face. Furthermore, it is held to be more cost-effective in general. This is in line with the 'better regulation' maxim discussed in chapter five. More specifically, it

[32] ibid.

[33] ibid.

[34] *Bowman v Fels* [2005] EWCA Civ 226.

[35] SI 2007 No 2157.

[36] Implementing the Third Money Laundering Directive: a consultation document available at http://www.hm-treasury.gov.uk/media/E/D/moneylaundering310706.pdf (last accessed 1 June 2008).

[37] Money Laundering Regs 2007: Regulatory Impact Assessment, July 2007 available at www.hm-treasury.gov.uk/d/moneylaundering_ria250707.pdf (last accessed January 2012).

represents a commitment by the state to demonstrate regulatory simplification alongside the introduction of new regulations. HM Treasury emphasised that the UK used its 2005 EU presidency to secure international standards across the EU in the adoption of the 2005 Directive. Perhaps this is the reason why there are very few critical observations in the otherwise ambitious report, even though HM Treasury consulted widely and published a draft for further consultation in 2007.[38] Moreover, the HM Treasury is currently conducting a post-implementation review of the 2007 Regulation, which is to be completed by end of 2011.[39]

An important change introduced by the 2005 Directive, is the requirement for the Member States to keep statistics. Specifically, Article 33 of the Directive requires the Member States to ensure the effectiveness of their systems in combating money laundering and terrorist financing by maintaining and publishing comprehensive data. In this respect, the UK Government has undertaken a consultation with representatives from all the relevant sectors to include statistics on the effectiveness of the system, the result of a number of recommendations for improvement of the regime. The UK also believes that the overall UK principle of better regulation and the need for impact assessments satisfies Article 35 of the Directive, which states that Member States shall ensure that, wherever practicable, timely feedback on the effectiveness of and follow-up to reports of suspected money laundering or terrorist financing is provided.[40] More specifically, the UK Government believes that the outcome of the further review consultation will satisfy the requirements laid out in the Directive. Indeed, the responsibility imposed by the 2005 Directive appears to be viewed in a wider context, with the Treasury emphasising an effective regime, which includes collaboration with industry and law enforcement to improve quality and to provide more effective feedback mechanisms. Part of the plan to implement the report includes a further detailed consultation on a performance management framework.[41]

With respect to enforcement issues, no changes were made in this respect in connection with the 2005 Directive compared to the previous legislation. Therefore, the Government suggested replicating the current regime, where compliance with Treasury-approved industry guidance can be used as a defence against certain offences.[42] Nevertheless, it was recognised that the UK still had to provide for the application of appropriate penalties.

The UK has also encouraged the development of supplementary guidance by private parties.[43] For example, the following groups have been approved:

[38] Implementing the Third Money Laundering Directive (above n 36).

[39] HM Treasury, Consultation on proposed changes to the money laundering regulations 2007. The previous UK anti-money laundering regulations (with the exception of the *Joint Money Laundering Steering Group* guidance) did not specify politically exposed persons as examples of high-risk customers in money laundering.

[40] Implementing the Third Money Laundering Directive: a consultation document (above n 36) 113.

[41] ibid.

[42] ibid.

[43] See Mutual evaluation, fourth follow-up report available at www.fatf-gafi.org/dataoecd/44/8/44048060.pdf (last accessed January 2012).

— the Joint Money Laundering Steering Group (JMLSG) (guidance for the financial services sector);
— the Combined Committee of Accountancy Bodies (guidance for accountants) and
— the Notary Profession (guidance for notaries).

i. The UK and a Risk-based Approach

The concept of a risk-based approach constitutes a key part of the UK's money laundering regime as required by the 2005 Directive.[44] In order to determine the level of supervision in the UK, the financial institutions are divided according to the level of 'impact' on the financial sector, based initially on the firm's total assets, but which can then be raised or lowered according to a number of factors. As explained in chapter five, under the risk-based approach, private actors, such as lawyers and banks, are expected to make risk assessments of their customers and divide them into low and high risk.[45] It has been suggested that for a risk-based approach to be successful there must be adequate information from the Government and law enforcement agencies on the risks and vulnerabilities involved, and relevant assessments must be undertaken. A full-scale and highly professional study needs to be undertaken of the assessment of the risks of reprisal against those who make disclosures in compliance with the anti-money laundering regime, since unlike the assessment of risk in the commercial world, human beings cannot necessarily be expected to react rationally where a perceived breach of personal trust is involved.[46]

This is 'risk management', as discussed in chapter five. Unfortunately, there are many ideas in the Treasury impact assessment, which are never really evaluated nor explained, such as the notion of an 'effective' anti-laundering approach and terrorist financing control, or even the concept of 'risk' as such. The point is that these words, which are not sufficiently well analysed, are still used as templates when concluding the need for further legislation.[47]

E. Gold Plating, Money Laundering and Suspicious Reporting

As noted, the UK was one of the main actors behind the 2005 Directive, partly because of its presidency at the time of the birth of the 2005 Directive, and partly

[44] ibid at 25.

[45] This is the so-called customer due diligence requirement (know-your-customer) and forms part of the risk-based confidence and transparency policy. Customer due diligence is to be applied in four cases. First, when establishing a 'business relationship'; secondly, when carrying out larger transactions; thirdly, regardless of any derogation, exemption or threshold, where there is a suspicion of money laundering or terrorist financing; and fourthly, where there are doubts about the veracity or adequacy of previously obtained customer identification data.

[46] J Fisher, 'Lack of Confidence' *Money Laundering Bulletin*, November 2006 available for subscribers at www.i-law.com/ilaw/doc/view.htm?id=61955 (last accessed January 2012).

[47] Money Laundering Regs 2007: Regulatory Impact Assessment, July 2007 (above n 37).

because of the pioneering role the UK has played more generally in the adoption of a risk-based approach and its emphasis on 'effectiveness' in anti-money laundering legislation. Indeed, with respect to the 2005 Directive, the UK legislator has been innovative and introduced the criminalisation of money laundering offences, although as noted in chapter five, this Directive requires the adoption of effective, proportionate and dissuasive penalties.

Moreover, the Drug Trafficking (Offences) Act had already been agreed in 1986, seven years before the first 1991 Directive was adopted.[48] This Directive was implemented into UK legislation in the form of a money laundering regulation in 1993. Thereafter, a new regulation in 2003 implemented the 2001 Directive that came into force in 2004.[49] In connection with the implementation of the 2001 Directive it has been noted, however, that the UK system already met the relevant requirements as it was already more thorough than the EU legislation in question.[50] Accordingly, the UK appears to have taken a strong role in the international struggle against money laundering and, as will be evaluated below, the UK has also been one of the major trend setters on the international stage.[51] After all, the UK is a major international centre for investment and private banking and has one of the largest commercial banking sectors in the world.[52]

However, many commentators have stressed the 'gold plating' phenomenon, or over-implementation, in connection with the anti-money-laundering regime in the UK.[53] In particular, regarding the First and Second Directives, Parliament went considerably beyond what was required. This section intends to highlight the issue of gold plating and the controversial rules governing the reporting of suspicious reporting. It will become clear that these concepts are related.

For example, it has been pointed out that the notion of 'suspicion' in relation to the source of the proceeds of crime appears to have constituted a crucial theme in UK anti-money-laundering legislation. Thus, rather than stipulating the requirement of 'knowledge' – that is, 'intent' – the UK legislator seems to rely on 'suspicion', which constitutes a lower threshold for prosecution on the criminal law scale. This is interesting, as the Directives in question refer to the requirement of 'knowledge' rather than an objective test consisting of 'having reasonable grounds to suspect'. Clearly, this is a considerable extension beyond the demands of the Directive[54] and confirms the extraordinarily wide-ranging scope of the PoCA. For this reason it has been suggested that when the PoCA implemented the Directive it created onerous extensions to these provisions, which made it much wider than one would have expected.[55]

[48] ibid.
[49] SI 2003/3075.
[50] Padfield (above n 20).
[51] ibid.
[52] FATF report (above n 4).
[53] Mitsilegas (above n 25).
[54] ibid.
[55] ibid.

Moreover, the anti-money laundering network in the UK has had a considerable impact on the national legislation on privacy rules. For example, it has been observed that the UK was the first European country to have extended the reporting obligation in its anti-money laundering legislation to lawyers.[56] This resulted in a debate in the UK on whether in the light of the 2001 Directive, the reporting obligations – and the attached privilege (for example, information related to a process) – should be extended to other occupations such as accountants. However, when the PoCA was debated in Parliament, the Government opposed the extension of the application of professional privilege in the manner envisaged by the Directives. However, the Government subsequently made a u-turn. The Money Laundering Regulation 2003 was amended in line with the Directives to include a wider group of professionals, such as accountants, that could rely on the privilege normally reserved for lawyers.[57] Therefore, introducing criminal rules inevitably has implications for the broader structure of the legal regime. The problem has been that reporting suspicious transactions in the UK has certainly not been risk-free, as the legislation in question did not protect those who reported suspicious activity in the case of mistaken reporting from liability for breach of confidentiality.[58] As explained in chapter five, the 2005 Directive requires Member States to take all appropriate measures to protect employees and others who make suspicious activity reports from being exposed to threats or hostile action. Therefore, prior to the third money-laundering instrument, the question of confidentiality was on the agenda in the Court of Appeal judgment of *Bowman v Fels*.[59] In this case, the claimant had lived with the defendant for ten years in a house registered solely in the defendant's name and, after the end of their relationship, she asserted a right to a beneficial interest in the property arising out of a constructive trust. In the course of litigation, the claimant's solicitors notified, pursuant to their understanding of Section 328 PoCA, their suspicion that the defendant was engaged in VAT fraud. The crucial issue that arose was to what extent Section 328(7) of the 2002 Act (stating that 'a person commits an offence if he enters into or becomes concerned in an arrangement which he knows or suspects facilitates the acquisition, retention, use or control of criminal property by or behalf of another person')[60] was applicable where during the course of legal proceedings a lawyer receives information leading to knowledge or suspicion of money laundering. In short, the Court upheld the fundamental principle that information passed to a lawyer during the course of litigation did not constitute disclosed information. In doing so, the Court focused mainly on the

[56] Gely (above n 29).

[57] J Fisher, '*Bowman v Fels*: The Continuing Fallout on Legal Privilege and Relevant Professional Advisers' (2006) *Money Laundering Bulletin*, available at www.mcgrigors.com/pdfdocs/bowman_fels.pdf (last accessed January 2012).

[58] *Padfield* (above n 20).

[59] *Bowman v Fels* [2005] EWCA Civ 226.

[60] Subsection 2 of the same section states that this does not apply if the person in question makes an authorised disclosure under s 338 and the disclosure is made before the act mentioned in subsection 1 is committed, and he has the appropriate consent, or he intended to make such a disclosure but had a reasonable excuse for not doing so.

relationship between the PoCA and the 2001 Directive and highlighted the notion of over-criminalisation of money laundering offences and the protection of the confidentiality principle between lawyer and client in the UK.[61] Although this judgment is generally celebrated as a welcome case, as the Court looked at the EU dimension in question and decided to limit the scope of the national law implementing it, the main criticism of this ruling has been that the PoCA created an undesirable discrepancy between the implementation of anti-money laundering regulation policy at both the domestic and the EU level.

The Court of Appeal discussed the gold-plating phenomenon. The judges[62] concluded that:

> it was open to the United Kingdom Parliament to go further than the Directives [1991 and 2001], and in some respects it did . . . Because of this fact, and of the possibility that Parliament might have had some different purpose in mind when it went further than the two directives strictly required, we will also examine whether in so doing it can have intended to override important principles of English law without clearly indicating its intention to do so. [63]

It is worth examining this ruling in further detail as it highlights how the European dimension has affected the UK's anti-money laundering framework. It was recently noted that the UK courts have generally been very reluctant to become involved in judging whether or not the transposing measure in question was gold-plated and thus should be left to the legislator.[64] So *Bowman v Fels* is exceptional in this regard and illustrates how EU law penetrates the principles of English criminal law. In particular, it has been stressed that great caution must be exercised in the future to ensure that the constantly evolving international initiatives dealing with money laundering are not hastily compromised by over-eager domestic legislation.[65] More specifically, the Court stressed the importance of the fundamental rights and values represented by the protection of lawyer–client confidentiality (legal privilege) and argued that the driving principles behind EU law, the European Convention on Human Rights (ECHR) and UK domestic law are 'virtually identical'.[66] This reasoning led the Court to conclude that Section 328 was not intended to cover or affect the ordinary conduct of litigation by legal professionals, and in any case there was nothing in the language of Section 328 PoCA to suggest that Parliament expressly intended to override legal professional privilege.[67]

[61] *Bowman v Fels* [2005] EWCA Civ 226; E Powles, 'All that Glisters is not Gold: Laundering the UK Money Laundering Regime' (2006) 65 (1) *CLJ* 40.

[62] Lord Justice Brooke, Lord Justice Mance and Lord Justice Dyson.

[63] para 45 in *Bowman v Fels* [2005] EWCA Civ 226.

[64] R Thomas and G Lynch-Wood, 'Transposing European Union Law in the United Kingdom: Administrative Rule-Making, Scrutiny and Better Regulation' (2008) 14 *European Public Law* 177.

[65] Powles (above n 61).

[66] *Bowman v Fels* [2005] EWCA Civ 226, para 82.

[67] paras 83–86, Mitsilegas (above n 25).

In this context it is also appropriate to mention the judgment of *Montila*,[68] where the House of Lords (now the Supreme Court) was asked, prior to the PoCA, to ascertain whether in a prosecution the Crown needed to prove that the property actually constituted the proceeds of a crime or drug trafficking in the knowledge of the defendant. Here, the Lords embarked upon an extensive examination of international anti-money laundering measures and the EU Directives in force – which required knowledge that the property in question constituted the proceeds of crime – in order to compare these measures with the national legislation. Again, the UK court used the EU Directives and international provisions to limit an over-extensive interpretation of domestic money laundering law.[69] In short, it appears as if the UK legislator has adopted a 'maximum criminalisation' trend where the money laundering regulations are used to promote a broader mission of fighting crime generally.

The UK Government's policy is that the transposition of EU Directives should mirror as closely as possible the requirement of the Directive except where there is a clear reason for not doing so. It appears less clear what such a reason could be in the context of money laundering since, as noted above, this is an area characterised by over-eager implementation.[70] More generally, according to the Transposition Guide, gold plating can arise in a variety of ways where the national legislator adds substantive requirements to the EU framework. Examples of this include: substituting wider UK legal terms for those used in the Directive; failing to take full advantage of any derogations which keep requirements to a minimum; providing for sanctions or enforcement mechanisms that exceed the minimum requirements; and implementing earlier than necessary.[71] Nevertheless, the phenomenon of gold plating is not one-sided. The Davidson report, which was set up to reduce unnecessary regulatory burdens on the private, public and voluntary sectors, concluded that the allegation of gold plating in the UK was rarely correct and was to a large extent, simply a criticism of the EU legislation.[72] It has also been observed that the focus seems to rest on gold plating while little attention is paid to the notion of under-implementation. Another shortcoming in connection with the allegation of over-eager over-implementation was that no examination was made of the actual enforcement of the alleged gold-plated legislation in issue.[73] Therefore, it is uncertain whether the gold plating phenomenon has been a significant problem in the implementation of the Money Laundering Directives in the UK. In addition, the UK has also been under international obligations, which, as explained in chapter five, have influenced the content of the EU Directives.

[68] *R v Montila and others* [2004] UKHL 50.

[69] Mitsilegas (above n 25).

[70] Cabinet Office, *Transposition Guide: How to Implement European Directives Effectively* (Cabinet Office London, 2005) para 3.3 cited in Thomas and Lynch-Wood (above n 64).

[71] ibid.

[72] N Davidson, *Davidson Review: Implementation of EU Legislation* (London, Better Regulation Executive, 2006), available at www.bis.gov.uk/files/file44583.pdf (last accessed January 2012).

[73] Thomas and Lynch-Wood (above n 64).

As discussed in chapter five, the 2005 Directive included the financing of terrorism as part of the anti-money laundering framework. Therefore we need to look at the UK approach in this area.

F. The Ever-expanding Anti-terrorism Network in the UK

> Rejection of the US war model is to be welcomed, for, like the 'war on drugs' or the 'war on crime', that approach is conducive to a lack of accountability and proportionality and threatens an everlasting departure from civil society. Yet, there are several tensions [within the current UK regime] . . . It is evident that measures such as detention without trial and control orders do not reflect the ideal[74]

The UK has had a number of different measures in place to oppose terrorism generally[75] for a long time, most prominently in connection with the problems in Northern Ireland. Nevertheless, in the context of the UK's struggle against money laundering and the financing of terrorism it has been noted that the war on the financing of terrorism in the UK has done little if anything to limit the sources of finance available to terrorist groups.[76]

The Terrorist Act 2000 was radically altered in the aftermath of the terrorist attacks on 9/11. It creates offences relating to the funding of terrorism, money laundering and the failure to provide information relating to terrorism finance during the course of employment. The UK has also implemented UN Resolution 1373 and ratified the UN Convention for the Suppression of the Financing of Terrorism, which resulted in the enactment of five new offences relating to fundraising for terrorist organisations, namely: use and possession, funding arrangements, money laundering and failure to disclose information.[77] The Terrorist Act also provided, among other things, for the right to seize terrorist assets, and the imposition of freezing and restraint orders. In addition, the Anti-Terrorism Crime and Security Act 2001 deals with the freezing of money connected to terrorism. Part II of this Act permits HM Treasury to freeze the assets of overseas governments or residents who have taken or are likely to take action to the detriment of the UK's economy, or action constituting a threat to life or property of a national or resident of the UK. However, in order to obtain such a freezing order there must be a reasonable belief that action threatening such objects has taken place or is likely to take place.[78] In short, a freezing order prevents all persons in

[74] C Walker, 'Clamping Down on Terrorism in the United Kingdom' (2006) 4 *Journal of International Commercial Law Journal* 1137.

[75] For an overview of these measures, see C Eckes, 'The Legal Framework of the European Union's Counter-terrorist Policies: Full of Good Intentions?' in C Eckes and T Konstadinides (above n 1) 127. See also more generally, C Eckes, *EU Counter-Terrorist Policies and Fundamental Rights* (Oxford, Oxford University Press, 2009).

[76] N Ryder, 'A False Sense of Security? An Analysis of Legislative Approaches towards the Prevention of Terrorist Finance in the United States and the United Kingdom' (2007) *Journal of Business Law* 821.

[77] ibid.

[78] HM Treasury Office *The Financial Challenge to Crime and Terrorism*, (February 2007) available at www.hm-treasury.gov.uk (last accessed January 2012).

the UK from making funds available to or for the benefit of a person specified in the order in question.

In any case, in the aftermath of the terrorist attacks in the UK in 2005, another Terrorism Act was passed in 2006, which introduced some new terrorism-related offences.[79] In particular, the 2006 Act extends police and investigatory powers in relation to terrorism, such as allowing the extension of detention of terrorist suspects with judicial approval for up to 28 days.[80] This Act also implemented the Council of Europe Convention on the Prevention of Terrorism of 2005. The 2006 Act, among other things, amended the definition of terrorism in the 2000 and 2001 Acts to eliminate disparities between its definition in domestic law and that in various international conventions to which the UK is a party. Asset freezing has been carried out in two ways, both of which are supervised by the Asset Freezing unit in the Treasury.[81] The first is the more general terrorist financing regime implemented by the Terrorist Order 2006. It provides the HM Treasury with powers to freeze accounts of suspected terrorists, pursuant to UN Resolution (2001) 1373. The second is the more specific measures against persons associated with al-Qaida. The UK gives effect to UN Resolution 1390 (2002) under the al-Qaida and Taliban Order 2006.

Thus, things developed further and in 2008, the Counter Terrorism Act introduced a procedure for setting aside decisions on financial restrictions taken by the Treasury.[82] More specifically, the Counter-Terrorism Act 2008[83] came into effect on 27 November 2008.[84] Schedule 7 of this act sets out new powers for the Treasury to direct financial and credit institutions to apply a range of financial restrictions in respect of business with persons in a non EEA country of money laundering or terrorist financing or proliferation concern (eg the spreading of weapons). As observed by commentators, the 2008 Act was introduced in haste to comply with a possible change of direction in the FATF and gives the Treasury the power to give directions to freeze assets or prohibit transactions where it reasonably believes that terrorism, money laundering or the development of chemical, biological, radiological or nuclear weapons is taking place, or on the grounds of designation as a non-cooperating country by the FATF. It also gives it the power to enforce due diligence, surveillance systematic reporting and winding-up orders

[79] Third Report of the Independent Reviewer pursuant to Section 14(3) of the Prevention of Terrorism Act 2005 available at www.statewatch.org/news/2008/mar/uk-carlile-3rd-terr-rep.pdf (last accessed January 2012).

[80] Explanatory Notes to Terrorism Act 2006 available at www.opsi.gov.uk/ACTS/acts2006/en/ukpgaen_20060011_en_1 (last accessed January 2012).

[81] P Sproat, 'Counter-terrorist Finance in the UK: A Quantitative and Qualitative Commentary based on Open Source Materials (2010) 13 *Journal of Money Laundering Control* 315.

[82] The legislative history of this act is provided in case *Her Majesty's Treasury (Respondent) v Mohammed Jabar Ahmed and others (FC), UK Supreme Court* [2010] UKSC 2, judgment given on 27 January 2010.

[83] Counter-Terrorism Act 2008 c 28, available at www.legislation.gov.uk/ukpga/2008/28/contents (last accessed January 2012).

[84] See also amendment 2009 No 58 (c 6), Prevention and Suppression of Terrorism.

(to shut down business) as well as to search any premises they suspect without a warrant.[85]

The key pieces of legislation on terrorist finance in the UK are:

—Terrorism Act 2000 (c 11) and Terrorism Act 2006 (c 11) and Counter
—Terrorism Act 2008 (c 28);
—Anti-Terrorism Crime and Security Act 2001 (c 24);
—Terrorism (United Nations Measures) Order 2001 (no 3365);
—al-Qaida and the Taleban (United Nations Measures) Order 2002 (SI 2002/111); and
—Prevention of Terrorism Act 2005 (c 2).

The concept of terrorism financing is defined as including money or other property, which is likely to be used for the purposes of terrorism or proceeds in relation to acts of terrorism. There is also, as in the context of 'traditional' money laundering offences, an obligation on the regulated sectors to train employees about these offences under the Terrorism Act as well as specific reporting obligations. Here too, HM Treasury emphasises a risk-based approach.[86] In doing so, it stresses the importance of striking a balance between the need to protect citizens' privacy and fundamental rights on the one hand, and ensuring their on-going security on the other. Nevertheless, as noted in chapter five, the inclusion of terrorist financing in the Money Laundering Directive poses problems. More specifically, since the purpose of financing terrorism is political rather than financial profit, the traditional money laundering definition breaks down.[87] Nonetheless, HM Treasury insists that the financial measures in this area deter crime and terrorism by increasing the risk of being 'caught'. Furthermore – unsurprisingly – the importance of 'effectiveness' is highlighted in its anti-terrorist financing agenda. This includes an increased understanding of the underlying threat, which should be increased continually and requires direct action to mitigate it. There is also the possibility of 'closed source' evidence in asset freezing cases, where there are strong operational reasons to impose a freeze, and where insufficient open source evidence is available. In order to ensure the fairness of any court challenge to the imposition of a freeze, the Government has discussed the possibility of introducing a procedure for the appointment of special advocates to represent the interests of the applicant with respect to closed evidence. Accountability to Parliament is also being increased through quarterly reporting to Parliament on the operation of the UK asset-freezing regime.[88]

However, the Terrorism Acts criminalise not only the offence of fundraising for terrorist purposes but also the use or possession of any asset where the perpetrator intends that it should be used, or has reasonable cause to suspect that it may be used, for the purposes of terrorism. Moreover, the measure provides for strict

[85] Sproat (above n 81).
[86] *The Financial Challenge to Crime and Terrorism* (above n 78).
[87] Alexander (above n 15).
[88] Walker (above n 74).

liability offences, though defences include that there was no reasonable ground for the defendant to suspect or make a disclosure. The legislation also establishes a requirement to disclose any suspicion 'that another person has committed an offence [of terrorist financing]' where the suspicion is based 'on information which comes to his attention in the course of a trade, profession, business [other than a business in the regulated sector] or employment'.[89]

Yet the power of the HM Treasury to freeze the assets of suspected terrorist organisations has been criticised as an 'inappropriate use of emergency legislation and constitutes a headlong rush to drive Anti-Terrorism Crime and Security Act through Parliament with little or no time to consider whether a more appropriate and effective system for forfeiture of terrorist cash could be devised'.[90] HM Treasury, conversely, simply stresses that the importance of freezing funds cannot be underestimated, as it remains an important weapon in the war on terrorist finances.[91]

Indeed, the powers of the Treasury have been significantly extended by the introduction of the Counter-Terrorism Act 2008 and in particular Schedule 7. According to some commentators, the Treasury can now choose whether to follow the recommendations of the FATF, or can simple decide whether a state or elements of it pose a terrorist, money laundering or proliferation risk to the interests of the UK without Parliament's approval.[92] This is a dangerous trend from a legitimacy perspective as well as from a fair trial point view. After all, an individual could go to prison for up to two years on the decision of the Treasury alone.[93]

i. *Judicial Review*

The judgment of *A et al v HM Treasury* an interesting example of a UK judgment where the freezing of assets for the purposes of terrorist financing has been discussed, although admittedly not in the specific context of money laundering.[94] The question posed was whether the Terrorism and al Qaida Orders of 2006 concerning freezing orders were ultra vires to the UK's United Nations Act of 1946. In particular, the applicants argued that the Terrorism Order contravened the principle of legal certainty as the freezing in question covered a seemingly endless circle of families, friends and associates.[95] Whereas Resolution 1373 required UN Member States to freeze the assets of any individual 'who is' a terrorist supporter,

[89] *The Financial Challenge to Crime and Terrorism* (above n 73).

[90] P Binning, 'In Safe Hands? Striking the Balance between Privacy and Security Anti-terrorist Finance Measures' (2002) 6 *European Human Rights Law Review* 737; and Ryder (n 76).

[91] *The Financial Challenge to Crime and Terrorism* (above n 73).

[92] G Rees and T Moloney, 'The Latest Efforts to Interrupt Supply Lines: Schedule 7 to Counter Terrorism Act' 2008 (2010) *Criminal Law Review* 127.

[93] ibid.

[94] *A, K, M, Q & G v HM Treasury* [2007] EWHC 869 (Admin), 24 April 2008.

[95] ibid; and www.statewatch.org/news/2008/apr/04financial-guantanamo.htm (last accessed January 2012).

in implementing it, the UK went further by allowing asset freezes to be imposed on any individual 'who may be' a terrorist supporter. To begin with the High Court stipulated the right to legal certainty. In doing so, it referred to the Opinion of AG Maduro in *Kadi* and the adequate protection of fundamental rights.[96] Due to the lack of legal certainty the High Court concluded that the orders in question needed to be annulled.

The High Court in this case referred to the inadequacy of relying on the 1946 Act alone. Subsequently, the Court of Appeal disagreed in upholding the freezing orders, although it noted that what was required was a case-by-case approach and not an annulment of the legal measures. Although the Court of Appeal[97] recognised the difficulties in the situation from a due process point of view, it did not consider that sufficient to nullify the order itself. Accordingly, the Court of Appeal ruled that: 'There must be procedures to enable [the applicant], again so far as possible, to discover the case against him, so that he may have an opportunity to meet it'. Subsequently, the case reached the Supreme Court. The Supreme Court ruled that both orders were ultra vires. However, it based its judgment on a slightly different ground.[98] The Supreme Court stressed the 'Simms principle'[99] under which Parliament can only depart from fundamental rights through express and unambiguous language. Thus, when the measures required by a Security Council resolution affect the individual, the Court held that there were limits to their adoption by means of Orders in Council under the general enabling power of the 1946 Act.[100]

Moreover, it could be argued that these judgments highlight the old common law question of legality and legal certainty in criminal law. After all, although the days of common law offences ought to be long gone, as Ashworth once put it, the elasticity of the European Court of Human Right's (ECtHR) reasoning in the common law context remains undefined.[101] For instance, in the judgment in *CR and SW v UK* the ECtHR concluded in approving a common law variation of the applicable law that the very nature of the offence in question needed to be in line with moral standards. In that case the Strasbourg court held that the removal of the marital rape exemption by the House of Lords did not amount to a retrospective change in the elements of the offence.[102] Again, this relates partly to what has already been touched on, namely the question of whether the whole issue of the freezing of terrorist assets at the EU and the UN level are more properly dealt with under the auspices of criminal law in order to guarantee fair trial principles. However, in the UK the question is more complicated as the Terrorism Acts criminalise the matter. In spite of this, the UK does not guarantee legal certainty due to

[96] Case 402/05P *Kadi* [2008] ECR I-6351 Opinion delivered on 16 January 2008. See ch 4 Pt II.

[97] *A, K, M, Q & G v HM Treasury* [2008] EWCA Civ 1187, judgment of 30 October 2008.

[98] For a commentary see, A Johnston and E Nanopoulos, 'The New UK Supreme Court, the Separation of Powers and Anti-terrorism Measures' (2010) *CLJ* 217.

[99] *R v Home Secretary ex p Simms* [1999] 1 AC 69.

[100] For an analysis, see A Johnston and E Nanopoulos (above n 98).

[101] A Ashworth, *Principles of Criminal Law* (Oxford, Oxford University Press, 2006) ch 2.

[102] *CR and SW v UK* (1995) 21 EHRR.

the use of so-called closed source evidence in asset freezing cases where there are strong operational reasons to impose a freeze and where there is insufficient open source evidence available.[103] At issue here is the concept of strict liability in criminal law cases, which is a reality in the UK but more fragile in other Member States, for example, in Sweden (except for petty crimes).

It should also be noted that recently, the issue arose of whether the Financial Services Authority (FSA) had the power to prosecute offences of money laundering contrary to sections 327 and 328 of the PoCA.[104] The claimant argued that the FSA power to prosecute criminal offences were limited to the offences referred to in sections 401 and 402 of the Financial Services Authority Act 2000, which did not include offences under the PoCA.[105] In response, the FSA stated that its powers were not limited and that it had the common law authority to bring common law offences in respect to other offences. In this case the Supreme Court held that the ability of the FSA to bring private prosecutions for money laundering offences made sense. It held that where offences form part of the same criminality as offences that the FSA has undoubted power to prosecute under the Financial Services Act[106] these could be included in the same indictment and that the FSA should be able to act as the single prosecutor instead of having to bring in another prosecuting authority. For this reason the Supreme Court concluded that: 'The fact that the FSA does not have statutory powers of investigation in relation to offences under PoCA tells one nothing about its power to prosecute those offences'.[107] So common law criminal law is still going strong.

In the more recent case of *Bank Mellat v HM Treasury*[108] concerning the interpretation of Schedule 7 of the 2008 Act, the Court of Appeal upheld an order by the Treasury. The order concerned financial restrictions against Iran and had been made by the Treasury on the basis that the Treasury reasonably believed that the development or production of nuclear weapons in Iran posed a significant risk to the national interests of the UK. In short, the order excluded Bank Mellat from the UK financial market. The main justification by the Treasury for issuing the order was that Bank Mellat was well placed to assist organisations to facilitate the development of nuclear weapons by providing them with banking facilities, in particular trade finance. Bank Mellat challenged this, mainly on the grounds of proportionality concerns and a lack of fair trail. However, the Court of Appeal concluded that Schedule 7 afforded Bank Mellat a reasonable opportunity to challenge the order and that in case of urgency there would be an opportunity to grant interim relief. Therefore, the Court of Appeal held that there was no breach of

[103] See for a recent survey, House of Lords, 10th Report 2007–2008 Select Committee on the Constitution, *Counter Terrorism Bill: The Role of the Ministers, Parliament and the Judiciary*.

[104] *R v Rollins* [2010] UKSC 39, on appeal from *R v Rollins* [2009] EWCA Crim 1941, see case comment by N Taylor, 'FSA Prosecutions: Offences of Money Laundering – Power to Prosecute' (2010) *Crim LR* 772.

[105] ibid.

[106] Financial Services Act 2000 (c 8), see also the newer Act of 2010 (c. 28).

[107] Sir John Dyson, delivering the judgment.

[108] *Bank Mellat v HM Treasury* [2011] EWCA Civ 1.

Article 6 of the ECHR or of Protocol No 1 of the Convention as attached to the ECHR. However, the Court of Appeal also stressed that the party must be given 'sufficient information to enable it actually to refute, in so far as that is possible, the case made out against it'. Given the outcome in this case it is perhaps difficult to imagine any scenario which would be considered to be in breach of fair trial guarantees in the fight against money laundering and terrorist financing in the area of suppression of terrorism.

G. Conclusion: the UK

The UK has one of the highest rates of compliance with FATF recommendations among the signatory states.[109] In reaching such a result, the UK combines civil law, criminal law and regulatory law in the suppression of dirty money. As a general conclusion it can be observed that the money laundering provisions in the UK have always been characterised by an all-crimes approach. As stated, this poses questions of legality and foreseeability. Moreover, it appears as if the money laundering framework in the UK has developed in an ad hoc fashion, from a non-regulatory grid to a far-reaching network of interacting – EU, UN and FATF – laws against money laundering and financing of terrorism. Despite the piecemeal evolution of anti-money laundering legislation, one might ask whether the increased impact of EU law reflects a society undergoing change. Commentators have criticised the UK's over-implementation of anti-money laundering instruments. It seems that the most significant impact on English law has been the duty to report suspicion and the PoCA has had a revolutionary impact on both the rules on confidentiality and on the confiscation regime. The issue of trust between lawyer and client has been a subject of particular debate in the present context. We may well ask whether money launderers will simply stop consulting lawyers now. As Sproat remarked in 2007, the legislation at issue has 'one way or another allowed the State to take approximately £300m from the hands of those it calls criminals'.[110]

Moreover, as noted above, the UK's policy reflects a strategy of using money laundering offences to ensure a general 'tough-on-crime' approach, with the imposition of heavier penalties than strictly required by the European measures. Therefore, as demonstrated by *Bowman v Fels*, the UK courts have questioned the tactics of the UK legislators by drawing inspiration from the EC instruments and managing to some degree to stop legislative and prosecutorial pressure to over-extend the money laundering offences.[111] In any case, it seems clear that the UK

[109] Based on a comparison of pre and post-2003 compliance with the FATF's Forty Recommendations and Nine Special Recommendations made using both self-assessment and mutual assessment data, see J Johnson, 'Third Round FATF Mutual Evaluations indicate Declining Compliance' (2008) 11 *Journal of Money Laundering Control* 47.

[110] Sproat (above n 7).

[111] Mitsilegas (above n 25).

legislator has used the money laundering framework and the implementation of EU legislation as an excuse to introduce tougher sanctions.

However, at no point has there been any discussion of whether the UK's approach – to go further than the Directive requires by gold plating its measure – could hinder the free movement of capital or be contrary to the proportionality principle.

Thus, a theme running through much of the literature studied here concerns ineffectiveness and the rushed legislation in the area in question. As discussed in previous chapters, the problem is that criminal law is far from effective per se. The UK legislator may gain some comfort from the fact that this problem is unique to the UK; it appears to be a common theme running through the EU, UN and FATF anti-money laundering legislation more generally. It appears to be a general consequence of the attacks of 9/11 and the fear of global terrorism finance. In contrast to most EU Member States, the UK has had experience of terrorism in Northern Ireland. However, it remains to be seen whether this experience will help the UK to successfully develop the EU's anti-money laundering scheme through a risk-based approach.

With respect to the current threat of terrorism in the UK more generally, it is worth mentioning that Europol issued a survey the results of which showed that terrorist plots in Europe had been almost exclusively focused on the UK.[112] In this respect, it is interesting to note that although terrorism is the most obvious security threat faced by the UK, other threats and state responses to them have also had a significant effect on the development of UK human rights law. In fact, it has been argued that in human rights cases the British Government cites the threat of terrorism less often than the threats of organised crime and illegal immigration.[113] As discussed in chapter two, there is also a clear EU law dimension to the discussion of fundamental human rights in the area of national criminal law and the EU law framework has had – and continues to have – a significant impact on the UK.

III. SWEDEN'S IMPLEMENTATION OF THE ANTI-MONEY LAUNDERING DIRECTIVES

A. Introduction

The Swedish government's approach to the 2005 Directive has been rather more lax than the anti-money laundering framework in the UK. Furthermore, there is very little scholarship about the EU's anti-money laundering network and its relationship to Swedish law.[114]

[112] www.europol.europa.eu/publications/TESAT/TESAT2008.pdf. (last accessed January 2012).

[113] B Goold et al, 'Public Protection, Proportionality, and the Search for Balance' available at www.justice.gov.uk/docs/270907.pdf (last accessed January 2012).

[114] For a recent overview, see however M Bergstrom, 'EU Anti-money Laundering Regulation: Multilevel Cooperation of Public and Private Actors' in above (n 1) 97.

In any case, the Swedish implementation of the Third Money Laundering Directive was considerably delayed. The new law (lag 2009:62) implementing the 2005 Directive was eventually adopted in February 2009. Before looking more closely at the process of Swedish implementation of the Third Money Laundering Directive, it is useful to briefly set out the basics of lawmaking in Sweden.

B. The Swedish Legislature

Parliament is Sweden's legislative assembly. The majority of parliament's decisions are based on proposals for new laws or amendments to existing laws presented by the government.[115] Before the government proposes legislation, the matter in question is analysed and evaluated, a task which may be assigned to officials from the ministry concerned, a commission of inquiry or a committee.[116] These evaluation documents in turn are published in the State Official Reports (the official abbreviation is SOU). Before the government takes a position on the recommendations in question, its report is referred for consideration to the relevant bodies. These referral bodies may be central government agencies, special interest groups, local government authorities or other bodies whose activities may be affected by the proposals. This is similar to the consultation process in the UK.

Once the referral bodies have submitted their comments, the ministry responsible drafts the bill that will be submitted to Parliament. If the proposed law has important implications for private citizens or public welfare, the government should first refer the proposal to the Council of Legislation to ensure that it does not conflict with existing legislation. This is where the implementation of the Money Laundering Directive was held up, although it should have been implemented by 15 December 2007 it was in fact, delayed for more than a year. Consequently, the Commission issued a letter informing the Swedish Foreign Ministry of the failure to implement the Directive and requested an explanation of the delay.[117] The question asked by the Commission was, of course, whether Swedish legislation already met the Directive's requirements. The explanation returned by the Swedish Government was simply that it was still evaluating the matter and that the new law would enter into force on 1 January 2009. Therefore, the Commission instituted proceedings before the Court.[118] On 11 June 2009, the Court ruled that Sweden's failure to implement the 2005 Directive had put

[115] See eg, www.lagrummet.se (last accessed January 2012).

[116] www.riksdagen.se/templates/PageWFrame____6577.aspx (last accessed January 2012).

[117] Official Notification K (2008) 382/24, breach 2008/0212 received on 29 January 2008. See also europa.eu/rapid/pressReleasesAction.do?reference=IP/08/1522&format=HTML&aged=0&language=EN&guiLanguage=en (last accessed January 2012).

[118] Case C-546/08 *Commission v Sweden*, judgment of 11 June 2009. See also Case C-185/09, *Commission v Sweden*, judgment of 4 February 2010 not yet reported concerning late implementation of Directive 2006/24/EC 'on the retention of data generated or processed in connection with the provision of publicly available electronic communications services or of public communications networks and amending Directive 2002/58/EC' [2006] OJ L105/54.

Sweden in breach of its obligations under Article 45(1) of the Directive. It is not the first time that Sweden has been late with the implementation of directives. The Swedish legislator was one and a half years late in implementing the 2001 Directive too.[119]

C. The Money Laundering Directives in Sweden

The war against dirty money started life as part of the struggle against drug dealing in Sweden. The Swedish National Economic Crimes Bureau estimated that the yearly proceeds of crime in Sweden in 2006 were approximately 130 billion SEK.[120] As stated, the implementation process of the Third Money Laundering Directive was delayed. The official report was issued on 30 March 2007, referred to as SOU 2007:23, but something delayed the process. This report was submitted to the Council on Legislation, which has been evaluating the matter. According to a spokesperson at the Ministry of Finance, the Council should have submitted their report in June 2008 but this process was delayed.[121] Instead, the final draft proposal for the implementation of the Third Money Laundering Directive was introduced in November 2008, almost a year after the implementation deadline.[122] One of the reasons for such a delay was the extended discussion about how and by whom supervision was to be organised.[123] The Swedish Agency for Public Management (*Statskontoret*) had been commissioned by the Swedish Government to investigate whether one government agency should be assigned the task of exercising the supervision required under the third AML Directive.[124] In general, the Government Bill stressed the importance of a flexible supervisory system since forms of money laundering change over time[125]

As mentioned, the new legislation implementing the Directive entered into force in February 2009. There appears to have been no intention to discuss the criminal law dimension of the Money Laundering Directive or to consider the impact of the Lisbon Treaty on the Swedish constitution.[126]

The afore-mentioned legislative preparatory works are informative. For example, it is held that there is no need to change the current definition of money laundering in connection with the 2005 Directive, though a general clause,

[119] A Calisendorff, 'Skärpta regler mot penningtvätt; advokater i en ny och oprövad roll som angivare av klienter' (2005–2006) *Juridisk Tidskrift* 553.

[120] FATF evaluation Sweden available at www.fatf-gafi.org/dataoecd/26/35/36461995.pdf (last accessed January 2012).

[121] Telephone interview with Mr Wilborg, head of section, Ministry of Finance and Banking, 24 April 2008.

[122] November 2008, Lagrådsremiss, issued for publication 14 October 2008, available at www.regeringen.se/sb/d/10163/a/113463 (last accessed January 2012).

[123] Bergstrom (above n 1).

[124] www.statskontoret.se/upload/Publikationer/2008/200802.pdf (last accessed January 2012).

[125] Prop (2008/09: 70) 'Genomförandet av tredje penningtvättsdirektivet' Government Bill 2008/09: 70 on the implementation of the third AML Directive. See also Bergstrom (above n 1).

[126] The final report was not published on the Swedish Government's website until the spring of 2009.

perhaps in the preamble, would be needed to aid the public understanding that the money laundering law only deals with administrative sanctions while the Penal Code – which according to the Swedish legislator is unaffected by this law – deals with criminal law.[127] Therefore, before analysing Sweden's implementation any further, it is useful to look briefly at the history of Swedish legislation of EU anti-money laundering measures.

i. The 1991 and 2001 Directives

Even before EU legislation entered the picture, Swedish legislation was adapted to the UN Vienna and Palermo Conventions. This brought changes to the Penal Code, which dealt with the proceeds of crime and what should be counted as money laundering. The influence of EU law on the Swedish anti-money laundering regulation has been extended as a result of the 1991 and 2001 Directives. In connection with the implementation of the 2001 Directive, the government noted, as in the UK, that Swedish legislation was already much more far-reaching than existing EU legislation in relation to the prohibition of the receipt of stolen goods.[128] Moreover, according to the Swedish preparatory works in connection with the 2001 Directive, Swedish legislation encompassed a much wider area than required by the Directive.[129] It is, however, less clear whether this has been an instance of the gold plating phenomenon or an independent initiative of the Swedish legislator. This is particularly true for criminal law regulation. Although the Swedish approach is, in slightly exaggerated terms, to keep the Money Laundering Directives away from their national criminal law, the concept of money laundering is nevertheless criminalised in the Penal Code. Indeed, the penal code criminalises not only aiding and abetting money laundering but also attempted laundering. For this reason, the Swedish penal code goes further than the Money Laundering Directive. The drafters of the preparatory works implementing the 2001 Directive recognised this and discussed whether it would be wise to adopt a more restrictive approach in the Penal Code, but no such amendment was made.[130]

Another important example of difference to the Directives is that Swedish legislation traditionally does not criminalise 'self-laundering'.[131] More specifically, the Supreme Court has ruled that self-laundering is not punishable separately under current Swedish Law.[132] However, it did not indicate whether punishing self-laundering would be contrary to the Constitution or other fundamental principles of Swedish legislation. There has, moreover, been a discussion about whether the level of punishment in Swedish legislation met the requirements of

[127] SOU 2007:23, 96.
[128] Prop. 2003/04:156, *Skärpta regler mot penningtvätt.*
[129] ibid.
[130] ibid.
[131] ibid.
[132] SOU 2007:23.

the relevant Directive. In this respect, the preparatory works stated that in the view of the legislator, the 'penal value' (that is, the indicator for what kind of punishment a certain crime deserves) of money laundering did not merit imprisonment. In fact, the legislator simply left it at that and did not discuss the requirement of an effective, proportionate and dissuasive sanction.[133]

In any event, Sweden, like the UK, has adopted an 'all-crimes' approach to the criminalisation of money laundering, with all criminal offences which generate proceeds being predicate offences to money laundering. This means, that any criminal act mentioned in the Penal Code and other penal acts (including terrorist offences under the Act on Criminal Responsibility for Terrorist Offences (2003:148, discussed below) and terrorist financing (Act on Criminal Responsibility for the Financing of Particularly Serious Crime in Some Cases[134] (2002:444 also discussed below)) could constitute predicate offences to money laundering. So could any criminal act mentioned in other legislation (that is, tax offences, customs offences and so on).[135] Consequently, as noted, Sweden has adopted an 'all-crimes' approach to the criminalisation of money laundering, and the penal code and other criminal laws cover the designated categories of offences, although participation in an organised criminal group is not a specific criminal offence. For example, while conspiracy applies to the aggravated offences of many crimes in the Swedish Penal Code (such as murder, kidnapping and robbery), it is not clear if conspiracy applies to the full range of profit-generating activities in which criminal groups engage. Without going into the matter in further detail, it should be noted that the Swedish Financial Supervisory Authority is authorised to impose fines for money laundering transactions.[136] This authority supervises and monitors companies operating in financial markets and is a public agency. As pointed out by Bergstrom, even though private bodies such as the Banking Association are engaged in the issue of anti-money laundering, the Swedish model is very conventional when it comes to the private/public divide.[137] Nevertheless, despite this conventional approach to the public law, it is interesting that during the late implementation of 2005 Directive by the Swedish government, the Bank Association and the Financial Supervisory Authority were early movers in this area. In fact, they adapted their regulations to fall in line with FATF recommendations and proposed changes in the national legislation prior to such changes taking place.

[133] ibid at 38–41.

[134] Author's translation.

[135] FATF report (above n 7).

[136] The Swedish Financial Supervisory Authority, Finansinspektionen, available at www.fi.se (last accessed January 2012).

[137] Bergstrom (above n 1).

D. The 2005 Directive – Confidentiality and Swedish Law

As with the implementation of the 2005 Directive in the UK, the extension of the targeted group to include lawyers and accountants will have a significant impact on Swedish legislation.[138] The 2001 Directive broadly extended the scope of the reporting obligation to lawyers.[139] Again, this intrusion on the privacy domain and the relationship between clients and lawyers has been criticised and concerns have been expressed with respect to dangers associated with this sort of limitation of fair-trial rights.[140] Therefore, the preparatory works noted that although the law would now be extended to cover accountants – as a result of the Directive – it stressed that the loyalty obligation for lawyers, as stated in the general rules for advocates, is the crux of this matter. According to the Swedish Bar Association's guidance rules, an advocate has an obligation of loyalty towards his or her client. Clearly, there is a potential conflict with the Money Laundering Directive's reporting obligation. It has been pointed out that 'the criminal law is trespassing into the domain of contract law here which could cause confusion and difficulties'.[141] After all, punishing someone for a crime presupposes personal autonomy, meaning that the person concerned had the option to choose whether to do *x* or *y*. Therefore, the argument is that there can be no criminal liability if this option does not exist.[142] But how can this be measured – when, for example, is 'something' counted as negligent behaviour? Obviously, intent is required, the lawyers must 'know'. Not all cases are clear, however, which can be seen from the rather foggy relationship between *mens rea* and *actus reus* in the context of civil law traditions, where the notion of *dolus eventualis* or 'could not care less intent' is difficult to distinguish from 'gross negligence'.[143] In other words, such a problem arises where there is no *pactum turpe*[144] at issue, but a more trivial situation where a lawyer receives money from a client and only much later realises that the money was 'dirty'. Nevertheless, the Swedish legislator is optimistic here and points out that it has to be assumed that the intention of EU anti-money laundering legislation was not to change the fundamental relationship of trust between client and lawyer.[145] Specifically, the preparatory work points out that a lawyer would always have the option to resign and in cases where the lawyer has advised the client not to engage in money laundering or terrorist financing he or she could simply inform the client that he or she did not wish to get involved in a crime. However,

[138] Third Mutual evolution of Money Laundering and the combatting of terrorism, country report Sweden, available at www.fatf-gafi.org/dataoecd/26/35/36461995.pdf (last accessed January 2012).

[139] The so-called '24-hour rule' will be also abolished as a result of the Directive. This rule had stated that in cases where a report was made, there was a requirement not to inform the client until the first 24 hours had elapsed. Calissendorff (above n 119).

[140] ibid.

[141] S Wennberg, 'Advokaters ansvar för penningtvätt' (2003/04) *Juridisk Tidskrift* 841.

[142] ibid.

[143] eg N Jareborg, *Allmän kriminalrätt* (Uppsala, Iustus, 2001) on civil law traditions.

[144] Unethical or unfair terms.

[145] SOU 2007:23.

as the preparatory work rightly observes, it is possible in that case that the client would then realise that there had been a report of suspicious transactions.[146] Moreover, there may also be a damages claim dimension at issue in the case of a report which turns out to be wrong even though according to the Swedish rules on civil liability this would be unlikely.[147] Instead, what would be more likely is a disciplinary fine by the Bar Association.[148] However, not all cases are 'easy'. The point is that there is no protection for mistaken reporting. It is nevertheless suggested that the rules on suspicious reporting, which form part of the law on associations, should be kept intact. Here, the preparatory works argued that although there are different ways of dealing with accountants, the smoothest way would be to exempt the law concerning associations from the scope of the money laundering law. Instead, it is proposed to include a section in the law on associations with a cross-reference to the money laundering legislation, to the effect that an accountant would be required to make a report in accordance with the 2005 Directive. Accordingly, the preparatory works refers to the fact that accountants would be required to report to the board of the investment about audit matter of governance interest in any case in accordance with international standards for 'good governance for accountants'.[149] Moreover, it is held that there are potential conflicts with the auditor's ethical and legal obligations of confidentiality.[150] Accordingly, it is suggested that it is 'enough' if there is an obligation on accountants to report suspicious transactions to the head of the business in question.

Finally, the latest FATF report from 2005 criticised the rules for credit card providers in Sweden. Under the current regime, they are exempt from the obligation to report suspicion. The FATF did not see any reason why they should be exempted. The preparatory work in question did not consider any changes necessary in this respect.[151]

i. *Corporate Criminal Liability, the Swedish Problem*

According to fundamental principles of Swedish law, legal persons incur no criminal liability. This principle evolved through a series of decisions by the Supreme Court in the 1870s to 1890s.[152] In these cases, the Supreme Court regularly overturned decisions by the lower courts and rejected the criminal liability of legal persons, for the express reason that the indictments had not been directed against identified physical persons. It has been observed that such reasoning was in line with the reform of the Swedish criminal law, which emphasised the concepts of

[146] SOU 2007:23, at 137.

[147] Statement by A Calissendorff, partner, Roschier law firm, (informal email correspondence 25 April 2008).

[148] ibid.

[149] Prop 2008/09:73, Penningtvätts direktivet.

[150] ibid.

[151] ibid at 64.

[152] eg Jareborg, (above n 143) 141–49.

legality and individual responsibility.[153] It has also been pointed out that the rejection of legal responsibility by the Supreme Court must be understood in the context of its rather late industrialisation – which took place between 1870 and 1950 – which might explain the absence of a code of criminal liability for legal persons given the dearth of corporations.[154] Absence of criminal liability for legal persons has remained the rule, although there is no explicit provision in the Swedish penal code which prohibits the punishment of legal persons. Even though it is true that legal persons cannot be subject to criminal liability, legal persons can nonethelessthrough wide interpretation of the term 'entrepreneur' or 'company' – be subject to quasi-criminal sanctions in certain circumstances. This is the so-called 'business responsibility'. Thus, while statute law is silent, praxis has – with a dash of common law inspiration – developed a kind of quasi-criminal law by punishing the physical person responsible for the business in question where the requirement of *mens rea* (in Sweden, intent) or negligence could be deemed to be fulfilled.[155] Although legal persons are not punished *stricto sensu* as they lack criminal responsibility, they could nonetheless be subject to a 'corporate fine', which is a special arrangement with respect to the proceeds of crime.[156] This is an economic non-criminal sanction similar to competition law fines. However, such a fine has only been used in a very few cases as the requirements for its imposition are very high – it presupposes gross negligence in connection with the running of the enterprise.[157] It has also been observed that there is a lack of experience among the public prosecutors in this area.[158] Therefore, as with the old question of whether the EC had a criminal law competence or not before the ruling in Case C-176/03, it all comes down to what we mean by 'sanctions' – that is, criminal law or administrative ones. The problem is obviously that if the corporate fine is counted as coming under criminal law, this type of vicarious liability is not in line with the principle of legality, as a person would be criminally liable for something which the legal person could not be held criminally responsible for. Here, the question is whether the Swedish legislation needs to be changed, rather than turning a blind eye to possible problems in the future and the increasing EU law dimension. Nevertheless, the position of the Swedish Government is that a system of corporate fines is sufficient to meet the legal standards of EU legislation, such as the requirement for effective sanction against legal entities.[159]

In any case, according to Chapter 36, Section 7 of the Penal Code, an 'entrepreneur' shall be ordered to pay a 'corporate fine' for a 'crime committed in the exercise of business activities' if: (1) the crime has entailed a gross disregard for

[153] S Jönsson, 'Criminal Legal Doctrine as a Spanner in the Works? The Swedish Experience' in A Stanislas et al (eds) *Corporate Criminal Liability in Europe* (Brussels, La charte, 2008) ch 14.

[154] ibid.

[155] ibid.

[156] ibid.

[157] E Henriksson, *Straffansvar för juridiska personer – en möjlighet i svensk rätt?* (unpublished Master's thesis, University of Lund, 2003).

[158] ibid.

[159] Jönsson (above n 153).

the special obligations associated with the business activities or is otherwise of a serious kind; and (2) the entrepreneur has not done what could reasonably be required of him for the prevention of the crime. There are, however, exceptions to this rule if the crime in question was directed against the entrepreneur or if it would otherwise be manifestly unreasonable to impose a corporate fine. The concept of an 'entrepreneur' is a general one that is used in many different statutes.[160] The customary understanding of the term is 'any natural or legal person that professionally runs a business of an economic nature' and it also covers state-owned and municipal trading companies. It should also be noted that under Swedish labour law there is a kind of principal agent liability.[161] There are also special arrangements for criminal liability in environmental law cases with strict liability. Therefore, despite there being no criminal law liability for legal persons in a strict sense, a fine could be imposed for a crime committed by a natural person in the conduct of business activities.[162]

As noted above, the 2005 Directive does not require criminalisation but leaves it to the Member States to decide what kind of effective, proportionate and dissuasive sanctions to impose. As discussed in previous chapters, the EU's institutions have already demonstrated that there is a willingness to intrude on the national criminal law platform. It would therefore be naive to suggest that Swedish criminal law legislation could be kept intact.

ii. Risk-based Approach

The notion of a risk-based approach is new to Swedish financial legislation, although it is a far from a new actor on the Scandinavian environmental law stage. The adoption of the 2005 Directive will effect changes in this respect. Therefore, the Swedish legislation already had in place a rule stipulating the requirement for identification of customers. How such an identification should be made is, however, found elsewhere in the guidance rules issued by the Financial Supervisory Authority (Finans Inspektionen).[163] Its meaning is set out in the general guidance rules issued by this Authority, but it is not legislation as such. In short, these guidelines set out principles for the identification of physical and legal persons, including for those cases when the customer is absent. The Swedish legislator argues that these guidance rules on 'know your customer' issued by the Swedish Financial Supervisory Authority reflect the 2005 Directive and hence could be adopted in the legislation. In particular, the Government points to the national identity scheme which issues personal registration numbers. The official investigation therefore proposes that the rules previously found in the Swedish Financial

160 ibid.

161 Jareborg (above n 143).

162 It should be noted, however, that there are special arrangements in the environmental area for some kind of strict liability in order to remedy the problem of absence of evidence, which often characterises such cases.

163 Finans Inspektionen:s författningssamling (FFFS) (2005:5).

Supervisory Authority guidance rules need to be brought in to the core of the legislation in order to live up to the 2005 Directive.[164] Another headache for the Swedish legislator has been the question of determining at what point the customer should be identified. In 'normal' non-money laundering circumstances, control should not impede business.

E. Sweden and the Financing of Terrorism

As explained, the scope of the 2005 Directive includes the financing of terrorism. With respect to the implementation of such regulation in Swedish legislation, the aforementioned preparatory works refer to the law concerning the financing of serious crime (2002:444, lagen *om straff för finansiering av särskilt allvarlig brottslighet i vissa fall*) hereafter the Financing Law. More specifically, it is suggested that the same principles for the suppression of terrorism should also apply to anti-money laundering legislation, although no such assessment appears to have been made so far. Moreover, it is stated that the definition of financing of terrorism should be the same as the above-stated law, although this would constitute a more far-reaching definition than the one offered by the Directive. The Financing Law could also be made clearer by referring to the law implementing the Directive. However, there are no proposed changes here. As explained, the 2005 Directive does not require explicit criminalisation, although the Commission's Communication and the Lisbon Treaty explicitly puts 'money laundering' within criminal law.

With respect to the changes to Swedish legislation as a result of the Money Laundering Directive's inclusion of the financing of terrorism within the scope of the Directive, here it appears as if the relevant changes to the Swedish legislation have already been made in connection with Sweden's accession to the 1999 United Nations International Convention for the Suppression of the Financing of Terrorism.

Despite the fact that the threat of terrorism is relatively low in Sweden, the preparatory works frequently stressed that what has happened in Denmark and the UK, for instance, illustrates the need for caution. In particular, Sweden is close to Denmark not only geographically but also through the Nordic cooperation network. The Danish cartoons scandal has also had some impact in Sweden, as some Swedish newspapers chose to print similar cartoons by a Swedish artist, which led to some fundamentalist threats. This, at least, is an aspect discussed by ministers in a recent working document.[165] There seems moreover, to be general concern about Sweden becoming a haven for the financing of terrorism. Therefore, the preparatory work points out that Sweden has been used for the purposes of terrorism financing and that this must be dealt with and measures put in place to

[164] SOU 2007:23, 109.

[165] Open letter from Foreign Minister C Bildt and Minister of Justice B Ask, February 2008 available at www.regeringen.se (last accessed January 2012).

prevent this happening in the future. In addition, Sweden is the home of the alleged terror financer, Al Barakaat.[166] The freezing of funds has obviously also been used in this Member State.

In any case, the above-mentioned FATF evaluation of Sweden in 2006 stated that Sweden's criminalisation of terrorist financing is largely in line with international standards – in particular, with the Terrorist Financing Convention.[167] Nevertheless, it was suggested that Sweden should amend its legislation to ensure that the offence specifically covers the collection or provision of funds without the need to demonstrate intent to commit a terrorist act, as well as providing higher penalties for the specific offence of terrorist financing, which would more properly take into account the grave nature of the offence. Rules on forfeiture are found in Chapter 36 of the Penal Code and in special penal laws.[168] The provisions provide for criminal confiscation of the proceeds of any crime with a minimum penalty of at least one year's imprisonment (which covers money laundering offences); property of corresponding value; instruments used in or intended for use in the commission of the offence; as well as property that is derived directly or indirectly from the proceeds of crime.[169]

One would have thought that the Lisbon Treaty would require the Swedish legislator to consider whether to change the Swedish Constitution. After all, the Swedish Constitution still claims that the legislator has exclusive competence in criminal law, in Chapter 10 Regerings Formen (RF). Chapter 8 RF in turn states that only the Government has the competence to enact laws and Chapter 10 paragraph 5 stipulates that Parliament can delegate power to the EU as long as it does not concern Swedish constitutional principles. One such principle is the requirement that only Parliament can enact laws and decide on criminalisation, and that any criminalisation must be in line with fundamental human rights. This means that any delegation of power to the EU presupposes that fundamental rights are respected and in harmony with the ECHR. Moreover, according to the RF, any such delegation must be granted by Parliament. It is questionable whether the RF is still fit for purpose. Indeed, there is currently a debate in Sweden about the need to change the Constitution.[170] There is also a debate as to whether Sweden would need a Constitutional Court.[171]

[166] Case C-415/05P and C-402/05P *Kadi* [2008] ECR I-6351.

[167] FATF, country report (above n 7).

[168] On special criminal law and the Swedish system, see J Zila, *Specialstraffrätten· en introduction* (Uppsala, Iustus, 2009).

[169] ibid.

[170] DS 2007:48 Lissabonfördraget, available at www.regeringen.se/content/1/c6/09/49/81/107aa077.pdf (last accessed January 2012), concluding that no change of the constitutional law is needed. See, however, CF Bergström et al, Lissabonfördraget 2008:11 SIEPS available at www.sieps.se/en/publikationer/the-lisbon-treaty-and-the-swedish-constitutions-regulation-of-the-eu-200813epa (last accessed 20 March 2009).

[171] Bergström, ibid.

F. Brief Overview of Denmark and Finland

Denmark and Finland both implemented the Directive on time. In fact, Denmark was the first Member State to transpose it into national law in 2006. Both Denmark and Finland prevent money laundering through different actors participating in the anti-money laundering regulation system. In Finland, the situation is slightly different as the anti-money laundering monitoring exercise is supervised mainly by two institutions: the Financial Supervisory Authority and the Insurance Authority. There is, however, a current debate in Finland about whether to merge these two authorities under one legal body. In any case, as in Sweden, both the Danish and the Finnish Bar Associations supervise the reporting obligations of lawyers. More specifically, members of the Danish Bar and Law Society may notify suspicions to the Secretariat of the Society, which will forward the notification to the Public Prosecutor for Serious Economic Crime after specific assessment.[172] Denmark has enacted a money receipt offence that serves as its money laundering provision. It meets the requirements for money laundering criminalisation set out in the Vienna and Palermo Conventions. Denmark's approach, which is through the offence of receiving stolen goods, is set out in Section 290(1) of the Criminal Code. As with Sweden, self-laundering is not criminalised in Denmark. Danish authorities indicate that self-laundering is not covered because of a fundamental principle in the Danish legal system that no-one can be convicted of two different crimes that concern the same assets.[173] It is an underlying precondition of the criminal law system that a person cannot be punished for the receipt of stolen goods (Section 290) and at the same time be held criminally liable as the principal perpetrator of the predicate crime, or for complicity in relation to the predicate crime.

In Finland the Penal Code was amended in 2003 in connection with the implementation of the 2001 Directive and the current money laundering offences were added and were made independent of the receipt offence. Accordingly, the Finnish application of anti-money laundering offences is broader than that required by the Directive. Self-laundering is thus not an offence in Finland either. Curiously however, while the FATF country report evaluation recommended that Sweden and Finland criminalise the offence of self-laundering, no such recommendation seems to have been made for Denmark.[174] As noted, the question currently under discussion in Sweden is whether it would be wise to allocate anti-money laundering regulation to different agencies or to keep such a monitoring system, in line with Finland, under the auspices of a single main authority.

[172] FATF report Kingdom of Denmark, available at www.fatf-gafi.org/dataoecd/1/26/37588381.pdf (last accessed January 2012).

[173] ibid.

[174] ibid, and FATF, third mutual evaluation of Sweden, (n 116) and the FATF report on money laundering and combating of the financing of terrorism, Finland www.fatf-gafi.org/dataoecd/20/46/39794392.pdf (last accessed January 2012).

G. Conclusion: Sweden

As discussed above, the Swedish approach to the anti-money laundering framework of the EU is that the 2005 Directive is not concerned with criminal law. Therefore, the possible implications for the national criminal law were not discussed in the preparatory works. It is thus easy to state that this is a somewhat lax attitude given the Lisbon Treaty and the strong influence of EU law in this area. With respect to the responsibility to report suspicious money laundering, it is less clear (which is also recognised by the Swedish legislator) whether the law in question needs to be amended. In particular, and as with the UK, it seems less clear whether 'civil liability' might follow in the case of reports that have turned out to be wrong. But perhaps the most delicate business is the question of criminal responsibility for legal persons. It has been suggested that the existing system is rather unfair and does not mirror modern society.[175] As discussed above, there appears to be a kind of quasi-criminal responsibility for legal persons through the concept of 'business responsibility'. Therefore, although there is no criminal law liability for legal persons *stricto sensu*, as explained, a fine could, in certain circumstances, be imposed for a crime committed by a natural person in the exercise of business activities. Nevertheless, the legal area governing when and how to impose such a responsibility is rather murky. The FATF conclusions also recommended that Sweden should criminalise self-laundering. If taken, such a step would bring Sweden closer to, if not Europe, at least the UK.

IV. GENERAL CONCLUSION

In summing up this chapter, it is tempting to conclude that the EU's involvement in the anti-money laundering struggle is a positive contribution to an existing patchy system in the UK and Sweden, where the legal picture has been rather foggy as a result of UN and FATF involvement. One of the main problems with the fight against terrorism at the global level has been the lack of an internationally-accepted definition of terrorism The EU has been surprisingly innovative here, as there is, at least, a definition at the EU level. This is seen in the Framework Decision on Combating Terrorism,[176] mentioned in chapter five. More generally, it should be noted that this measure has had a revolutionary impact on the Member States, partly because of the very short time limit (six months) to transpose it into national law, and partly because it was no longer regarded as sufficient to address the threat of terrorism through common offences. Therefore, as pointed out by Nuotio, 'the terrorist nature of these offences was now required to

[175] Henriksson (above n 157).

[176] Framework Decision 2002/475/JHA and amending Framework Decision 2008/919/JHA [2008] OJ L300/42.

be part of the definition'.[177] In the war against the financing of terrorism the Member States have used criminal law in contrast with the US's use of military force. However, the question is more complicated – the UN and EU freezing orders are seen as non-criminal. Apart from questions of effectiveness, as discussed in chapter five, the EU's anti-money laundering agenda highlights not only the awkward question of whether the combination of combating money laundering and the suppression of terrorism constitute an effective partnership as part of the same legal instrument, but also issues of legality, civil liberties and competence (discussed in chapter four) and the civil law obligations for incorrect reporting. Furthermore, the reporting obligation still seems to be one of the most sensitive questions at the national level in connection with the Money Laundering Directive.

The biggest difference between the UK and Sweden in this context is that while the UK has changed its criminal law legislation repeatedly in order to keep in step with EU Directives, the Swedish legislator lags behind and insists that the 2005 Directive does not have any 'impact' on the Swedish Penal Code. Another difference is the lack of academic scholarship in Sweden compared to the almost over-analysed academic study of 'dirty money' in the UK. A further distinction between the UK and Sweden is that 'self-laundering' is not criminalised in Sweden but is in the UK. It is unclear whether Swedish legislation will have to change. Moreover, while the UK has allocated responsibilities to private actors such as the JMLSG, which has presented recommendations, the Swedish model is more traditional in keeping the public law dimension. Finally, one of the biggest differences is the regulation of responsibility for legal persons; there is no corporate liability in Sweden *stricto sensu* while there is in the UK. It remains to be seen for how long the Swedish criminal law system will remain 'intact' in this regard while continuing to live up to the effectiveness requirement in EU law. Therefore, this demonstrates the force for change at the national level of 'EU criminal law'.

[177] K Nuotio, 'Terrorism as a Catalyst for the Emergence, Harmonization and Reform of Criminal Law' (2006) 4 *Journal of International Criminal Justice* 998.

7

The Lisbon Treaty: Anything New Under the Sun?[1]

I. INTRODUCTION

THE AIM OF this chapter is to go back to the theoretical domain to explore the impact of the Lisbon Treaty[2] on criminal law. Indeed, given the sensitive nature of criminal law, it is promising that the preamble of the Lisbon Treaty states that it draws inspiration not only from the cultural and religious inheritance of Europe but also from its broader humanist values.[3] Indeed, the EU places the individual at the centre of the stage. Article 2 TEU reminds us that:

> The Union is founded on the values of respect for human dignity, freedom, democracy, equality, the rule of law and respect for human rights, including the rights of persons belonging to minorities. These values are common to the Member States in a society in which pluralism, non-discrimination, tolerance, justice, solidarity and equality between women and men prevail.

Article 3 makes it clear that not only does the Union aim to promote the well-being of its people, but it also offers its citizens an area of freedom, security and justice (ASFJ) without internal frontiers, in which the free movement of persons is ensured in conjunction with appropriate measures with respect to, among other things, the prevention and combating of crime. Moreover, as explained in chapter two, Article 6 TEU stipulates that the Union recognises the rights, freedoms and principles set out in the Charter of Fundamental Rights of the European Union (the Charter). It is also stated that the Union shall accede to the European Convention on Human Rights (ECHR) which constitutes general principles of the Union's law. From the perspective of protection of human rights and effective judicial protection, this offers something new. However, the whole area is under development which makes it difficult to speak about a fully formed regime in EU criminal law.

[1] The title and some of the content draws on E Herlin-Karnell, 'The Lisbon Treaty and the Criminal Law: Anything New Under the Sun?' (2008) 10 *European Journal of Law Reform* 321.

[2] Treaty of Lisbon amending the Treaty on European Union and the Treaty establishing the European Community, Lisbon, of 17 December 2007, 13 December 2007, OJ C306.

[3] V Mitsilegas, *EU Criminal Law* (Oxford, Hart Publishing, 2009) 107–10.

One of the most significant changes to the criminal law introduced by the Lisbon Treaty, apart from the new competence provisions discussed above, is the emergency brake provision. The following section examines this in greater detail.

II. THE EMERGENCY BRAKE – IT LOOKS SAFER

The purpose of this section is to advance the ideas put forward in chapter four part IV and apply them in the context of the Lisbon Treaty. As explained above, the provisions of Articles 82(2) and 83(1) and (2) also stipulate in their respective paragraph 3 the possibility of applying a so-called 'emergency brake' if the law in question would affect fundamental aspects of a Member State's criminal justice system. If such an emergency brake scenario occurs, a Member State may request that the measure be referred to the European Council. In that case, the ordinary legislative procedure is suspended, and after discussion and 'in case of a consensus, the European Council shall, within four months of this suspension, refer the draft back to the Council, which shall terminate the suspension of the ordinary legislative procedure'. There is, however, no such emergency possibility with respect to the notion of mutual recognition in Article 82(1), which will remain the main theme in EU criminal law cooperation. This appears odd, as the phenomenon of mutual recognition in EU criminal law is vulnerable to the accusation that it has too easily adopted the internal market template of free movement to the area of EU criminal law cooperation.[4]

Clearly, the notion of an emergency brake looks attractive to Member States with a strong relationship between the criminal law and the nation state, and hence remedies Member State anxiety about the loss of their national sovereignty in criminal law matters. Regarding the merits of such an emergency brake, and as touched upon in chapter four part V, it can be argued that the procedure is too much of a smooth political solution. In fact and as stated elsewhere:

> One gets the impression that the emergency brake, in reality, is not supposed to be used in the first place . . . Instead, it seems to be as it says on public transport 'refrain from abuse' or in the worst scenario 'abusers will be prosecuted'. It is easy to make the statement that such a possibility is not the ideal solution as regards future problems, although, certainly, it looks safer (after all, we all know that we usually don't need to pull it very often).[5]

A policy analysis of the Lisbon Treaty uses the same analogy with an emergency brake (this time specifically on a train) but argues that the prohibition sign is there for a reason: the Member States should refrain from applying the brake in

[4] S Peers, *EU Justice and Home Affairs* (Oxford, Oxford University Press, 2011) ch 9.

[5] E Herlin-Karnell, 'Recent Developments in the Area of European Criminal Law' (2007) 14 *Maastricht Journal of European and Comparative Law* 15 at 35.

order to avoid unnecessary halts.[6] The point the commentators make is that too much flexibility will lead to too much complexity. Although it is true that an emergency brake scenario will generate fragmentation, the problem is more fundamental than that. The crux of the matter is that the mere inclusion of an emergency brake does not automatically constitute a guarantee of successful European criminal law. The point is that the very notion of the transformation of criminal law to the supranational stage prompts the question of whether the Lisbon Treaty was drafted carefully enough in the first place to live up to the freedom, security and justice paradigm. This is particularly important, as the issue is not only a question of 'taming' protectionist states but also of the adequate protection of the individual at the EU level.[7] However, as explained in chapter four part IV, whether or not a single Member State applies the emergency brake, the Lisbon Treaty provides for the possibility of enhanced cooperation for the remaining (nine or more) Member States to move forward by establishing enhanced cooperation. However, as the question of the establishment of enhanced cooperation has already been discussed, this issue will not be dealt with in further detail here. Instead, the purpose was to show that the issue of EU criminal law is more complicated than the mere inclusion of emergency brakes, as it appears ambiguous in the context of the establishment of enhanced cooperation – as explained in chapter four part IV – and the broader issue of 'moving forward' with the Union project.

A. A European Public Prosecutor?

The Lisbon Treaty broadens the opportunities for enhanced cooperation by extending it to police cooperation and to the establishment of the European Public Prosecutor (Article 86 TFEU), an innovation comparable to the Constitutional Treaty. The prosecutor will be responsible for investigating, prosecuting and bringing to judgment, where appropriate in liaison with Europol, the perpetrators of and accomplices in offences against the Union's financial interests, as determined by the regulation provided for in Article 86 TFEU. It is beyond the scope of this analysis to discuss the general pros and cons of establishing a European Public Prosecutor.[8] It should be pointed out that there has been a debate as to whether such a Prosecutor should have a wider criminal law mandate

[6] S Carrero and F Geyer, 'The Reform Treaty and Justice and Home Affairs', available at www.libertysecurity.org/IMG/pdf_The_Reform_Treaty_Justice_and_Home_Affairs.pdf (last accessed January 2012) 9.

[7] E Herlin-Karnell, 'The Lisbon Treaty and the Area of Criminal Law and Justice (2008) 11 *Eurparattslig tidskrift* 646.

[8] eg C Van den Wyngaert, 'Eurojust and the European Public Prosecutor' in N Walker (ed), *Europe's Area of Freedom, Security and Justice* (Oxford, Oxford University Press, 2004) 224; and A Suominen, 'The past, present and the future of Eurojust (2008) 15 *Maastricht Journal of European and Comparative Law* 217, G Conway, 'Holding to Account a Possible European Public Prosecutor: Supranational Governance and Accountability across Diverse Legal Traditions' forthcoming manuscript (on file with the author).

than that of the financial sphere.[9] Indeed, Article 86(4) provides the opportunity for a future European Council to adopt a decision amending the competences of such a prosecutor to include serious crime with a cross-border dimension in the broader sense. According to the Stockholm programme,[10] the Commission intends to issue a communication on the establishment of a European Public Prosecutor in 2013.[11] As pointed out by Peers, however, there is a fundamental flaw in the creation of a European Public Prosecutor. The point is that it is difficult to separate on the one hand rules relating to investigations and prosecutions (at the EU level), and on the other hand, trials (Member State level). According to Peers, the Commission should have considered other possibilities of more limited measures to achieve the same objectives such as the harmonisation of the national prosecutions rules in this area.[12]

III. THE EMBRYONIC CONCEPT OF A 'GENERAL PART' OF EU CRIMINAL LAW[13]

As discussed in the previous chapters, the Lisbon Treaty, as well as the Stockholm programme, increases the focus on security in the Union. Article 67 TFEU paints a picture of crime prevention at the EU level as discussed in previous chapters, by providing for a more general EU law competence for the prevention of crime. In addition, as noted, the TFEU includes sanctions against individuals, in Article 75 TFEU, the so-called general crime prevention chapter. This section highlights the implications of Chapter 1 of Title V TFEU from the perspective of crime prevention and its relationship with Chapter 4 of Title V TFEU and the sector-specific clauses on criminal law from a theoretical perspective.

Indeed, in criminal law theory it is common to refer to the general part (general principles of criminal law) and the special part (specific criminal provisions) of criminal law. One commentator has argued that in the EU context, the general part of EU criminal law takes shape, and should take shape, as general principles are crystallised by the judiciary.[14] Alternatively, I have previously argued that applied in the context of the Lisbon Treaty and with a dash of imagination, it is possible to refer to Chapter 1 of Title V as the general part of EU criminal law, while Chapter 4 of Title V – Articles 82 and 83 TFEU – constitutes the special part with specific EU core crimes such as money laundering and terrorism, as well as

[9] J Monar, 'Justice and Home Affairs in the EU Constitutional Treaty. What Added Value for the "Area of Freedom, Security and justice"?' (2005) 1 *European Constitutional Law Review* 226.

[10] The Stockholm programme An open and secure Europe serving and protecting the citizen (Council of the European Union Brussels, 2 December 2009.

[11] Commission, 'Action Plan on the implementation of the Stockholm programme, annexed time proposal' COM (2010) 171.

[12] S Peers, *EU Justice and Home Affairs Law* (Oxford, Oxford University Press, 2011), 858–60.

[13] This part draws on E Herlin-Karnell, 'Waiting for Lisbon . . . Constitutional Reflections on the Embryonic General Part of EU Criminal Law' (2009) 17 *European Journal of Criminal Law and Criminal Justice* 227.

[14] A Klip, *European Criminal Law* (Antwerp, Intersentia, 2009) 167, refers to 'fragments of a general part'.

explicit grounds for adopting legislation to facilitate mutual recognition.[15] Admittedly, Chapter 1 does not set out the definition of intent or recklessness so the comparison is weaker from this perspective. The key point, however, is simply that Article 67 TFEU – the portal provision of Chapter 1 – should be read in conjunction with the specific provisions on criminal law as discussed above: it sets the scene and tells us what values the Union seek to enforce – freedom, security and justice and respect for fundamental rights. Consequently, these aspirations should be achieved by fighting crime and ensuring a high level of crime prevention and security. As explained in chapter four, the distinction between the 'general' crime prevention in Chapter 1 of Title V on the area of freedom, security and justice (ASFJ) and Chapter 4 on the specific part is important. The clarification is significant as there is no emergency brake opportunity for the Member States within this general part in the event of a clash with fundamental aspects of a Member State's criminal law.

This leads us to one of the most important innovations in the Lisbon Treaty: the extended jurisdiction of the Court of Justice.

IV. THE COURT OF JUSTICE AND CRIMINAL LAW

As noted in chapter two, one of the most significant changes to be introduced by the Lisbon Treaty is the extension of the Court's jurisdiction to cover the former third pillar area. This is one of the most important constitutional restructurings compared to the period before the entry into force of the Lisbon Treaty. It should be remembered that before the Lisbon Treaty, the Court's jurisdiction was based on a voluntary declaration by Member States as to whether to accept such jurisdiction in accordance with ex Article 35 TEU.[16] The Lisbon Treaty changes this, by significantly extending the Court's jurisdiction within the AFSJ field.[17] However, the Lisbon Treaty Protocol on Transitional Provisions provides a five-year transition – or alteration – period before the existing third-pillar instruments can be treated in the same way as Community instruments. Article 10 of this Protocol stipulates that:

> 1. As a transitional measure, and with respect to acts of the Union in the field of police cooperation and judicial cooperation in criminal matters which have been adopted before the entry into force of the Treaty of Lisbon, the powers of the institutions shall be following the date of entry into force of that Treaty: the powers of the Commission under Article 258 of the Treaty on the Functioning of the European Union shall not be applicable and the powers of the Court of Justice of the European Union under Title VI

[15] Herlin-Karnell (above n 13).

[16] E Denza, *The InterGovernmental Pillars of the European Union* (Oxford, Oxford University Press, 2002) ch 9.

[17] eg D Leczykiewicz, '"Effective Judicial Protection" of Human Rights After Lisbon: Should National Courts Be Empowered to Review EU Secondary Law?' (2010) 35 *EL Rev* 326; A Hinarejos, *Judicial Control in the European Union* (Oxford, Oxford University Press, 2009); and P Craig, *The Lisbon Treaty* (Oxford, Oxford University Press, 2010) ch 9; as well as S Peers, (above n 12).

> of the Treaty on European Union, in the version in force before the entry into force of the Treaty of Lisbon, shall remain the same, including where they have been accepted under Article 35(2) of the said Treaty on European Union.
>
> 2. The amendment of an act referred to in paragraph 1 shall entail the applicability of the powers of the institutions referred to in that paragraph as set out in the Treaties with respect to the amended act for those Member States to which that amended act shall apply.
>
> 3. In any case, the transitional measure mentioned in paragraph 1 shall cease to have effect five years after the date of entry into force of the Treaty of Lisbon.

As a result of the transitional rules, there will be mixed jurisdiction over different measures concerning the same subject matter, and the most feasible regime (and favourable from the perspective of the individual) should then be preferred. In the light of the Court's history in promoting European integration, the Court would conceivably favour the most 'Communitised' reading of when an act is 'amended' as noted in chapter two, so as to fall outside the scope of the transitional protocol.

However, despite the reformation of the Court of Justice's jurisdiction as provided by the Lisbon Treaty, the Court will still not have the power to review the validity or proportionality of operations carried out by the police or other law enforcement agencies of a Member State or the exercise of responsibilities incumbent upon Member States with regard to the maintenance of law and order and the safeguarding of internal security. This is likely to create interpretation problems in relation to the notion of 'internal Member State security' as opposed to EU security. In fact, the Lisbon Treaty goes further than 'internal security'. As touched upon above, Article 71 TFEU states that a standing committee shall be established within the Council in order to ensure that operational cooperation on internal security is promoted and strengthened within the Union. Article 72 TFEU in turn stipulates that 'it shall be open to Member States to organise between themselves and under their responsibility forms of co-operation and co-ordination as they deem appropriate between the competent departments of their administrations responsible for safeguarding national security'. Furthermore, it has been argued that the conceptual difference between 'internal security' and 'national security' suggests that the institutions and ultimately the Court will apply a narrow understanding of 'national security'.[18] It has also been noted that although this constitutes an express restriction on the Court's ability to rule on certain acts committed by national authorities, it does not restrict the Court from ruling on the validity or interpretation of EU acts.[19] After all, the general principles of EU law, such as non-discrimination, solidarity and loyalty towards the Union, would arguably apply anyway as it is difficult to draw a clear dividing line between internal and external activity in the fight against crime.

[18] C Ladenburger, 'Police and Criminal Law in the Treaty of Lisbon' (2008) 4 *European Constitutional Law Review* 20.

[19] S Peers, *EU Justice and Home Affairs* (Oxford, Oxford University Press, 2011) 45–46.

Moreover, as briefly touched on above, an area which will become a challenging testing ground for the Court's jurisdiction is the complicated opt out/or opt in system. The complexity of the opt-out/opt-in system and how it will work in future poses challenges for the coherence of the EU criminal law area and goes beyond the scope of this section. In short, this system means that an instrument adopted under the AFSJ will not bind the UK and Ireland unless they choose to 'opt-in'.[20] It could, of course, be argued that the UK and Ireland would still be bound by the EU general principles. Clearly, this is one of the most dynamic areas for the future, which requires attention and examination. This chapter will set out some of the most important aspects of the Court's jurisdiction in the area of EU criminal law.

A. Expedited Procedure

Most importantly, the Lisbon Treaty introduces the possibility of expedited procedures for people in custody. More specifically, the Lisbon Treaty stipulates in Article 267 TFEU that if a question is raised in a case pending before a court or tribunal of a Member State with regard to a person in custody, the Court shall act with the minimum of delay. This is an extremely important change and reflects the interest in speedier justice in Europe. In practice, it means that the urgent preliminary ruling procedure will apply.[21] The Lisbon Treaty thus introduces the possibility of expedited procedures for people in custody, though such a possibility has been on the Commission's table since 2006 when the Commission delivered a communication – in the absence of the Constitutional Treaty (CT) – on the need to use the bridging clause of ex Articles 67(2) and 68 EC to speed up preliminary procedures within the ASFJ.[22] In fact, even the Court itself participated in the debate on speedier justice in Europe by issuing a letter to the Commission on the establishment of emergency preliminary procedures.[23] Indeed, the so-called urgent preliminary ruling process with respect to third pillar matters has been in force since March 2008.[24] Even though the regulation of expedited procedures constitutes a welcome development for those on bail, we could nonetheless speculate whether the Court will become a criminal tribunal now. But could it become one? As highlighted in AG Maduro's opinion in *Kadi* there is a clear lack

[20] E Fahey, 'Swimming in a Sea of Law: Reflections on Water Borders, Irish (- British -) Euro Relations and Opting Out and Opting-In After the Lisbon Treaty' (2010) 47 *CML Rev* 673.

[21] JC Piris, *The Lisbon Treaty, A Legal and Political Analysis* (Cambridge, Cambridge University Press, (2010) 167.

[22] Commission 'Adaptation of the provisions of Title IV of the Treaty establishing the European Community relating to the jurisdiction of the Court of Justice with a view to ensuring more effective judicial protection' (Communication), COM (2006) 346 final of 28 June 2006.

[23] Letter from V Skouris, 25 September 2006, available at www.statewatch.org/news/2006/oct/ecj-and-third-pillar-13272-06.pdf (last accessed January 2012).

[24] Council Decision of 20 December 2007 amending the Protocol on the Statute of the Court of Justice and amendments to the Rules of Procedure of the Court of Justice adopted by the Court on 15 January 2008, [2008] OJ L24, 39.

of experience in these matters in the EU.[25] After all, the Court is used to dealing with fundamental freedoms other than issues of criminal law policy.

Another major dispute in the national criminal law arena appears to have been whether the national courts would be competent to uniformly interpret criminal provisions at the European level. There is also the associated issue of forum shopping.[26] Therefore, it could be suggested that an EU criminal law court, a special Chamber[27] or a pre-trial court in criminal matters, would be a prerequisite for any further transfer of criminal law to the supranational level. Thus, there seems to have been a common view held among many criminal lawyers that the CT was not an ideal solution from the perspective of criminal law and justice.[28] A team of scholars drafted the 'Alternative Constitution for a European Criminal Law and Procedure'.[29] This draft was written as a response to the increased focus on repressive aspects within the Union and amounted to a call for a 'second enlightenment' in the EU. Therefore, as indicated in the introduction to this book, it should be remembered that, historically, 'Europe' stood for humanity and legality.[30] Expressed bluntly, today it appears to represent the opposite, where basic criminal law principles such as legality and criminalisation as last resort seem largely forgotten.[31] This lack of attention to the genuine problems of single market analogies in criminal law has constituted a major source of the criticism presented in the alternative draft. In particular, one of the main points of this draft was the creation of a 'Eurodefensor' institution (defence rights) as a counterpart to the creation of a Prosecutor. Nevertheless, in the horse-trading for a new Treaty there seems to have been no room for such consideration on the European Council stage. It is anticipated that the matters advocated in the alternative draft are far from being dead although the possibility of the creation of a European criminal law code of the same calibre as that of private law seems at present highly unrealistic.[32]

The fact that the Lisbon Treaty has promoted the Charter as a legally binding document, and that the ECHR will become a more explicit part of the Union *acquis* once the EU has acceded to it, are certainly positive developments for the rights of the individual.

[25] C-402/05P *Kadi* Opinion of AG Maduro delivered on 16 January 2008.

[26] A Klip and H van der Wilt (eds), *Harmonisation and Harmonising Measures in Criminal Law*, (Amsterdam, Royal Netherlands Academy of Arts and Sciences, 2002).

[27] At present this would only be possible in respect to the General Court, Art 257 TFEU.

[28] A von Hirsh, 'Alternative Draft for European Criminal Proceedings' (2007) 18 *Criminal Law Forum* 195.

[29] B Schünemann, 'Alternative-Project for a European Criminal Law and Procedure' (2007) 18 *Criminal Law Forum* 227. See also Manifesto on European criminal law policy drafted by criminal law scholars available at sites.google.com/site/eucrimpol/manifest/manifesto (last accessed January 2012).

[30] eg A Norrie, *Crime, Reason and History* (London, Butterworths, 2003) ch 1.

[31] B Schünemann, 'Europäischer Sicherheitstaat=Europäischer Polizeistaat?' (2007) 14 *Zeitschrift für Internationale Strafrechtsdogmatik* 528.

[32] See, however, for an early contribution on the possibility of a model code: A Cadoppi 'Towards a European Criminal Code?' (1996) 4 *European Journal of Crime, Criminal Law and Criminal Justice* 21.

B. Accession to the ECHR and the Legally Binding Status of the Charter of Fundamental Rights

The Lisbon Treaty stipulates the EU shall accede to the ECHR. Nevertheless, Article 6(2) TEU adds that such accession shall not affect the Union's competences as defined in the Treaties. As noted in chapter two, it is clear that this accession has great symbolic value, particularly in the areas of criminal law and the adequate protection of the individual. Such an accession would also require unanimity in the Council and ratification by the Member States. Similarly, the Charter has finally become legally binding. It is, of course, true that even though the Charter is now legally binding, it is stated in Article 6 TEU that the provisions of the Charter shall not extend the EU's competences which would significantly limit its scope if read literally. Moreover, Article 51 of the Charter is clear that the Charter is directed at the Union's institutions and to the Member States when they are implementing Union law. Given this, one could ask what the point of the Charter is. One could speculate on whether the Court will use its traditional case law on general principles and view the Charter as part of this case law, but such an interpretation would run counter to the express will of the Member States. Or, as noted by one commentator, it is possible that the Court would continue its old case law based on general principles and then have a separate agenda for the EU's institutions and Member States when implementing EU law.[33] The Charter, in Article 52, distinguishes between principles and rights. The problem is how to identify fully justiciable rights as opposed to partially justiciable principles.[34] Interestingly, the principle of legality is referred to as a principle in the Charter while Article 7 ECHR refers to the ban on retroactive criminal law[35] as an absolute right.

Moreover, as briefly discussed in chapter two, even if the Charter – according to Article 51 – only binds the EU's institutions and the Member States when they are implementing Union law, it still has an important function as a source of interpretation. As with criminal law, Articles 47 to 50 of the Charter have a huge influence as they guide the Union's action in this area and draw up the theoretical framework. Most importantly, Article 49 of the Charter provides for the guarantee of legality and proportionality in a more extensive way than the ECHR. In addition, Article 47 of the Charter guarantees the right to a fair trial, while Article 48 stipulates the presumption of innocence and the right of defence. This provision also makes it clear that the severity of penalties must not be disproportionate to the criminal offence. As explained in chapter four Part IV, this is actually a more extensive guarantee than the ECHR framework (and its promise of Article 6 ECHR – fair trial – as only guarantee of proportionality). It should also be noted that the Charter in Article 50 states the *ne bis in idem* principle (double jeopardy).

[33] M Dougan, 'The Treaty of Lisbon 2007: Winning Minds, Not Hearts' (2008) 45 *CML Rev* 613.

[34] For a much more detailed account, see Dougan (ibid).

[35] Apart from the international law exception drafted in the aftermath of the Second World War.

Nevertheless, one could ask to what extent the ECHR represents a sufficient guardian of the individual in EU criminal law. As is well known, the *Bosperous*[36] case law, where the European Court of Human Rights (ECtHR) took it for granted that EU judicial protection standards were sufficiently high, taught us that 'equivalent protection' might not mean that much in practice.[37] It is cross-referring between the ECtHR and the Court of Justice which has been the main theme here. Obviously, it remains to be seen how this relationship will be shaped by the EU's future accession to the ECHR where the EU becomes a signatory. Interestingly it was recently argued that the ECHR cases are taken with specific reference to the single case decided by the ECtHR and are, therefore, not intended to construe general binding principles.[38] Therefore, the argument goes, this would be the main difference from the European law jurisprudence. There is a further difference here. After all, the ECtHR takes up cases only after all domestic remedies have been exhausted and it gives judgments on overall fairness. It is to be hoped that the doctrine of 'equivalent' protection will develop to that of 'maximum protection' of the individual in this area.

V. CITIZENSHIP AND CITIZEN INITIATIVE

As briefly mentioned in chapter two, the Lisbon Treaty opens up a new area for the application of citizenship to the AFSJ. Indeed, it is often suggested that the Lisbon Treaty and the merging of the pillar structure would reform the doctrine of citizenship to cover former third pillar matters not previously applicable.[39] It is true that a closer inspection of ex Articles 17 and 18 EC (now Articles 20 and 21 TFEU) reveal that although citizenship grants the right for all EU citizens possessing the nationality of a Member State to move and reside freely within the Union, the rights conferred were the rights as granted by the ex EC Treaty. Nevertheless, the very concept of citizenship of the Union implied a broader scope even before the Lisbon Treaty. After all, the Charter also claims to place the individual at the heart of its activities by establishing the concept of citizenship of the Union and by creating an AFSJ. Equally, the Hague programme[40] and the Stockholm programme emphasised the idea of citizenship by stressing the constitutional impact of Directive 2004/38/EC as strengthening the former third pillar sphere and thus

[36] *Bosphorus Hava Yollari Turizm ve Ticaret Anonim Sirketi v Ireland* (45036/98) [2006] 42 EHRR 1 (ECHR). See S Douglas-Scott, 'A Tale of Two Courts: Luxembourg, Strasbourg and the Growing European Human Rights Acquis' (2006) 46 *CML Rev* 629.

F van den Berghe, 'The EU and Issues of Human Rights Protection: Same Solutions to More Acute Problems' (2010) 16 *European Law Journal* 112.

[37] Douglas-Scott, ibid.

[38] S Allegrezza, 'Critical Remarks on the Green Paper on Obtaining Evidence in Criminal Matters' (2010) *Zeitschrift für Internationale Strafrechtsdogmatik* 569.

[39] eg Editorial comment, 'Two-speed European Citizenship? Can the Lisbon Treaty Help Close the Gap?' (2008) 45 *CML Rev* 1.

[40] The Hague programme: Strengthening Freedom, Security and Justice in the EU [2005] OJ C53/1.

bringing clarity and simplicity to this area. It could, therefore, be argued that the notion of citizenship was already applicable to the former third pillar sphere and that the Lisbon Treaty merely asserts this.

The question of citizenship and application of the non-discrimination axiom to the former third pillar and the European Arrest Warrant (EAW) in particular, was on the table in the *Wolzenburg* case[41] as touched on in chapter two. In this case the Court, although not elaborating on citizenship, confirmed that these principles were also applicable to the third pillar framework. Surely there is no doubt that the notion of citizenship is destined to have an exciting future as the most dynamic of the freedoms. Equally, this means that citizenship is relevant to the existing third pillar Acts that are still in force, during the transitional period according to Protocol No 36 as discussed above.

In any case, as noted the Lisbon Treaty places the individual at the heart of its activities in Article 2 and 3 TEU by stating that the Union in founded on the value of respect for human rights and, among other things, that its aim is to promote peace and the well-being of its citizens. Indeed, the new mechanism of 'citizen initiative' is important here. Article 11 TEU is central here as it gives citizens and representative associations the opportunity to make known and publicly exchange their views in all areas of Union action. This gives citizens a direct right to bring a so-called 'citizens' initiative' signed by not less than one million citizens who are nationals of a significant number of Member States. It is a symbolic provision to counteract the alleged lack of democracy in the Union by stipulating, in Article 10 TEU, that it is founded on 'representative democracy'. [42]

It should be observed, as briefly discussed in chapter four, part IV, that criminal law is a hugely sensitive subject. The point is that, to reiterate from the previous chapters, and in particular in political debate on criminal law, penal populism is not uncommon. Citizens might sign up to extremely harsh penalties if they had been mislead by empirical data that was not collected in a sound way. This approach might not necessary lead to a more *effective* criminal law system. On the contrary, increased repression could be a dangerous direction for EU criminal law policy.[43] Nevertheless, it is of course true that the very existence of citizen initiatives if is of crucial importance for the legitimacy of criminal law policy. Clearly, this is an area which is highly complex and cannot be simplified. 'Initiatives' may be important in some areas (such as the protection of the victim) and more complicated in other areas (such as the level of sentences) that criminal law policy and human rights.

[41] Case C-123/08 *Wolzenburg*, judgment of 6 October 2009 not yet reported. Discussed in ch 2.

[42] JC Piris, *The Lisbon Treaty, A Legal and Political Analysis* (Cambridge, Cambridge University Press, 2010) 133.

[43] See eg, Nolan M, 'Law Reform, 'Beyond Mere Opinion Polling and Penal Populism' in A Norrie et al (eds), *Regulating Device* (Oxford, Hart Publishing, 2009) 165. With further references.

VI. CONCLUSION

One can ask, and as touched on in chapter four part VI, whether the Lisbon Treaty amounts to anything new in relation to competences, or whether such a restructuring actually concerns capacity in terms of more efficient and transparent law-making. Nevertheless, it is hardly possible to distinguish so sharply between capacity and competences. This chapter examined the emergency brake in some detail and argued that it rather represents a politically smooth solution than a genuine safeguard of fundamental principles of criminal law, since nine remaining Member States can still move ahead by establishing enhanced cooperation between them. The purpose of this chapter has been to illustrate the relationship between the general and specific EU criminal law supplied by the Lisbon Treaty. As shown, this relationship remains rather vague and leaves unexplained the extent to which it would be possible to harmonise under Chapter 1 of Title V rather than Chapter 4 of Title V TFEU. Such a clarification is important as there is no clear basis for an emergency brake in respect of Chapter 1.

Furthermore, this chapter investigated the role by the Court of Justice in this area and discussed the extent to which it could become a criminal law court. This section also touched on the expedited procedure mechanisms. Nevertheless, and most significantly, due to the highly sensitive nature of criminal law, there is the risk of scoring own goals in respect to the adequate protection of fundamental rights and the never-ending task of enhancing respect and trust for the Union project, but this is an area where extensive research and data is needed. Nevertheless, it is clear that the Lisbon Treaty offers a far more attractive framework in the terms of competences and protection of the individual than the previous regime. This is particularly true if we consider not only the symbolic inclusion of the Charter and the accession to the ECHR,[44] but also the proclamation of the Union's values. There is a willingness among the Member States and the EU to make the ASFJ a reality. It remains to be seen whether this will actually happen, as it depends on what kind of security, freedom and justice we are referring to. Nevertheless, there is reason to be optimistic. After all, the declaration of the Union's values is new and is intended to breed trust and enhance the broad legitimacy of European criminal law. Assuming these values are substantially and legally attainable – and taking the conundrums outlined in this book seriously – it is certainly something new under the sun. What is more, it brings us neatly to the conclusions of this book.

[44] Protocol relating to Article 6(2) TEU.

8

Conclusion

I. CONCLUSION

THE PURPOSE OF this study has been to explore the meaning of effectiveness as a constitutional principle in EU criminal law. The specific focus has been the constitutional dimension of the judgment in Case C-176/03 and the use of effectiveness as a lever of EU law to open up legislative competences; but the scope has been broader than that. The intention has been to construct a theoretical framework of European criminal law and discuss how it emerged as part of the depillarisation trend initiated by the *Pupino*[1] and Case C-176/03[2] rulings. In short, such a trend confirms not only the famous patchwork of criminal law on the EU scene, but also the ambiguous impact of effectiveness more generally as both an enforcement mechanism and a competence parameter. This study also highlights the fact that there is no clear-cut division between enforcement and competence, and that the effectiveness axiom is a truly chameleonic concept. As covered in chapter three, this principle dictates the classical enforcement game, yet as explained in chapter four it also serves a competence-allocating function. This poses difficulties when applied to the area of the criminal law, as 'effectiveness' in criminal law is a difficult concept where over-criminalisation often means *ineffectiveness.* Chapter four embarked on an exegesis of these issues, by analysing 'effectiveness' against the objectives of the EU and the wider question of competence allocation, particularly in the light of Article 114 TFEU. This chapter also charted the history of ex Article 47 TEU, and how it dictated these issues to favour the supranational arena. The aim of this chapter was to highlight the 'carte blanche' function of 'effectiveness' in this context, as a precept for harmonisation. The chapter also analysed how closely ex Article 47 EU favoured the supranational sphere, even when the competence for such a result appeared less clear.

Thereafter, the book examined the principles of subsidiarity and proportionality and investigated these notions from both the EU law point of view and the criminal law angle, and discussed their fundamental importance in relation to criminal law legislation. Chapter four also considered the mechanisms of enhanced cooperation and examined them in relation to the emergency brake and the concept of loyalty. It was argued that what will emerge in this area is

[1] Case C-105/03 *Criminal proceedings against Maria Pupino* [2005] ECR I-5285.
[2] Case C-176/03 *Commission v Council* [2005] ECR I-7879.

something similar to a proportionality test, a balance, which would better recognise the sensitive nature of criminal law (without denying the difficulty of pinning down the exact meaning of proportionality). The final part of this chapter addressed the broader question of competences in the EU and the extent to which criminal law could be considered in the same way as other EU law policies.

The issue of the EU's market creation powers and criminal law was taken a step further in chapter five, where the intention was to look at the EU's financial crime agenda. The driving principles in this area are not only the effectiveness mantra but also notions of security and risk, which, when read together, appear to point in the direction of preventive criminalisation. In particular the purpose was to contrast the EU's approach to preventive market legislation with the concept of paternalistic legislation. In doing so the chapter looked at the justification for EU action in this area, by examining the famous 'confidence in the market' concept. The conclusion here was that the confidence *ratio* is far too vague to justify harmonisation or criminalisation, as it leaves too much uncertainty about what the EU is trying to achieve and why.

Chapter six turned to what happens in practice at the intersection of national law and EU law by discussing a case study on the implementation of the Third Money Laundering Directive in the UK and Sweden. It was concluded that EU law involvement was a positive contribution to an area which was already fragmented by international law obligations. Thereafter chapter seven charted the Lisbon Treaty by looking specifically at the newly-won Court's jurisdiction as well as discussing which values the EU wants to ensure and their importance for the emergence of EU criminal law. This chapter also discussed the emergency brake. In addition, this chapter touched upon the notion of citizenship and considered the extent to which it could enhance the credibility of the phenomenon of EU criminal law. Finally, this chapter touched on the citizenship initiative provision in relation to criminal law and highlighted the fact that although this is a great improvement in terms of democracy, there might also be some aspects with regard to criminal law that could be problematic, such as increased penal populism.

II. EU SUPRANATIONAL CRIMINAL LAW, THE (GRAND?) FINALE

From the standpoint of criminal law, which has traditionally been a core nation state question, it could be asked whether the concept of European criminal law is an oxymoron. However, from the perspective of the EU it seems as if the development of criminal law has constituted an exercise in effectiveness without any normative debate about what kind of criminal law the EU is aiming to achieve.[3] Yet, this is a mistake. If the EU wants to develop a common criminal law then it

[3] See also Mitsilegas, *EU Criminal Law* (Oxford, Hart Publishing, 2009) ch 7. In national criminal law see A Ashworth, 'Is the Criminal Law a Lost Cause?' (2000) 116 *LQR* 225.

needs a more sophisticated approach. At a theoretical level, the key issue is whether the notion of a supranational EU criminal law is at all possible, beyond the explicit mandate granted by the Lisbon Treaty. This book has confronted EU law principles with criminal law axioms and questioned whether these sometimes conflicting values might be reconciled. So can they be reconciled? Any attempt to comprehensively predict whether the concept of supranational criminal law is possible, and whether it would be effective would, at first sight, be a task fit for the Oracle at Delphi. Regardless, the Lisbon Treaty simplifies this question by not asking it and thereby setting the ball rolling for an EU criminal law developed through the motto of 'learning through experience'. The crux of the matter is that there has been no specific competence within the former third pillar as the Treaties previously stood to legislate on legal safeguards for the individual, and the legislative competence on criminal law was generally very limited, and specifically to cross-border criminality. As explained, the competence picture was even less clear within the former first pillar. And yet, one might surely ask whether there was anything in EU criminal law that could not have been achieved without the Treaty of Lisbon. From a legitimacy perspective, the answer is yes. After all, the legal basis for the transformation of criminal law in the EU rested on rather shaky legal grounds. In other words, if one requires better evaluated reasoning as to why the full effectiveness of EU law required the supranationalisation of criminal law in the first place, then the formula provided by the Court was not a sufficiently sound justification. It is simply not good enough to develop criminal law on an ad hoc basis if one wants to respect not only the legitimacy of Union action, but also the principle of legality. It is here that the Lisbon Treaty made a significant contribution in providing for Treaty-based support as well as for the possibilities of approximation of legal safeguards in this area.

It could be argued, however, that despite the broader mandate given by the Lisbon Treaty, it would be wise for the EU legislator to limit itself to two areas. The first is the field of financial crimes that in one way or another could be linked to the concept of market creation. The reason for this, as explained above, is that the EU has already been relying on quasi-penal law in terms of administrative sanctions in this area, so the difference would not be very great. As discussed, the true danger, however, is that there is a tendency in the EU's institutions to consider divergent criminal laws as constituting obstacles to trade, which amounts to a very low threshold when justifying action under Article 114 TFEU. As shown in this book and more crucially from the constitutional dimension of European criminal law, it is far from clear that such a regime would be effective or have any impact on 'confidence' in the market.

The second field where the EU could become a successful actor, and where it has for a long time been an active player – even before the Lisbon Treaty entered the scene – is of course that of cross-border criminality (which, with the usual imagination of the EU legislator, could prove to have wide-ranging repercussions).

The main concern here is that any expansion of EU activity in this area needs to be carefully thought through and should be based on the effectiveness principle in a more sophisticated way than the previous over-reliance on the principle. In other words, there is a clear lacuna in the legal reasoning applied by the EU's institutions, which demonstrates not only a lack of underlying research, but arguably also an unwillingness to get involved in the substance. Most importantly, this book has tried to show that there is a danger in the current focus on effectiveness as a driving principle in this area, not only as a constitutional issue but also in forming part of the broader ambitions of the area of freedom, security and justice. Therefore the book has elaborated on this dimension by tying this question to the more general concern of the effectiveness of EU law and the wider issue of risk regulation in this area.

Nonetheless, the real difficulty with the creation of EU criminal law from a national perspective is the need to develop accompanying principles of procedural protection. How this could be done, regardless of the extended EU competence in criminal law procedure, is a question for future evaluation. The EU is currently active on this front, with the recent plans for strengthening procedural rights of suspected or accused persons in criminal proceedings – one of the latest, and welcome, developments in this area. This forms part of the ambitious Stockholm programme for making Europe more secure and serving the citizen.[4] But it is regrettable that in relation to the measures contained in the plans outlined by the Stockholm programme there is no clarification regarding the precise procedural stage at which they should be guaranteed.[5] Clearly, this is a work in progress. At a more sophisticated level, it could be argued that the most important aim is to create a common European sense of fairness which genuinely cares for the individual.

For any advancement of the concept of EU criminal law to legitimately take place it is crucial for the EU's institutions to adopt a more nuanced approach.. Whether such attentiveness is to be found in the creation of a criminal law division in the Court and/or a European ombudsman as well as the potential need for a European defence lawyer as a counterpart to the creation of a EU prosecutor, poses a conundrum for the future. One thing seems clear however – and bears repeating. There has been a clear over-reliance on effectiveness at the EU level which renders the current supranationalisation of the criminal law problematic.

In conclusion, inadequate attention is paid to the question of why there should be a 'common' criminal law at the EU level at all, and how far it might damage national tradition. The problem is that 'effectiveness' is simply not enough on its own to allow the development of EU criminal law. That has been the central message of this book. There is a need for a realistic understanding of *effectiveness* as an

[4] (2009/C 295/01), Resolution of the Council, of 30 November 2009 on a Roadmap for strengthening procedural rights of suspected or accused persons in criminal proceedings. See also S Allegrezza, 'Critical Remarks on the Green Paper on Obtaining Evidence in Criminal Matters' (2010) *Zeitschrift für Internationale Strafrechtsdogmatik* 569.

[5] M Jimeno Bulnes, 'Towards Common Standards on Rights of Suspected and Accused Persons in Criminal Proceedings in the EU?' CEPS analysis (2010) available at aei.pitt.edu/15104/1/Jimeno-Bulnes_on_rights_of_suspects.pdf (last accessed January 2012).

ambiguous conceptwhich should not be read as equivalent to EU legislation *for its own sake.* But more crucially, there is a need for a normative debate on the development of EU criminal law and justice. What kind of criminal law for Europe? This is the burning question for the future.

Bibliography

Accetto M and Zleptnig S, 'The Principle of Effectiveness: Rethinking its Role in Community Law' (2005) 11 *European Public Law* 375.

Albrecht H and Braum S, 'Deficiencies in the Development of European Criminal Law' (1999) 5 *European Law Journal* 293.

—— and Kilchling M, 'Crime Risk Assessment, Legislation, and the Prevention of Serious Crime Comparative Perspectives' (2002) 12 *European Journal of Crime, Criminal Law and Criminal Justice* 23.

Aleagere S and Leaf M, 'Mutual Recognition in European Judicial Cooperation: A Step Too Far Too Soon?'(2004) 11 *European Law Journal* 200.

Alexander R, 'Insider Dealing and Money Laundering in the EU: Law and Regulation' (Aldershot, Ashgate, 2007).

Alexy R, *A Theory of Constitutional Rights* (Oxford, Oxford University Press 2002).

Allegrezza S, 'Critical Remarks on the Green Paper on Obtaining Evidence in Criminal Matters' (2010) *Zeitschrift für Internationale Strafrechtsdogmatik* 569.

Amtenbrink F and Kochenov D, 'Towards a more Flexible Approach to Enhanced Cooperation', in A Ott and E Vos (eds), *50 Years of European Integration: Foundations and Perspectives* (The Hague, TMC Asser, 2009) 181.

Apps K, 'Case C-176/03, *Commission v Council*: Pillars Askew: Criminal Law EC-Style', (2006) 12 *Columbia Journal of European Law* 625.

Ashworth A, 'Is the Criminal Law a Lost Cause?' (2000) 116 *LQR* 225.

——, 'Principles of Criminal Law' (Oxford, Oxford University Press, 2006).

——, 'Criminal Law, Human Rights and Preventive Justice' in A Norrie et al (eds), *Regulating Deviance* (Oxford, Hart Publishing, 2009).

—— and Zedner L, 'Preventive Orders: a Problem of Undercriminalization?' in RA Duff et al (eds), *The Boundaries of the Criminal Law* (Oxford, Oxford University Press, 2011) ch 3.

Asp P, *EG: S sanktionsrätt* (Uppsala, Iustus, 1998).

——, *EU & Straffrätten* (Uppsala, Iustus, 2002).

——, 'Two Notions of Proportionality' in K Nuotio (ed) *Festschrift in honour of Raimo Lathi,* (Helsinki, Helsinki University Press, 2007).

Auel K, 'Democratic Accountability and National Parliaments: Redefining the Impact of Parliamentary Scrutiny in EU Affairs' (2007) 13 *European Law Journal* 487.

Baker E, 'Taking European Criminal Law Seriously' (1998) *Criminal Law Review* 361.

Bantekas I and Nash S, *International Criminal Law* (London, Cavendish, 2003).

Baratta A, 'Droits de l'homme et politique criminelle' (1999) 23 Deviance et Société 246.

Barents R, 'The Internal Market Unlimited: Some Observations on the Legal Basis of the Community Legislation' (1993) 30 *Common Market Law Review* 85.

Barnard C, *The Substantive Law of the EU* (Oxford, Oxford University Press, 2007).

Beaumont P and Weatherill S, *EU Law* (London, Penguin, 1999)

Beauvais P, 'Droit penal de l'Union européen' (2010) 46 *RTD eur* 722.

Bedingfield D and Sallon S, 'Drugs, Money and the Law' (1993) *Criminal Law Review* 165.

Bernitz U, et al (eds) *The General Principles of EC Law in the Process of Development* (The Hague, Kluwer Law International 2008).

Bergström C et al, *Lissabonfördraget* 2008:11 Swedish Institute for European Policy Studies, available at http://www.sieps.se/sites/default/files/2008_11_nytryck_0.pdf.

Bergstrom M, 'EU Anti-money Laundering Regulation: Multilevel Cooperation of Public and Private Actors' in C Eckes and T Konstadinides *Crime within the Area of Freedom, Security and Justice* (Cambridge, Cambridge University Press, 2011) 97.

—— et al, 'A New Role for Profit Actors? The Case of Anti-money Laundering and Risk Management' (2011) 49 *Journal of Common Market Studies* 5, 1024.

Bermann G, 'Proportionality and Subsidiarity' in C Barnard and J Scott (eds), *The Law of the Single European Market* (Oxford, Hart Publishing, 2002) 75.

Bernard N, 'The Future of European Economic Law in the Light of the Principle of Subsidiarity' (1996) 33 *Common Market Law Review* 633.

Besson S, 'From European Integration to European Integrity: Should European Law Speak with Just One Voice?' (2004) 10 *European Law Journal* 257.

Binning P, 'In Safe Hands? Striking the Balance between Privacy and Security Anti-terrorist Finance Measures' (2002) 6 *European Human Rights Law Review* 737.

Biondi A, Annotation, *Mûnoz* (2003) 40 *Common Market Law Review* 1241.

——, '*Francovich* Fifteen Years Later' in M Maduro (ed) *The Past and Future of EU Law, The Classics of EU Law revisited on the 50th Anniversary of the Rome Treaty* (Oxford, Hart Publishing, 2010) 413.

—— and Mastroianni R, Case Comment (2006) 43 *Common Market Law Review*.

Boom S, 'The European Union after the Maastricht Decision: Will Germany be the Virginia of Europe' (1995) 43 *American Journal of Comparative Law* 177.

Borgers M, 'Regulating and Combating Underground Banking' (2009) 22 *Criminal Law Forum* 97.

Bradley A and Ewing K, *Constitutional and Administrative Law* (Harlow, Longman 2007).

Bungenberg, VM, 'Dynamische Intergration, Art 308 und die Forderung nach dem Kompetenzkatalog' (2002) *Europarecht* 879.

Cadoppi A, 'Towards a European Criminal Code?' (1996) 4 *European Journal of Crime, Criminal Law and Criminal Justice* 21.

Calisendorff A, Skärpta regler mot penningtvätt; advokater i en ny och oprövad roll som angivare av klienter (2005–2006) *Juridisk tidskrift* 553.

Carrero S and Geyer F, 'The Reform Treaty and Justice and Home Affairs' available at www.libertysecurity.org/IMG/pdf_The_Reform_Treaty_Justice_and_Home_Affairs.pdf.

Chalmers J and Leverick F, 'Fair Labelling in Criminal Law', (2008) 71 *Modern Law Review* 217

Chalmers, D, Davies G and Monti G, *EU Law* (Cambridge, Cambridge University Press, 2010).

Christie N, *Crime Control as Industry* (London, Routledge, 2001).

Clarkson C and Keating H, *Criminal Law, Text and Materials* (London, Sweet & Maxwell, 2003).

Claes, M, *The National Court's Mandate in the European Constitution* (Oxford, Hart Publishing, 2006).

Conway G, 'Conflicts of Norms in EU Law and the Legal Reasoning of the ECJ' (2010) 11 *German Law Journal* 966.

——, 'Holding to Account a Possible European Public Prosecutor: Supranational Governance and Accountability across Diverse Legal Traditions', forthcoming manuscript (on file with the author).

Cooper I, 'The Watchdogs of Subsidiarity: National Parliaments and the Logic of Arguing in the EU' (2006) 44 *Journal of Common Market Studies* 281.

Corriras L, *The Passivity of Law: Competence and Constitution in the European Court of Justice* (Dordrecht, Springer 2011).

Corstens G, 'Criminal Law in the First Pillar?' (2003) 11 *European Journal of Crime, Criminal Law and Criminal Justice* 131.

—— and Pradel J, *European Criminal Law* (The Hague, Kluwer Law Publishing, 2002).

Craig P, 'Competence, Clarity, Conferral, Containment and Consideration' (2004) 29 *European Law Review* 323.

——, *EU Administrative Law*, (Oxford, Oxford University Press, 2006).

——, 'The Lisbon Treaty, Process, Architecture and Substance' (2008) 33 *European Law Review* 137.

——, 'The Legal Effects of Directives: Policy, Rules and Exceptions' (2009) 34 *European Law Review* 349.

——, Case Comment (2009) 46 *Common Market Law Review* 1265.

——, *The Lisbon Treaty, Law, Politics and Treaty Reform* (Oxford, Oxford University Press, 2010).

——, 'Integration, Democracy and Legitimacy' in Craig and De Burca, *The Evolution of EU Law* (Oxford, Oxford University Press, 2011).

—— and De Burca G, *EU Law, Text Cases and Materials*, (Oxford, Oxford University Press 2011).

Cremona M, 'External Relations of the EU and the Member States: Competences, Mixed Agreements, International Responsibility and Effects of International Law' EUI Working paper LAW No 2006/22.

——, 'EC Competence, "Smart Sanctions" and the *Kadi* Case' (2009) 28 *Yearbook of European Law* ch 15.

da Cruz Vilaca J, 'The Precautionary Principle in EC law' (2004) 10 *European Public Law* 369.

Dashwood A, 'Article 308 and the Outer Limit of Expressly Conferred Community Competence' in C Barnard and O Odudu, *The Outer Limits of European Union Law* (Oxford, Hart Publishing, 2009) 35.

—— 'Article 47 EU and the Relationship between First and Second Pillar Competences' in A Dashwood and M Marcesceau, *Law and Practice of EU External Relations* (Cambridge, Cambridge University Press, 2008) 70.

Davidson N, *Davidson Review: Implementation of EU Legislation* (London, Better Regulation Executive, 2006).

Davies G, 'Can Selling Arrangements Be Harmonised?' (2005) 30 *European Law Review* 371.

——, 'Subsidiarity: The Wrong Idea, in the Wrong Place, at the Wrong Time' (2006) 43 *Common Market Law Review* 63.

——, 'The Post-Laeken Division of Competences' (2003) 28 *European Law Review* 686.

——, 'Understanding Market Access: Exploring the Economic Rationality of Different Conceptions of Free Movement Law' (2010) 11 *German Law Journal* 671.

De Busser E, (2010) 'Transatlantic adequacy and a certain degree of perplexity' 1 *eucrim* 31.

De Burca G, 'The Principle of Subsidiarity and the Court of Justice as an Institutional Actor' (1998) 36 *Journal of Common Market Studies* 217.

——, 'Setting Constitutional Limits to EU Competence?' Francisco Lucas Pires Working Paper Series on European Constitutionalism 2001/02.

De Burca G, 'The European Court of Justice and the Evolution of EU Law' in Börzel T and Cichowski R *Law, Politics and Society*, (Oxford, Oxford University Press, 2003) 48.

——, 'Reappraising Subsidiarity's Significance after Amsterdam', Jean Monnet Paper 7/1999 available at http://centers.law.nyu.edu/jeanmonnet/papers/99/990701.html.

—— and De Witte B, 'Delimitation of Powers between the EU and its Member States' in A Arnull and D Wincott (eds), *Accountability and Legitimacy in the European Union* (Oxford, Oxford University Press, 2002).

—— and Craig P, *The Evolution of EU Law* (Oxford, Oxford University Press, 2011) 407.

De Hert P, 'Division of Competences between National and European levels with regards to Justice and Home Affairs' in J Aap (ed), *EU Justice & Home Affairs* (Cheltenham, Edward Elgar, 2004).

De Sade, D *Justine or the Misfortunes of Virtue* (Hertfordshire, Wordsworth, 1996) cited in C Lernested, *Kriminalisering* (Uppsala, Iustus, 2002) ch 1.

De Sadeleer N, 'The Precautionary Principle in EC Health and Environmental Law' (2006) 12 *European Law Journal* 139.

De Witte B, 'Non-market Values in Internal Market Legislation' in N NicShuibne (ed) *Regulating the Internal Market* (Cheltenham, Edward Elgar, 2006).

——, 'A Competence to Protect: The Pursuit of Non-Market Aims through Internal Market Legislation' paper delivered in Antwerp 8-9 March 2010 (on file with the author).

—— (ed), *Ten Reflections on the Constitutional Treaty of Europe* (EUI, booklet, Florence 2003).

Dehousse R, *The European Court of Justice* (London, Macmillan, 1998) 161.

Delmas-Marty M, 'The European Union and Penal Law' (1998) 4 *European Law Journal* 87.

—— and Vervaele J, *The Implementation of Corpus Juris in the Member States*, vol 1 (Antwerp, Intersentia, 2000).

Demetis D and Angell O, 'The Risk-based Approach to AML: Representation, Paradox and the 3rd Directive' (2007) 10 *Journal of Money Laundering Control* 412.

den Boer M, 'Crime and the Constitution: A Brief Chronology of Choices and Circumventions' (2004) 11 *Maastrict Journal of European and Comparative Law* 143.

Denza E, *The Intergovernmental Pillars of the European Union* (Oxford, Oxford University Press, 2002).

Dougan M, 'Minimum harmonization and the Internal Market' (2000) 37 *Common Market Law Review* 853.

——, *National Remedies before the Court of Justice: Issues of Harmonization and Differentiation* (Oxford, Hart Publishing, 2004).

——, 'Legal Developments', (2006) 44 *Journal of Common Market Studies* 119.

Dougan M, 'When Worlds Collide! Competing Visions of the Relationship between Direct Effect and Supremacy' (2007) 44 *Common Market Law Review* 931.

——, 'The Treaty of Lisbon 2007: Winning Minds, Not Hearts', (2008) 45 *Common Market Law Review* 613.

——, 'The Unfinished Business of Enhanced Cooperation: Some Institutional Questions and their Constitutional Implications' in A Ott A and E Vos (eds), *50 Years of European Integration: Foundations and Perspectives* (The Hague, TMC Asser Press, 2009) 157.

——, 'The Vicissitudes of Life at the Coalface: Remedies and Procedures for enforcing Union Law before the National Courts' in G De Burca and P Craig, *The Evolution of EU Law* (Oxford, Oxford University Press, 2011).

Douglas-Scott S, 'The Rule of Law in the EU – Putting the Security into the Area of Freedom, Security and Justice' (2004) 29 *European Law Review* 219.

Drake S, 'Twenty Years after *von Colson*: The Impact of Indirect Effect on the Protection of the Individual's Community Rights' (2005) 30 *European Law Review* 329.

Duff RA, *Criminal Attempts* (Oxford, Clarendon Press, 1996).

—— et al (eds), *The Boundaries of the Criminal Law* (Oxford, Oxford University Press, 2011).

Eckes C, *EU Counter-Terrorist Policies and Fundamental Rights* (Oxford, Oxford University Press, 2009).

——, 'The legal framework of the European Union's counter-terrorist policies: full of good intentions?' in C Eckes and T Konstadinides *Crime within the Area of Freedom, Security and Justice* (Cambridge, Cambridge University Press, 2011) 127.

Editorial 'The Scope of Application of the General Principles of Union Law', (2010) 47 *Common Market Law Review* 1589.

Eeckhout P, 'The European Court of Justice and the Legislator' (1998) 17 *Yearbook of European Law* 1.

——, *External Relations of the EU* (Oxford, Oxford University Press, 2004).

——, General report Fide congress Cyprus 2006, available at www.fide-europe.eu/index.php/congresses?catid=5&start=10.

Egan M, *Constructing a European Market* (Oxford, Oxford University Press, 2001).

Elhom T, *EU Svieg* (Copenhagen, Jurist, 2002).

Emiliou N, 'Subsdiarity: An Effective Barrier against "the Enterprise of Ambition"' (1992) 17 *European Law Review* 383.

——, *The Principle of Proportionality in European Law* (The Hague, Kluwer Law Publishing, 1996).

Estella A, *The EU Principle of Subsidiarity and its Critique* (Oxford, Oxford University Press, 2002).

Faber A, 'Theoretical approaches to EU Deepening and Widening A Multi-disciplinary Overview and Some Tentative (Hypo)theses', EU-CONSENT Project Publications, 2006. Available at www.eu-consent.net/library/brx061012/WP%20II%20III%20Paper redefiningconcepts.pdf.

Fahey E, 'Swimming in a Sea of Law: Reflections on Water Borders, Irish (- British)-Euro Relations and Opting Out and Opting- In After the Lisbon Treaty' (2010) *Common Market Law Review* 673.

Faure M, 'European Environmental Criminal Law: Do we really Need it?' (2004) 13 *European Environmental Law Review* 18.

Feinberg J, *Harm to Others* (Oxford, Oxford University Press, 1981).

——, *Offense to Others* (Oxford, Oxford University Press, 1986).

Fennelly N, 'The European Arrest Warrant: Recent Developments' (2007) 8 *ERA Forum* 519.

Ferrarini G, 'The Market Abuse Directive' (2004) 41 *Common Market Law Review* 711.

Ferris A, 'The European Investigation Order: Stepping Forward with Care' (2011) 2 *New Journal of European Criminal Law* 426.

Fichera M, 'The implementation of the European Arrest Warrant in the European Union: Law, Policy and Practice (Antwerp, Intersentia 2011).

——, 'Organized crime: developments and challenges for an enlarged European Union' in C Eckes and T Konstadinides *Crime within the Area of Freedom, Security and Justice* (Cambridge, Cambridge University Press, 2011) 159.

Fisher J, '*Bowman v Fels*: The continuing fallout on legal privilege and relevant professional advisers', Money Laundering Bulletin, 2006 available at www.mcgrigors.com/pdfdocs/bowman_fels.pdf .

——, 'Lack of Confidence', *Money Laundering Bulletin*, November 2006 available at www.i-law.com/ilaw/doc/view.htm?id=61955.

Fisher L, *Risk Regulation and Administrative Constitutionalism* (Oxford, Hart Publishing, 2007).

Fitzmaurice G, '*Vae Victis* or Woe to the Negotiators! Your Treaty or Our "Interpretation" of It?' (1971) 65 *American Journal of International Law* 358, 373.

Fletcher M, 'EU Criminal Law Justice: Beyond Lisbon' in C Eckes and T Konstantinides, *Crime within the AFSJ* (Cambridge, Cambridge University Press 2011) 10.

Frände D, *Den straffrättsliga legalitetsprincipen* (Ekenäs, Juridiska Föreningens i Finland, Publikationsserie No 52, 1989).

Gallant M, *Money Laundering and Proceeds of Crime* (Cheltenham, Edward Elgar, 2005).

Geiger H and Wuensh O, 'The Fight against Money Laundering: An Economic Analysis of a Cost-benefit Paradoxon' (2007) 10 *Journal of Money Laundering Control* 91.

Gely M, 'Tax Offences: The Hidden Face of Money Laundering?' (2003) 10 *International Tax Review* 328.

Gennert M, 'Les Parlements Nationaux dans le Traité de Lisbonne: Evolution ou Révolution' (2010) 17 *Cahiers de droit Europeen* 46/1–2.

Gilmore G and Rijpma J, 'Case Note' (2007) 44 *Common Market Law Review* 1092.

Gilmore W, *Money Laundering* (Council of Europe, 2004).

——, 'International Financial Counterterrorism Initiatives' in C Fijnaut and others (eds), *Legal Instruments in the Fight against International Terrorism* (Leiden, Brill Publishing, 2004) 189.

Goold B et al, 'Public Protection, Proportionality, and the Search for Balance' available at www.justice.gov.uk/docs/270907.pdf.

Gormley L, 'Competition and Free movement: Is the Internal Market the Same as a Common Market?' (2002) 14 *Electronic Business Law Review* 517.

Grief N, 'EU Law and Security' (2007) 33 *European Law Review* 752.

Gröning L, *EU Staten och rätten att straffa* (Stockholm, Sandeus, 2008).

Guild E, *Crime and the EU's Constitutional Future in an Area of Freedom, Security and Justice* (2004) 10 *European Law Journal* 218.

——, (ed) *Constitutional Challenges to the EAW* (The Hague, TMC Asser, 2006).

Gutman K, 'Case Comment' (2006–2007) 12 *Columbia Journal of European Law* 147.

Haekkerup N, *Controls and Sanctions in the EU Law* (Copenhagen, Djoef Publishing, 2001).

Haltern U, 'On Finality' in A von Bogdandy and J Bast (eds), *Principles of European Constitutional Law* (Oxford/Munich, Hart, Beck, Nomos 2010) 205.

Handoll J, *Capital Payments and Money Laundering in the European Union*, (London, Richmond, 2006).

Harding C, 'Member State Enforcement of European Community Measures: The Chimera of Effective Enforcement' (1997) 4 *Maastrict Journal of European and Comparative Law* 5.

——, 'European Regimes of Crime Control: Objectives, Legal Bases and Accountability' (2000) 7 *Maastrict Journal of European and Comparative Law* 224.

——, 'Exploring the Intersection of European law and National Criminal Law (2000) 25 *European Law Review* 374.

——, 'The Identity of European Law: Mapping out the European Legal Space' (2000) 2 *European Law Journal* 128.

Harlow C, 'A Common European Law of Remedies?' in Kilpatrick et al (eds), *The Future of Remedies in Europe* (Oxford, Hart Publishing, 2000).

Henkel C, 'Allocation of Powers in the European Union', (2002) 20 *Berkeley Journal of International Law Journal* 359.

Henriksson E, *Straffansvar för juridiska personer – en möjlighet i svensk rätt?* (unpublished LLM thesis, University of Lund, 2003).

Herlin-Karnell E, 'EU Competence in Criminal Law After Lisbon', chapter in Biondi, A et al, (eds), *European Union Law after the Treaty of Lisbon* (Oxford, Oxford University Press, forthcoming 2012).

——, '*Commission v Council*: Some Reflections on Criminal Law in the First Pillar', 15 (2007) 15 *European Public Law* 69.

——, 'Recent Developments in the Area of European Criminal Law' (2007) 14 *Maastricht Journal of European and Comparative Law* 15.

——, 'In the Wake of Pupino: Advocaten voor der Wereld and Dell'Orto', (2007) 8 *German Law Journal* 1147.

——, 'The Swedish Supreme Court and the European Arrest Warrant', (2007) 8 *Europarattslig tidskrift* 883.

——, 'Is there more to it than the Fight against Dirty Money? Article 95 EC and the Criminal Law' (2008) 19 *European Business Law Review* 555.

——, '"Light Weapons" and the Dynamics of Art 47 EU – The EC's Armoury of Ever Expanding Competences' (2008) 71 *Modern Law Review* 998.

——, 'The Lisbon Treaty and the Area of Criminal Law and Justice' (2008) 11 *Europarattslig tidskrift* 646.

——, 'The Question of Communautaire reasoning in the Third Pillar – the Case in *Segi* and Beyond', (2008) 19 *Kings Law Journal* 624.

——, 'The Lisbon Treaty and the Criminal Law: Anything New Under the Sun?' (2008) 10 *European Journal of Law Reform* 321.

——, Case comment, *Ship source pollution* judgment (2008) 14 *European Public Law* 533.

——, 'Waiting for Lisbon . . . Constitutional Reflections on the Embryonic General Part of EU Criminal Law,' (2009) 17 *European Journal of Criminal Law and Criminal Justice* 227.

——, Annotation, Case C-301/06 (2009) 46 *Common Market Law Review* 1667

——, 'Subsidiarity in the Area of EU Justice and Home Affairs – A Lost Cause?' (2009) 15 *European Law Journal* 351.

——, 'European Arrest Warrant Cases and the Principles of Non-discrimination and EU Citizenship' (2010) 73 *Modern Law Review* 824.

——, 'The Development of EU Precautionary Criminalization' (2011) 1 *European Criminal Law Review* 149.

—— 'The EU's Anti Money Laundering Agenda: Built on Risk?' in C Eckes and T Konstadinides (eds) *Crime within the Area of Freedom, Security and Justice* (Cambridge, Cambridge University Press, 2011).

Hijmans H and Scirocco, A, 'Shortcoming in EU Data Protection in the Third and Second Pillars. Can the Lisbon Treaty be Expected to Help?' (2009) 46 *Common Market Law Review* 1443.

Hinarejos A, *Judicial Control in the European Union* (Oxford, Oxford University Press, 2009).

Hinterseer K, *Criminal Finance, The Political Economy of Money Laundering in a Comparative Legal Context* (The Hague, Kluwer Law Publishing, 2002).

Hinton E, 'Strengthening the Effectiveness of Community Law: Direct Effect, Art 5 EC and the European Court of Justice' (1998–99) 31 *NYU Journal of International Law and Politics* 307.

Husabo J, 'The Implementation of New Rules on Terrorism through the Pillars of the European Union' in Husabo K and Strandbakken A, *Harmonization of Criminal Law in Europe* (Antwerp, Intersentia, 2005) 58.

Husak D, *Overcriminalization* (Oxford, Oxford University Press, 2007).

Jareborg N, 'What kind of Criminal Law Do We Want?' in A Snare (ed) *Beware of Punishment: On the Utility and Futility of Criminal Law* (Oslo, Scandinavian Studies in Criminology, 1995) 17.

——, *Allmän Kriminalrätt* (Uppsala, Iustus, 2001).

——, 'Criminalization as Last Resort (*ultima ratio*)' (2005) 2 *Ohio State Journal of Criminal Law* 531.

Jimeno Bulnes M, Towards Common Standards on Rights of Suspected and Accused Persons in Criminal Proceedings in the EU?, CEPS analysis (2010) available at aei.pitt.edu/15104/1/Jimeno-Bulnes_on_rights_of_suspects.pdf.

Johnson J, 'Third Round FATF Mutual Evaluations indicate Declining Compliance', (2008) 11 *Journal of Money Laundering Control* 47.

Johnston A and Nanopoulos E, 'The New UK Supreme Court, the Separation of Powers and Anti-terrorism Measures' (2010) *Cambridge Law Journal* 217.

Jung H, 'Criminal Justice – A European Perspective' (1993) *Criminal Law Review* 244.

——, 'L'Etat et moi: Some Reflections on the Relationship between the Criminal Law and the State' (1998) 6 *European Journal of Crime, Criminal Law and Criminal Justice* 208.

Jönsson S, 'Criminal Legal Doctrine as a Spanner in the Works? The Swedish Experience', A Stanislas et al (eds), *Corporate Criminal Liability in Europe* (Brussels, La charte, 2008).

Kaiafa Gbandi M, 'The Development towards Harmonization within Criminal Law in the European Union – A Citzen's Perspective' (2001) 7 *European Journal of Crime, Criminal Law and Criminal Justice* 239.

——, 'Towards a New Approach of Organized Crime in the EU: New Challenges for Human Rights' (2007) 3 *Zeitschrift für Internationale Strafrechtsdogmatik* 537.

Kant I, *Perpetual Peace and Other International Essays* (Indianapolis, Hackett Publishing, 1983).

Kaye N, 'Freezing and Confiscation of Criminal Proceeds' (2006) 77 *Revue Internationale de Droit Penal* 326.

Kersten A, 'Financing of Terrorism – A Predicate Offence to Money Laundering?' in Pieth M (ed,) *Financing Terrorism* (The Hague, Kluwer Law Publishing, 2002) 49.

Keyaerts D 'Ex ante evaluation of EU Legislation Intertwined with Judicial Review? Comment on Vodafone' (2010) 35 *European Law Review*, 869.

Kiiver P, 'The Early Warning System for the Principle of Subsidiarity: The National Parliament as a Conseil d'Etat for Europe' (2011) 36 *European Law Review* 98.

——, 'The Lisbon Judgement of the German Constitutional Court: a Court-OrderedStrengthening of the National Legislature in the EU' (2010) 16 *European Law Journal* 578.

——, 'The Treaty of Lisbon: the National Parliaments and the Principle of Subsidiarity' (2008) 15 *Maastrict Journal of European and Comparative Law* 77.

Klamert M, 'Conflicts of Legal Basis: No Legality and Basis but a Bright Future under the Lisbon Treaty?' (2010) 35 *European Law Review* 497.

Kliching M, 'Financial Counterterrorism Inititatives in Europe' in C Fijnaut et al (eds), *Legal Instruments in the Fight against International Terrorism* (Leiden, Brill Publishing, 2004) 203.

Klip A, 'The Constitution for Europe and Criminal Law: A step Not Far Enough?' Editorial (2005) 12 *Maastricht Journal of European and Comparative Law* 115.

——, *European Criminal Law: An Integrative Approach* (Antwerp, Intersentia) 2009).

—— and H Wilt (eds), *Harmonisation and Harmonising Measures in Criminal* Law (Amsterdam, Royal Netherlands Academy of Arts and Sciences, 2002).

Konstadinides T, *Division of Powers in the European Union* (Deventer, Kluwer Law Publishing, 2009).

——, 'Wavering between Centres of Gravity: Comment on *Ireland v Parliament and Council*' (2010) 35 *European Law Review* 88.

——, 'Between Circumvention and Gap-filling: The Conceptual Limits around the Treaty's Flexibility Clause', forthcoming (2011) *Yearbook of European Law.*

Kumm M, 'Constitutionalising Subsidiarity in Integrated Markets: The Case of Tobacco Regulation' (2006) 12 *European Law Journal* 503.

——, 'The Idea of Socratic Contestation and the Right to Justification: The Point of Rights-based Proportionality Review' (2010) 4 *Law & Ethics of Human Rights* 141.

Koutrakos P, *EU International Relations Law* (Oxford, Hart Publishing, 2006).

Kurcz B, 'Harmonisation by Means of Directives – Never-ending Story?' (2001) 11 *European Business Law Review* 287.

Kurpas S et al, 'The Treaty of Lisbon: Implementing the Institutional Innovations' (2007) available at www.ceps.eu/files/book/1554.pdf.

Labayale H, 'L'ouverture de la jarred de Pandore: reflexions sur la competene de la Communaute en materiere penale' *Cashiers de Droit Europeen* (2006) 382.

Lacey N et al, *Reconstructing Criminal Law* (London, Butterworths, 2003).

Ladenburger C, 'Police and Criminal Law in the Treaty of Lisbon' (2008) 4 *European Constitutional Law Review* 20.

Lang JT, 'The Developments of the Court of Justice on the Duties of Cooperation of National Authorities and Community Institutions under Article 10 EC' (2008) 31 *Fordham International Law Journal* 1483.

——, The Duties of Cooperation of National Authorities and Courts under Article 10 EC (2001) 26 *European Law Review* 84.

Lavenex S, 'Justice and Home Affairs' in H Wallace et al (eds), *Policy-Making in the European Union*, (Oxford, Oxford University Press, 2010) Ch 19.

——, 'Mutual Recognition and the Monopoly of Force: Limits of the Single Market Analogy' (2007) 14 *Journal for European Environmental and Planning Law* 762.

—— and Wagner W, 'Which European Security? Sources of Imbalance in the European Area of Freedom, Security and Justice' *European Security* 16 (2007) 225.

Leczykiewicz D, '"Effective Judicial Protection" of Human Rights After Lisbon: Should National Courts Be Empowered to Review EU Secondary Law?' (2010) 35 *European Law Review* 326.

Lee M *EU Environmental Law* (Oxford, Hart Publishing, 2005).

Lenaerts K, 'Constitutionalism and the Many Faces of Federalism' (1990) 38 *American Journal of Comparative Law* 205.

—— and Nuffel K, *Constitutional Law of the European Union* (London, Sweet & Maxwell, 2005).

—— and Corthaut T, 'Of Birds and Hedges: The Role of Primacy in invoking Norms of EU Laws' (2006) 31 *European Law Review* 287.

Lernestedt C, *Kriminalisering: problem och principer* (Uppsala, Iustus, 2003).
Ludwigs M, Annotation C-380/03 (2007) 44 *Common Market Law Review* 1159.
Lynsky O and Dawnes A, 'The Ever-longer arm of EC law: The Extension of Community Law into the field of Criminal Law' (2008) 45 *Common Market Law Review* 131.
Lyons C, 'Closer Co-operation and the Court of Justice' in G de Burca and J Scott (eds) *Constitutional Change in the EU, From Uniformity to flexibility?* (Oxford, Hart Publishing, 2000) 95.
Lööf R, 'Shooting from the Hip: Proposed Minimum Rights in Criminal Proceedings throughout the EU' (2006) 12 *European Law Journal* 421.
MacCormick, N, *Questioning Sovereignty* (Oxford, Oxford University Press, 1999).
Magnusson D, 'The Costs of Implementing the Anti-money Laundering Regulations in Sweden' (2009) 12 *Journal of Money Laundering Control* 101.
Maguire M, et al, *The Oxford Handbook of Criminology* (Oxford, Oxford University Press, 2007).
Majone G, 'What price safety?' (2002) 40 *Journal of Common Market Studies* 89.
——, 'One Market, One Law, One Money? Unintended Consequences of EMU, Enlargement and Eurocentricity' LSE Law, Society and Economy Working Papers 1/2007, available at www.lse.ac.uk/collections/law/wps/wps.htm.
Marin L, 'The European Arrest Warrant and Domestic Legal Orders. Tensions between Mutual Recognition and Fundamental Rights: the Italian Case' (2008) 15 *Maastrict Journal of European and Comparative Law* 473.
Marshall P, 'Part 7 of the Proceeds of Crime Act 2002: Double Criminality, Legal Certainty, Proportionality and Trouble Ahead', (2003) 11 *Journal of Financial Crime* 111.
Martinico G, 'From the Constitution for Europe to the Reform Treaty: A Literature Survey on European Constitutional Law' in (2009) *Perspectives on Federalism* available at www.on-federalism.eu/attachments/024_download.pdf.
Meessen K, 'Hedging European Integration: The Maastricht Judgment of the Federal Constitutional Court of Germany' (1994) 17 *Fordham Internationall Law Journal* 511.
Meuwese A, *Impact Assessment in EU Lawmaking* (The Hague, Kluwer Law Publishing, 2008).
Mill J, *On Liberty* (London, Routledge, 1991).
Mitsilegas V, 'Defining Organized Crime in the European Union' (2001) 26 *European Law Review* 565.
——, 'The Ambivalent Concept of Transnational Orgnized Crime' in M Beare (ed), *Critical Reflections on Transnational Organized Crime: Money Laundering and Corruption* (Toronto, Toronto University Press, 2003) 72.
——, *Money Laundering Counter-Measures in the EU: A New Paradigm of Security Governance versus Fundamental Legal Principles* (The Hague, Kluwer Law Publishing, 2003).
——, 'Countering the Chameleon Threat of Dirty Money' in A Edwards and P Gill, *Transnational Organised Crime* (London, Routledge, 2003).
——, 'International Regulation of Money Laundering and Terrorist Finance' in Bantekas I and Keramides G (eds) *International and European Financial Criminal Law* (London, Butterworths, 2006) 305.
——, 'The Constitutional Implications of Mutual Recognition in EU Criminal Law' (2006) 43 *Common Market Law Review* 1277.
——, 'Constitutional Principles of the European Community and European Criminal Law' (2007) 9 *European Journal of Law Reform* 303.

——, 'The Third Wave of Third Pillar Law. Which Direction for EU Criminal Justice?' (2009) 34 *European Law Review* 523.
——, 'Global standards in Domestic Legal Cultures: The Money Laundering Offences in English Law' in S Braum (ed) *Droit Pénal Européen des Affairs* (Berliner Wissenschaftsverlag, 2009).
——, 'The Transformation of Criminal Law in the Area of Freedom, Security and Justice' (2007) 26 *Yearbook of European Law* 1.
——, *EU Criminal Law* (Oxford, Hart Publishing, 2009).
——, 'European Criminal Law and Resistance to Communautarisation after Lisbon, (2010) 1 *New Journal of European Criminal Law* 456.
——, 'The External Dimension of EU Action in Criminal Matters', (2007) 12 *European Foreign Affairs Review* 457.
—— and Gilmore B, 'The EU legislative framework against money laundering and terrorist finance: a critical analysis in the light of evolving global standards' (2007) 56 *International and Commercial Law Quarterly* 119.
Moloney N, *EC Securities Regulation* (Oxford, Oxford University Press, 2002).
——, 'Investor Protection and the Treaty' in G Ferrarini et al (eds), *Capital Markets in the Age of the Euro* (The Hague, Kluwer Law Publishing, 2003).
——, 'Confidence and Competence: The Conundrum of EC Capital Market Law' (2004) 4 *Journal of Corporate Law Studies* 44.
Monar J, 'The EU as an International Actor in the Domain of Justice and Home Affairs' (2004) 9 *EU Foreign Affairs Review* 395 at 398.
——, 'Justice and Home Affairs in the EU Constitutional Treaty. What added Value for the Area of Freedom, Security and Justice?' (2005) 1 *European Constitutional Law Review* 226.
——, 'The Area of Freedom, Security and Justice' in A Von Bogdandy and J Bast (eds), *Principles of European Constitutional Law* 2nd edn (Oxford, Hart, 2010) 551.
Murphy C, 'The European Evidence Warrant: Mutual Recognition and Mutual (Dis) Trust?' in C Eckes and T Konstadinides (eds), *Crime within the Area of Freedom, Security and Justice: A European Public Order* (Cambridge, Cambridge University Press, 2011) 224.
Möller K, 'Balancing and the Structure of Constitutional Rights' (2007) 5 *International Journal of Constitutional Law* 453.
Nardo M, 'Economic Crime and Illegal Markets Integration: A Platform for Analysis' (2011) 18 *Journal of Financial Crime* 47.
Neagu N, 'Entrapment between Two Pillars: The European Court of Justice Rulings in Criminal Law' (2009) 15 *European Law Journal* 536.
Nebbia P, 'Internal Market and Harmonization of European Contract Law' in P Nebbia and T Tridimas (eds) *European Law for the Twenty-First Century* (Oxford, Hart Publishing, 2004) 89.
——, 'Do the Rules on State Aid have a Life on their Own? National Procedural Autonomy and Effectiveness in the Lucchini Case' (2008) 33 *European Law Review* 427.
Neframi E, 'The Duty of Loyalty: Rethinking its Scope through its Application in the field of EU External Telations' (2010) 47 *Common Market Law Review*, 323.
Nettesheim M, 'UN Sanctions against Individuals – A Challenge to the Architecture of European Union Governance' (2007) 44 *Common Market Law Review* 567.
Nolan M, 'Law Reform, Beyond mere opinion polling and penal populism' in A Norrie et al (eds), *Regulating Device* (Oxford, Hart Publishing, 2009) 165.

Norrie A, *Crime, Reason and History* (London, Butterworths, 2001).

Nuotio K, 'Terrorism as a Catalyst for the Emergence, Harmonization and Reform of Criminal Law' (2006) 4 *Journal of International Criminal Justice* 998.

——, 'The Emerging Concept of European Criminal Law' in P Asp (ed) *Festskrift till Nils Jareborg* (Uppsala, Iustus, 2002).

Odeby A, 'The European Union and Money Laundering' in Bantekas I and Keramides G (eds), *International and European Financial Criminal Law* (London, Butterworths, 2006).

O'Keeffe D and Twomey P, *Legal Issues of the Maastricht Treaty* (Chichester, Wiley, 1994).

Padfield N, 'Country Report: Anti-money laundering rules in the United Kingdom' in Pieth M and Aiolfi G (eds), *A Comparative Guide to Anti-Money Laundering* (Cheltenham, Edward Elgar, 2004).

Payandeh M, 'Constitutional Review of EU Law after Honeywell: Contextualizing the Relationship between the German Constitutional Court and the EU Court of Justice' (2011) 48 *Common Market Law Review* 9.

Peers S, 'EU Responses to Terrorism' (2003) 52 *International and Commercial Law Quarterly* 227.

——, 'Salvation outside the Church: Judicial Protection in the Third Pillar after the *Pupino* and *Segi* Judgments', (2007) 44 *Common Market Law Review* 883.

——, 'EU Criminal Law and the Treaty of Lisbon' (2008) 33 *European Law Review* 507.

——, 'The European Community's Criminal Law Competence: The Plot Thickens' (2008) 33 *European Law Review* 399.

——, 'The EU's JHA agenda for 2009,' available at www.statewatch.org/analyses/eu-sw-analysis-2009-jha-agenda.pdf.

——, 'Divorce, European Style: The First Authorization of Enhanced Cooperation' (2010) *European Constitutional Law Review* 339.

——, Case note (2010) 35 *European Law Review* 849.

——, *EU Justice and Home Affairs* (Oxford, Oxford University Press 2011).

Pernice I, 'Multilevel Constitutionalism in the European Union' (2002) 27 *European Law Review* 511.

——, 'The Treaty of Lisbon and Fundamental Rights' in S Griller and Z Ziller (eds) *The Lisbon Treaty EU Constitutionalism without a Constitutional Treaty?* (New York, Springer, 2008) 235.

Piris J-C, *The Constitution for Europe – A Legal Analysis* (Cambridge, Cambridge University Press, 2006).

——, *The Lisbon Treaty, A Legal and Political Analysis* (Cambridge, Cambridge University Press, 2010).

Powles E, 'All that Glisters is not Gold: Laundering the UK Money Laundering Regime' (2006) 65 *Cambridge Law Journal* 40.

Prechal S, 'EC Requirement for an Effective Remedy' in Lonbay and Biondi (eds), *Remedies for Breach of EC Law* (Chichester, Wiley, 1997).

——, *Directives in EC Law* (Oxford, Oxford University Press, 2005).

——, 'Direct Effect, Indirect Effect, Supremacy and the Evolving Constitution of the European Union' in C Barnard (ed) *The Fundamentals of EU Law Revisited* (Oxford, Oxford University Press, 2007).

Rees G and Moloney T, 'The Latest Efforts to Interrupt Supply Lines: Schedule 7 to Counter Terrorism Act 2008' (2010) *Criminal Law Review* 127.

Rijken C, 'Re-balancing Security and Justice: Protection of Fundamental Rights in Police and Judicial Cooperation in Criminal Matters' (2010) 47 *Common Market Law Review* 1455.

Ross M, 'Effectiveness in the European Legal Order(s): Beyond Supremacy to Constitutional Proportionality' (2006) 31 *European Law Review* 476.

Ryder N, 'A False sense of Security? An Analysis of Legislative Approaches towards the Prevention of Terrorist Finance in the United States and the United Kingdom' (2007 *Journal of Business Law* 821.

——, 'The Financial Services Authority and Money Laundering a Game of Cat and Mouse', (2008) 67 *Cambridge Law Journal* 635.

Safferling J, '*Europe as Transnational Law* – A Criminal Law for Europe: Between National Heritage and Transnational Necessities' (2009) 10 *German Law Journal* 1383

Sazarek-Mason P, 'EU Policy against Corruption' in C Eckes and T Konstadinides (eds) *Crime within the Area of Freedom, Security and Justice* (Cambridge, Cambridge University Press, 2011) 43.

Schonsheck J, *On Criminalisation* (The Hague, Kluwer Law Publishing, 1994).

Schünemann B, 'Alternative-Project for a European Criminal Law and Procedure' (2007) 18 *Criminal Law Forum* 227.

Schünemann B, 'Europäischer Sicherheitstaat=Europäischer Polizeistaat?' (2007) 14 *ZIS* 528–34.

Schütze R, *From Dual to Cooperative Federalism: The Changing Structure of European Law* (Oxford, Oxford University Press, 2009).

——, 'Organized Change towards an "Ever Closer Union": Art 308 EC and the Limits to the Community's Legislative Competence' (2003) 22 *Yearbook of European Law* 79.

——, 'Subsidiarity after Lisbon: Reinforcing the Safeguards of Federalism?' (2009) 68 *Cambridge Law Journal* 525.

Seidel M, 'Präventive Rechtangleichung im Bereich des Gemeinsamen Markets', (2006) *Europarecht* 26.

Senden L, *Soft Law in European Community Law* (Oxford, Hart Publishing, 2004).

Shaw M, *International Law* (Oxford, Oxford University Press, 2003).

Sieber U, 'Memorandum avseende en europeisk modellstrafflag' (1997) 84 *Nordisk Tidskrift for Kriminalvidenskab* 237.

Singer R, 'Proportionate Thoughts About Proportionality' (2010) 8 *Ohio State Journal of Criminal Law*, 217.

Smith G, 'Competition in the European Financial Services Industry: The Free Movement of Capital versus the Regulation of Money laundering' (1992) *University of Pennsylvania Journal of International Business Law* 101.

Snyder F, 'The Effectiveness of European Community Law: Institutions, Process, Tools and Techniques'(1993) 56 *Modern Law Review* 19.

Somek A, *Individualism* (Oxford, Oxford University Press, 2008).

——, *Engineering Equality* (Oxford, Oxford University Press, 2011).

Sparenta, E 'Remembrance of Principles Lost: on Fundamental Rights, the Third Pillar and the Scope of Union Law' (2006) 25 *YEL* 153.

Sproat P, 'The UK's Anti Money Laundering and Asset Recovery Regime' (2007) 47 *Crime Law and Social Change* 169.

——, 'Counter-terrorist Finance in the UK: A Quantitative and Qualitative Commentary based on Open Source Materials (2010) 13 *Journal of Money Laundering Control* 315.

St Bradley K, 'Powers and Procedures in the EU Constitution: Legal Bases and the Court' in P Craig and G De Burca, *The Evolution of EU Law* (Oxford, Oxford University Press, 2011) 85.

Stessens G, 'Money Laundering' (2006) 77 *International Review of Penal Law* 201.

Stone Sweet A, 'All Things in Proportion? American Rights Doctrine and the Problem of Balancing' available at works.bepress.com/cgi/viewcontent.cgi?article=1034&context=alec_stone_sweet.

Suominen A, (2011) *Juridiska Foreningen Tidskrift* 122.

——, *The European Arrest Warrant and its Implementation in the Nordic Countries* (PhD thesis, Bergen University, 2011).

——, 'The Past, Present and the Future of Eurojust (2008) 15 *Maastrict Journal of European and Comparative Law* 217.

Swenden, W 'Is the European Union in need of a Competence Catalogue? (2004) 42 *Journal of Common Market Studies* 381.

Symeonidou-Kastanidou E, 'Towards a Definition of Organized Crime in the European Union' (2007) 16 *European Journal of Crime, Criminal Law and Criminal Justice* 83.

Tadros V, 'Crime and Security' (2008) 71 *Modern Law Review* 940.

Taylor N, 'FSA Prosecutions: Offences of Money Laundering – Power to Prosecute' (2010) *Criminal Law Review* 772.

Thomas R and Lynch-Wood G, 'Transposing European Union Law in the United Kingdom: Administrative Rule-Making, Scrutiny and Better Regulation' (2008) 14 *European Public Law* 177.

Thym D, 'In the name of Sovereign Statehood: A Critical Introduction to the Lisbon Judgment of the German Constitutional Court' (2009) 46 *Common Market Law Review* 1795.

Timermanns C, 'Subsidiarity and Transparency' (1999) 22 *Fordham International Law Journal* 106.

Tobler C, Annotation 'Case 176/03' (2006), 43 *Common Market Law Review* 835.

Tomuschat C, Annotation *Yusuf* and *Kadi* (2006) 43 *Common Market Law Review* 537.

Torriti J, 'Impact Assessment in the EU: A Tool for Better Regulation, Less Regulation or Less Bad Regulation', (2007) 10 *Journal of Risk Research* 239.

——, 'The Unsustainable Rationality of Impact Assessment' (2011) 31 *European Journal of Law and Economics* 307.

Trachtman J, 'Trade and Problems, Cost Benefit Analysis and Subsidiarity' (1998) 9 *European Journal of International Law* 32.

Tridimas T, 'Liability for Breach of Community Law: Growing up or Mellowing Down?' (2001) 38 *Common Market Law Review* 301.

——, *General Principles of EU Law*, (Oxford, Oxford University Press, 2006).

Tridimas G and Tridimas T, 'The European Court of Justice and the Annulment of the Tobacco Advertisement Directive' (2002) 14 *European Journal of Law & Economics* 171.

Van den Berghe F, 'The EU and Issues of Human Rights Protection: Same Solutions to More Acute Problems' (2010) 16 *European Law Journal* 112.

Van den Wyngaert C, 'Eurojust and the European Public Prosecutor' in N Walker (ed), *Europe's Area of Freedom, Security and Justice*, 224 (Oxford, Oxford University Press, 2004).

Van Elsuwege P, 'EU external action after the collapse of the pillar structure. In search of a new balance between delimitation and consistency' (2010) 47 *Common Market Law Review* 987.

Van Gerven W, 'Of Rights, Remedies and Procedures' (2000) 37 *Common Market Law Review* 501.

——, 'Harmonization of Private Law: Do we really need it?' *Common Market Law Review* 41 (2004) 505.

Van Ooik R, 'Cross-Pillar Litigation Before the ECJ: Community and Union Competences'(2008) 4 *European Constitutional Law Review* 399.

Van Sliedriegt E and Keijzer N (eds) *The EAW in practice* (The Hague, Asser Press 2009)

Veng Mei Leong A, 'Chasing Dirty Money: Domestic and International Measures against Money laundering' (2007) 10 *Journal of Money Laundering Control* 140.

Vogenauer S and Weatherill S (eds), *The Harmonisation of European Contract Law: Implications for European Private Laws, Business and Legal Practice* (Oxford, Hart Publishing, 2006) 89.

Von Bogdandy A, 'Founding Principles' in von Bogdandy and J Bast, *European Constitutional Law* (Oxford/Munich, Hart Publishing /Beck, 2011) 29.

Von Bogdandy A and Bast J, 'The Vertical Order of Competences' (2002) 39 *Common Market Law Review* 227.

——, 'The Vertical Order of Competences' in A Bogdandy and J Bast (eds), *Principles of European Constitutional Law* (Oxford, Hart Publishing, 2006) 335.

——, 'The Federal Order of Competences' in A von Bogdandy and J Bast, *Principles of European Constitutional Law* (Oxford/Munich, Hart/Beck/Nomos, 2010) 275.

Von Hirch A and Jareborg J, 'Gauging Criminal Harm: A Living Standard Analysis' (1991) 11 *Oxford Journal of Legal Studies* 1.

Von Hirsh A, 'Alternative Draft for European Criminal Proceedings' (2007) 18 *Criminal Law Forum* 195.

Walker C, 'Clamping Down on Terrorism in the United Kingdom' (2006) 4 *Journal of International Commercial Law* 1137.

Walker N, *Punishment, Danger and Stigma: The Morality of Criminal Justice* (Oxford, Blackwell, 1980).

Ward A, 'Effective Sanctions in EC Law: A Moving Boundary in the Division of Competences', (1995) 1 *European Law Journal* 205.

——, *Judicial Review and the Rights of Private Parties in EC Law* (Oxford, Oxford University Press, 2000) 328.

——, 'The Case for Uniform Remedies', in J Prinssen and A Schrauwen (eds), *Direct Effect, Rethinking a Classic of EC Legal Doctrine* (Groningen, Europa Law Publishing, 2002).

——, case note *Willy Kempter* (2008) 33 *European Law Review* 739.

——, 'National and EC Remedies under the EC Treaty' in C Barnard and O Odudu, *The Outer limits of EU Law* (Oxford, Hart Publishing, 2009) 329.

Wasik M, 'The Hodgson Committee Report on the Profits of Crime and their Recovery' (1984) *Criminal Law Review* 708.

Weatherill S, 'Beyond Preemption? Shared Competence and Constitutional Change in the European Community' in D O'Keffee (ed), *Legal Issues of the Maastricht Treaty* (London, Chancery Law Publishing, 1994)

——, 'After *Keck*: Some Thoughts on How to Clarify the Clarification' (1996) 33 *Common Market Law Review* 885.

——, 'Safeguarding the *Acquis Communautaire*', in T Heukles et al(eds), *The European Union after Amsterdam* (Amsterdam, European Institute Amsterdam, 1998) 153.

——, 'If I'd wanted you to understand I would have explained it better': What is the Purpose of the Orovisions on Closer Co-operation introduced by the Treaty of Amsterdam? in D O'Keeffe and P Twomey (eds), *Legal Issues of the Amsterdam Treaty* (Oxford, Hart Publishing, 1999) 21.

——, *Law and Integration in the European Union*, (Oxford, Clarendon Press, 1995).

Weatherill S, 'The Common Market – Mission Accomplished?' In Heiskanen and Kulovesi (eds), *Function and Future of European Law*, (Helsinki, Helsinki University Press, 1999).

——, 'Addressing Problems of Imbalanced Implementation in EC law.' in C Kilpatrick et al (eds), *The Future of Remedies in Europe*, (Oxford, Hart Publishing, 2000).

——, 'Finding Space for closer Cooperation in the Field of Culture' in De Burca and J Scott (eds) *Constitutional Change in the EU, From Uniformity to Flexibility*? (Oxford, Hart Publishing, 2000) 237.

——, 'Is Constitutional Finality Feasible or Desirable? On the case for European Constitutionalism and the European Constitution' (2002), available at www.wiso.uni-hamburg.de/fileadmin/sowi/politik/governance/ConWeb_Papers/conweb7-2002.pdf.

——, 'Why Object to Harmonization of Private Law by the EC?' (2004) 5 *European Review of Public Law* 663.

——, 'Competence Creep and Competence Control' (2004) 24 *Yearbook of European Law* 1.

——, 'Reflections on the EC's Competence to Develop a European Contract Law' (2005) 13 *European Review of Public Law* 405.

——, *EC Consumer Law* (Cheltenham, Edward Elgar, 2005).

——, 'Better Competence Monitoring' (2005) 30 *European Law Review* 23.

——, 'Constitutional Issues – How Much is Best Left Unsaid?' (2006) in S Vogenauer and S Weatherill (eds), *The Harmonisation of European Contract Law: Implications for European Private Laws, Business and Legal Practice* (Hart Publishing 2006).

——, 'Recent Developments on the Free Movement of Goods' (2006) 55 *International & Comparative Law Quarterly* 457.

——, (ed) *Better Regulation* (Oxford, Hart Publishing, 2007).

——, 'The Challenges of Better Regulation' in Weatherill (ed), *Better Regulation* (Oxford, Hart Publishing, 2007) 7.

——, 'Competence and Legitimacy' in C Barnard and O Odudu (eds) *The Outer Limits of EU Law* (Oxford, Hart Publishing, 2009) 1.

——, 'The Limits of Legislative Harmonisation Ten Years after Tobacco Advertising: How the Court's case law has become a "drafting guide"' (2011) 12 *German Law Journal* 827.

——, 'European Contract Law: Taking the Heat Out of Questions of Competence' (2004) 16 *European Business Law Review* 23.

——, 'The Commission's Options for Developing EC Consumer Protection and Contract Law: Assessing the Constitutional Basis' (2002) 13 *European Business Law Review* 497.

—— and Menon A, 'Legitimacy, Accountability and Delegation in the European Union', in A Arnull and D Wincott, *Accountability and Legitimacy in the European Union* (Oxford, Oxford University Press 2002).

Weber M, *Economy and Society* vol 1, (Berkeley, CA, University of California Press, 1978).

Weiler J, 'The Transformation of Europe' (1990–91) 100 *Yale Law Journal* 2400.

——, *The Constitution of Europe* (Cambridge, Cambridge University Press, 1999).

Wennberg S, 'Advokaters ansvar för penningtvätt' (2003/04) *JuridiskTidscrift* 841.

Wessel R, 'The Inside Looking Out: Consistency and Delimitation in EU External Relations' (2000) 37 *Common Market Law Review* 1135.

Weyembergh A, *L'harmonisation des legislation pénals: Condition de l'espace penal Européen et révélateur de ses tensions* (Brussels, Univetrsity of Brussels, 2004).

Wiener JB, 'Better Regulation' (2006) *Current Legal Problems* 447.

Wilhelmsson T, 'The Abuse of the Confident Consumer' (2004) 27 *Journal of Consumer Policy* 317.
——, 'Jack-in-the-Box Theory of European Community Law', in Krämer, Micklitz and Tonner, *Law and Diffuse Interests in the European Legal Order* (Baden-Baden, Nomos, 1997).
Williams A, *The Ethos of Europe* (Cambridge, Cambridge University Press, 2010)
Williams S, 'The Mandatory Exclusions for Corruption in the New EC Procurement Directives' (2006) 31 *European Law Review* 711.
Wyatt D, 'Community Competence to Regulate the Internal Market', Oxford Legal Working Paper No 9/2007 July 2007.
——, 'Could a Yellow Card for National Parliaments strengthen Judicial as well as Political policing of Subsidiarity?' (2006) 2 *Croatian Yearbook of European Law & Policy* 1.
——, 'Is Subsidiarity too Vague as a Legal rinciple' in Nicolaidis K and Weatherill, *Whose Europe? National Models and the Constitution of the European Union*; (OUP/European Studies at Oxford 2003) 86, available at www.europeanstudies.ox.ac.uk/.
—— et al, *European Union Law* (London, Sweet & Maxwell, 2006).
Zedner L, 'The Concept of Security: An Agenda for Comparative Analysis' (2003) *Legal Studies* 153.
Ziegler K, 'Strengthening the rule of law but fragmenting international law: the Kadi decision of the ECJ from the perspective of human rights' (2009) 9 *Human Rights Law Review* 288
Zila J, *Specialstraffrätten : en introduction* (Uppsala, Iustus 2009).

Other sources

House of Lords, European Union Committee, 42 Report of Session 2005–06, *The Criminal Law Competence of the European Community*.
——, European Union Committee 14th Report of Session 2004–05 *Strengthening national parliamentary scrutiny of the EU – the Constitution's subsidiarity early warning mechanism*.
——, EU select committee 10th Report of session 2007–08, 13 March 2008 '*The Treaty of Lisbon: An Impact Assessment*'.
——, 10th Report 2007–2008 Select Committee on the Constitution, *Counter Terrorism Bill: The Role of the Ministers, Parliament and the Judiciary*.
HM Treasury office *The Financial Challenge to Crime and Terrorism*, published (February 2007).
—— report *Implementing the Third Money Laundering Directive: A consultation Document*, 31 July 2006.
Cabinet Office, *Transposition Guide: How to Implement European Directives Effectively* (London, Cabinet Office, 2005).
Open letter from Foreign Minister C Bildt and Minister of Justice B Ask, February 2008 available at www.regeringen.se.
Letter from Mr V Skouris, 25 September 2006, available at www.statewatch.org/news/2006/oct/ecj-and-third-pillar-13272-06.pdf.
Comments on the Reform Treaty provided by Prof Steve Peers, Statewatch www.state watch.org/news/2007/aug/eu-reform-treaty-texts-analyses.htm (last accessed 30 August 2007).
Statement by F Frattini, 5 September 2007 available at europa.eu/rapid/pressReleases Action.do?reference=SPEECH/07/505&format=HTML&aged=0&language=EN&guiLa nguage=en.

Open letter from Swedish Foreign Minister C Bildt and Minister of Justice B Ask, February 2008 available at www.regeringen.se.

Commission staff working document, *An examination of the links between organized crime and corruption*. Sec (2008) 196, 8.2.2008.

Lagrådsremiss, 14 October 2008 available at The Swedish government's website www.regeringen.se/sb/d/10163/a/113463.

FFFS (2005:5), Finansinspektions föreskrifter och allmänna rekommendationer Review of the UK Prevention of Terrorism Act 2005 available at www.statewatch.org/news/2008/mar/uk-carlile-3rd-terr-rep.pdf.

Interview with A Calissendorff, partner Roschier law firm, (informal email correspondence 25 April 2008).

Interview with Prof M Borgers, Free University of Amsterdam (informal email correspondence 22 March 2009).

Roundtable discussion on 'Kadi', Bristol University Law School 3 November 2008.

Web-links

DG internal market website ec.europa.eu/internal_market/top_layer/index_3_en.htm

Gateway to the EU available at //europa.eu/index_en.htm

Dublin declaration on tackling organized crime, available at europa.eu/legislation_summaries/justice_freedom_security/judicial_cooperation_in_criminal_matters/l33264_en.htm.

Explanatory Notes to Terrorism Act 2006 available at www.opsi.gov.uk/ACTS/acts2006/en/ukpgaen_20060011_en_1.

The Swedish gateway for law, www.lagrummet.se.

Official notification, K (2008) 382/24, breach 2008/0212 received on 29 January 2008 at europa.eu/rapid/pressReleasesAction.do?reference=IP/08/1522&format=HTML&aged=0&language=EN&guiLanguage=en.

FATF, 40 recommendations available at www.fatf-gafi.org/document/28/0,3343,en_32250379_32236930_33658140_1_1_1_1,00.html.

FATF Country reports:

FATF report on the UK, at www.fatfgafi.org/dataoecd/55/29/39064399.pdf.

FATF, report on Sweden, 17 Feb 2006, at www.fatfgafi.org/dataoecd/26/35/36461995.pdf.

FATF report on money laundering and combating of the financing of terrorism, Finland, www.fatf-gafi.org/dataoecd/20/46/39794392.pdf.

FATF report Kingdom of Denmark, at www.fatfgafi.org/dataoecd/1/26/37588381.pdf.

OLAF office, anti fraud at ec.europa.eu/dgs/olaf/mission/index_en.html.

The Swedish supervisor of the financial market www.fi.se.

The Serious Organized Crime Agency, the UK available at www.soca.gov.uk/financialIntel/suspectActivity.html.

The Stockholm programme – An open and secure Europe serving and protecting the citizen (Council of the European Union Brussels, 2 December 2009), available at www.se2009.eu/polopoly_fs/1.26419!menu/standard/file/Klar_Stockholmsprogram.pdf.

Statewatch report 'The exceptional and draconian become the norm' www.statewatch.org/analyses/exceptional-and-draconian.pdf.

Index